The Turki:
Indepe

The Turkish War of Independence

A Military History, 1919–1923

Edward J. Erickson

BLOOMSBURY ACADEMIC
NEW YORK · LONDON · OXFORD · NEW DELHI · SYDNEY

BLOOMSBURY ACADEMIC
Bloomsbury Publishing Inc
1385 Broadway, New York, NY 10018, USA
50 Bedford Square, London, WC1B 3DP, UK
29 Earlsfort Terrace, Dublin 2, Ireland

BLOOMSBURY, BLOOMSBURY ACADEMIC and the Diana logo
are trademarks of Bloomsbury Publishing Plc

First published in the United States of America by ABC-CLIO 2021
Paperback edition published by Bloomsbury Academic 2024

For legal purposes the Acknowledgments on p. xi constitute
an extension of this copyright page.

Author photo: (Rene Diaz Photography)
Cover photo: Mustafa Kemal Atatürk, Turkish War of Independence. (Peter Horree/Alamy Stock Photo)

Bloomsbury Publishing Inc does not have any control over, or responsibility for,
any third-party websites referred to or in this book. All internet addresses given
in this book were correct at the time of going to press. The author and publisher
regret any inconvenience caused if addresses have changed or sites have
ceased to exist, but can accept no responsibility for any such changes.

Library of Congress Cataloging-in-Publication Data
Names: Erickson, Edward J., 1950-author.
Title: The Turkish War of Independence : a military history, 1919–1923 /
Edward J. Erickson.
Description: Santa Barbara, California : Praeger, an imprint of ABC-CLIO,
LLC, [2021] | Includes bibliographical references and index.
Identifiers: LCCN 2021008010 (print) | LCCN 2021008011 (ebook) |
ISBN 9781440878411 (hardcover) | ISBN 9781440878428 (ebook)
Subjects: LCSH: Turkey—History—Revolution, 1918–1923. | Turkey—History,
Military—20th century. | Turkey—Politics and government—1918–1960. |
Turkey—History—Revolution, 1918–1923—Historiography. |
Turkey—History, Military—Historiography.
Classification: LCC DR589 .E757 2021 (print) |
LCC DR589 (ebook) | DDC 956.1/023—dc23
LC record available at https://lccn.loc.gov/2021008010
LC ebook record available at https://lccn.loc.gov/2021008011

ISBN: HB: 978-1-4408-7841-1
PB: 979-8-7651-3012-4
ePDF: 978-1-4408-7842-8
eBook: 979-8-2161-5782-3

To find out more about our authors and books visit www.bloomsbury.com
and sign up for our newsletters.

This book is dedicated to my wife,
Jennifer Collins,
for her unstinting and tireless understanding
and for encouraging me to reengage and
pursue this long-delayed book.

Contents

Illustrations

TABLES

Acknowledgments

I could not have completed this book without the assistance and advice of my good friend and colleague, Professor Konstantinos Travlos of Özyeğin University. I am incredibly indebted to Konstantinos's brilliant analysis and keen eye for mistakes in the draft manuscripts. Moreover, he is the keystone in the architecture of nonpartisan academic balance that I believe this book represents.

I also owe a personal and special thanks to my dear Turkish friend and colleague Dr. Mesut Uyar, dean of the School of Business and Social Sciences at Antalya Bilim University, whose knowledge and understanding of the Ottoman and Nationalist Armies during this period is unrivalled in the world today.

I am fortunate to count among my personal friends Dr. Yücel Güçlü of the Turkish Ministry of Foreign Affairs and Dr. Maxime Gauin, whose knowledge of Armenian activities in Cilicia is unmatched anywhere in the world. Their work and support have been particularly useful in understanding the war against the French.

I am indebted to the scholarly works of the authors mentioned in my introduction and, in particular, Richard Hovannisian for his monumental study of the First Armenian Republic and Ismet Görgülü for his efforts in assembling Ottoman and Turkish orders of battle.

This book could not have been produced without the encouragement and assistance of my acquisitions editor at Praeger Publishers, Dr. Vince Burns. Vince's immediate interest and critical support of this project during the COVID-19 pandemic was critical to shepherding it through to a contract. I am also grateful for the excellent and thorough copyediting of Angel Daphnee as well as for the advice of my production editor Bridget Austiguy-Preschel.

Introduction

On this world so torn with strife I dread to see you let loose the Greek armies—for all our sakes and certainly for theirs.[1]

Winston S. Churchill to David Lloyd-George

March 24, 1920

DÉBUT

There is a large gap in the extant military historiography of the post–World War I era because there has never been a comprehensive work in the English language that integrates the various military fronts and operations conducted in the Turkish War of Independence (1919–1923). In what is sometimes called the Greco-Turkish War, the Turkish Nationalists, led by Mustafa Kemal, fought a bitter and costly war to expel the Greek, French, British, Italian, and Armenian occupying forces, many pursuing national stakes of their own, to restore Turkish sovereignty to the Anatolian heartland. Many World War I histories, written in English, end with the signing of the Mudros Armistice on October 30, 1918 (which led to the occupation of Istanbul, the Turkish Straits, and the railway passes in the Toros Mountains by the British and French). However, the narrative ought not to end there. The subsequent failure of the Allies to negotiate a fair and durable peace treaty with the Turks in 1919 led to further crises and war. The issue of who had claim to Anatolia and the Aegean littoral became a cause célèbre in the early 1920s.

The Turkish War of Independence: A Military History, 1919–1923 is a strategic, operational, and tactical history of the Turkish War of

Independence. It is a synthesis based on the Turkish, Greek, British, French, and Italian official military histories, as well as the extant field of secondary sources (although, as the literature review reveals, all the official histories and much of the secondary material, especially the work of Hovannisian and Shaw, derive directly from primary sources in the official archives). *The Turkish War of Independence* completes a trilogy of books that I aspired to write concerning the conventional wars of the Ottoman and Turkish armies in the early twentieth century. The first two of these are *Defeat in Detail: The Ottoman Army in the Balkans, 1912–1913* (Praeger), published in 2003 and *Ordered to Die: A History of the Ottoman Army in the First World War* (Praeger), published in 2001. In my defense, I was waylaid by the centenary of World War I, which focused me more narrowly on writing about the Gallipoli and Palestine campaigns. *The Turkish War of Independence* also complements and adds to my study of the Ottoman campaigns of counterinsurgency fought in the period 1876–1918, which was published as *Ottomans and Armenians: A Study in Counterinsurgency* (Palgrave Macmillan) in 2013. Taken together, these four books present a comprehensive treatment of the organization, command, and combat operations of the Ottoman Army and its successor Turkish Nationalist Army in the period 1900–1923.

DEFINING THE TURKISH WAR OF INDEPENDENCE

World War I in the Middle East did not end the fighting with the armistice at Mudros on October 30, 1918, nor did it settle the problem of what to do with the territory and peoples of the Ottoman Empire. Indeed, the fighting continued over the next five years, finally ending with the establishment of the modern Republic of Turkey. The Turks call this period of sustained war *İstiklâl Harbi* (the Independence War) and *Millî Mücadele* (the National Struggle), while many English-language histories call it the "Turkish War of Independence" or the "War of National Liberation."[2] The fighting in western Anatolia and the Aegean littoral is often called the "Greco-Turkish War," but this is an incomplete description when considering the multifront entirety of the war. It was a multifront war, although there was essentially no coordination between the Greek, Armenian, and French opponents of the Nationalists, justifying the view that each of the conflicts was distinct for those nations. However, from the Nationalist perspective, these three fronts were interconnected and formed one strategic whole.

Indeed, the complexity of the war, its character, and its participants make defining it with a single descriptive phrase quite difficult. It was, in many ways, never about independence as we understand that word but more about liberation from foreign occupation and resistance to foreign domination. For most Greeks and Armenians, their wars were part of national liberation struggles consummating ancient territorial claims against what they saw as a genocidal master. For the Muslims of the Anatolia and Muslim refugees who made Anatolia their last refuge—the people who increasingly saw themselves as Turks—their struggle was justified in the principle of nationality and sovereign independence. While it is trivially true that defeat would not have eliminated a Turkish state in Anatolia, that state would likely have suffered a historical trajectory similar to that of Iran, from division into foreign spheres of influence, continuous penetration of domestic politics by foreign powers, further territorial loss, and authoritarian rule by absolutists contending with regional warlords, all cumulating into an Islamist, Marxist, or mixed mass revolution. Like the American Civil War, this was a war made of wars and an existential struggle for a vast future.

Starting in November 1918, foreign powers—Britain, France, Italy, Greece, and Armenia—occupied significant parts of Anatolia and Thrace, leaving the rump Ottoman state with only the city of Istanbul and Mustafa Kemal's Nationalists with only the Anatolian plateau. In the beginning stages of the war, nonstate secret societies organized to smuggle arms and equipment out of the areas of Allied occupation. Then the Nationalists defied the Ottoman government and declared a national movement dedicated to freeing the Anatolian heartland from foreign occupation. The Ottoman Army was largely persuaded to abandon its own government and join the Nationalists. In the Aegean littoral against the Greeks and in eastern Anatolia against the Armenians, the Nationalists raised conventional armies from the detritus of defeat to fight large-scale, multifront conventional wars. As the fighting intensified against the French occupation of Cilicia (south-central Anatolia), the hard-pressed Nationalists responded with irregular and militia groups. Moreover, they had to contend simultaneously with dozens of uprisings and rebellions as tribal entities, ethnic minorities, and political groups sought autonomy and independence. As the war progressed, Kemal used his growing military strength to deter the British and French in the 1922 Chanak Crisis. Kemal and the Nationalists fought overlapping and simultaneous wars of differing types in the period 1918–1923.

Using contemporary twenty-first century military terminology, these overlapping conflicts can be characterized as hybrid warfare. In 2020, NATO defines a "hybrid threat" as a combination of threats that are military and nonmilitary and employ covert and overt means, including disinformation, cyberattacks, economic pressure, and deployment of irregular armed groups in coordination with the use of regular forces.[3] NATO further adds the idea of blending the activities of deniable forces (volunteers who are sometimes called "green men" today) and nonstate actors into the hybrid mix as well. The concept of hybrid warfare, therefore, might be identified as the simultaneous accretion and employment of many forms of warfare. The difficulty of responding effectively to hybrid threats cannot be overstated. This was the situation confronting Kemal and the Nationalists in 1919. Retrofitting this modern concept into the world as it existed in 1919–1923, we might consider that Kemal's Nationalists simultaneously waged conventional wars against the Greeks and Armenians, irregular and conventional war against the French, counterinsurgency campaigns against their own citizens, a civil war and rebellion against the Ottoman government in Istanbul. Moreover, the Nationalists conducted deterrence operations against the British and French in the straits region, information warfare (mostly propaganda) against the Allied occupation forces and the sultan, arms smuggling by secret societies, resistance to economic blockade and the occupation of strategic points, cooperative diplomacy to gain the support of nonstate actors such as the early Bolsheviks, and nation-building activities to restore military capability and capacity. Lastly, an elegant solution to the problem of defining these overlapping wars is a phrase originated by Professor Konstantinos Travlos characterizing the Turkish War of Independence as a "war made of wars."[4]

ORGANIZATION AND CONTENT

The Turkish War of Independence presents a chronological narrative that is organized thematically around the different fighting fronts on which the Nationalist armies and forces fought—chapter 1: "The End of World War I," chapter 2: "Call to Arms," chapter 3: "To the First İnönü Campaign," chapter 4: "The Long War against Insurgents," chapter 5: "A Short War on the Eastern Front," chapter 6: "The Franco-Turkish War," chapter 7: "Second

İnönü and Kütahya-Eskişehir," chapter 8: "The Culminating Point at Sakarya," chapter 9: "Operational and Strategic Pause," chapter 10: "The Great Offensive and the Pursuit to Izmir," chapter 11: "The Advance to the Straits and the Armistice," and chapter 12: "The Treaty of Lausanne and the Establishment of the Turkish Republic."

The Turkish War of Independence focuses on the Nationalist strategy and the operational-level campaigns that were waged to fulfill their strategic objectives. It is a broad survey with a focus on understanding why and how the Nationalists balanced ends, ways, and means to achieve their strategic objectives. The book is not a cultural, diplomatic, or social history of these events, although, from time to time, these subjects must be introduced to provide context for explaining military operations. The book is also not intended as an extended biography of Mustafa Kemal Atatürk—although he played a prominent and decisive role in these wars. I have not intentionally left out airpower and sea power from the story, but these capabilities were never particularly important in these wars. Airplanes were used by all participants but almost exclusively for reconnaissance and scouting, and I have included where these were tactically useful. Some readers will likely be disappointed because I have left out first-person narratives of the experience of war on individuals, particularly refugees and displaced persons. Moreover, others will be disappointed that I have left out many details of atrocities and crimes committed against the civilian populations of the war zones, including those against Greeks, Armenians, Kurds, Nestorians, Circassians, and Turks. While these threads are all important, these kinds of details are not critical to an understanding of why and how military operations were planned and undertaken. Further, in this regard, Churchillian and western-centric epigraphs are provided at the head of each chapter for contemporary context, as Europeans and Americans observed these events at the time. None of the preceding choices are meant to de-emphasize component parts of the history, individuals, or ethnic groups.

In this book, I refer to Mustafa Kemal's Nationalists in Ankara as the "Nationalists" and its military forces as the "Nationalist Army" rather than as "Turks" and the "Turkish Army." The extant literature in English mostly refers to the Ankara government as "Turks," and, during the period 1920–1923, the Europeans often referred to the Nationalists as "Kemalists." While "Turks" they may have been—and "Turks" they had been called by the Europeans since the 1300s—the term is historically inaccurate, as is the term "Kemalists." After the Treaty of Lausanne in July 1923 and the establishment of the Republic of Turkey later that year, the proper term is indeed "Turks"—but not before. Likewise, it is inaccurate to refer to the government of the Ottoman Empire as "Turks," and I refer to the sultan's government in Istanbul as the "Ottomans." To be clear, not all citizens of the Ottoman Empire were "Turks" and not all adherents of the Nationalist cause were "Kemalists." For the sake of brevity, I use the term "Greek Army" when the proper term is the Royal Hellenic Army, as well as associated terms such as the "Greek General Staff" (rather than Royal Hellenic General Staff). For the names of individuals and organizations, I have used the most commonly found spellings in English, simply because the Ottoman Turkish, Greek, and Armenian scripts must be transliterated into the English and European alphabets, rendering direct translation impossible.[5] With a few exceptions noted in the text, I have used modern Turkish place names (followed by a western or Greek place name, as appropriate) should the reader wish to refer to a modern map of the theater of war. Last, in what I think adds fidelity to the narrative, I have used the term Asia Minor when describing Greek operations and the term Anatolia when describing Nationalist operations on the Greek-Turkish fronts.

LITERATURE AND SOURCES

This book is a broad survey covering several overlapping wars, conflicts, and rebellions based primarily on the Turkish, Greek, British, French, and Italian official military histories, as well as on the work of American historian Richard Hovannisian (the importance of which I will explain below). The overlapping modern official military histories of the component wars are readily available in European alphabets, and all were based on the military archives of the nation. Consequently, *The Turkish War of Independence: A Military History, 1919–1923* integrates the extant field of official military histories with the smaller field of secondary literature and memoirs to achieve a balanced synthesis for writing an overall narrative. A brief summary of these official histories follows.

The Turkish Official Military Histories

The Turkish official military histories are based entirely on the massive archival records held by the Turkish General Staff's history and archives division (ATASE) in Ankara. They were written in the period 1930–1970 by retired army general staff officers who had served in the wars and were fluent in the written version of the Ottoman Turkish language (their names may be found in the bibliography). They also took advantage of the existence of reserve officers of Ottoman Greek descent, who were able to translate some of the Greek literature into Turkish. Those translations are in the ATASE archives.[6] The volumes used in this study are published in modern Turkish (with the publication dates following in ellipses).[7]

World War I

This book used three of the 27 World War I official histories.

- *1918 Yılı Hareketleri, Vnci Cilt (1967)*
- *Hicaz, Asir, Yemen Cepheleri ve Libya Harekâtı (1978)*
- *Birinci Dünya Harbı Idarı Faalıyetler ve Lojistik (1962)*

Mudros Armistice

- *Mondros Mütarekesi ve Tatbikatı (1962)*

Western Front (Greek-Turkish War)

- *Batı Cephesi (15 Mayıs–4 Eylül 1919) (1999)*
- *Batı Cephesi (4 Eylül 1919–9 Kasım 1920) (1999)*
- *Batı Cephesi (9 Kasım 1920–15 Nisan 1921) (1994)*
- *Kütahya, Eskişehir Muharebeleri (15 Mayıs 1921–25 Temmuz 1921) (1974)*
- *Sakarya Meydan Muharebesinden Önceki Olaylar ve Mevzi İlerisindeki Harakât (25 Temmuz–22 Ağustos 1921) (1972)*
- *Sakarya Meydan Muharebesi (23 Ağustos–13 Eylül 1921) ve Sonraki Harekât (14 Eylül–10 Ekim 1921) (1973)*
- *Büyük Taarruza Hazırlık ve Büyük Taarruz (10 Ekim 1921–31 Temmuz 1922) (1967)*
- *Büyük Taarruz (1–31 Ağustos 1922) (1968)*
- *Büyük Taarruzda Takip Harekâtı (31 Ağustos–18 Eylül 1922) (1969)*
- *Son Safhası (18 Eylül–1 Kasım 1923) (1969)*

Eastern Front (Armenian-Turkish War)

- *Doğu Cephesi (1919–1921)* (1965)

Southern Front (Franco-Turkish War)

- *Güney Cephesi* (2009)

Rebellions and Uprisings

- *Ayaklanmalar (1919–1921)* (1974)

Naval and Air Operations

- *Deniz Cephesi ve Hava Harekâtı* (1964)

Logistics and Administration

- *İdari Faaliyetler (15 Mayıs 1919–2 Kasım 1923)* (1975)

Biographies of National, Front, Corps, Group, and Division Commanders

- *Tümen ve daha Üst Kademelerdeki Komutanların Biyografileri (İkinci Baskı)* (1989)

Special Studies

- *Kütahya ve Eskişehir Muharebeleri* (2006)
- *2nci Kolordu (1918–1921)* (2006)
- *Sakarya'dan Mudanya'ya* (1972)
- *Büyük Taarruz* (1992)

The Greek Official Military History

The Hellenic Army History Directorate published an English language concise history of the Greek-Turkish War in 2003. The authors are Demetrios Gedeon, Eupraxia Paschalidou, and Angeliki Dima-Dimitrou, and the work is titled *A Concise History of the Campaign in Asia Minor 1919–1922* [English Edition] (hereafter in the text and end notes as the Concise Greek History).[8] The 530-page Concise Greek History was consolidated from the following official histories, published in Greek by the Hellenic Army History Directorate, which were based on the army archives:[9]

- *The Greek Army in Smyrna* (1957)
- *Operations of Philadelphia, Prusa, Ishak* (1958)
- *Reconnaissance in Force December 1920–March 1921* (1963)
- *Operations June–July 1921* (1965)
- *Operations Towards Ankara* (1965)
- *The Events Preceding the Turkish Attack* (1960)
- *The End of the Campaign, Part 1: Struggles Related to the Withdrawal of Army Corps A and B* (1962)
- *The End of the Campaign, Part 2: Retreat of Army Corps C* (1962)
- *Operations in Thrace 1919–1923* (1969)

Armenian Military History

The Republic of Armenia has produced no official military histories in a European Roman alphabet. However, the monumental work of American historian Richard G. Hovannisian, based on his original research in the Armenian state archives (as well as in western archives and Turkish sources), stands as a near-peer and reliable partner to the works previously discussed. Professor Hovannisian's work comprises the following:

- *The Republic of Armenia: The First Year, 1918–1919*, vol. 1 (1971)
- *From Versailles to London, 1919–1920*, vol. 2 (1982)
- *From London to Sèvres, February–August 1920*, vol. 3 (1996)
- *Between Crescent and Sickle: Partition and Sovietization*, vol. 4 (1996)

British Official History

The British World War I official histories are based on the military archives and are well respected by military historians. The three volumes used in this book:

- *Military Operations, Egypt & Palestine: From June 1917 to the End of the War* (1930)
- *Military Operations Macedonia: From the Spring of 1917 to the End of the War* (1935)
- *The Occupation of Constantinople 1918–1923* (1944, unpublished until 2010)

French Official History

The single French volume used in this study is:

- *Les Armées Françaises dans la Grande Guerre: Les Fronts Secondaires*, Tome IX, Ier Volume (1936)

Italian Official History

The single Italian volume used in this study is:

- *Il Corpo di Spedizione Italiano in Anatolia (1919–1922)* (2010)

Given the length of these wars and the scope of these events, the official histories are numerous and robust. However, the secondary field of literature about the military history of these wars and events for the English language reader is surprisingly limited. In addition to the works listed above, the most useful of the English language field includes W. E. D. Allen and Paul Muratoff's *Caucasian Battlefields: A History of the Wars on the Turco-Caucasian Border 1828–1921* (1953); Briton Cooper Busch's *Mudros to Lausanne: Britain's Frontier in West Asia, 1918–1923* (1976); Bruce Clark's *Twice a Stranger: The Mass Expulsions that Forged Modern Greece and Turkey* (2006); Winston S. Churchill's *The World Crisis: The Aftermath*, vol. 5 (1929); David Fromkin's *A Peace to End All Peace: The Fall of the Ottoman Empire and the Creation of the Modern Middle East* (1989); George W. Gawrych's *The Young Atatürk: From Ottoman Soldier to Statesman of Turkey* (2015); Michael Llewellyn-Smith's *Ionian Vision: Greece in Asia Minor 1919–1922* (1973); Andrew Mango's *Atatürk: The Biography of the Founder of Modern Turkey* (1999); Justin McCarthy's *Death and Exile: The Ethnic Cleansing of Ottoman Muslims, 1821–1922* (1995); Sean McMeekin's *The Ottoman Endgame: War, Revolution, and the Making of the Modern Middle East 1908–1923* (2015); Michael A. Reynold's *Shattering Empires: The*

Clash and Collapse of the Ottoman and Russian Empires, 1908–1918 (2011); Heinz A. Richter's *The Greek-Turkish War 1919–1922* (2016); Jeremy Salt's *The Last Ottoman Wars: The Human Cost, 1877–1923* (2020); Stanford Shaw's *From Republic to Empire: The Turkish War of National Liberation*, 5 vols. (2000); David Walder's *The Chanak Affair* (1969); and Robert F. Zeidner's *The Tricolor over the Taurus: The French in Cilicia and Vicinity, 1918–1922* (2005).

There are several additional works in the Turkish language, including memoirs and secondary sources. I have listed these in the bibliography for those interested in a more thorough understanding of the references used in this book.[10] There is also a massive amount of literature in Greek, which I cannot read, but of which numerous relevant parts were provided to me by Professor Konstantinos Travlos. According to Professor Travlos, almost all the commanders of the Field Army of Asia Minor who survived the war produced memoirs or books about their experience (e.g., Leonidas Paraskevopoulos and Anastasios Papoulas), and there is a hard-to-find and overpriced apologia for Georgios Chatzanestes. Some commanders of major units, such as Nikolaos Trikoupes, published apologia as well. Some access to the early Greek military history can be found in the various entries of the *Great Military and Naval Encyclopedia*, printed between 1924 and 1928, which essentially became the first official Greek history.[11]

Professor Travlos notes that the decision-makers who were privy to the debates on Greek strategy also produced works, often apologia and often reprinting archival documents (including Victor Dousmanes and Xenophon Strategos). A large secondary literature has developed, but it is marred by the continued legacy of the National Schism and is mostly focused on the Asia Minor Disaster; the destruction of the Ottoman Greek community because of the war; or issues of diplomacy, politics, or grand strategy.

Both the Turkish and Greek secondary literature lack operational- and tactical-level critical analysis studies of battles and military operations of the kind that dominate the study of World Wars I and II (what is often called guns-and-trumpets history). Professor Travlos asserts, for example, that the only critical military history analysis of a specific operation that he is aware of is the limited-print two-volume work by Lieutenant General Christos Karrasos (published in 1968) of the Greek offensive of March/April 1921 (which is exceedingly hard to come by).[12] Recently, Brigadier General (ret.) Basileios Loumiotes began engaging in the kind of archive-based, cross-referencing sources with battlefield archaeology study of specific actions during the war (specifically the activity of Colonel Plasteras). In

Turkey, amateur battlefield archaeologists such as Serdar Aydın or ones working for the few national military history parks, such as Dr. Selim Erdoğan, are introducing the type of battlefield archaeology studies that have become a hallmark of modern military history, complementing the work of Loumiotes.

However, the lack of trained military historians who both command the new methodologies and have the linguistic command of Greek and Turkish, or Armenian and Turkish, is noticeable. Also problematic is the shadow cast by the Greek-Turkish and Armenia-Turkish interstate rivalries and the lack of any resolution on a common understanding of the shared history of these states, which makes collaboration across borders difficult and opens those who try to write robust military history at the operational and tactical level to attacks by the self-appointed adherents of politicized national and diaspora narratives. Hopefully this work will help provide a foundation for a younger generation of scholars to delve into the "as yet unexploited history" of these conflicts to produce high-quality, balanced military history in English.

All translations of Turkish, French, and Italian are my own, and I hope that I have not introduced any factual or contextual errors into the narrative. I have used the modern European calendar in all cases in this book, rather than the old-style Greek calendar (which differs by 13 or 14 days, depending on the month and year) or the Ottoman calendar (which differs in both month and year). Any errors I have introduced regarding specific dates are unintentional and due to my conversions of Greek and Ottoman calendars.

FINIS

The resilience and capacity of the Nationalist Army surprised the world in the early 1920s in the same way that its Ottoman predecessor surprised the world in 1914–1918. In World War I, the Allies expected the armies of the Sick Man of Europe to be easy prey. But they were not easy prey . . . and even in late 1918, the Ottoman Army remained in the field, fighting. In 1919 and 1920, in the same way, the Allies—especially the Greeks—expected the Ottoman Empire to collapse in the same way as the Romanov, Hapsburg, and Hohenzollern Empires had collapsed, leaving them with geographical prizes unimaginable in 1914. Instead, while the rump Ottoman government clung to tenuous legitimacy in Istanbul, a powerful Nationalist movement began in central Anatolia, led by Mustafa Kemal. And there the unthinkable happened "among the stern hills and valleys of the 'Turkish Homelands' in Anatolia, there dwelt that company of poor men . . . who would not see it settled so."[13]

NOTES

1. Winston S. Churchill, *The World Crisis, The Aftermath*, vol. 5 (London: Thornton Butterworth Limited, 1929), 378.

2. I am grateful to Professor Konstantinos Travlos for this information regarding how this war is named. A more radical suggestion is to name the series of wars the Wars of Anatolian Succession, since they might make more sense as a complex of wars rather than as one war. Similar conditions characterize the Russian Civil War, which connects with a series of wars and civil wars, and could be seen as the Wars of Eurasian Succession. Indeed, if we shear these wars of their ideological or national patina, is it that paradoxical to see them as wars of succession between competing territorial stakes and, thus, cousins to the great wars of the succession of the eighteenth century?

3. See North Atlantic Treaty Organization (NATO), "NATO's Response to Hybrid Threats," https://www.nato.int/cps/en/natohq/topics _156338.htm.

4. Applying the phrase "a war made of wars" to the Turkish War of Independence originates in the fertile mind of my friend and colleague Professor Konstantinos Travlos. In my opinion, it is the perfect characterization for these events.

5. It is important to keep in mind that many of the individuals living at the end of the Imperial Ottoman and early Turkish Republican periods did not have a surname. Atatürk's Surname Law of 1934 required all Turkish citizens to adopt and maintain a hereditary surname.

6. Interestingly, the publication of the official Turkish history followed the initiation in 1957 of the publication of the official Greek history.

7. In a truly generous act, the Turkish general staff has put scanned PDF versions of all books online. This website can be reached at no cost and without copyright infringements at https://msb.gov.tr/ArsivAskeriTarih /icerik/turk-istiklal-harbi-serisi, though the scanning quality varies. Hopefully the Greek General Staff will also follow suit. Both set of books are not readily available outside of the secondhand and antiquarian book markets.

8. For many years, this was the only military history of the conflict written in English. It should be noted that the translation, outsourced to translators in the United States, is very problematic—at times contradicting the narrative or the included maps. A new translation is very much needed, and the centenary of the war should offer the opportunity.

9. Once more, as in the case of the Turkish official histories, the Greek Army, especially in the 1930s when the study of military history as part of the tasks of the General Staff took off, relied on Greek translations of the earlier works of Turkish authors. These translations are deposited in the Army History Directorate of the Army General Staff (DIS) in Athens.

10. A good guide for the literature in Turkish can be found in chapters 1, 2, and 3 of Erik-Jan Zürcher, *The Young Turk Legacy and Nation Building* (New York: I.B. Tauris, 2010).

11. This is available for free at the excellent Anemi Digital Library of Modern Greek Studies: https://anemi.lib.uoc.gr/metadata/e/3/e/metadata -01-0001601.tkl.

12. This book is so rare that only two libraries in Greece have copies, and potentially the only copy available in Turkey is in the hands of Dr. Konstantinos Travlos. The work is available in the antiquarian bookstores in Athens at inflated prices.

13. Churchill, *The Aftermath*, 368.

ONE

The End of World War I

Venizelos is entitled to plead that in going to Smyrna he acted as mandatory for the four greatest powers. But he went as readily as a duck will swim.[1]

Winston S. Churchill, 1919

INTRODUCTION

As late as September 1, 1918, the Ottoman government could believe that the war might end on favorable terms. The Treaty of Brest-Litovsk ended the Russian threat. The fronts in Palestine, Mesopotamia, and Macedonia appeared to be holding fast, and the Pozantı tunnel complex traversing the Taurus Mountains was nearly completed (October 9, 1918). Moreover, Ottoman armies in the Caucasus had conquered Armenia and Azerbaijan and were advancing north to Derbent, Russia, along the west side of the Caspian Sea. Under these circumstances, a favorable negotiated peace seemed possible. However, the Ottomans did not understand the full effects of the failed German spring 1918 offensives in France on the German strategic position. Likewise, they did not understand the psychological impact of the Battle of Amiens, August 8–11, 1918, which resulted in the "black day of the German Army."[2] In truth, the Germans, as well as the Austro-Hungarians and the Bulgarians, were on their last legs, and the Ottoman Empire's strategic position was more like a house of cards than anything else. Moreover, the British economic blockade affected the Ottoman Empire to a far more damaging degree than its Central powers allies.[3]

In early October 1918, the sudden collapse of the fronts in Palestine and Macedonia led to a strategically unrecoverable position, and, just a month later, the Allies occupied Istanbul, and the Ottoman Young Turk regime fled, seeking asylum in Germany.

An armistice concluded at Mudros Harbor (known as Mondros by the Turks) on the island of Lemnos ended World War I in the Middle East on October 30, 1918. The Ottomans had held out far longer than anyone thought possible, and they expected a fair peace, based largely on Wilsonian principles. However, the crippling terms imposed on the Ottomans at Mudros shocked the government, the military, and the population and led to conditions that matured into a war to the finish between Greece and the Turkish Nationalists.

THE MUDROS ARMISTICE

By late September 1918, the end of World War I in the Middle East was in sight. British general Sir Edmund Allenby's Egyptian Expeditionary Force had shattered the Ottoman Army's Yildirim Army Group in Palestine and was advancing northward through Syria toward Damascus and Aleppo. In Europe, an Anglo-French offensive had broken open the Macedonian front, and General Sir George Milne's British force was advancing on Istanbul (then called Constantinople by Europeans). In the east, on the shores of the Caspian Sea, the Ottoman Army of Islam had shattered the Armenian Army, seized Baku, and was advancing on Derbent, Russia. The Ottoman Army overall, however, was on its last legs—its reserves used up and its manpower pool depleted.[4] Thus, on October 4, 1918, the sultan sent Rüştü Bey (Tevfik Rüştü [Aras] who was a high-ranking member of the government) to Switzerland with peace proposals not only to end the war but also to begin the process of overthrowing the ruling Committee of Union and Progress (CUP) regime. The sultan's proposals were ignored but, at nearly the same time, CUP Minister of the Interior Talaat Pasha extended peace feelers as well.[5]

With the war ending catastrophically, the regime began to break apart, with Talaat Pasha resigning on October 13, 1918. The sultan asked retired general and war hero Ahmet İzzet (Furgaç) Pasha to form a peace cabinet and, on October 19, Ahmet İzzet secured approval to negotiate an armistice.[6] Importantly, because their armies were still fighting, the Ottomans believed a generous peace was possible based on American president Woodrow Wilson's Fourteen Points.[7] Armistice negotiations took place aboard the HMS *Agamemnon* in Mudros Harbor over four days (October 27–30, 1918). The new minister of marine, Rauf (Orbay) Bey, led the Ottoman delegation that was negotiating with British admiral Arthur Gough-Calthorpe. Rauf was hamstrung by instructions from the sultan that, above all else, the armistice was to allow the continuation of the sultanate.[8] Gough-Calthorpe used this as leverage to achieve far more than he had hoped for.[9] In order to save the sultanate, Rauf was forced to sign an agreement that amounted to a British ultimatum.

Like its counterpart, the Compiègne armistice (signed on November 11), the Mudros armistice was designed to leave the Ottoman Empire defenseless and unable to oppose humiliating and damaging peace terms subsequently imposed by the Allies. The agreement was signed on October 30 and contained 25 clauses. The clauses that are important to this narrative are summarized here:

Clause 1. The Allies would immediately occupy the Dardanelles and Bosporus fortifications.

Clauses 2/3. The Ottomans would assist with and ensure the demining of the straits.

Clause 4. The Ottomans would collect in Istanbul and release all Allied prisoners of war and Armenian interned persons.

Clause 5. The Ottomans would immediately demobilize military forces, except for those authorized by the Allies as necessary for frontier and internal security.

Clause 7. The Allies would be allowed to occupy strategic points.

Clause 8. The Allies had the right to use Istanbul and all Ottoman ports as naval bases.

Clause 10. The Allies would occupy the Taurus and Amanus tunnel systems.

Clause 11. The Ottomans would retreat their forces in the Transcaucasus and in Persia to the 1914 frontier.

Clause 12. The Allies would supervise all Ottoman telephone, telegraph, and cable stations.

Clause 15. Entente supervisory officers would supervise all Ottoman railroads.

Clauses 16/17. The Ottomans would surrender all forces in the Arabian Peninsula, Libya, Syria, and Cilicia.

Clause 18. All German and Austrian personnel would surrender to the nearest British or Entente commander.

Clause 22. Ottoman prisoners of war would remain under the control of Entente forces.

Clause 24. The Allies reserved the right to occupy any part of what they called "six Armenian provinces" to protect Ottoman Armenians.

Clause 25. Hostilities would cease at noon local time, Thursday, October 31, 1918.

Rauf returned to Istanbul on November 1 and was, alternately, hailed as a hero by the population who badly misunderstood the terms of the armistice and as a traitor by the sultan and the military. In upper Mesopotamia, British general Sir William Marshall, on instructions from London, immediately violated the armistice by seizing the oil-rich city of Mosul on November 2.[10] There was immediate disagreement about the meaning of much of the terminology, and Ahmet İzzet unsuccessfully attempted to alter some of the clauses. In particular, the ambiguous identification of "strategic points" enabled the British to subsequently occupy any place they chose, and the clause regarding the railroad tunnels enabled the French to occupy all of the territory between Aleppo and the tunnels themselves.

On the night of November 2–3, the CUP triumvirate who were the de facto wartime rulers of the empire—Enver Pasha, Talaat Pasha, and Cemal Pasha—fled on a German freighter for ports in the Ukraine, which was still occupied by the German Army. Most certainly, Ahmet İzzet knew of their plans and let them escape, but, on November 3, he "went through the motions of demanding that the Germans return the fugitives."[11]

THE OCCUPATION

On November 6, Admiral Gough-Calthorpe was appointed British high commissioner for the Ottoman Empire, while the French appointed Vice Admiral Jean Amet on November 13. From November 6–12, the British 28th Infantry Division occupied the Dardanelles fortifications, and the Ottomans demined a path through the straits. An allied fleet, led by HMS *Superb*, placed Istanbul under the guns of its battleships, landing a French brigade on November 12 and a British brigade the following day. Istanbul was, in the technical sense, not occupied by the Allies, but they immediately established an allied control commission in the city to arrange armistice-related matters. However, the commission and its garrison constituted such a pervasive presence that it amounted to a de facto occupation. The Allies occupied the Bosporus fortifications on November 13. The famous Ottoman Fifth Army, the victor of the 1915 Gallipoli campaign, withdrew from the peninsula to garrisons in Thrace on November 28.[12]

Ahmet İzzet's government proved to be short-lived, as it resisted British encroachments on the Mudros Agreement and was replaced on November 11 by a more malleable government led by Tevfik Pasha. Additional armistice violations appeared in the form of French incursions. Although France had played a very minor role in the defeat of the Ottomans, French premier Georges Clemenceau was furious with the British, who had cut the French out of the armistice talks, but he acted quickly to take advantage of Ottoman weaknesses. On December 7, the French occupied Adana and Mersin and occupied Gaziantepe 10 days later.[13] By March 1919, they also took Maraş and Urfa.

The British and French War Offices reached an agreement in late November regarding Allied command and control in the soon-to-be occupied territories of the Ottoman Empire. The Allied commander-in-chief of the Macedonian front, French general Franchet d'Espèrey, retained command of European Turkey (eastern Thrace), and British general Sir George Milne took control of the Istanbul police.[14] In Cilicia and what is now southeast Turkey, British general Sir Edmund Allenby assumed control of the strategic points. The Black Sea littorals were, however, figuratively up for grabs in that no firm decisions regarding occupation had been reached.

The sultan dissolved the parliament on December 21, but Tevfik continued in a caretaker role until March 4, 1919, when the sultan's son-in-law, Damat Ferit, organized another government. The uncertainty of the terms and details of the Anglo-French occupation did not stop the British from sending troops to occupy Batum on December 22 (see chapter 5). This occupation led the British to establish the British Army of the Black Sea, which, by the spring of 1919, was composed of two infantry divisions with headquarters in Tiflis (Tbilisi) and Haydarpasha in Istanbul.[15]

Like the French, the Italians were enraged by the unilateral nature of the British armistice negotiations, but they sent Count Carlo Sforza as their high commissioner to Istanbul anyway. The Italians had held the Dodecanese Islands since 1911, and they had waged a minor counterinsurgency campaign against the Ottoman-led Senussi tribe members in Libya during the war. Overall, they played an even lesser role in defeating the

Ottomans than had the French. Nevertheless, by mid-May 1919, the Italians occupied Antalya, Bodrum, Fethiye, and Konya.[16] However, in many locations, the Allied occupation forces were tiny elements of a platoon or detachment size.

DEMOBILIZATION

The Ottoman Army sustained terrible losses during the war but still had some 900,000 men on its rolls, organized into 26 infantry divisions, at the armistice.[17] Although the armies in Syria, Mesopotamia, Asir, and Yemen were badly worn down by combat and desertion, the armies in the Caucasus, Thrace, and Gallipoli were mostly at their established war strength. In November 1918, the Ottoman Army did not, as Lenin famously remarked about the Russian Army when it quit the war in 1917, vote with its feet and return home. Instead, the Ottoman Army remained a disciplined force under competent command authority. Unlike Germany, the Ottoman Empire signed an armistice that did not require the immediate demobilization of its army and the surrender of its weapons.[18] Rather, the Ottoman demobilization would be coordinated with the British authorities and would be contingent on internal and external security requirements. In contrast, under the terms of the armistice with Germany, the German Army had to surrender almost immediately 5,000 artillery guns, 3,000 mortars, 1,700 military aircraft, 5,000 motor lorries, and 25,000 machine guns.[19]

The Ottoman General Staff, under direction from Ahmet İzzet Pasha, sent out telegraphic instructions concerning the implementation of the armistice to all armies and garrisons on October 31.[20] Further instructions followed in November 1918, outlining the timelines and geographic parameters of the turnover of strategic points to the Allies. The Yildirim Army Group and the Seventh Army were inactivated on November 4 and the surviving units subsumed into the Second Army in Adana. The Eastern Army Group and the 1st Caucasian Corps were inactivated on November 21, followed by the inactivation of the Army of Islam on 27th.[21] By late November, the Ottoman General Staff had completed the reorganization process and issued orders to all corps and divisions, assigning them to peacetime garrisons within the Anatolian heartland.[22] By December, several armies and corps, as well as seven infantry divisions were inactivated, including the Eighth Army, which was being reconstituted near Izmir after its destruction in Palestine.

However, in western Arabia, Fahrettin Pasha still commanded more than 10,500 men and maintained control of Medina and its hinterlands.[23] British officers attached to Emir Ali's headquarters notified Fahrettin of the signing of the Mudros armistice, especially of paragraph 16, which specified that the Ottoman Army would withdraw from Yemen, the Asir, and the Hejaz. However, Fahrettin was unsure if the information was true and how to proceed if it were, so he wrote to Ahmet İzzet Pasha, for instructions while holding his position.[24] It was not until January 20, 1919 that Fahrettin received instructions from Istanbul ordering him to stand down and surrender his men. As his story spread in the postwar Ottoman Empire, he became known to the public as the "Lion of the Desert" and the "Defender of Medina."[25]

General Ali İnsan Pasha's Sixth Army continued to guard the southeastern frontier approaches along the Euphrates and Tigris rivers. However, it was also inactivated in mid-February 1919. The surviving XIII Corps absorbed the remnants of the army and withdrew behind the agreed-upon lines under the armistice.

British high commissioner Gough-Calthorpe dictated the Allied demobilization schedule on November 26, 1918.[26] According to the British schedule, all men in year groups 1866–1884 were to demobilize beginning on November 6 (and this was apparently already in progress); all men in year groups 1885–1893 were to be demobilized beginning on November 28; and the 1897–1899 year groups would begin demobilization on January 6, 1919. About 10,000 officers and 264,339 men were discharged under this schedule by January 22, 1919, which still left the army with about 60,000 more men than the British thought appropriate to Ottoman military requirements at that point.[27] Reducing the number further was left on the table, but the Turks were willing to repatriate 10,000 Arab and 4,300 Greek soldiers who were then serving in the Ottoman Army to areas outside the rump Ottoman State. Demobilization resumed in February on a massive scale, as forces returned home from the Caucasus. By the end of March 1919, the Ottoman Army had discharged another 337,615 soldiers, leaving 61,223 men on active duty.[28]

THE ARMISTICE ARMY

The Ottoman General Staff finalized its plans for the new peacetime active army on January 21, 1919.[29] The army inactivated most of its surviving field army headquarters and returned to its prewar system of army inspectorates. Under the inspectorate system, a field army–level commander was responsible for the training and mobilization of military forces within his geographic area of responsibility. In keeping with its reduced land mass, the Ottoman General Staff planned to activate three inspectorates by June 7, 1919: the First Army Inspectorate in Istanbul, the Second Army Inspectorate in Konya, and the Third Army Inspectorate in Erzurum.[30] The Ninth Army, which was retreating from Persia, was briefly named the Ninth Army Inspectorate, but it was inactivated on April 3, 1919, providing the staff for the new Third Army Inspectorate. However, by May 14, the plan completely fell apart with the government decision to inactivate all three inspectorates.[31]

The army authorized a postwar establishment of 20 infantry divisions organized into nine army corps. Rather than reactivating sequential numbered army corps (from I to IX) or divisions (from 1 to 20) the General Staff retained the wartime designations and colors (see table 1.1).

Table 1.1   Ottoman Army Corps, May 14, 1919

Corps	Headquarters	Subordinate Divisions & Regiments—Locations
I Corps	Edirne	49th Division—Kırklareli
		60th Division—Keşan
III Corps	Sivas	5th Caucasian Division—Amasya
		15th Division—Samsun
VIII Corps	Diyarbakir	2nd Division—Silvan
		5th Division—Mardin
		5th Cavalry Regiment—Siverek
		11th Cavalry Regiment—Malatya
XII Corps	Konya	11th Division—Niğde
		24th Division—Ereğli
		41st Division—Karaman
		7th Cavalry Regiment—Beyşehir

Table 1.1   (continued)

Corps	Headquarters	Subordinate Divisions & Regiments—Locations
		20th Cavalry Regiment—Aksaray
XIV Corps	Bandirma	61st Division—Bandırma
		55th Division—Tekirdağ
XV Corps	Erzurum	3rd Caucasian Division—Tortum
		9th Caucasian Division—Erzurum
		11th Caucasian Division—Van
		12th Division—Horasan
XX Corps	Ankara	23rd Division—Afyonkarahisar
XXV Corps	Istanbul	1st Division—İzmit
		10th Caucasian Division—Istanbul
XVII Corps	Izmir	57th Division—Aydin
		56th Division—Izmir

Source: Tevfik Bıyıklıoğlu, *Türk İstiklâl Harbi I, Mondros Mütarekesi ve Tatbikatı* (Ankara: Genelkurmay Basımevi, 1962), Map 8, between pages 184 and 185.

The General Staff returned to a scaled-down version of the cadre organization that the active army used prior to the war, and each division was authorized 1,540 riflemen, 36 machine guns, and 8 artillery pieces.[32] Additional artillery was held at the corps level, as were more machine guns. Altogether, there were roughly 41,000 men and 256 artillery pieces in the active Ottoman field army in late spring 1919. The total strength of the army, including staff, schools, and garrisons, was approximately 61,000 officers and men. These active strengths were governed by the strict economies of the bankrupt Ottoman Empire, but the army held the substantial reserves of a far larger force—791,000 rifles, 2,000 machine guns (light and heavy), and 945 artillery pieces, as well as large quantities of ammunition.[33] However, much of this material lay in magazines located in areas controlled by the Allies. As will be seen, the retention and storage of these armaments would prove critically important to the resurrection of the Nationalist Army in 1920 and 1921.

The prewar triangular structure of infantry divisions was retained, as was an independent assault battalion in some of the divisions. When called to full mobilization under this plan, the Ottomans would have an active army of 20 combat divisions, fielding about 250,000 men. Moreover, using the reserve equipment stockpiled in Anatolia, they retained the capacity to activate another 10 infantry divisions. Additionally, the Ottoman General Staff itself continued to exist and continued to function as a directing staff. The professional corps of trained general staff officers was, likewise, retained and, as would be expected, continued to hold the important command and staff posts within the army (see map 1.1).[34]

THE RETREAT FROM THE CASPIAN

Events in the Caucasus in 1918 had moved in unpredictable directions. The collapse of the Russian Army in the wake of the Bolshevik Revolution led to the Ottoman Army drawing down its strength in the region as well. By the end of 1917, the Ottomans had reduced their strength there by half, withdrawing the entire Second Army and leaving the Third Army (composed of nine infantry divisions). At the same time, the staff received reports that the Armenians were building strength and Muslim Azeris were being massacred. In early January 1918, the ever-aggressive Enver Pasha decided to conduct a Caucasian offensive to recover the territory lost in 1916, which had been abandoned by the Russians and claimed by the Armenians.[35] Enver reinforced the Third Army with several infantry divisions and additional equipment and supplies. The Armenians, with the help of the Russian general headquarters on the Caucasian front, had formed a small national army of two infantry divisions and three infantry brigades.[36] On February 12, 1918, General Vehip Pasha's Ottoman troops went forward, capturing Erzincan and Trabzon. The Treaty of Brest-Litovsk, signed on March 3, 1918, restored the 1878 Russo-Ottoman border, thereby returning three provinces to the empire, including the cities of Kars, Batum, and Sarıkamış. Vehip immediately seized Erzurum, destroying most of the

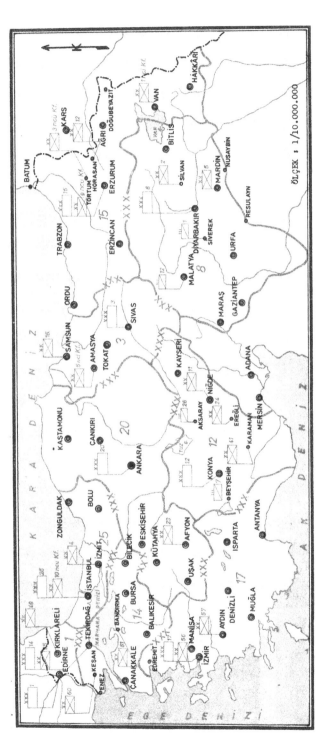

Map 1.1 The Ottoman Army (May 14, 1919)

As the Ottoman Army demobilized following World War I, its surviving divisions and corps headquarters returned to the army's garrisons in Anatolia. The postwar army had 20 reduced-strength cadre infantry divisions and four cavalry regiments. Rather than renumbering the surviving divisions from 1 to 20 and the surviving corps headquarters from I to IX, the General Staff retained the wartime division and corps designations.

Courtesy of the Turkish General Staff Military History and Strategy Institute (ATASE).

small Armenian Army. His army then marched to the 1914 border on March 25. Flush with victory and having eliminated Armenian resistance, Enver decided to push on to the 1878 border, and then to Azerbaijan. Batum fell on April 14, 1918, and Kars fell 10 days later.[37]

In May 1918, the short-lived Transcaucasian Federation dissolved, and its three republics, Azerbaijan, Armenia, and Georgia declared independence. Germany assumed a protectorate over the new Georgian republic, causing difficulties between the Ottomans and the Germans. On June 7, the hot-tempered Enver Pasha reorganized his armies for a drive to Baku on the Caspian Sea. Ottoman forces swiftly conquered Armenia and invaded Azerbaijan, capturing Baku itself on September 15, 1918.[38] Offensive operations in Azerbaijan and Persia continued beyond the Mudros armistice, but the agreement called for withdrawals back to the 1914 borders.

The British were quick to occupy Caucasian strategic points under the terms of the armistice. On November 14, Major General William Thomson's North Persia Force landed at Baku.[39] The Ottoman ministry of war thought the withdrawal would take two months, and, on November 17 and 18, the Ottoman armies in the east began the withdrawal from Baku and Tabriz, respectively. Since the Ottomans had restored the railways, the artillery and most of the army's supplies returned from Baku to Kars by rail. Determined to exert control in the east, General Milne's newly established Army of the Black Sea ordered Major General George Forestier-Walker's 27th Division to Batum, with a headquarters to be established in Tiflis (Tbilisi). Royal Navy detachments took control of Batum's port on December 19, clearing the way for Forestier-Walker's men to land on 22nd.[40]

There was much Ottoman unhappiness over the Mudros clause requiring a withdrawal to the 1914 border because three largely Muslim inhabited *sanjacks* (a county-like municipal area), Ardahan, Batum, and Kars, lay beyond that frontier. The Ottoman Ninth Army commander, General Yakup Şevki (Subaşı) Pasha, encouraged the Kars Municipal Council to organize resistance, which resulted in the Great Congress at Kars on November 30, 1918. This proto-Nationalist gathering began stockpiling weapons and advocated for a plebiscite. One hundred thirty-one delegates attended a subsequent congress on January 17–19, 1919, adding other Ottoman inhabited towns and proclaiming the Provisional National Government of the Southwest Caucasus.[41] They wrote a constitution and formed a government that included Russians and Greeks. At the same time, Forestier-Walker and Şevki entered into negotiations that were designed to install British garrisons in key infrastructure to deny it to the rapidly advancing (and revived) Armenian Army, as well as to coordinate the withdrawal of Ottoman Army units by sea to Istanbul.[42] On January 18, the Ottoman 5th Caucasian Division marched out of Batum, and, five days later, the Ottoman commander, General Cemal, departed by sea for Istanbul as well.

The British initially recognized the Kars government, but they were unable to prevent outbreaks of violence against Muslim inhabitants, attributed to Armenian forces that were led by the well-known Armenian general Andranik (Ozanian).[43] Andranik had led Armenian irregulars throughout World War I and brutally occupied Kars and Sarıkamiş. His men continued raiding as far south as Van, and hundreds of atrocities against Muslim inhabitants of the disputed area were reported.[44] Yakup Şevki protested vigorously but to no avail. On April 12, the British occupied Kars and arrested 11 members of the quasi government putting an end to the self-proclaimed Nationalist government.

The orderly withdrawal of the Ottoman Army from the Caucasus continued, and the Ottoman General Staff inactivated the Ninth Army on April 2, with Yakup Şevki returning to the capital on the 14th. Command and control of the area fell to General Kâzım Karabekir Pasha, commander of the XV Corps, which was then reorganizing in Erzurum. Kâzım was an experienced and resourceful soldier who proved to be an excellent choice for command of the critical eastern theater. In the following months, both Kâzım and British Colonel Anthony Rawlinson reported to their respective capitals that the Armenians perpetrated large numbers of massacres and atrocities on the Muslim inhabitants of the newly proclaimed Armenia and in the contested 1878–1914 border area.[45] Historian Stanford Shaw gravely understated the problem, noting, "The result was tremendously increased tension."[46]

Tensions were not limited to the Armenian frontier. The Muslim inhabitants of the Black Sea port city of Trabzon became worried by the vocal Nationalist aspirations of the Pontic Greeks and formed Muslim militia groups in January 1919, as well as a Trabzon Defense of National Rights Society. Several congresses were held and plans made to resist a takeover by Pontic Greeks.[47] However, the Pontic Greek leaders knew that armed rebellion would be a foolish move, and they opted for political agitation. This strategy was fostered by the Greek government itself, which sent a mission under Colonel Dimitrios Katheniotis to coordinate with the Pontic Greeks. However, in his report to Athens, Katheniotis said that Greek-supported independence for the Pontus was unfeasible, and he suggested that the Pontic Greeks ask the Armenians for support. In any case, as 1919 unfolded, violence against Pontic Greeks by Muslims and, reciprocally, against Muslims by Pontic Greeks increased in frequency.

THE GREEKS, ITALIANS, AND THE OCCUPATION OF IZMIR

As early as January 1915, British foreign secretary Sir Edward Grey dangled the idea of the acquisition of the eastern Aegean littoral in front of an eager Prime Minister Eleutherios Venizelos of Greece. On January 23, 1915, Grey wired the British minister in Athens to offer "most important territorial compensation on the coast of Asia Minor"[48] in exchange for Greece joining the Allies in the war. Venizelos was an ardent Nationalist and a fierce proponent of what was called the Great Idea (*Megali Idea* or simply *Megali*) of a revived Greek Empire, encompassing the lands inhabited by Greeks in ancient times. These included Epirus, Thessaly, Macedonia, the Peloponnese, Crete, Cyprus, and the Dodecanese and Aegean islands. Importantly, *Megali* also included Thrace and Istanbul, Izmir (then known as Smyrna), the west and southwest Anatolian coast and hinterlands, and the Pontus (the Anatolian Black Sea coast). These regions were heavily populated by ethnic Greeks, and their recovery fit neatly into the irredentist schemes of Venizelos. As a matter of practical concern, however, Ottoman Muslims outnumbered their Greek neighbors in many of these places. Moreover, 2,000 years of cultural diffusion created such anomalies as the Karamanli, who were Turkish Orthodox Christians who spoke and wrote in Greek, as well as Greeks who had converted to Islam and only spoke Turkish. Adding to the confusion were several million displaced refugees from the wars of 1877–1878, 1898, 1912–1913, and most recently 1914–1918, many of whom were Muslims.

Venizelos, who was originally from Crete, was 55 years old in 1919, and he was serving his third term as prime minister (1910–February 1915, August–September 1915, and June 1917–November 4, 1920). Venizelos was at the center of an internecine Greek political struggle called the National Schism between pro-Allied Greeks like himself and pro-German Greeks like King Constantine.[49] The divide tore Greece apart, but slowly—starting in 1915, when Venizelos allowed the Allies to bring their armies into Lemnos and Salonika—Greece leaned toward an Entente with the Allies. Over the next year, the Allies decided to depose King Constantine and permit

Venizelos to unite the country under his government. In a way, the Allies installed Venizelos as the de facto leader of the country. Throughout this period, Venizelos negotiated with the Allies to secure postwar territorial gains in exchange for entering the war, similar to the promises that the Allies had made to lure Italy into abandoning the Central Alliance and joining the Entente. Britain and France recognized the Venizelos government in December 1916, and the king went into exile a few months later. Greece joined the Allies in May 1917 and her army participated in the Macedonian campaign against Austria-Hungary, Bulgaria, and Germany. As Venizelos desired, at the end of the war, Greece was positioned to demand territorial compensation for her cooperation and efforts in defeating the Central Powers.

Like the French and the Italians, Britain cut the Greeks out of the armistice talks, much to the dismay of Venizelos. However, this did not stop the Greeks from occupying irredentist claims. In late 1918, General Milne's British forces occupied the area between Xanthi and Alexandropoulis, which had been awarded to Bulgaria in 1913, but the main Greek Army remained well to the west, near Salonika.[50] On January 14, 1919, the Greek Army sent officers east to monitor the railway stations of western Thrace from the Bulgarian border to Hadımköy. According to historian Stanford Shaw, the appearance of uniformed Greek officers caused local Greeks to "express their joy by pillaging and burning Turkish and Jewish homes and shops."[51] However, the Greeks did not stop there, and they prepared for further encroachments on Ottoman territory.

The wartime Agreement of St.-Jean-de-Maurienne between Britain, France, and Italy divided parts of the Ottoman Empire among the three signatories. Signed on April 17, 1917, it never came into force because the British and French had second thoughts about an Italian occupation of southeastern Anatolia and repudiated the agreement.[52] Under the agreement, Italy would receive most of southwest Anatolia, including Izmir, Bodrum, Antalya, and Konya. The overanxious and impatient Italians landed troops at Antalya and Marmaris in March 1919, ostensibly to keep order, and appeared poised to land troops at Izmir. By April, the Italian Army landed the 33rd Division, composed of the Livorno Brigade (the 33rd and 34th Infantry Regiments and two bersaglieri battalions) and supporting divisional troops.[53] Italy referred to this force as the Anatolian Expeditionary Corps and stationed its headquarters in the port city of Antalya. This overt act energized British prime minister Lloyd George to push American president Woodrow Wilson (both leaders were then at

Versailles working on the peace treaty with Germany) to intervene to stop the Italians. The Americans had not gone to war with the Ottoman Empire and were more or less neutral. Wilson threatened to send in the U.S. Navy, forcing the Italians to withdraw from the peace conference for consultations at home.[54] The Italians returned to Versailles on May 7 and, at the suggestion of Lloyd George (who did not want the Italians in Izmir), agreed to ask the Greeks to land men to keep civil order.[55]

The Greeks were ready for such a request. Previously, the Greek Navy had sailed the destroyer *Leon* into the Gulf of Izmir on December 24, 1918, raising a wave of celebrations among the Greek inhabitants of Izmir.[56] The ship carried a high representative—in this case, Captain Ilias Mavroudes, the well-known captain of the famous armored cruiser *Georgios Averof.* A few days later, Greek transports landed a Greek Red Cross element in the city. Venizelos then surfaced the proposals for occupations in parliament in January 1919, and the Greek staff began to plan seriously for expeditionary operations in Asia Minor. The Army Staff Service alerted the 1st Infantry Division, which was available, commanded by Colonel Nikolaos Zafeiriou, for the occupation of Izmir.

On the Ottoman side of the hill, the Eighth Army, which had been destroyed in Palestine in September 1918, was in the process of being reactivated, with the XVII and XXI Corps assigned to it. However, these plans were terminated after the armistice, leaving the XVII Corps in Izmir with the 56th and 57th Infantry Divisions under its command (both previously organized in the fall of 1916). On January 20, General Nurettin (Sakallı) took command of the Aydin military area and the forces stationed therein (including Izmir).[57] Nurettin was a professional soldier who had come up through the officer ranks, but he was not member of the elite Ottoman General Staff officer corps. Rather, he was promoted because he was a fighting general. Nurettin had won the battle of Ctesiphon and then pursued and encircled British major general Charles Townshend at Kut al-Amara in 1915, although the credit for the 1916 victory went to Enver Pasha's uncle Halil (Kut) Pasha.

Nurettin stepped into a domestic hornet's nest. According to the Turks today, similarly to the unrest in Thrace and in the Pontus, minority groups began to conduct episodes of banditry and violence directed against their Muslim neighbors. In fact, the so-called bandits were returning Ottoman Greek citizens who had been sent involuntarily to Greece in the Venizelos-CUP population removals of 1913–1914 and who were determined to recover their confiscated property (see chapter 12 for an explanation of the forcible population exchanges). They returned to find their homes confiscated and the property gone, causing justifiable outbursts of anger and violence. The Ottomans did not see it that way. Moreover, inflammatory articles supporting the *Megali Idea* appeared in Greek and British newspapers, which were extremely worrisome to General Mustafa Fevzi (Çakmak), chief of the Ottoman General Staff, who alerted all area commanders to be on the watch for outbreaks of banditry. Nurettin immediately had to confront a growing problem of uprisings and banditry in Urla (a town west of Izmir), where, on January 5, 1919, an armed gang of 20 to 30 Greeks stopped a vehicle and killed two travelers.[58] The Greek bandits (Turkish: *Rum çetesi*—translated, depending on context, as bandits, rebels, or guerrillas) began to prey on local Muslims and Jews. The problem accelerated in February with the landing of some Greek soldiers in nearby Ayvalık, who provided weapons and assistance to the bandits—who the Ottoman government now termed rebels.[59] Nurettin rushed to attack the bandits by mobilizing local Jandarma and police forces and crushed them. He was also careful to keep the local British, French, and Italian Allied Control Commission representatives apprised of his actions by reassuring them that he guaranteed the safety of the local Christians.

Episodes such as the Urla and Ayvalık incidents as well as localized violence in southwest Anatolia provided the Italians with plenty of reasons to intervene in an area they believed belonged to Italy. However, due to the active diplomacy of Lloyd George and Wilson, the Greeks reached Izmir first. Escorted by a combined Royal Navy-Greek Navy squadron, the Greek 1st Division began landing in Izmir at 7:50 a.m., Thursday, May 15.[60] Minister of War Ahmet İzzet Pasha instructed Ottoman XVII Corps commander, General Ali Nadir Pasha, not to oppose the landings and for his soldiers to remain in their barracks. The Turks assert that the Evzone Regiment (elite light infantry) of the Greek division marched in a victory parade to the joy of local Greeks and Armenians, who celebrated en masse, resulting in violence against local Muslims. A victory parade was not what army colonel Zafeiriou had planned. Instead naval captain Mavroudes intervened in Zafeiriou's initial plans and made a crucial change in the itinerary of the 3rd Battalion of 2/39th Evzone Regiment, making the march highly visible, which inflamed the situation.

Violence broke out almost immediately when gunshots were heard at the customs house. Various histories present the events differently. According to the Greeks, Nurettin planned to resist the occupation and prepared groups of soldiers and civilians to attack the occupiers.[61] The Greeks maintain that a raging firefight broke out in which 13 Turkish military, 47 civilians, and two Greek soldiers were killed, after which corps commander Ali Nadir Pasha, 56th Division commander Lieutenant Colonel Hürrem, 150 officers, and 540 soldiers were taken prisoner (along with 2,000 irregular fighters) and confined to the Greek steamship *Patris*.[62] Turkish sources claim that Ali Nadir Pasha kept his men in barracks but that 141 officers and men were killed that day.[63] Both agree on the number imprisoned on the *Patris*, but the Turks assert that some 2,000 died on the ship from maltreatment before urgent Allied appeals forced the Greeks to release the survivors on May 18. A British scholar wrote that 300–400 Turks and about 100 Greeks were killed or wounded on May 15 and that many atrocities were committed against Turks in the days that followed.[64] In any case, the violence accompanying the Greek landings at Izmir foreshadowed the grim events to come in the next four years.

The Greek Army restored order to the city and returned the remaining Ottoman Jandarma and local police to duty. However, a gathering Turkish resistance movement was now real and growing by the moment. The remnants of Ali Nadir Pasha's men, perhaps as many as 800 soldiers and 4,000 irregulars armed with machine guns and some artillery, withdrew to Aydin and established a strong presence there. With Ali Nadir detained, the newly appointed chief of the Ottoman General Staff, Cevat Pasha, ordered the XVII Corps chief of staff, Colonel Bekir Sami (Günsav) to assume command of the corps.

To protect their coastal enclave, the Greeks felt they had to expand their perimeter, and they pushed north toward Ayvalık, west to Kuşadası, and east toward Manisa. On May 27, the Greek Army pushed the Turkish Nationalists out of Aydin. Unfortunately, this enabled angry and now propertyless returning Greek refugees to subject local Muslims to a three-day spree of massacre and robbery.[65] Although Venizelos pressured the army to stop such incidents, conduct such as this inflamed the sensibilities of the Muslim Ottoman population and contributed to the gathering wave of anti-Allied Nationalist sentiment.

THE HUNT FOR WAR CRIMINALS

World War I unleashed waves of varied cause célèbres and generated a worldwide sense of humanitarianism that would come to characterize the 1920s. Violation of neutral nations' sovereignty, unrestricted submarine warfare, indiscriminate aerial bombing, and the killing of noncombatants were some of the humanitarian concerns affecting the ongoing negotiations in Versailles in the spring of 1919. In the Middle East, the Allies were concerned about the treatment of prisoners of war—especially those surrendered at Kut in 1916, the relocation of parts of the Ottoman Greek population, and the massacres perpetrated against Ottoman Armenians during the wartime relocations. The escape of Cemal, Enver, and Talaat brought these concerns to a head when the Allies forced the Ottoman government to request their extradition from Germany on November 11, 1918. The subsequent accusations, investigations, arrests, and trials of Ottoman officials charged with war crimes went on for three years and remains a bitterly politicized and contested history to this day.[66] In any case, Admiral Gough-Calthorpe was the man on the spot and now had to balance judicial demands from London (mainly from British solicitor general Sir Ernest Pollock) against the actions and reactions of the Ottoman government.

During the war itself, some 1,673 Ottoman civil and military officials were tried and sentenced to death or hard labor by the Ottoman judiciary for crimes committed against Ottoman Armenians.[67] After the armistice, there were two sources of Ottoman inquiry and judicial action against what would today be considered war crimes and crimes against humanity. In the first case, deputies in the Ottoman parliament investigated from November 5–December 21, 1918. Commissions at the national and provincial level were established—the most well-known today is the Istanbul Court Martial—to try Ottoman officials and soldiers for crimes against Ottoman Armenians and Greeks. There was much objection to these trials in parliament, but when parliament dissolved, Damat Ferit continued cooperating with the Allies and assembled dossiers on individuals accused of crimes. On January 3, 1919, Admiral Gough-Calthorpe, frustrated by armistice violations and inaction by the Ottoman government, cabled London, asking permission to imprison the accused.[68] Gough-Calthorpe expanded his definition of crimes to include such thing as insulting Allied officers and breaches of the customs of war. Gough-Calthorpe's roundup of accused war criminals began on January 5 and continued for two months. Most of the accused were former members or supporters of the routed Committee of Union and Progress. In May 1919, the British imprisoned the accused on Malta to await trial, which pleased the anti-CUP Damat, who had asked for their removal.

The dossiers assembled by the government were heavily politicized because most of the accused were members of the CUP. Often the documents were forged or constructed piecemeal to build a cherry-picked narrative. The most well-known forged document to appear was the infamous *Ten Commandments of the Committee of Union and Progress*, acquired by Royal Navy intelligence officer Commander C. E. Heathcote-Smith on February 4, 1919, which originated from an Armenian-Greek Committee in Izmir.[69] The document purported a plan to exterminate the Ottoman Armenian population and, although undated, was supposedly written in December 1914 or January 1915. More forged documents surfaced, which purportedly showed extermination orders flowing from the CUP government in Istanbul to Cemal Pasha in Syria. The authenticity of these documents is bitterly contested today, but many contemporary politically neutral scholars dispute them.

Not all the accused were genuine war criminals. The French demanded the arrest of all wartime cabinet officials simply because they might have committed crimes or supported the continuation of the war. Damat told the British on March 8, 1919 that he was arresting every individual on the British list of suspects, and he apprehended an additional 60 Ottoman officials. This sweep included not only government officials but also journalists and editors who had expressed sympathy for the gathering resistance movement in Anatolia. Simultaneously, with the extradition of the Allied suspects to Malta, the Ottoman government conducted the now well-known 1919 trials, which began with the first conviction on April 8 of Mehmed Kemal Bey for massacring Ottoman Armenians; he was sentenced to death by hanging.[70] Kemal Bey's funeral caused massive demonstrations against the government in Istanbul and in provincial capitals. The entire inner committee CUP regime was tried in absentia, including Enver, Talaat, Cemal, Bahattin Şakir, and Dr. Nazim Bey, who were all sentenced to death. The trials continued through July 5, when the indictments and remaining suspects then in custody were turned over to the British for transport to Malta. The British ultimately sent more than 100 Ottoman officials and civilians to Malta, including Third Army commander Mahmud Kâmil Pasha, Sixth Army commander Ali İnsan Pasha, Medina commander Fahrettin Pasha, Prime Minister Said Halim Pasha, Chief of the General Staff Cevat Pasha, Minister of the Marine Rauf Bey, Minister of War Cemal (Mersinli) Pasha, Nationalist writer Ziya Gökalp, journalists Celal Nuri (İleri) and Ahmet Emin (Yalman), and Kurdish Nationalist Süleyman Nazif.[71] Within the British government itself, their legal status was much in dispute, but by mid-1921, about a third had been released, while some escaped—notably Rauf and Ali İnsan.[72] On October 23, 1921 the remaining 59 prisoners were released in exchange for a handful of

British prisoners held in Anatolia. In the end, due to a lack of authentic evidence, none of the Malta prisoners were tried by the British.

THE POSTWAR OTTOMAN GOVERNMENT

The last Ottoman sultan, Mehmed VI Vahdettin (1861–1926), took the throne on July 4, 1918 upon the death of Mehmed V Reşad. Sultan Vahdettin's reign lasted until November 1, 1922 when the Turkish Grand National Assembly abolished the sultanate. The 57-year-old new sultan spent most of his time trying to maintain the legitimacy of his dynasty and remain the titular head of the Ottoman Empire.

The Ottoman parliament had existed since 1876 but had not met from 1878 until 1908 when the empire functionally became a constitutional monarchy. The Ottoman prime minister also held the post of grand vizier, a position that dated back to the earliest days of the sultanate. During World War I, the CUP Triumvirate (Enver, Talaat, and Cemal), rather than Said Halim Pasha, the prime minister, made all the important decisions in the operation of the government. In the armistice period, there were 12 governments and seven prime ministers, which grew gradually weaker as the Nationalist movement in the Anatolia interior grew stronger.

Ahmet Tevfik replaced Ahmet İzzet Pasha on November 11, 1918, and Ottoman politics entered an extremely turbulent period. The CUP was formally disbanded and its property confiscated, although it had previously dissolved itself. Damat Ferit revived the Liberal Union Party under his own leadership, and he adopted the position that it was the CUP, rather than the Ottomans, that had lost the war.[73] The surviving members of the CUP mostly joined the new Regeneration Party, which embraced secular and Nationalist ideologies, or the Ottoman Freedom-Loving People's Party, which advocated a liberal agenda retaining the sultanate. Other new parties sprang into existence, complicating parliamentary unity. An attempt at political unification came from the newly formed National Congress, organized by some well-known Istanbul professionals, which held several meetings in November and December. According to historian Stanford Shaw, "In the face of the CUP revival and the proliferation of political groups opposing the peace settlement and Allied occupation, the Sultan finally dissolved parliament (21 December 1918) to deprive them of a forum and enable the government to rule by decree without the need for popular consultation."[74]

Over the next few months, patriotic organizations, Nationalist societies, military and naval associations, and university student organizations—in other words, those who might publicly cause trouble and dissent—were dissolved or disbanded. This period of centralized rule came to an end on March 4 when Damat Ferit formed a government with himself as prime minister. Structurally, the cabinet remained fundamentally unchanged from the wartime cabinet, and the Ministry of the Interior was the principal administrative office working with the Allied Control Commission. During most of 1919, the most influential man in the Ottoman government was Damat Ferit (1854–1923), who was married to Sultan Abdülmecid I's daughter, in turn becoming Sultan Mehmed VI's brother-in-law. Although he had served many years in the Foreign Service in Paris, Berlin, St. Petersburg, and London, he was judged "of limited competence and narrow vision."[75] As a lifelong enemy of the CUP, Damat was devoted to the idea of the Sultanate. His government lasted until October 2, 1919 when Ali Riza Pasha became prime minister.

Damat was pro-British and supported Admiral Gough-Calthorpe in almost all the demands and requests made by the commissioners. Moreover, the Ottoman prime minister could not do anything substantial without the approval of the Allies. In truth, much of what Britain did in those days, in terms of trying to limit Greek and Italian expansion in Anatolia, as well as their willingness to imprison former CUP members, aligned with the sultan and Damat's political objectives. Damat was so successful in marginalizing members of the party that had brought the empire into the war that on February 1, 1919, the Istanbul government abolished the CUP as a legal political party in the empire.

CONCLUSION

While the armistice and Damat preserved the sultanate, the dysfunction and authoritarian actions of the Ottoman government served to increase feelings of nationalism among those who called themselves Turks. The Allies contributed to this with their high-handed de facto occupation of Istanbul and their support for Venizelos and his efforts to carve parts of the Ottoman Empire away from the Turks. There was a growing sense among the Turkish part of the Ottoman population that the Allies were something of a pack of hungry wolves circling for the kill. Likewise, there was a growing sense among the Greeks, Armenians, and some of the non-Turkish Muslim minorities that a window of opportunity for throwing off the shackles of Ottoman rule was opening.

NOTES

1. Winston S. Churchill, *The World Crisis: The Aftermath*, vol. 5 (London: Thornton Butterworth Limited, 1929), 366.

2. John Terraine, *Douglas Haig, The Educated Soldier* (London: Hutchinson, 1963), 460–461.

3. Archibald C. Bell, "The Turkish Breakdown," in *A History of the Blockade of Germany and of the Countries Associated with Her in the Great War: Austria-Hungary, Bulgaria, and Turkey 1914–1918* (London: Her Majesty's Stationary Office, 1937), unpaginated. See also Marion C. Siney, "British Official Histories of the Blockade of the Central Powers during the First World War," *The American Historical Review* 68, no. 2 (1963): 392–401, https://doi.org/10.2307/1904539.

4. Stanford J. Shaw, *From Empire to Republic: The Turkish War of National Liberation, The Rise and Fall of the Ottoman Empire, 1300–1918*, 5 vols. (Ankara: Türk Tarih Kurumu Basımevi, 2000), 65–67. See also Briton Cooper Busch, *Mudros to Lausanne: Britain's Frontier in West Asia, 1918–1923* (Albany: State University of New York Press, 1976), 12–20.

5. David Fromkin, *A Peace to End All Peace: The Fall of the Ottoman Empire and the Creation of the Modern Middle East* (New York: Henry Holt & Company, 1989), 368–369. Although somewhat dated, Fromkin's narrative of the armistice negotiations is by far the most readable.

6. Metin Ayışığı, *Mareşal Ahmet İzzet Pasha* (Ankara: Türk Tarih Kurumu Basımevi, 1997), 163–172.

7. Shaw, *From Empire to Republic*, vol. 1, 72–75.

8. Erik-Jan Zürcher, "The Ottoman Empire and the Armistice of Moudros," in *At the Eleventh Hour: Reflections, Hopes, and Anxieties at the Closing of the Great War, 1918*, eds. Hugh Cecil and Peter H. Liddle (London: Leo Cooper, 1998), 266–275.

9. Shaw, *From Empire to Republic*, vol. 1, 78–93. The late Professor Shaw's exposition of the armistice negotiations is the most comprehensive in the English language.

10. Tevfik Bıyıklıoğlu, *Türk İstiklâl Harbi I: Mondros Mütarekesi ve Tatbikatı* (Ankara: Genelkurmay Basımevi, 1962), 80–81.

11. Fromkin, *A Peace to End All Peace*, 372.

12. Bıyıklıoğlu, *Mondros Mütarekesi ve Tatbikatı*, 113–115.

13. A note on city names. In 1973 the city of Maraş was renamed Kahramanmaraş; however, for brevity I have used the 1920s name Maraş. Antep (or Ainteb) was renamed Gaziantepe in February 1921. Urfa is the central city in Şanlıurfa Province.

14. Cyril Falls and A. F. Becke, *Military Operations Macedonia: From the Spring of 1917 to the End of the War* (London: Her Majesty's Stationery Office, 1935), 306.

15. Ibid., 308–309.

16. Ismet Görgülü, *On Yıllık Harbin Kadrosu 1912–1922* (Ankara: Türk Tarih Kurum Basımevi, 1993), 197.

17. Fahri Belen, *Birinci Cihan Harbinde Türk Harbi 1914 Yılı Hareketleri, Vnci Cilt* (Ankara: Genelkurmay Basımevi, 1967). Ek: Harpte kurulan tümenler (Chart: Divisions organized in the war), pages 250–251. Twenty-six divisions remained on establishment of the 62 infantry divisions organized during the war. None of the five cavalry divisions organized during the war survived.

18. The armistice, signed at Mudros Harbor on October 30, 1918, called for the surrender of strategic points such as the Dardanelles and the Toros and Amanus tunnel complexes, but it left the Ottoman Army's leadership intact. See Fromkin, *A Peace to End All Peace*, 373.

19. Cyril Falls, *The Great War* (New York: G. P. Putnam's Sons, 1959), 416.

20. Bıyıklıoğlu, *Mondros Mütarekesi ve Tatbikatı*, 46–47.

21. Zekeriya Türkmen, *Mütareke Döneminde Ordunun Durumu ve Yeniden Yapılanması (1918–1920)* (Ankara: Türk Tarih Kurumu Basımevi, 2001), 30–31.

22. Bıyıklıoğlu, *Mondros Mütarekesi ve Tatbikatı*, 68–69.

23. Şükrü Erkal, *Birinci Dünya Harbinde Türk Harbi VIncı, Hicaz, Asir, Yemen Cepheleri ve Libya Harekâtı 1914–1918* (Ankara: Genelkurmay Basımevi, 1978), 375.

24. Ibid., 385.

25. İsmail Bilgin, *Medine Müdafaası: Çöl Kaplanı Fahrettin Paşa* (Istanbul: Timaş Yayınları, 2009), 291.

26. Bıyıklıoğlu, *Mondros Mütarekesi ve Tatbikatı*, 184–185. This source erroneously identifies Admiral Sir John de Robeck as the officer responsible for the demobilization schedule.

27. Ibid., 185.

28. Ibid., 185.

29. Ibid., 177–178.

30. Görgülü, *On Yıllık Harbin Kadrosu*, 200.

31. Bıyıklıoğlu, *Mondros Mütarekesi ve Tatbikatı*, Map 8, following 184.

32. Ibid., 180.

33. Necmi Koral, Remzi Önal, Rauf Atakan, Nusret Baycan, and Selâttin Kızılırmak, *Birinci Dünya Harbı Idarı Faalıyetler ve Lojistik, Xncü Cilt* (Ankara: Genelkurmay Basımevi, 1962), 583.

34. Görgülü, *On Yıllık Harbin Kadrosu*, 197–213.

35. Edward J. Erickson, *Ordered to Die: A History of the Ottoman Army in the First World War* (Westport, CT: Greenwood Press, 2001), 182–184.

36. W. E. D. Allen and Paul Muratoff, *Caucasian Battlefields: A History of the Wars on the Turco-Caucasian Border 1828–1921* (Cambridge: Cambridge University Press, 1953), 458–459.

37. Mesut Uyar, *The Ottoman Army and the First World War* (London: Routledge, 2021), 396–416.

38. See Erickson, *Ordered to Die*, 179–192 for a narrative of these campaigns.

39. Richard G. Hovannisian, *The Republic of Armenia: The First Year, 1918–1919*, vol. 1 (Los Angeles: University of California Press, 1971), 60–61.

40. Falls and Becke, *Military Operations Macedonia*, 307–309.

41. Shaw, *From Empire to Republic*, vol. 2, 924–925.

42. Bıyıklıoğlu, *Mondros Mütarekesi ve Tatbikatı*, 164–165

43. Ibid., 167. The Turkish official history uses the phrase "systematic massacre" to describe Andranik's activities, but this is contested by Armenian sources. See Hovannisian, *The First Year, 1918–1919*, 427.

44. Ibid., 162.

45. Shaw, *From Empire to Republic*, vol. 2, 934–937.

46. Ibid., 937.

47. Ibid., 938–942.

48. Edward Grey to Sir Francis Elliot, F. O. Papers, Series 371, Volume 2242 (Jan. 23, 1915), quoted in Michael Llewellyn-Smith, *Ionian Vision: Greece in Asia Minor 1919–1922* (New York: St. Martin's Press, 1973), 35.

49. For a superb view of Venizelos, see Konstantinos Travlos et al., "The Correlates of Obsession: Selectorate Dynamics and the Decision of Venizelos for Military Intervention in Asia Minor," in *Salvation and Catastrophe: The Greek-Turkish War, 1919–1922*, ed. Konstantinos Travlos (Lanham, Maryland: Lexington Books, 2020), 67–107.

50. James E. Edmonds, *The Occupation of Constantinople 1918–1923 (Provisional)* (Draft manuscript written in 1944, transcribed by Neil J. Wells and published in 2009) (Brambleside, East Sussex: The Naval and Military Press, 2010), 3.

51. Shaw, *From Empire to Republic*, vol. 2, 463.

52. Paul C. Helmreich, "Italy and the Anglo-French Repudiation of the 1917 St. Jean De Maurienne Agreement," *The Journal of Modern History* 48, no. 2 (1976): 99–139, http://www.jstor.org/stable/1877819.

53. Giovanni Cecini, *Il Corpo di Spedizione Italiano in Anatolia (1919–1922)* (Rome: Stato Maggiore Dell'Esercito, Ufficio Storico, 2010), 77–78.

54. Fromkin, *A Peace to End All Peace*, 392–393.

55. Shaw, *From Empire to Republic*, vol. 2, 480–495.

56. Demetrios Gedeon, Eupraxia Paschalidou, and Angeliki Dima-Dimitrou, *A Concise History of the Campaign in Asia Minor 1919–1922*, English ed. (Athens: Hellenic Army History Directorate, 2003), 7. The dates in this book conform to the Old Greek calendar and are 13 or 14 days earlier than the European calendar (depending on the month and year). Therefore, when I present a date from this book, I convert the date using the following online program: http://aulis.org/Calendar/Old_%26 _New_Style_Dates.html.

57. Necati Ökse, Nusret Baycan, and Salih Sakaryalı, *Türk İstiklâl Harbi'ne Katılan Tümen ve daha Üst Kademelerdeki Komutanların Biyografileri (İkinci Baskı)* (Ankara: Genelkurmay Basımevi, 1989), 229–231.

58. Bıyıklıoğlu, *Mondros Mütarekesi ve Tatbikatı*, 136.

59. Ibid., 137.

60. Shaw, *From Empire to Republic*, vol. 2, 493–507. Professor Shaw provides the most coherent account of the complex diplomacy behind these events.

61. Gedeon, Paschalidou, and Dima-Dimitrou, *A Concise History of the Campaign in Asia Minor*, 16–18.

62. Ibid.

63. Shaw, *From Empire to Republic*, vol. 2, 510–511; and Ökse, Baycan, and Sakaryalı, *Komutanların Biyografileri*, 243.

64. Llewellyn-Smith, *Ionian Vision*, 90.

65. Ibid., 91.

66. For a short summary taken exclusively from western sources see Michelle Tusan, "'Crimes against Humanity': Human Rights, the British Empire, and the Origins of the Response to the Armenian Genocide," *The American Historical Review* 119, no. 1 (February 2014): 47–77. For

opposing perspective taken almost entirely from Ottoman sources see Shaw, *From Empire to Republic*, vol. 1, 303–329. There is vast extant literature on this topic related to the debate of whether the relocation and massacres of Ottoman Armenians in 1915–1916 constituted a genocide.

67. Pulat Tacar and Maxime Gauin, "State Identity, Continuity, and Responsibility: The Ottoman Empire, the Republic of Turkey and the Armenian Genocide: A Reply to Vahagn Avedian," *The European Journal of International Law* 23, no. 3 (2012): 827–828.

68. Arthur Gough-Calthorpe to F. O. Papers, No. 14 Secret, FO 371/4172/2391 (Jan. 3, 1919), quoted in Shaw, *From Empire to Republic*, vol. 1, 309–310.

69. Shaw, *From Empire to Republic*, vol. 1, 312.

70. Ibid., 321.

71. Ökse, Baycan, and Sakaryalı, *Komutanların Biyografileri*, 192–193.

72. See Shaw, *From Empire to Republic*, vol. 1, 303–344 for a comprehensive narrative of the legal positions of the British government based on documents from the British archives.

73. Stanford J. Shaw and Ezel Kural Shaw, *History of the Ottoman Empire and Modern Turkey: Reform, Revolution, and Republic: The Rise of Modern Turkey, 1808–1975*, vol. 2 (Cambridge: Cambridge University Press, 1977), 332.

74. Ibid., 333.

75. Shaw, *From Empire to Republic*, vol. 1, 156.

TWO

Call to Arms

There has now arrived at Erzeroum the Inspector-General of the Turkish Eastern armies, who has since become famous as Mustapha Kemal Pasha, a great Turk.[1]

Lt. Col. Anthony Rawlinson, 1919

INTRODUCTION

It was remarkable that the Osmanlı dynasty continued in power after the collapse of its Romanov, Hapsburg, and Hohenzollern counterparts at the end of World War I. However, that the famously named sick man of Europe endured until 1922 was not as much a tribute to its strength but rather an indictment of its malleability in the hands of the Allies. Soon after the armistice, Nationalist officers in the army conspired to form a resistance to Allied occupation and to the encroachments of the agreed terms of Mudros. At first, the Nationalists thought to act within the apparatus of the Ottoman government, but they soon realized that the Sultan and his government were simply pawns of the victors. This led to a growing sense of alarm and to the evolution of a Nationalist movement led by Mustafa Kemal in Anatolia. A Nationalist assembly grew into a Nationalist government centered in Ankara, which claimed political legitimacy based on maintaining the territorial integrity of the nation.

MUSTAFA KEMAL AND THE ARMISTICE

Mustafa Kemal was 38 years old in spring 1919. It is hard to imagine that a man so young could have such an effect on his times and on history, but Kemal was, in the words of Winston Churchill, a man of destiny.[2] He was well prepared to step onto the stage of world history and had served with distinction at Gallipoli and in Palestine in World War I. By the end of the war, he commanded the Ottoman Seventh Army, saving it from destruction in Syria. He was highly educated, a graduate of the Ottoman War Academy—a three-year curriculum stressing operations and national-level strategy. In addition to Ottoman Turkish, Kemal spoke German and French and read voraciously in all three languages.[3] Kemal was an ardent Nationalist and modernizer and had been an early member of the Young Turks (the CUP), but his attempts to break into the inner circle of party leadership were unsuccessful.

In January 1918, Mustafa Kemal was moderately well known to the Ottoman public for his brilliant performance during the Gallipoli campaign of 1915; however, his criticisms of Enver and the Germans had led to his dismissal in 1917.[4] As 1918 arrived, Kemal was without an appointment and sick, and he watched from the sidelines as the Ottoman Empire became progressively weaker. Upon the succession of Sultan Vahdettin, who was an admirer, Kemal was professionally and politically rehabilitated to command the Ottoman Seventh Army in Palestine. He arrived there in late August and was caught up in the disastrous defeat at Megiddo in September. During the retreat from Palestine, Kemal was constantly in touch with the new cabinet in Istanbul, seeking a political appointment. When he received the full text of the armistice on November 3, 1918, Kemal was furious with the terms, which turned over control of such key strategic locations as Istanbul, the Dardanelles, the Pozantı tunnel, and Mosul to the allies. This caused him to send telegrams to the capital opposing certain clauses of the armistice and stating that he intended to oppose the British occupation of Iskenderun by force. Ahmet İzzet ordered him to peacefully turn over the city and then promptly resigned as prime minister—but not before relieving Kemal of his post.[5] On November 10, 1918, Kemal turned over command of the Second Army and departed from Adana by train for the capital. Kemal arrived in Istanbul on November 13, once again without an appointment and seemingly finished career-wise, to find the Allied fleet anchored off the city's Golden Horn.[6]

Andrew Mango's magisterial biography *Atatürk: The Biography of the Founder of Modern Turkey* captures the zeitgeist of the armistice period with the chapter title "Figures in a Ruined Landscape."[7] The figures that Mango refers to broadly fall into two categories: those colluding with the Allies to save the sultanate at any expense and those who chose a path of resistance to Allied occupation and encroachments. Moreover, Mango's use of the phrase "ruined landscape" captures not only the penury and damage caused by the war but also the psychological impact of the magnitude of the defeat. Mustafa Kemal was one of a number of professional military officers who have come to be known in Turkish history as "the Nationalist group of officers."[8] When it became clear that World War I would end in the defeat of Germany and the Ottoman Empire, these men became politically active with a view toward preserving the independence and territorial integrity of a Turkish successor state. In the summer of 1918, Kemal was in contact with a number of these officers, including Fethi (Okyar) and Rauf (Orbay), who were conspiring to replace the CUP government.[9] Kemal hoped to be appointed minister of war in a new government.

Throughout his service in the retreat to Aleppo, Kemal remained in contact with his Nationalist friends and maintained a constant finger on the pulse of the political affairs in Istanbul. However, he was still deeply engaged in the military campaign when the CUP cabinet collapsed on October 10, and retired general Ahmet İzzet formed a new government, with himself as prime minister. Kemal pressed his associates hard and tried unsuccessfully to secure a place for himself in the new government. Although Rauf secured a cabinet post, the Nationalists were unable to convince İzzet to reject the British armistice agreement. Within a short period of time, the Allies occupied the capital, the straits, and most of Cilicia. Subsequently, the peace process in 1919 began the breakup of the Ottoman Empire of its Middle Eastern provinces (Arabia, Yemen, Iraq, Lebanon, Palestine, and Syria), leaving it with what was essentially the Turkish heartland of Anatolia. Moreover, a succession of ineffective cabinets was unable to prevent the Italians, French, Greeks, and Armenians from occupying even more parts of Anatolia than the victors anticipated. As a result, resistance from the group of Nationalist officers to this piecemeal destruction of the country began almost immediately after the first days of occupation.

In Istanbul, Kemal continued his political machinations, but he was unsuccessful in advancing himself for a command or a key army staff position. He met secretly with his friends, but he was unable to generate much government support for his cause of halting foreign intervention and ejecting foreign forces from the territory remaining to the empire.[10] Beyond securing the war minister's portfolio in the government for himself, Kemal's most compelling concern was the ongoing demobilization of the Ottoman Army. In spring 1919, Allied control commission officers, the most aggressive of which were British, fanned out across the truncated empire to count and collect weapons for demilitarization.

Kemal was encouraged when the government appointed a number of Nationalist officers to important command positions, including Cevat (Çobanlı) as minister of war, Mustafa Fevzi (Çakmak) as chief of the general staff, and İsmet (İnönü) as assistant chief to study military aspects of the armistice agreement.[11] Other important Nationalist-leaning officers were appointed to key commands in the spring of 1919, including Fahrettin (Altay) in the XII Corps in Konya, Ali Fuat (Cebesoy) in XX Corps in Sivas and Kâzım (Karabekir) in XV Corps in Erzurum.[12] All these men had served during the war with Kemal, and they commanded some of the largest remaining formations in the armistice army. Moreover, the government gave Kemal's friend İbrahim Refet (Bele) command over the Ottoman Jandarma, a large and well-trained paramilitary gendarmerie, stationed throughout the empire's cities and towns. (Refet left the Jandarma and took command of the III Corps in Ankara in May 1919).[13] According to one historian, Kemal, Rauf, and these officers were "the original military planners of the Turkish War of Independence."[14] Of future significance, Kemal's former trusted subordinate from Palestine, İsmet, was a frequent visitor at his house and helped formulate the plan of action. Karabekir left for the east, determined to hold back the advancing Armenians, while the others took up their posts equally determined to conceal weapons from the Allied inspectors. They were taking their lives in their hands since the sultan went to any lengths to please the Allies, and their actions effectively made them criminals.

At the same time, the hunt for, and imprisonment of, former CUP leaders, who were now considered war criminals, began in earnest, as the Ottoman government sought to appease the Allies regarding the ill-treatment of prisoners of war and the Armenian massacres. Several of Kemal's political and military associates were arrested, but he was not. Whether the Allies wanted Kemal arrested is unclear, although the Italian high commissioner Count Sforza later claimed that the British were preparing to arrest him and send him to Malta.[15] In March 1919, the Italians seized the Mediterranean port city of Antalya, while the Greek government announced claims to

Izmir and its hinterlands, as well as to the Pontus region of the Black Sea coast. But it was the encroachments of the Armenians and the Greeks that affected Kemal. According to Ali Fuat, this disorder in eastern Anatolia led Interior Minister Mehmet Ali to recommend Kemal for an appointment as Ninth Army Inspector.[16] Kemal met with the minister of war and the assistant chief of the general staff and agreed to terms of reference that conformed to the Allied plan for demobilization and occupation.

The government gave Kemal unusually wide authority over both military and civil administration in eastern Anatolia. He was charged with restoring order, confiscating and storing weapons, and stamping out Nationalist and revolutionary councils. On April 30, 1919, he was appointed Ninth Army Inspector, which, in the German-derived peacetime Ottoman command architecture effectively amounted to the position of army commander. This was no small success for Kemal, as the Ninth Army area contained Karabekir's XV Corps of four infantry divisions and Ali Fuat's III Corps of two infantry divisions. Kemal was given so much power that his counterpart Second Army Inspector, Cemal (Mersinli), complained to the minister of war. This was not the high-level political position that Kemal had envisioned, but, providentially, the appointment put him in the best possible location to lead the Nationalist revival.

Throughout this period, Kemal had extensive meetings with Mustafa Fevzi, the outgoing chief of the general staff, and his successor, Cevat, who were Nationalists themselves and clandestinely supportive of what Kemal wanted to accomplish. On May 15, while Kemal was still in Istanbul, the Greek Army landed in Izmir with the intent of annexing it. This was a surprise to the government, which had not taken seriously Greek Prime Minister Venizelos's *Megali*, which advanced the notion that a greater modern Greece must encircle the Aegean Sea and include Istanbul, as well as ancient Ionia (the eastern Aegean littoral and most of western Anatolia). Kemal's final call on the grand vizier that day found the government stunned by these events.

UNIFYING THE RESISTANCE

The British were aware of Kemal's Nationalist aspirations and of his collusion with fellow Nationalists. The British liaison officer at the Ottoman ministry of war, John G. Bennett, hesitated to issue a travel permit to Kemal but the government assured him that Kemal could be trusted to carry out his instructions.[17] In the meantime, Greek forces occupied Izmir and began to push into the interior. On May 16, 1919, Kemal boarded the elderly steamer *Bandırma*, bound for Samsun on the Black Sea coast. Before the ship's departure, British inspectors searched it looking for weapons and contraband, leading Kemal to later assert that during the inspection, he exclaimed, "We are not taking contraband or arms, but faith and determination!"[18] Kemal and his personal staff landed in Samsun on May 19 and initiated a campaign to unite the disjointed Nationalist resistance movement. Belatedly, that day, the British high commission asked the government why it was sending a man to command the Ninth Army, which was designated for demobilization. In fact, the Ninth Army was inactivated on April 3, 1919, and the Third Army Inspectorate was activated in its place on June 7; however, this was irrelevant to Kemal, who was already slated to oversee the transfer of headquarters designations.[19] The Turks have celebrated May 19 as a Turkish national holiday since 1935 and, according to Andrew Mango, "in Turkish popular thinking it marks the beginning of the Turkish War of Independence."[20] I would agree and, from this point in the narrative, I will refer to Mustafa Kemal and his adherents as the Nationalists, and the sultan and his government as the Ottomans.

British inspectors in Samsun were alerted to monitor closely Kemal's actions. A British relief officer, Captain L. H. Hurst, warned him repeatedly and strongly about supporting anti-government Nationalist groups. Undeterred by these admonitions, Kemal spent a few days encouraging local Nationalists and stirring up anti-Greek sentiment. He departed the city, bound for the interior, on May 25 in a Benz automobile, leaving Refet in change in his absence. The automobile soon broke down, but Kemal, on foot and by wagon, then visited army and Jandarma garrisons. In the town of Havza, Kemal opened the army's magazines and distributed weapons to local Nationalists, encouraging resistance to Armenian and Greek occupation. Captain Hurst, having learned this, met with Kemal in Havza on June 1 to warn him again, but Kemal reassured him that he was not leading a resistance movement. Hurst was not stupid and left "with a feeling that mischief was afoot."[21] His messages to Admiral Gough-Calthorpe in Istanbul warned that organizing resistance would lead to massacres of non-Turks, but Gough-Calthorpe felt that trying to stop the Nationalists was hopeless.

Kemal relentlessly sent telegraph messages to all army headquarters, urging commanders to demand independence from foreign occupation. On May 28, he sent similar messages to provincial officials, famously flooding the telegraph system to the point of excluding normal traffic.[22]

Encouraged by Kemal's proclamations, Turkish Nationalist protest groups formed in the empire's cities, often coalescing around military commanders and units. Kemal's provocative actions immediately caused the British to demand his relief. The government recalled him on June 8, but he delayed by sending a reply asking why they had done so. Captain Hurst continued to report accurately from Samsun and watched helplessly as Kemal organized the resistance.

Rauf left the capital to join Kemal but only made it as far as Ankara where he joined Ali Fuat on June 6. There, Rauf learned that Kemal, fearing arrest by the British, had gone on to Amasya, a town deeper in central Anatolia, where Refet's III Corps and 5th Caucasian Division were garrisoned and provided a safe refuge. Refet, Ali Fuat, and Rauf left to join Kemal in Amasya on June 12. By now, the government was sufficiently alarmed that Kemal's activities would compromise the Ottoman delegation's position at Versailles that it forbade the telegraph and postal transmission of Nationalist messages encouraging resistance. Rauf and Ali Fuat reached Amasya on June 18, and spent several days in discussions with Kemal about the future of the resistance. Refet joined them on June 21, and they (Kemal and Refet) sought and obtained support from Second Army Inspector Cemal in Konya and XV Corps commander Kâzım Karabekir in Erzurum. Kemal was now poised to issue what amounted to a revolutionary call to arms.

Most telegraph officials ignored the government's directive, and Kemal was able to send his now famous Amasya Circular on the night of June 21/22, 1919 explaining the need for a national parliamentary body and giving notice to hold national congresses in Sivas and Erzurum. In fact, provisional Nationalist congresses already existed in several provinces and cities. Kemal's signature on the circular was essentially an act of open rebellion against the Ottoman government. It also brought him into conflict with Karabekir, who thought his actions were too strong.

The Amasya Circular essentially had three parts: a problem statement, a proposed solution, and a recommendation about what to do next. The problem, according to Kemal, was twofold: (1) the territorial integrity of the country and the independence of the nation were in danger, and (2) the central government proved unable to discharge the duties for which it was responsible. As a result, the independence of the nation was essentially nonexistent. Kemal's solution was revolutionary—only the will and resolution of the people could save the independence of the nation. He ended with a plea to conduct a regional Nationalist conference in Erzurum, followed by a Nationalist congress in Sivas. The government's reaction was conflicted because some of the cabinet sympathized with the Nationalists, with only the interior minister, Ali Kemal,[23] demanding his return to Istanbul. In turn, arguments in the cabinet drove the minister of war (Şevket Turgut) and the minister of the interior to resign. Some local officials tried unsuccessfully to arrest Kemal.

Kemal and Ali Fuat left for Erzurum on June 28 by way of Erzincan and met Karabekir 10 miles outside the city on July 2. Over the next few days, the government attempted to have Refet persuade Kemal to resign from the army and abandon the Nationalists. This caused Kemal to send out his last telegraph message, advising that army formations should not demobilize further and that no more arms or munitions should be handed over to the allies.[24] This action proved too much for the sultan's government and provoked a strong response from Istanbul. Admiral Gough-Calthorpe also weighed in, demanding that the government recall Kemal, Cemal, and Refet.

On the night of July 8/9, 1919, Kemal in Erzurum traded angry telegrams with Ferit Pasha, the new minister of war in Istanbul, at the end of which Kemal resigned from the army. It was not immediately clear at the time what would happen next, sending Kemal into a bleak period of despair. There is dispute about what occurred during this period, and Kemal's recollections conflict with those of Karabekir and Rauf.[25] The government appointed Karabekir to replace Kemal as Third Army Inspector, expecting him to conform to the Allies' demands for demobilization and the turnover of weapons. In the end, Karabekir stood by his friend, and he refused to alter the basic tenants of Kemal's directives. This was a key moment for the Nationalist movement because, in doing so, Karabekir removed himself as the only real competitor to Kemal's self-appointed role as the movement's leader. On July 13, Refet resigned from the army in support of the Nationalists. Colonel Çolak Selâhattin (Köseoğlu) (hereafter referred to as Selâhattin [Köseoğlu]), who unknown to the ministry of war favored the Nationalists, replaced him.

The sultan was then persuaded to issue a directive (a firman) prohibiting convening unconstitutional congresses that might provide the Allies with further provocation for interventions. The ministry of war sent instructions to all army commands to ignore any requests or directives from Kemal and the Nationalists. Kemal and the Nationalists persevered and, on July 23, the regional Erzurum Congress opened to elect delegates to send to Sivas, at which the Nationalists planned to convene a national congress.[26] Still wearing his uniform and supported by Karabekir, Kemal wrangled politically with the Trabzon representatives and finally prevailed to lead the delegation destined for the national congress in Sivas. A 10-point political doctrine was drawn up that rejected the dismemberment of the empire by foreign occupation and affirmed that the army was responsible for its territorial integrity. More importantly, Kemal ensured that the idea of a national territory composed of a Muslim Turkish and Kurdish majority within the boundaries agreed to at the Mudros Armistice was embedded in the document. Belatedly, on July 27 and for two days after, the government tried to stop the congress and issued arrest warrants for Kemal and the Nationalist leaders, but these were ignored. The Nationalists sent out invitations countrywide, inviting delegates to Sivas. The tidal wave of Turkish nationalism, at this moment, was inevitable and unstoppable.

THE SIVAS AND THE AMASYA CONTAGION[27]

The Sivas Congress opened on September 4, 1919. The government ordered Kemal's arrest and sent a troop of Kurdish cavalry to apprehend him. Kemal received warnings, and an Ottoman Army cavalry detachment successfully intercepted the Kurds. Under the protective cover of Ali Fuat's XX Corps in Ankara and Colonel Selâhattin's III Corps in Sivas, both of whom disregarded instructions from Istanbul, the Sivas Congress opened on September 4. According to Andrew Mango, the Sivas Congress was not representative and "brought together Nationalist militants who were largely self-appointed."[28] Mango also asserted that many of the delegates were former members of the disbanded and illegal CUP. Of over 200 delegates invited, less than 40 actually attended, enabling Kemal to dominate the proceedings and convince many of the delegates to reach the Nationalist consensus, which adopted the ideas of the regional Erzurum Congress. The Sivas Congress adjourned on September 11 with several important outcomes; a Representative Committee with Mustafa Kemal as its president was elected, charged with unifying the national movement under the tenants outlined in the Erzurum and Sivas doctrines.[29] For all intents, the Representative Committee became the executive body for the Nationalist movement. In the end, the Sivas Congress was a de facto declaration of war on foreign occupation of Anatolia and European Turkey.

One of the Representative Committee's first actions was to issue a directive organizing national defense around a national army (*Milli Ordu*), which would consist of the already organized Ottoman army corps and the

National Forces.[30] The idea behind the National Forces was to bring the various dissident Nationalist groups under centralized control. These irregular ad hoc forces would keep order in their towns; protect the inhabitants from the depredations of Greeks, Armenians, and Kurds; and help the army as needed. The army's corps commanders in Anatolia favored the Nationalists, and the Representative Committee ordered them to distribute the stockpiled weapons to these local irregular organizations and groups. The National Forces were organized into two kinds of units: mobile field units (*seyyar*) and static/stationary units (*sabıt*). The stationary units were defensive and charged with the protection of towns and citizens, and the field units were capable of limited offensive actions. The National Force units were supposedly organized into companies and regiments, but such formal designations broke down, and the units were designated as groups and were normally named for the place of origin—for example, the Hamza Grubu or the Grup Elemanları. Since all Ottoman men had previously served in the military and many had recent combat experience, this was not a difficult task. The establishment of mobile National Forces under competent command proved fortuitous in the coming year when revolts broke out throughout Anatolia (see chapter 4).

The Representative Committee charged Ali Fuat with organizing the National Army from the existing Ottoman Army architecture in Anatolia. Four corps responded to him, and he organized them into three districts. District One: XX Corps (Ankara) and XII Corps (Konya), District Two: III Corps (Sivas), and District Three: XIII Corps (Diyarbakır).[31] Functionally, these districts performed the same tasks as the Ottoman Army inspectorates and were responsible for the integration of the National Forces and National Army into a cohesive whole. Kâzım Karabekir, commanding the army's largest XV Corps in Erzurum, was a staunch Nationalist but chose to remain outside the formal architecture of Ali Fuat's National Army. The British mission in Samsun reported that this process was developing rapidly, which greatly troubled the Allies. The sultan's government was, likewise, troubled by the Sivas Congress and by the establishment of a Nationalist military forces and sent General Mustafa Fevzi Pasha (First Army Inspector) on a fact-finding mission to eastern Anatolia. Mustafa Fevzi arrived in Sivas on October 25, 1919 to find most of the Nationalist commanders already there at a planning meeting.[32] He spoke with several commanders, including Kemal, Karabekir, and İsmet. Mustafa Fevzi had close personal and professional ties to the Nationalist commanders and officers in Anatolia and rendered an apparently innocuous report on November 3.[33]

Unsurprisingly, throughout the coming months, the Ottoman Army corps commanders in Anatolia continued to receive orders and instructions from the ministry of war in Istanbul. Kemal made efforts to bring the remaining Ottoman Army corps and divisions over to the Nationalist cause and sent cables to Cafer Tayyar Pasha, commanding the I Corps in Edirne and Yusuf İzzet Pasha, commanding the XIV Corps in Balıkesir, as well as the commanders of the 56th and 61st Divisions. These efforts came to naught. However, the XVII Corps in Aydin, under the command of Colonel Bekir Sami (Günsav), had been in action against the Greeks at Izmir since the middle of May and came over to the Nationalists.[34]

On October 9, Grand Vizier Ali Rıza sent Minister of Marine Salih Hulusi to Amasya to carry messages to Kemal, Bekir Sami, and Rauf to try to repair relations between the government and the Nationalists. During the Amasya Conference, October 18–22, 1919, Kemal responded positively, but conditionally, to the government's overtures. He demanded that the decisions made by the Erzurum and Sivas congresses be respected and adhered to; that parliamentary elections be held with assurances that Nationalists could run for office; and that the Representative Committee be given a voice in political, financial, and military decisions. He also demanded that no special privileges be allowed for non-Muslim minorities and that the Malta prisoners be released. While the cabinet broadly sympathized with the Nationalists, Ali Rıza could not possibly accept all these conditions. Kemal agreed to negotiate through Minister of War Cemal (Mersinli) Pasha. On October 22, they issued the Amasya Declaration (not to be confused with the Amasya Circular), which contained five main protocols.[35] The most important parts stated that the sultanate and caliphate would continue; the territories identified at Sivas and specified by the Mudros agreement, including Thrace, Cilicia, the Kurdish areas, and the province of Aydin, could not be separated from the polity; no foreign mandates were acceptable, except for economic assistance; officials who opposed the Nationalists were to be replaced; and a new parliament was to be elected and convened outside of Istanbul.

Kemal and Rauf returned to Sivas believing they had a deal, but it fell apart in days when Cemal Pasha balked at some of the terms. Those in Istanbul who favored appeasing the occupation forces, as well as minority groups such as the Greeks and Armenians, bitterly opposed the declaration. Ali Rıza insisted on maintaining parliament in Istanbul, while Kemal demanded that it move to somewhere in Anatolia and out from under the thumb of the Allies. In the end, the agreement broke down completely.

However, what General Fahri Belen called the "Amasya Contagion" was now abroad and, in the elegant prose of Sir Winston Churchill,

> All of the raked-out fires of Pan-Turkism began to glow again. That Greeks should conquer Turks was not a Decree of Fate that any Turk would accept. . . .
>
> But among the stern hills and valleys of "the Turkish Homelands" in Anatolia, there dwelt that company of poor men . . .who would not see it settled so; and at their bivouac fires at this moment sat in the rags of a refugee the August Spirit of Fair Play.[36]

VISITORS TO VERSAILLES AND ANATOLIA

The evolution and history of the Treaty of Versailles, signed on June 28, 1919 in the Hall of Mirrors, is well known, and its effects are largely outside the scope of this book. It did not formally end World War I in the Middle East, which technically continued until the sultan's government signed the Treaty of Sèvres on August 10, 1920. However, many of the promises, both explicit and implicit, made before and during the negotiations directly and immediately affected the Ottomans. This situation was complicated by wartime agreements made between the Allies and the restive minorities in the Ottoman Empire. Adding even more convolutions was the intervention of the Americans, who became caught up in the Allies' desire to create a mandate system under the supervision of the soon-to-be establish League of Nations.

Naturally, the Ottomans were not invited to send a formal delegation to participate in the Peace Conference, "either to present their own case or to make the necessary rejoinders when false information or matters of dispute arose during the conference."[37] However, as a result of the internecine Allies' arguments over Antalya and Izmir, on June 1, the Allies invited Damat Ferit to send a formal Ottoman delegation to Versailles. The delegation arrived in Paris two weeks later and was composed of Grand Vizier Damat Ferit, Finance Minister Tevfik Bey, Ambassador Reşad Halis Bey, Senate President Rıza Tevfik, and former Grand Vizier Tevfik Pasha. On June 17, 1919, Damat Ferit presented the Ottoman Empire's case to the conference's supreme council, blaming the war on the CUP. Damat's rambling statement asked for the retention of the sultanate and its territory and an ending of the occupation, as well as the return of western Thrace from Bulgaria. Over the next few days, while Lloyd George, Georges Clemenceau, and Woodrow Wilson were discussing what to do with the Ottomans, Damat Ferit provided them with a more explicit formal memorandum. Essentially, he asked the Allies, with minor concessions, to restore the empire to its *status quo ante bellum*.[38] The Allies were quick to reject Damat Ferit's proposals and sent the Ottoman delegation packing. The delegation left insulted, angry, and concerned about the future; however, this did not stop Damat Ferit in July from blaming the Anatolian resistance for his failure to secure concessions from the Allies at Versailles. Importantly, Damat's repeated and strident demands only served to stoke Venizelos's fears that Greece would not materially benefit from its support of the Allies in World War I.

British prime minister Lloyd George had already engaged the attentions of American president Woodrow Wilson to intervene on behalf of Greece against the Italians. Lloyd George continued to pressure Wilson in May 1919 to accept a mandate for Anatolia, including the provinces claimed by Armenians. Wilson was already under considerable domestic political pressure from Armenian diaspora political groups in the United States and from Armenian Nationalist delegations at Versailles. In particular, the American Committee for the Independence of Armenia, led by former Ambassador James Gerard and listing over 100 well-known Americans, including William Jennings Bryant, Justice Charles Evans Hughes, AFL union leader Samuel Gompers, and New York governor Al Smith, as well as the powerful Armenian National Union of America, led by naturalized expatriate Vahan Kardashian, continually pushed Wilson and the congress for action. Additionally, a delegation at Versailles, led by Armenian statesman Avetis Aharonian, represented the newly established Republic of Armenia.[39] He was assisted by Sir Mark Sykes, who supported the Armenian cause, and by the well-known Armenian Nationalist Boghos Nubar, who represented the western Armenians. A Kurdish delegation seeking independence, led by Şerif Pasha also arrived at Versailles to advocate for the Ottoman Kurds. Faced with such vocal and prominent domestic and international pressure, Wilson responded by organizing two commissions to investigate conditions and make recommendations as to whether the United States should accept a League of Nations mandate in Anatolia. Since the United States had not declared war with the Ottoman Empire, both the Allied delegates and the Ottoman delegates at Versailles hoped that the neutral American commissions would produce results favorable to their respective interests.

The first to arrive in Istanbul on June 7, 1919 was the King-Crane Commission, led by Oberlin University president Henry King and industrialist Charles Crane. They were accompanied and advised by Professor Albert

Lybyer from the University of Illinois, who had written extensively on Ottoman institutions, and Presbyterian Reverend George Montgomery. Lybyer's body of work was taken exclusively from non-Ottoman sources since he neither read nor spoke any Middle Eastern languages, and both King and Montgomery were well known for their abysmal opinions of Turks.[40] They were, however, accompanied by an experienced American oil field explorer, who is almost forgotten today, named William Yale, who had been a Department of State special agent in Cairo before and during the war.[41] The King-Crane Commission was charged with investigating the area known as the Levant, including Syria, Palestine, and what is today southeast Turkey.

The commission proceeded to Syria via Beirut and returned to the capital on July 21. The commission interviewed leading provincial officials, Ottoman political figures, journalists, Nationalists, academics, Kurds, Greeks, and Armenians, and the Allied high commissioners.[42] Accompanying the commission as an advisor to Crane was journalist Louis Edgar Browne. Crane desired to interview Kemal and the Nationalists but felt that it was unwise to do so officially since they were considered quasi rebels. Instead, Crane sent Browne as his unofficial representative to meet the Nationalists. Browne went east by train to Ankara where he met with Ali Fuat, and then proceeded to Sivas for 18 days, meeting both Kemal and Rauf, much to the indignation of the Greeks, Browne's dispatches to the *Chicago Daily News* presented Kemal and the Nationalists in a more favorable light than did previous reports. Later, at the Sivas Congress, Kemal presciently told the delegates that Browne thought that America "might well reject" the mandate for Anatolia.[43] The commission left Istanbul on August 21 and submitted its report to the American Delegation at the Paris Peace Conference on August 28. Since Wilson had already returned to America, the delegation held the King-Crane Report as a basis for future negotiations regarding the mandate.

The King-Crane Report recommended forcibly dividing the Ottoman Empire into mandates supervised by the Allied Powers. The division of Arabia, Mesopotamia, Palestine, and the Levant into British and French mandates is well known today, generally following the lines drawn by Mark Sykes and François Georges-Picot in January 1916. Regarding Anatolia, the commission recommended an American mandate for Istanbul and the Turkish straits, an American mandate for Armenia, an unspecified mandate for Anatolia (constituted around what they called "the bulk of the Turkish people"), and an autonomous Greek region around Izmir and its hinterlands. King and Crane pointed out that such a plan would be very expensive and would require several thousand soldiers to enforce and manage the implementation.

A second American investigative commission was dispatched from France, led by U.S. Army Major General James G. Harbord, chief of staff of the American Expeditionary Force. Harbord was instructed to proceed to eastern Anatolia and Armenia to investigate considerations relating to possible American interests in the region. He left Paris on August 13 and arrived in Sivas on September 20, 1919. Two days later, Harbord met with Kemal, who explained the Nationalist positions and told Harbord that the Turks would only accept an American mandate that did not interfere in Turkey's internal affairs. Harbord and his 26-man commission then went on to Erzurum, where they met Kâzım Karabekir on September 25.[44] Initially, Harbord was sympathetic to the plight of the Armenians, both refugees and the nascent republic, but when confronted with evidence of Armenian atrocities and encroachments, he changed his views. The commission went on to the Caucasus, visiting Tiflis, and then returning to Istanbul on October 11. Harbord submitted his extensive 13-volume report to the American Delegation at Versailles on October 16. Harbord was explicit in his analysis. He stated that Ottoman Anatolia, including Edirne in Thrace and Tiflis in Georgia, was economically interdependent and should compose a single mandate. Further, Harbord stated that the three Transcaucasian republics were not viable politically and economically, and he recommended placing them under a single mandate as well. As an experienced military planner, Harbord was able to estimate America's potential investment as $90 million ($1.33 trillion in 2020 USD) in the first year, as well as 60,000 to 200,000 soldiers.[45]

The Americans were not the only ones to meet with the Nationalists in Anatolia that fall. France sent veteran diplomat François Georges-Picot to Kayseri to meet with agents of the Representative Committee in Konya on September 27–28 to seek a rapprochement in Cilicia. Later, in response to a letter from Kemal expressing concern for outrages committed in the areas under French control, Picot returned to meet with Ali Fuat on November 21, 1919 in Kayseri, where Picot hinted that French policy supporting the Armenians might soon change and that France favored a strong Turkey. Kemal then invited Picot to Sivas for discussions on December 8, at which Picot told him that the French occupation of Cilicia was temporary. Furthermore, Picot offered a rapid and complete evacuation of Cilicia in return for exclusive economic privileges for France, which Kemal rejected out of hand.[46] In return for a French promise to withdraw the Armenian legions from Cilicia and protect Muslim lives and property, Kemal agreed to halt attacks on French forces. According to Andrew Mango, discounting the story about Kemal meeting Count Sforza in Istanbul, "it was his first important contact with an important Allied representative (discounting Harbord since America was not an actual Allied Power and had participated in the war as an Associated Power)."[47]

The outcomes of these meetings with the Americans and French were not immediately apparent. The meetings did serve to expose the goals and opinions of the Turkish Nationalists to the world, unfiltered by Lloyd George, the British, the Greeks, and the Armenians. The extensive costs and responsibilities of an American mandate in Anatolia identified in the reports of the American commissions influenced the U.S. Senate, which refused to ratify the Treaty of Versailles or join the League of Nations, ending all interest in an American mandate. Recognition of this reality then forced Britain to continue its efforts in controlling the future of the Ottoman state.[48] Most importantly, however, these meetings served to legitimize and encourage the aspirations of the Nationalist government in Sivas, as well as alert the Allies that the sultan's government was no longer in full control of its territory and peoples.

SECRET SOCIETIES AND IRREGULARS

The role of secret societies, patriotic groups, and irregular militias in the early stages of the Turkish war of Independence cannot be overstated, as these played large roles in suppressing anti-Nationalist dissent and organizing resistance. The earliest established secret group arose from the ashes of the Teşkilat-ı Mahsusa, the Special Organization, set up by Enver Pasha to gather intelligence and foment revolution in Allied territory and dissolved at the end of World War I. The ex-members initially organized in Istanbul on November 13, 1918 and named the successor organization Karakol Cemiyeti (the Sentry Society), hereafter Karakol, under the direction of army Colonel Kara Vasıf (1872–1931) and ex-CUP minister Kara Kemal.[49] Karakol inherited an existing organizational architecture, weapons, money, and "above all experience in underground activities."[50]

Karakol maintained its headquarters in Istanbul and was instrumental in smuggling individuals accused of war crimes out of the city. It established a network of safe houses under the noses of the British and began to publish Nationalist propaganda for countrywide distribution. Karakol organized mass rallies against the occupation and established links with Bolsheviks in Russia to gather support against the Armenians in eastern Anatolia. It was very successful in smuggling arms concealed in Istanbul to the Nationalists and, by 1920, had reportedly sent 320 machine guns; 1,500 rifles; 2,000 cases of ammunition; and thousands of rifle parts, uniforms, and miscellaneous military equipment to the National Forces and the National Army.[51] Cumulatively, these were no small achievements. Mustafa Kemal had ambiguous feelings toward Karakol supporting their goals but was wary of its CUP roots infecting the Nationalist movement.[52] By spring 1920, Kemal dissolved Karakol and replaced it with a personal secret service named Hamza Grubu, under the leadership of Colonel Çopur Neşet (Bora), to continue the smuggling operations out of British-controlled Istanbul. Hamza Grubu was later renamed the Felah Grubu.

Other secret societies composed of army officers, who had access to arms and magazines, also organized and smuggled weapons to Anatolia.[53] The societies in Gallipoli and Akbaş shipped over 18,000 rifles, 400 heavy machine guns, and 5,500 cases of ammunition to Anatolia.[54] The army commanders in the XIV Corps area (where this happened), including 61st Division commander Colonel Kâzım and the Gallipoli fortress commander Colonel Şevket (Galatalı), actively helped the smugglers. One historian asserted, based on British records, that some 80,000 rifles were removed from Allied control in the Gallipoli sector alone.[55] Ottoman commanders later told the Allied commissioners that the French inspectors then supervising the demobilization in that area were lax in their responsibilities. Farther to the east in the XII Corps area, where there were very few Allied commissioners, staggering quantities of weapons and munitions were sent to the Nationalists, including 25,000 rifles, 60 machine guns, and 32 field artillery guns with 64,000 artillery shells.[56] Officers in the III, VIII, and XX Corps also provided large numbers of German Mauser rifles, howitzers, shells, and ammunition from their reserve magazines to Kemal. The smugglers also dispatched animals, such as oxen, horses, and even camels to haul the caissons and wagons necessary to support the army. Most of these weapons were not immediately put into the hands of soldiers (who were already armed) but were stored away in magazines and armories for the future.

Pro-Nationalist irregular armed groups began to coalesce and organize in many provincial towns. While there were numerous local names for these groups, a commonly used term in the extant Turkish literature is Defense of Rights Societies. These societies acquired arms and were often organized and led by ex-army officers and government officials. Well-organized societies formed powerful groups, particularly in the southeast where neither the government nor the Nationalists had a strong presence: in Gaziantepe on December 17, 1918; Maraş on February 22, 1919; and Urfa on March 24, 1919, as well as in Adana, Ceyhan, Mersin, Osmaniye, Pozantı, and Tarsus.[57] When Armenian atrocities against Muslims in Cilicia increased in the spring of 1919, these societies turned from a defensive posture to the offensive, engaging in guerrilla warfare against the French and their Armenian allies. Kemal decided to step up guerrilla activity and ordered the regular forces in the area to provide arms and equipment for the irregular societies. Key towns were taken over from the French, and their supply lines cut off. The success of the irregular societies and the inability of the French to combat them in summer 1919 were the driving factors in the decision to send Picot to negotiate with the Nationalists.

FRENCH INTERVENTION ON THE BLACK SEA COAST

While the armistice agreement had used the words "strategic points" in its text, these were poorly defined and offered opportunities to the Allies for progressive occupation. In addition to the military strategic points, such as the Pozantı tunnel complex or the Dardanelles, there were economic strategic points as well. The most important functional strategic resource in Anatolia in early 1919 was the coal mine complex at Zonguldak and Ereğli on the Black Sea coast. The mines were the sole remaining source of coal in the empire, but they were owned by a French concession, which wanted them returned to company control (the Germans had taken them over during the war). With rising unrest in the Pontus, the French intervened on March 8, 1919 by landing a large force of police and soldiers to maintain order in the Zonguldak-Ereğli area.[58] Exploitation of the mines went smoothly, but the French occupation of Cilicia (see chapter 6) led them to withdraw most of the garrison on April 12. The security situation in the area deteriorated steadily, and the Nationalists organized a Defense of Rights militia in late October 1919, causing Pontic Greek communities and repatriated Armenian refugees to form similar armed groups. Moreover, both the Ottoman government in Istanbul and the Nationalist government in Ankara claimed ownership of the coal mines and, by the spring of 1920, civil disorder reigned in the area.

The French reinforced their residual garrison on June 8, 1920, reoccupied the Zonguldak and Ereğli mines, and extended their control inland to

Kastamonu.[59] This expansion of the French zone cut the road from the western front to Ankara, causing Kemal to order the Zonguldak National Forces and the Nationalist Army to drive the French out. The Nationalists immediately began to ambush French detachments and convoys, causing the French to send in an additional 2,000 soldiers in July and bring in large numbers of weapons to arm Pontic Greek militias. By January 1921, the French had as many as 10,000 soldiers armed with artillery and machine guns in Zonguldak and Ereğli.[60] However, a reversal of French policy toward the occupation of Anatolia led the government to withdraw the entire French force on June 21, 1921. According to historian Stanford Shaw, the French evacuation "tremendously improved Nationalist morale" and also "removed a serious threat to the rear of the Nationalist Army as it was preparing for the Battle of Sakarya."[61]

CONTAINING GREEK EXPANSION

By June 1919, the Greek Army forces in Anatolia came under the command of Major General Konstantinos Nider, whose Army Corps A headquarters was located in Izmir. Nider's corps had five infantry divisions under its control: the 1st Division at Aydin, the 2nd Division at Izmir, the 13th Division at Manisa, the Archipelago Division at Pergamum, and the Smyrna Division at Izmir.[62] With the partial destruction of the Ottoman Army's 56th Division, the Ottomans had the 57th Division to the east and south of Aydin, commanded by Colonel Şefik (Aker), and the XIV Corps' 61st Division at Bandırma, commanded by Colonel Kâzım (Özalp), opposing the Greeks. Both divisions were understrength but were reinforced by groups of Nationalist irregular fighters. Fighting broke out as the Nationalists attempted to reclaim lost territory on what they called the Menderes River front.

As the Greeks occupied Izmir, Damat Ferit protested feebly to the Allies while the Ottoman General Staff ordered their forces in the region to contain the Greek Army's expansion. Instructions to this effect went out to the corps and division commanders from May 27 to June 1. On June 28–29, Şefik's 57th Division launched an attack against the Greek 4th Regiment in Aydin and pushed it out of the city to the west.[63] The Greeks retreated to Germancik, and then rapidly moved the 1st Division from Buca to Tire by motor transport. On July 3, a coordinated Greek counterattack coming from the north and west retook Aydin, pushing Şefik back to the south. The Greek Army reported terrible atrocities and massacres perpetrated on Greek inhabitants when they reoccupied the city.[64] By July 7, the Greeks had pushed the Nationalist 57th Division 20 kilometers to the southeast where Şefik's men bumped into an Italian combat group at the village of Çine. This caused Şefik to reestablish his headquarters to the east of Aydin and pull most of his infantry back into Nazilli.

In the fall, smaller groups of Nationalist soldiers conducted harassing raids against Greek outposts and columns. These were not as significant as the Nationalist raids attempting to cut the railway and telegraph lines to Aydin, which became more frequent as 1920 approached. The Greeks claim that these raids originated in the Italian Zone, and soon the raiders launched artillery strikes on Greek units and on Greek civilians in Aydin and Ömerli.[65] To avoid conflict with the Italian Army, which had reached Çine and Söke, Venizelos negotiated a demarcation line with Italian foreign minister Tommaso Tittoni on July 29, 1919 (the Venizelos-Tittoni Line).[66] The Italians had previously landed at Antalya and Marmaris and had pushed inland quickly. By August 1919, major Italian units held a large part of southwest Anatolia: the Italian expeditionary headquarters and the 33rd Infantry Regiment occupied Antalya, the 34th Infantry Regiment held Kuşadası, the Livorno Brigade headquarters occupied Milas, the Bersaglieri held Çine, the 136th Infantry Regiment held Akşehir and Konya, and the 13th Cavalry Regiment held Söke. Subunits of these regiments garrisoned the smaller ports and cities.[67]

In the north, General Yusuf İzzet (Met) Pasha moved his Ottoman XIV Corps headquarters from Tekirdağ across the Sea of Marmara to Balıkesir. On June 4, his 61st Division lay in Bursa, with the 172nd and 188th Infantry Regiments forward at Ayvalık and Soma respectively.[68] The 172nd was an orphan regiment from the now reduced 56th Division and was commanded by Lieutenant Colonel Ali (Çetinkaya). Yusuf İzzet reinforced these regiments with groups of Nationalist volunteers and designated Ali's group as the Ayvalık Zone Command (Mıntı Komutanı) and Lieutenant Colonel Akif's 188th Group as the Soma Zone Command.[69] The groups of volunteers were typically composed of 100–200 men with machine guns and an artillery piece; importantly, most were veteran soldiers under experienced officers.

By early June, the Greeks had occupied the town of Bergama, and Yusuf İzzet was determined to recapture it, sending out orders to this effect on June 11, 1919. On June 14, the Ayvalık and Soma commands launched a coordinated attack from the west and east encircling the 1st Battalion, 8th Cretan Regiment in Bergama.[70] Combat continued throughout the day, and, at 9:00 p.m., the Greek commander decided to retreat, and he quietly disengaged. The Nationalists did not impede his withdrawal, but he abandoned his artillery and combat trains. On the 80-kilometer retreat to Menemen, the Nationalists continuously assaulted the Greek survivors, inflicting many casualties and, according to the official Concise Greek History, committing numerous atrocities.[71] In turn, the Nationalists reported that the Greeks retaliated by massacring a large number of Muslims in the town of Menemen.[72] The Greeks reacted rapidly by launching a counterattack with the 5th and 6th Archipelago Infantry Regiments supported by artillery and cavalry. The Nationalists put up strong resistance, but the Greeks retook the town on June 20. The Nationalists were pushed back halfway to Soma, where the front stabilized.

These were significant battles, with both sides losing hundreds of soldiers. At the end of July, the Hellenic Army of Occupation in Asia Minor was comprised of 2,082 officers and 63,223 men,[73] while the Nationalists opposed it with mixed forces composed of regular and irregular soldiers. In response to Greek expansion, Mustafa Kemal reinforced his forces with the 23rd Division from Afyonkarahisar.

In mid-August, British general Milne attempted to encourage the Greeks and Nationalists to abide by the terms of the armistice agreements, and the tempo of operations declined. However, in late October 1919, the Greek commanders in Izmir were informed that the Allies in Versailles had redrawn the demarcation line between the Greek and Nationalist forces. On October 29, General Milne formalized this line into what was then called the Milne Line, which somewhat enlarged the Greek bridgehead in Asia Minor.[74] The Greeks pushed out to the Milne Line, which was lightly contested by the Nationalists.

To oppose Greek expansion, the Nationalists reorganized their forces on the southwest front. On November 16, 1919, Kemal detached the 23rd, 57th, and 61st Divisions from their respective corps, and he sent ciphered cables to Refet and Bekir Sami to consolidate their forces along the Milne Line.[75] Eleven days later, Kemal reorganized these units as the Western Anatolia National Force under the command of Colonel Refet, with a tactical mission as an army of observation (a term for an armed force that watches and guards the frontier against enemy intrusions). As the Nationalists drew into a well-organized defensive posture, the Greeks reorganized to a more effective offensive posture. On December 25, 1919, the Hellenic Army of Occupation in Izmir was redesignated as the Occupation Field Army of Asia Minor, commanded by Lieutenant General

Konstantinos Meliotes Komnenos, who arrived that day.[76] Two army corps headquarters were assigned to the new field army: Army Corps A, composed of the 1st, 2nd, and 13th Divisions under the command of Major General Konstantinos Nider, and the Army Corps of Smyrna, composed of the Smyrna and Archipelago Divisions under the command of Lieutenant General Dimitrios Ioannou. There were small increases in strength as several hundred officers joined the field army, as well as increases in the stockpiling of communication and logistical assets to support offensive operations. As 1919 ended, there were uprisings by Muslim Turks in Izmir and the adjacent areas occupied by Greece, which were forcibly put down.

THE OTTOMAN INVESTIGATION COMMISSIONS

The British demanded loudly and continuously for the Ottoman government to enforce the clauses in the Mudros Armistice pertaining to demilitarization. Messages to the corps and division commanders in spring 1919 failed to bring the errant army commanders into compliance. Under intense pressure from the Allied commissioners, Damat Ferit's cabinet sent high-ranking commissioners to investigate, correct, and verify compliance with the terms of the agreement.[77] Moreover, the large number of reports about massacres and atrocities were also of concern, and the investigation widened to include collecting information about these events. However, the cabinet was particularly concerned about the Nationalist activities of Kemal, Karabekir, and Ali Fuat, who exercised control over the military forces in central and eastern Anatolia, and wanted information on how to best eliminate the growing Nationalist movement. Active and retired senior generals were brought into the ministry of war and assigned sectors to investigate these activities.

Army Chief of Staff General Ali Fevzi headed the commission to Trabzon-Erzurum, arriving in Trabzon on August 20.[78] He travelled to Bayburt and six days later to Erzurum for discussions with Karabekir, and he reportedly observed the depredations of Greek Pontic rebels while travelling through the region (although this was not verified). While en route, Ali Fevzi sent several reports to the cabinet about the dangers of putting arms into storage where the Nationalists could steal them. Süleyman Şefik Pasha was assigned to inspect Konya-Afyonkarahisar-Antalya; however, this region was fairly quiet due to Italian forces in the area, and he returned to Istanbul on August 10. The government sent Galip Pasha to inspect Ankara-Kastamonu, and he submitted his report from Kastamonu on

August 14, 1919. These reports were sent via ciphered telegram and thus kept away from Allied eyes. The inspectors and the general staff were sympathetic to the idea of not fully disclosing the exact quantities of weapons held in Anatolia because they might be seized by the Allies, but after the Sivas Congress, it became very difficult to resist Allied demands.[79] In turn, Damat's government collapsed, and Ali Rıza Pasha became the grand vizier on October 2, 1919. Ali Rıza was known to support the objectives of the Nationalists, and General Milne renewed British demands to know the status of demobilization.

On December 17, Minister of War Cemal Pasha assigned Yakup Şevki (Sübaşı) Pasha, who had formerly commanded the Ninth Army at the end of the war, as chief of the investigation and classification commission.[80] Previously, in August, Yakup Şevki had been involved in planning for the resurrection of the army's reserve system, which was in contravention of the terms of the armistice—so he was certainly not the best choice to supervise the investigation into demobilization. Nevertheless, he proceeded to organize an eight-man commission but made no real effort to start work. On January 20, 1920, General Milne met unsuccessfully with Minister of War Cemal, Chief of the General Staff Cevat, and Yakup Şevki, the three of whom had conspired to provide the British with the absolute minimum amount of information collected under Ali Rıza.[81] Cooperation with the British regarding demobilization collapsed after this, and Cemal, Cevat, and Yakup Şevki were detained and sent to Malta. The Allies certainly knew about the failure to fully demobilize the army, as well as the smuggling and distribution of arms to irregular Nationalist groups, but the active obstruction of the sultan's generals and officers prevented them from ensuring that the terms of the Mudros Armistice were carried out.

CONCLUSION

Thus as 1919 ended, the Nationalists—organized, goaded, and led by Mustafa Kemal—issued an explicit call to arms to contest the intrusions of the Mudros Armistice. The sultan's government had, more or less, implicitly refused to comply fully with the terms of the armistice, and its ministry of war obstructed the implementation of the demobilization clauses. Several prominent general officers put their careers in jeopardy and their lives at risk by embracing the Nationalist cause proclaimed at Erzurum and Sivas. Among these were Kemal, Ali Fuat, Karabekir, Fahrettin,

İsmet, Refet, Cevat, Cemal, Yakup Şevki, Nurettin, and Bekir Sami—and the world would soon hear more of them.

The most important military outcomes from this period were the retention and stockpiling of arms in violation of the armistice terms, the preservation of army organizational structure, the identification of trusted and capable officers, and the establishment of friendly relations with the French and the Soviets. In 1920 these factors, in combination, enabled the Nationalists to reject the Treaty of Sèvres entirely and take the field against the west. In terms of humanitarian concerns, there were widespread reports of atrocities against both civilians and captured soldiers, the Turks blaming the Greeks and Armenians, and the Italians and Greeks blaming the Turks. It was a harbinger of the violence to come. What the Turks call the Turkish War of Independence (*Türk İstiklâl Harbi*) was about to begin.

NOTES

1. Anthony Rawlinson, *Adventures in the Near East, 1918–1922* (London: Andrew Melrose, 1924), 188.

2. Churchill, *The Aftermath*, 367.

3. George W. Gawrych, *The Young Atatürk: From Ottoman Soldier to Statesman of Turkey* (London: I.B.Tauris, 2015), 96.

4. For an explanation of Kemal's criticisms leading to his relief from army command in September 1917, see Erickson, *Ordered to Die*, 171–172.

5. İzzet Pasha was known to be a patron of Mustafa Kemal while both were serving in the Ottoman Army.

6. Fahri Belen, *Türk Kurtuluş Savaşı* (Ankara: Başbakanlık Basımevi, 1973), 43.

7. Andrew Mango, *Atatürk: The Biography of the Founder of Modern Turkey* (New York: The Overlook Press, 2002), 185.

8. Gwynne Dyer, "The Origins of the 'Nationalist' Group of Officers in Turkey 1908–18," *Journal of Contemporary History* 8, no. 4 (1973): 121–164.

9. Belen, *Türk Kurtuluş Savaşı*, 45–46.

10. Mango, *Atatürk*, 198–199. See also Ali Fuat Cebesoy, *Millı Mücadele Hatıraları* (Istanbul: Temel Yayınları, 2000), 51–54; and Kâzım Karabekir, *İstiklâl Harbimiz, 1 Cilt* (Istanbul: Yapı Kredi Yayınları, 2006), 14–16.

11. Mango, *Atatürk*, 200.

12. Görgülü, *On Yıllık Harbin Kadrosu*, 199–200.

13. Ökse, Baycan, and Sakaryalı, *Komutanların Biyografileri*, 99.

14. Dyer, "The Origins of the 'Nationalist' Group of Officers," 3.

15. See Mango, *Atatürk*, 204–205 for a discussion of Kemal's connections with the Italians in spring 1919.

16. Mango, *Atatürk*, 213–214.

17. Ibid., 218.

18. Ibid., 219.

19. Görgülü, *On Yıllık Harbin Kadrosu*, 200. The three army inspectorates were all inactivated on August 14, 1919.

20. Mango, *Atatürk*, 220.

21. Ibid., 225.

22. Shaw, *From Empire to Republic*, vol. 2, 666; and Mango, *Atatürk*, 223–224.

23. Ali Kemal was a liberal journalist who was fanatically anti-CUP and, interestingly, the grandfather of U.K. prime minister Boris Johnson.

24. Mango, *Atatürk*, 235.

25. Mango, *Atatürk*, 236–237.

26. Belen, *Türk Kurtuluş Savaşı*, 110–111.

27. Belen, *Türk Kurtuluş Savaşı*, 138. Belen used the phrase Amasya Contagion (*Amasya bulaşması*) to describe the gathering and widening number of soldiers, officials, and citizens who were drawn to the tenets of Kemal's Amasya Circular.

28. Mango, *Atatürk*, 244–245.

29. Shaw, *From Empire to Republic*, vol. 2, 715–716.

30. Ibid., 717.

31. Ibid., 719.

32. Cebesoy, *Millî Mücadele Hatıraları*, 281, 286.

33. Ökse, Baycan, and Sakaryalı, *Komutanların Biyografileri*, 57.

34. Ryan Gingeras, "The Sons of Two Fatherlands: Turkey and the North Caucasian Diaspora, 1914–1923," *European Journal of Turkish Studies* (online edition), November 30, 2011, parts 20–25, http://journals.openedition.org/ejts/4424.

35. Belen, *Türk Kurtuluş Savaşı*, 138–139; and Shaw, *From Empire to Republic*, vol. 2, 760–766.

36. Churchill, *The Aftermath*, 368.

37. Shaw, *From Empire to Republic*, vol. 2, 412–413.

38. Ibid., 414–420. Shaw's narrative contains an English translation of Damat's proposal.

39. Hovannisian, *The First Year*, 292–294.

40. Ibid., 425–426.

41. Scott Anderson, *Lawrence in Arabia: War, Deceit, Imperial Folly and the Making of the Modern Middle East* (New York: Doubleday, 2013), 488.

42. See Shaw, *From Empire to Republic*, vol. 2, 424–452 for a comprehensive narrative of who the commissioners interviewed.

43. Mango, *Atatürk*, 246–247.

44. Seçil Karal Akğun, "The General Harbord Commission and the American Mandate Question," in *Studies in Atatürk's Turkey, The American Dimension*, eds. George Harris and Nur Bilge Criss (Leiden: Brill Academic Publishers, 2009), 83–96.

45. Shaw, *From Empire to Republic*, vol. 2, 453–458.

46. Ibid., 912–914.

47. Mango's, *Atatürk*, 259. Mango narrative differs from Shaw's, listing Picot's meeting with Ali Fuat as occurring on September 20 and with Kemal between December 5 and 7, 1919.

48. Busch, *Mudros to Lausanne*, 252–253.

49. Fahrettin Çiloğlu, *Kurtuluş Savaşı Sözlüğü* (Istanbul: Livane Yayınları, 2004), 180; and Görgülü, *On Yıllık Harbin Kadrosu*, 202–203.

50. Shaw, *From Empire to Republic*, vol. 1, 346–347.

51. Ibid., 350.

52. Mango, *Atatürk*, 241–242.

53. Gedeon, Paschalidou, and Dima-Dimitrou, *A Concise History of the Campaign in Asia Minor*, 33.

54. Cevdet Timur, Rauf Atakan, Alişan Berktay, and Veli Ertekin, *Türk İstiklâl Hârbi VIInci Cilt, İdari Faaliyetler (15 Mayıs 1919–2 Kasım 1923)* (Ankara: Genelkurmay Basımevi, 1975), 53–54. These are the combined totals for the arms and munitions taken from the XIV Corps magazines and shipped from Akbaş.

55. Busch, *Mudros to Lausanne*, 202.

56. Timur, Atakan, Berktay, and Ertekin, *İdari Faaliyetler*, 57–58.

57. Görgülü, *On Yıllık Harbin Kadrosu*, 223–240.

58. Shaw, *From Empire to Republic*, vol. 2, 597.

59. Ibid., vol. 2, 601.

60. Ibid., 602–603.

61. Mango, *Atatürk*, 312; and Shaw, *From Empire to Republic*, vol. 2, 603.

62. Gedeon, Paschalidou, and Dima-Dimitrou, *A Concise History of the Campaign in Asia Minor*, 28–29.

63. Hakkı Güvendik, Cihat Akçakayalıoğlu, and Selim Turhan, *Türk İstiklâl Hârbi IInci Cilt, Batı Cephesi, 1nci Kısım (15 Mayıs–4 Eylül 1919)* (Ankara: Genelkurmay Basımevi, 1999), 120–124.

64. Gedeon, Paschalidou, and Dima-Dimitrou, *A Concise History of the Campaign in Asia Minor*, 26–27. The commanding officer of the Fourth Regiment, who had lost Aydin, Alexandros Schinas, was court-martialed and given a sentence of life imprisonment.

65. Ibid., 36–37.

66. Cecini, *Il Corpo di Spedizione Italiano in Anatolia*, 205–221.

67. Güvendik, Akçakayalıoğlu, and Turhan, *Batı Cephesi, 1nci Kısım*, 159. In addition, the Italian 135th and 136th Infantry Regiments arrived in August to reinforce the Italian expedition. See Cecini, *Il Corpo di Spedizione Italiano*, 272–274.

68. Güvendik, Akçakayalıoğlu, and Turhan, *Batı Cephesi, 1nci Kısım*, 133.

69. Görgülü, *On Yıllık Harbin Kadrosu*, 248–250.

70. Ibid., 128–136.

71. Gedeon, Paschalidou, and Dima-Dimitrou, *A Concise History of the Campaign in Asia Minor*, 26.

72. Güvendik, Akçakayalıoğlu, and Turhan, *Batı Cephesi, 1nci Kısım*, 136.

73. Gedeon, Paschalidou, and Dima-Dimitrou, *A Concise History of the Campaign in Asia Minor*, 31.

74. Timur, Atakan, Berktay, and Ertekin, *İdari Faaliyetler*, 34; and Gedeon, Paschalidou, and Dima-Dimitrou, *A Concise History of the Campaign in Asia Minor*, 36–37.

75. Timur, Atakan, Berktay, and Ertekin, *İdari Faaliyetler*, 32–33.

76. Gedeon, Paschalidou, and Dima-Dimitrou, *A Concise History of the Campaign in Asia Minor*, 39.

77. Shaw, *From Empire to Republic*, vol. 2, 700–701.

78. Türkmen, *Mütareke Döneminde Ordunun Durumu*, 196–197.

79. Ibid., 202–203.

80. Selma Yel, *Yakup Şevki Paşa ve Askerı Faaliyetleri* (Ankara: Atatürk Araştırma Merkezi, 2002), 201–203.

81. Ibid., 202.

THREE

To the First İnönü Campaign

*M. Venizelos has taken this inopportune moment to fall off his perch,
with the result that I expect we shall see all the Greek troops in Asia
Minor "hopping it."*[1]

General Sir Henry Wilson, 1920

INTRODUCTION

In the postwar years, Maurice Hankey accurately described Lloyd George's
way of getting things done as "diplomacy by conference."[2] While postwar
diplomacy was indeed characterized by conferences, it was the British
who provided the leadership for the postwar settlements in the Middle
East. The first actual treaty that technically ended World War I in the Middle East was the Treaty of Sèvres, which imposed such severe and catastrophic conditions on the Ottoman Empire that it immediately inflamed
the Nationalist cause. It is widely known today that the terms of the Treaty
of Versailles in 1919 inflamed nationalism in postwar Germany and
directly led to the rise of Adolf Hitler and the Nazi Party. However, this
did not occur immediately in Germany, and the full impact of the Versailles treaty did not mature politically until the late 1920s. In what would
become Turkey, the impact of the Sèvres treaty was immediate and
significant.

THE FIRST LONDON CONFERENCE

During the waning days of negotiations in Versailles, Woodrow Wilson suffered a debilitating stroke and went home. Partly due to his incapacitation, Wilson's party was defeated in the 1920 elections, losing not only the presidency but also the congress. A newly isolationist America refused to ratify the Treaty of Versailles or join the new League of Nations. Regarding the Ottoman Empire, it was obvious in fall 1919 that the United States was unlikely to assume the burden of any sort of mandate in the Middle East. The recognition of this drove the remaining Allies to plan a subsequent conference to hammer out solutions about what to do with the defeated Ottoman Empire. The Allied Supreme Council scheduled a meeting in London on February 12, 1920, which is known as the First London Conference. The British broadly shared a vision for the Ottoman Empire that included separating the Arab states from the empire, international control of the Turkish straits, continuing the sultanate in a more restricted form, limitations on Ottoman military forces, and special protections for non-Muslim minorities.[3] The French and Italians opposed much of the British agenda, but British foreign secretary Lord George Curzon offered them zones of economic domination, which brought them over. Because America was unwilling to assume any sort of mandate, earlier Allied assurances of independence for the Armenians and Kurds were put aside.

The Ottomans were not invited to London, but Greek prime minister Venizelos did attend and presented his opinion that Greece should occupy and administer Izmir and its hinterlands, followed by a plebiscite to determine complete annexation by Greece. Venizelos's proposals conformed to British interests, and Lloyd George supported him, but the French and Italians were vehemently opposed to the Greek occupation of Thrace and Izmir.[4] Nevertheless, by the conclusion of the conference two days later, Venizelos had secured Curzon's support for the future of Izmir, as well as for the Greek acquisition of eastern Thrace up to the Çatalca Line, including the city of Edirne. The British high commissioner in Istanbul only told the Ottomans on February 14 that Istanbul was to be left to the sultan, causing a misunderstanding by the public about the full scope of the First London Conference.[5]

In Athens, the lingering animosity caused by the National Schism between Venizelos and the anti-Venizelists again reared its head. The basic dilemma concerned whether Greece should expand its influence by military offensives or maintain a "defensible zone" around Izmir.[6]

Venizelos initially advocated for the defensive zone, which would allow the army to demobilize its reserve soldiers (for reasons of both fiscal economy and the negative political consequences of keeping reservists on prolonged active service). However, by the time of the First London Conference, Venizelos, with British encouragement, was brought over to an expansionist position. The Greek military, supported by the investigations and opinion of Lloyd George's private secretary Philip Kerr, claimed that it had the capability and capacity to shatter Kemal's Nationalists in an offensive military advance to Ankara.[7]

Not everyone outside of the Ottoman Empire was enthusiastic about trying to impose a punitive treaty that divided up the empire along lines that conformed to the political ambitions of the victors. The Supreme Council wrote to the Allied supreme commander, General Ferdinand Foch, then heading the Military and Naval Commission at Versailles, asking his advice about the means and costs necessary for imposing such a treaty. Foch replied in a report on March 30, 1920, concluding that an Allied occupation force of 27 divisions would be required for an indefinite duration.[8] British Chief of the Imperial General Staff, General Sir Henry Wilson, agreed with Foch and told Lloyd George that the Allies could not possibly undertake such a commitment while simultaneously undergoing postwar demobilization.[9] Wilson's diary noted that Venizelos was shocked at these estimates and retorted that Greece could provide 10–12 divisions, which would be more than sufficient to enforce such a treaty.[10] The "frocks," as General Wilson colorfully referred to the politicians in his diary, ignored his and Foch's advice and accepted Lloyd George's plans for creating a greater Greece.

THE GRAND NATIONAL ASSEMBLY

Ottoman parliamentary elections were held in November and December 1919, and the last Ottoman parliament convened on January 12, 1920 under Grand Vizier Ali Rıza. The constitution called for 170 deputies, but there were never more than 107 present at any given time, mainly because Ottoman Greeks and Ottoman Armenians boycotted the elections, as did Damat Ferit (because ex-CUP members whom he hated were permitted to participate). Importantly though, about 60 deputies were members of Nationalist Defense of Rights groups, including Rauf, Bekir Sami, and Kara Vasıf, which constituted a parliamentary majority.[11] They secretly organized an executive committee to try to push Kemal's Turkish National Pact through parliament. The Nationalists expanded their number to an overwhelming majority of 96 deputies, and, on January 24, Rauf introduced into committee a text agreed to by Kemal and the members of Felah, which had succeeded Karakol. The sultan, the grand vizier, and Defense of Rights Nationalists now traded messages about what to do, and Ali Rıza appointed a pro-Nationalist cabinet in the first two weeks of February. The text went to the floor on February 4, and, after debate, the Chamber of Deputies voted to approve the Turkish National Pact (*Misak-ı Millî*) on February 17. The pact demanded plebiscites to determine who would claim the various parts of the empire (rather than the Allies awarding provinces and cities according to their prewar agreements), a free vote in western Thrace to determine judicial ownership, the inclusion of Turks in any decision regarding the future of Istanbul and the straits, and complete independence and sovereignty for the country.

The Turkish National Pact was not a radical document, conforming largely to Wilson's Fourteen Points, but it contradicted the plans of the Allies. However, the pact officially affirmed the Nationalist position in parliament, thus enraging the British, who immediately plotted to establish a caretaker puppet government. The grand vizier tried to circumvent the Allies by asking Kemal, given the official approval of the National Pact, to recognize the Chamber of Deputies as the sole legitimate political entity representing the people. In effect, two governments, the sultan's and Kemal's, claimed legitimacy, and Ali Rıza proved unable to reconcile political authority. Simultaneously with this constitutional crisis in the Ottoman Empire, the Armenian delegation leader in Paris, Boghos Nubar, reported that 12,000 Armenians had been massacred in Maraş and that Turks were about to slaughter thousands more in Adana and Mersin. Using these pretexts, the dysfunction of the Ottoman government and the massacre of Christians, the British forced Ali Rıza to resign on March 3, 1920.

This ill-founded move drove many deputies, who were fence-sitters, into the arms of the Nationalists, and many subsequently fled into the interior to join Kemal. The sultan replaced Ali Rıza with well-known Nationalist Minister of Marine Salih Hulusi, who was not confirmed by the now truncated and Allied-leaning Chamber of Deputies. This left the Ottoman Empire without a functioning government. It is sometimes assumed that the absence of a cabinet or the ratification of the National Pact directly caused the second Allied occupation of Istanbul. In fact, having imposed a harsh treaty dividing up Anatolia among the victors, the Allies determined that the occupation of the Ottoman capital was a necessity. On March 5, Curzon informed the new British high commissioner, Admiral Sir John de Robeck, that the Supreme Council intended Istanbul to be occupied at once. De Robeck, along with the French and Italian high commissioners, was adamantly opposed to this, as was Lord Sir Charles Hardinge at the Foreign Office. Lloyd George pushed the Supreme Council by repeating Venizelos's assurances that "the Turks were paper tigers."[12] After bitter discussion, the council decided to place Istanbul under military occupation beginning at 10:00 a.m. on March 16, 1920.

The occupation was conducted mostly by British troops and had been well planned so as not to arouse resistance.[13] The local Ottoman Army garrisons were seized at 5:30 a.m. to avoid bloodshed. The ministry of war and ministry of marine were taken at 10:00 a.m. precisely, as were the telegraph and postal offices. French soldiers occupied the armories and military storehouses while British soldiers set up machine gun posts at key road intersections throughout the city. Deputies from the parliament and Nationalist journalists were arrested, while others went into hiding. The Allies then forced the sultan to install a reactionary puppet government led by Damat Ferit, which continued in power until October 1920, when he resigned and was replaced by Ahmet Tevfik Pasha.[14]

Upon learning that Istanbul had been occupied by the Allies, Kemal issued a call to elect a national assembly in Ankara, and several days later, he announced that the Turkish nation was establishing its own parliament in Ankara under the name Grand National Assembly. By early April, several deputies had made their way to Ankara, and on April 6, the president of the now-dissolved Ottoman Chamber of Deputies, Celalettin Arif, arrived. He issued a statement that because of the occupation, the chamber had transferred itself to Ankara. He issued a second statement on April 10 to the same effect, and ten days later, Minister of War Mustafa Fevzi stated that he could only serve the nation from Ankara. On April 23, with 115 deputies from the Ottoman parliament who had escaped from Istanbul and 190 elected delegates from around the country, the new Grand National Assembly convened for the first time. The following day, the Grand National Assembly immediately elected Kemal as the first president and İsmet as the army's chief of staff. Mustafa Fevzi was reappointed minister of war in the Nationalist cabinet, and the army went over to the Nationalist cause. Kemal gave a two and one-half hour speech in which he declared that the work of the Representative Committee was done and that the National Assembly was now charged with the defense of the nation.

THE SAN REMO CONFERENCE

The Ottoman question was only one of the issues concerning the Allies when they resumed discussions at San Remo, Italy, on April 18, 1920 (the others being relations with the Soviets and the disposition of Trieste on the Adriatic Sea). This is where the decisions that would frame the peace treaty with the Ottomans were made. Once again, the Ottomans were not invited to send an official delegation, but an unofficial Nationalist representative, former ambassador Galib Kemal, was in attendance. Lloyd George, Curzon, and Hankey were present for Britain. French premier Alexandre Millerand and Philippe Berthelot represented France, and Italian prime minister Francesco Nitti represented Italy.

Over the next few days, the delegations worked out the unanswered questions involving Greece, France, Italy, the Armenians, and the Kurds. The outcome was the San Remo Convention, which was negotiated on April 25, 1920. The important clauses included Britain's acceptance of a Mandatory for Palestine, and Iraq while France accepted a Mandatory for Syria (including what is now Lebanon); further, Britain accepted a limited Mandatory for Arabia. Greece would be allowed to occupy Izmir and southwest Anatolia, as well as Edirne and western Thrace. Italy was to be allowed to occupy Antalya and the southern coast while France would occupy Cilicia. The British, then occupying Batum on the Black Sea, agreed to evacuate the port and hand it over to the Republic of Georgia. The Allied delegations stepped away from decisions on the Armenians and the Kurds, promising an independent Armenia but leaving it to American President Wilson to determine its exact boundaries. The agreements in London and San Remo now became the blueprint from which the peace treaty with the Ottoman Empire would be drawn.

THE TREATY OF SÈVRES

The Allies handed the draft peace treaty to Riza Tevfik Pasha at Versailles on May 11, 1920 with instructions that the Ottoman government would have one month to submit its observations. The terms were devastating. In addition to the inter-Allied agreements previously made, President Wilson would decide an Armenian state's boundaries, which would likely include Van, Bitlis, Erzurum, and Trabzon. In an about-face to the French, Cilicia including Maraş, Urfa, and Mardin might transfer to the Armenians as well. If Wilson leaned this way, Armenia would have access to both the

Black Sea and to the Mediterranean Sea. France would be left only with southern Cilicia, including İskenderun and Antakya. The treaty reconfirmed the Arbitration Award of February 1914, which recognized Greek sovereignty of the Aegean islands and Italian possession of the Dodecanese islands, along with the occupation of Antalya and its hinterlands. Venizelos received Izmir and the entire southwest, although the Ottomans would be permitted to fly their flag over Izmir's ancient citadel. Greece could then hold a plebiscite after five years to annex the area. Non-Muslim minorities could open schools teaching non-Turkish languages and proselytize wherever they chose.[15] Control of the straits would be supervised by an international commission, the Capitulations (damaging economic concessions abolished during the war) would be restored, and reparations and damages paid to the victors. The Ottoman Army would consist of 50,700 men, 15,000 of whom would compose the Jandarma, and the navy was limited to 13 small coastal patrol boats. Conscription was prohibited. The terms imposed on the Ottomans made the terms of the Versailles Treaty imposed on the Germans generous by comparison.[16]

Riza Tevfik cabled the terms back to Istanbul, noting his opposition. The government and the Nationalists placed the blame squarely on Lloyd George. The recently formed Grand National Assembly condemned the treaty on May 22, 1920, and the nation from Edirne to Kars was soon aflame with anti-British sentiment.[17] American high commissioner Admiral Mark Bristol pointed out to the British that Anatolia was overwhelmingly Muslim, thereby defeating Allied plans to hold legitimate plebiscites. The Nationalists proclaimed Damat Ferit a traitor to the nation, and Istanbul erupted in protests and large demonstrations on May 21. Damat Ferit tried to delay responding by engaging the French and Italians, who were not pleased with parts of the treaty that favored Britain and British interests, and he left for Paris on June 10. Lloyd George and Venizelos worked feverishly behind the scenes to keep the Allies aligned with the original terms. On June 24, the Ottoman government officially responded with a list of counteroffers, and the Allies and Venizelos met at Spa on July 2 to consider the Ottoman positions. In the end, the Allies refused to make any changes, except for some minor modifications, in the draft treaty.[18] On July 10, 1920, they gave the Ottoman government 10 days to signify acceptance of the treaty. The Ottoman delegation acquiesced and signed the treaty on August 10, 1920, in Sèvres, Switzerland.[19] All of the Allied nations and the Republic of Armenia signed the treaty, but the Americans did not.

The signed treaty was a brilliant coup for Venizelos and Lloyd George, who got almost everything they wanted. The Ottoman parliament, which was not in session, never ratified the Treaty of Sèvres, nor did any of the Allies or Associated Powers. The Grand National Assembly in Ankara immediately renounced the treaty and used it as a rallying cry against occupation and partition. Since the treaty was never ratified, it never went into force as an international legal document.[20] Belatedly, on November 22, 1920, President Woodrow Wilson issued his "award," which identified the boundaries of the Republic of Armenia.[21] However, events would soon overtake both the Greeks and the Armenians, rendering their territorial claims nothing more than illusions. Historian Michael Llewellyn-Smith wrote, "A dour French lawyer-politician Raymond Poincaré was one of the first to observe the symbolism of the name Sèvres, the home of fine and fragile porcelain."[22]

THE FIRST GREEK OFFENSIVE

On January 29, 1920, Venizelos met with High Commissioner Aristeides Stergiades; Greek army commander in chief Leonidas Paraskevopoulos; and Generals Meliotes Komnenos, Nider, and Ioannou at a conference on the island of Chios to examine the situation in Asia Minor.[23] They decided that it was urgent to reinforce the Occupation Field Army of Asia Minor with an additional infantry division. The Army Staff Service shipped the 31st Infantry Regiment from the Cydonia Division and a regiment from the 8th Division in Thessaloniki to Izmir where they joined the Smyrna Garrison Regiment to form the new division. By late February, the Cydonia Division was consolidated and training for war. On February 28, 1920, the Greek General Headquarters arrived in Izmir from Thessaloniki, and the commander in chief General Paraskevopoulos assumed command of all Hellenic Army units in Asia Minor.[24] The Occupation Field Army of Asia Minor was inactivated, and the ministry of war assumed operational control of its forces in Macedonia and along the northeast frontier. The Greeks spent March through May 1920 bringing their units up to strength and shipping engineer, communication, and transportation units to Izmir. By May, the Greeks had 3,248 officers, 91,063 men, 28,804 pack animals, and 937 motor vehicles inside their Anatolian bridgehead.[25]

On the international scene, Venizelos met with British and French representatives in May and June 1920, attempting to persuade them that the

Greek Army was the only force capable of stabilizing the restive situation in western Asia Minor.[26] An attack by Nationalist forces on a British detachment near Izmit on June 14–15 seemed to confirm his position and lifted War Office objections to supporting the Greeks.[27] On June 19, the Supreme Allied Council decided to allow the Greeks to advance to the Sea of Marmara to secure the Dardanelles. The Greek Army intelligence staff estimate of the Nationalist forces opposing them was 42 infantry battalions, supported by irregular militias, and 50 artillery pieces—about 42,250 soldiers altogether.[28] The Field Army of Asia Minor planned a rapid campaign with two axes of advance—one axis of advance going north through Soma and Edremit to Bandırma, and the second going east to Alaşehir. The Greek offensive began on June 22, 1920 against the far weaker Nationalist forces.[29]

The Smyrna Army Corps launched the attacks to the north, with the Smyrna Division advancing toward Akhisar and the Archipelago Division taking Soma on June 23. The Nationalist 61st Division defending Soma briefly resisted and fell back to Balıkesir. Akhisar fell on 24th with the Nationalist 188th Infantry Regiment falling back to the east. After taking Soma, the Greek 13th Division and Archipelago and Smyrna Divisions, reinforced by the newly activated Cavalry Brigade (composed of the 1st and 3rd Cavalry Regiments), proceeded north to seize the small port town of Bandırma (Panormos to the Greeks). The Nationalists launched counterattacks in unsuccessful attempts to stop the Greeks at İvrindi and near Edremit. But by June 30, the Greeks had taken Balıkesir, Edremit, and the surrounding high ground. The Greek General Headquarters also planned a supporting amphibious attack from the north and staged the 15th and 27th Infantry Regiments on ships. On July 2, the 15th Regiment landed at the small port of Misakça (Edinjik) west of Bandırma while the 27th Regiment landed to the east at Dutliman (Tuz Liman), and they moved rapidly. Bandırma fell immediately, but the Greeks kept up their momentum with the 27th Regiment establishing contact with the Archipelago Division's advance guard that same day.[30] On July 3, the 15th Regiment met the advance guard of the Smyrna Division. Colonel Kâzim and the Nationalist 61st Division were powerless to stop the advancing Greeks. As will be seen, the fall of Bandırma gave the Greeks an important port on the Sea of Marmara for the Field Army of Asia Minor.

On June 30, the Greek General Headquarters asked the British headquarters in Istanbul for permission to exceed the agreed-upon limits of advance and seize the important city of Bursa (Prusa). The Greeks that stated this was necessary to crush the Kemalist forces. The British never answered, and the Greeks took that as approval and launched another offensive on July 6 with the Archipelago Division and the Cavalry Brigade. The Bursa garrison was composed of the 56th Division (173rd and 174th Infantry Regiments) under the command of Lieutenant Colonel Nazmi (Solok).[31] On the same day, Greek Army detachments landed from ships, seizing the ports of Mudanya and Gemlik. The British had previously seized Mudanya by landing about 100 soldiers there on June 25 and taking it after a brief skirmish.[32] Greek infantry and cavalry swept north and south of Lake Uluabat (Lake Artynina) and took Bursa on July 8. Two days later, Colonel Bekir Sami had established a defensive line 20 kilometers east of Bursa from Lake İznik south to Aksu; however, the Greeks took 2,500 Nationalists prisoner in the retreat from Soma to Bursa.[33] When Venizelos was informed of the capture of Bursa, he reprimanded the General Headquarters because he not given prior approval for the operation.[34]

To the south, the Greek Army Corps A launched its attacks on June 23 and pushed east with the 13th and 2nd Divisions encircling Alaşehir while the 1st Division held the southern flanks along the Great Menderes River and Aydin.[35] The Nationalist 23rd Division holding the center sector on the Gediz River "offered resolute resistance," losing almost 700 killed and 800 men taken prisoner.[36] Nationalist counterattacks by the 69th Infantry Regiment failed to recover the lost ground and led to further losses. The division's left wing at Kiraz was likewise crushed and driven back. By July 24, division commander Lieutenant Colonel Aşır (Atlı), ordered the general retreat of the 23rd Division to Uşak.[37] Likewise, on the Nationalist's left (southern) flank, Colonel Şefik's (Aker) 57th Division came under very heavy attacks from the Greek 1st Division launching its offensive east out of Aydin. Şefik managed a fighting withdrawal to the town of Nazilli, which he held against the Greeks on June 28.[38] Reinforcing their attacks, the Greeks took the town on July 3, 1919, pushing Şefik's lines five kilometers to the east. The defeat of the Nationalists had been catastrophic; however, as will be presented in the following chapters. Kemal and a large part of his forces were busy elsewhere putting down internal uprisings and fighting the Armenians in the east. This, of course, made the concentration against the Greeks impossible because Kemal decided to trade operational space in western Anatolia for the strategic time needed to solidify the Nationalist hold on the eastern and southeastern provinces and ensure the security of his internal lines of communication. This was a risky strategy that paid off handsomely in the following year.

By July 10, 1920, the Greeks had taken all their initial objectives and established positions in the north beyond what Venizelos had imagined. On July 13, the British occupied Izmit and Gebze, which stopped the Greeks from advancing north from Bursa. The Greeks timed their massive offensive to coincide with the negotiations that were then being conducted in Sèvres to send a direct message to the hesitant Ottoman government. Professor Stanford Shaw suggested that the fall of Bursa, the original capital of the Ottoman dynasty, was such a shock to the government and to the delegation at the treaty talks in Sèvres that it was a significant factor in the decision to accept the treaty.[39] The Nationalists were shocked by the scope and intensity of the Greek offensive, and both they and the public were shocked at the excesses perpetrated by the Greek Army during their advances. General Paraskevopoulos, as the offensive began, had issued a proclamation stating that the rights and property of Ottoman citizens who did not resist the Greeks either directly or indirectly would be preserved and guaranteed.[40] Unfortunately, a large number of episodes of criminal brutality occurred throughout the areas captured by the Greek Army, although the western press portrayed the Greeks as liberators welcomed warmly by the local inhabitants.[41] According to Professor Shaw, as had happened in Thessaloniki (Salonika) in 1912, "both Turks and Jews found themselves on the wrong end of bayonets and burning torches and were driven from their homes" in the thousands.[42]

THE OCCUPATION OF EASTERN THRACE

Venizelos and the Greek Army were encouraged by their comparatively easy victories over the Nationalist forces and excited by territory awarded to Greece under the imminent Treaty of Sèvres. General Paraskevopoulos cabled Venizelos on July 1 outlining two options for further operations. The first course of action involved standing fast in Asia Minor and detaching forces to occupy eastern Thrace, followed by a resumption of the offensive to crush the Nationalists, and the second considered ignoring Thrace and continue operations in Asia Minor until the Nationalists were destroyed.[43] Paraskevopoulos preferred the second course of action but was overruled by Venizelos, who told the Allies at Spa on July 7 that the Greeks were standing fast on the ground they had taken. In any event, Venizelos informed Paraskevopoulos to begin preparations to seize eastern Thrace. Venizelos's sense of urgency was driven, in part, by a rise in Nationalist political and military activity in eastern Thrace, as well as by his desire for rapid demobilization.

Several Nationalist congresses had been held in Edirne, the first on July 16, 1919, organized by the Committee for the Defense of Rights in Thrace. The second, the Great Edirne Congress, May 9–13, 1920, was much more dangerous from the Greek perspective, as it was explicitly conducted to organize Nationalist resistance in Thrace.[44] Thrace had been a hotbed of anti-Bulgarian sentiment ever since Bulgaria had taken western Thrace in 1913. The subsequent Greek occupation of western Thrace in 1919 transferred that sentiment against Greece. In 1919–1920, large and well-armed Turkish Nationalist groups organized in Edirne, Uzunköprü, Babaeski, and İpsala. More problematic for the Greeks was the position of Ottoman colonel Cafer Tayyar (Eğilmez), commander of the I Corps at Edirne, who became an ardent Nationalist after Kemal's call to arms in the summer of 1919. The I Corps composed three divisions, the 49th Division at Edirne, the 60th Division at Uzunköprü, and the 55th Division at Tekirdağ.[45] Cafer's sympathies became so well known that Damat Ferit unsuccessfully attempted to have him arrested in May 1920. After the Great Edirne Congress, the potential for a coordinated military response from the Defense of Rights groups and the Ottoman I Corps became an imperative, driving Venizelos. This dovetailed into his belief that Bulgarian guerrillas would also emerge as a threat to Greek interests.

The final Greek operational plan for the occupation of eastern Thrace envisioned a two-pronged offensive. Greek officers already supervised the railway and telegraph stations in eastern Thrace; moreover, Greek Army divisions lay just across the Meriç River (the Maritsa River, which today composes much of the Greek-Turkish border). Greek forces in western Thrace, the 9th Division and the Xanthi Division, would advance to seize Edirne while, simultaneously, the Greek Field Army of Asia Minor would amphibiously land the Smyrna Division to support the operation.[46] The Greek commanders were worried about Cafer's I Corps, which had over 18,000 officers and men, 53 artillery pieces of varying types, and 47 machine guns and could be reinforced immediately by the Defense of Rights groups. On July 22, 1920, the Greeks launched their offensive under the command of Lieutenant General Emmanouel Zamvrakakes's Field Army of Thrace.[47]

The Nationalists had some warning of these impending operations when they learned that the Smyrna Division was concentrating in the port of Bandırma, as well as from increased Greek activity along the Meriç River. Cafer put his 55th Division on coastal alert and deployed his other divisions in defensive positions.[48] However, when the Smyrna Division landed at Tekirdağ, on July 20, 1920, opposition by the 55th Division was almost nonexistent because of the wide area in which it was dispersed. Lieutenant Colonel Alâaddin (Koval) withdrew his 55th Division northwest to positions on the high ground overlooking the town of Muratlı.[49] On July 22, the Greeks attacked the Nationalist positions and overwhelmed the 170th and 171st Infantry Regiments in what the Turks call the Battle of Büyükkarıştıran (a small village nearby). The Nationalists withdrew into the town of Lüleburgaz (see map 3.1).[50]

General Zamvrakakes's 9th Division attacked the Nationalist 49th Division's defensive positions along the Meriç River on July 21, forcing the 153rd Infantry Regiment back to Babaeski. The 49th Division established new defensive positions there on July 23. To the south, the Xanthi Division's attacks on the Nationalist 60th Division forced it to retreat to Uzunköprü. At Keşan, the retreat of the 60th Division effectively cut off the 155th Infantry Regiment, the elements of which began to surrender.[51] Greek attacks on Babaeski continued on July 23, as did attacks on the 60th Division. With three Greek infantry divisions converging on Edirne and isolated from his fellow Nationalists in Anatolia, Colonel Cafer's tactical position was hopeless. He surrendered himself and the Nationalist units immediately under his command at Havza-Bostanlı on July 25.[52] However, before surrendering, Cafer granted freedom of action to 49th Division commander Lieutenant Colonel Şükrü Naili (Gökberk) to act as he saw fit.[53] As Edirne was abandoned to the Greeks on July 26, Şükrü Naili led 700 officers, 200 civil officials, 4,000 soldiers with 30 machine guns, 31 artillery pieces, and 1,147 draft animals, accompanied by 10,000 refugees fleeing the Greeks, across the border into Bulgaria where they were interned.[54] Lieutenant Colonel Şükrü Naili remained in Bulgaria until December 1920, rejoining the Nationalist forces in Anatolia on May 1, 1921 to take command of the 15th Division.[55]

The destruction of the I Corps removed three infantry divisions from the Nationalist order of battle, leaving 17 organized but understrength infantry divisions on the rosters as 1921 arrived. General Paraskevopoulos's campaign was exceptionally well planned and well executed, resulting in a decisive victory over the Nationalist forces in eastern Thrace. Colonel Cafer's situation was hopeless from the beginning because he was completely isolated by Greek and British forces. Venizelos declared the legal annexation of all of Thrace immediately upon the signing of the Treaty of Sèvres on August 10, 1920.[56] Unfortunately, the story of the Greek Army's blitzkrieg-like campaign to seize eastern Thrace was left

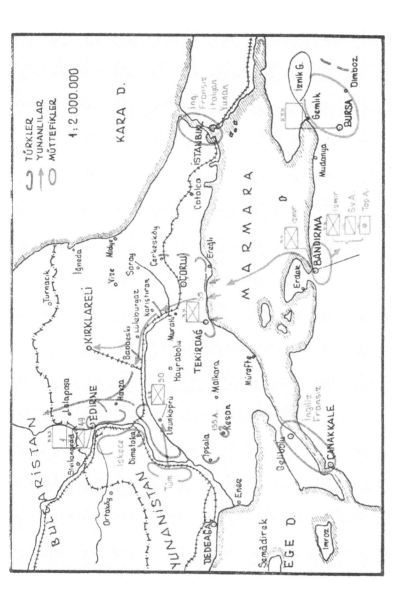

Map 3.1 The Greek Occupation of Eastern Thrace

On July 22, 1920, the Greeks began their campaign to occupy Eastern Thrace. The Field Army of Thrace crossed the Meriç River from the west while the Field Army of Asia Minor landed the Smyrna Division amphibiously at Tekirdağ. The Greeks converged on Edirne and successfully concluded the campaign on July 26. The Nationalist 49th Division commander Lieutenant Colonel Şükrü Naili (Gökberk) led some 5,000 soldiers into internment in Bulgaria, while the I Corps and 50th and 55th Infantry Divisions surrendered to the Greeks.

Courtesy of the Turkish General Staff Military History and Strategy Institute (ATASE).

out of the Concise Greek History, which focused on the campaigns in Asia Minor. Nevertheless, in a 35-day period, the Greek Army executed two extremely successful campaigns at low cost, which returned important positional advantages for future operations.

THE UŞAK CAMPAIGN

Greek anti-Venizelists made an unsuccessful attempt to assassinate Venizelos on August 12, 1920 in Paris. He escaped with light wounds and returned to Athens several days later. In midmonth, while awaiting ratification of the Treaty of Sèvres that never came, General Paraskevopoulos concluded that further offensive military operations were necessary to end the war on terms favorable to Greece.[57] The Greek General Headquarters recommended the seizure of Eskişehir and Afyonkarahisar, which would paralyze Nationalist communication and be of great value to Greek morale.[58] Further, they recommended the seizure of Konya, which would serve Allied interests (and connect the Greeks from Izmir with the French in Cilicia), as well as give the Greek Army almost unlimited freedom of action. In turn, the Field Army of Asia Minor began to reallocate forces in anticipation of a political decision to resume offensive operations. On August 22, 1920, the General Headquarters ordered Army Corps A to seize Uşak and Gediz. The 2nd and 13th Divisions were assigned the main effort from Alaşehir (Philadelphia) to Uşak while the 1st Division secured the right (southern) flank, and the Cydonia Division secured the left (northern flank).[59]

Opposing this on the avenue of advance to Gediz and Kütahya, Western Front commander General Ali Fuat organized the Ertuğrul Group, commanded by Colonel Kâzım (Özalp), composed of the 61st Division, the 11th Division (newly arrived on the front from Niğde), the 24th Division, and the First Mobile Force (a provisional irregular group commanded by Çerkez Ethem).[60] Colonel Fahrettin's (Altay) XII Corps held the southern approaches, with Lieutenant Colonel İzzettin's (Çalışlar) 23rd Division defending the town of Uşak, which Fahrettin reinforced with a Provisional Division commanded by Lieutenant Colonel Mehmet Sabri (Erçetin). To İzzettin's south, the 57th Division continued to hold the Menderes River sector. İzzettin had previously served as the chief of staff of the XX Corps, which was inactivated on July 24, 1920, and he was an experienced officer.[61]

The Greek offensive began on August 28 with the Greeks making contact with İzzettin's 68th, 69th, and 176th Infantry Regiments the next day.
After a brief early morning firefight, well supported by effective field artillery, the Greek Army's 2nd Division easily defeated the Nationalists
enabling them to seize Uşak that day. The town fell so quickly that the
Greeks were able to capture fully loaded trains in the railway station
before they could get away.[62] According to the Greeks, the Nationalists lost
160 killed, 263 prisoners, and 7 artillery guns, but İzzettin's 23rd Division
remained intact and retreated to Dumlupınar.[63] On July 30, the unopposed
Greek 13th Division advanced on the right flank of the victorious 2nd
Division. As that division consolidated its position in Uşak, the 13th Division slipped around the town to the north and continued its advance north,
taking Han on August 31, and the town of Gediz on September 3.[64] While
these battles were going on, the Cydonia Division advanced through
Demirci and took Simav on September 1. A detachment from its 32nd
Infantry Regiment took Dereköy the next day and made contact with the
13th Division in Gediz on September 3.[65]

During the month of August, both sides reinforced and reorganized
their tactical forces. The Greeks brought the headquarters of Army Corps
B, under the command of Major General Perikles Pierrakos Mauromichales, from Patras to Izmir on August 18. Accompanying the headquarters, the Greek General Headquarters sent the 3rd Division under the
command of Major General Nikolaos Trikoupes.[66] The Cavalry Brigade
was also reestablished, having been broken apart in the advance to Bursa
and stationed at Ahmetli. On September 23, the Greeks began to rotate the
Cydonia Division back to mainland Greece and replace it with the Cretan
Division, commanded by Major General Euthymios Tsimikales. By October 16, most of the Cretan Division had reached Izmir. The Nationalists
were working to activate a new 4th Division in the town of Bolu from III
Corps units and deploy it to the Western Front Command but were experi-
encing delays.[67] With the French threat in Cilicia diminishing, Kemal also
alerted the 41st Division, then in Pozantı, for movement to reinforce Ali
Fuat's Western Front Command against the Greeks.

In mid-October, Ali Fuat felt confident enough to order Ertuğrul Group
commander Colonel Kâzım to conduct a counterattack with a view toward
recovering Gediz. On October 15, Ali Fuat met with Kâzım and the commanders of the 11th and 61st Divisions and the First Mobile Force in
Eskişehir to outline his plan. Three days later, Kâzım met with his three

commanders at the Alayunt train station to finalize the details of the plan, which would attempt to encircle the Greek 13th Division in Gediz.[68] On October 22, the fresh 70th Infantry Regiment arrived at Alayunt to reinforce the 11th Division, and the Nationalists began moving their men into assault positions. The Greek 13th Division had two regiments composed of five infantry battalions in the town of Gediz, with one infantry battalion in reserve, and its remaining three battalions were in Simav. Moreover, the 13th Division was unsupported on its flank, and its forward position constituted an exposed thumb-like salient that was ripe for encirclement. Altogether, the Nationalists were able to bring about 8,000 soldiers, 28 machine guns, and 16 artillery pieces against the Greeks in Gediz.

Colonel Kâzım delayed his attack until 7:30 a.m. on October 24, taking advantage of heavy fog to obscure his attacking infantry. The main attack was composed of the seven infantry regiments from the 11th Division (reinforced by an additional infantry regiment) and the 61st Division. To add weight to the attack, Kâzım also sent in the 159th Depot Regiment (a training unit) and supported the attack with a 105mm howitzer battery. The First Mobile Force was composed of an infantry regiment and 13 irregular groups (most of which seem to have been cavalry) under the command of Çerkez Ethem. Kâzım sent the First Mobile Force racing toward the roads leading southwest out of Gediz to block them, but he also detached a cavalry group and a Bolshevik group, under the command of Recep Bey, to attack the rear of Gediz itself.[69] The intensity of the fighting peaked around noon, and the Nationalists cut the road between Gediz and Han to the south. The Nationalists renewed the attack about 6:00 p.m., but darkness halted their efforts. The 13th Division sent out patrols, which discovered that, although the road to Han remained blocked, the Nationalists' lines were porous.[70] In the early morning hours of October 25, the Greeks broke out of the encirclement and withdrew safely to their lines.

Fighting continued on October 26, as the Nationalists pushed south to Han and were met by a Greek counterattack. Army Corps A reinforced the 13th Division, and it pushed the Nationalists north about nine kilometers northeast of Han, where the front lines stabilized on October 28. Casualties on both sides were fairly light, and the ground gained and lost was not at all tactically decisive. However, the Gediz-Han battles were an extremely important harbinger of the rebirth of Nationalist offensive capability. The Concise Greek History asserted, "It was the first large-scale well organized offensive by the Kemalist forces."[71]

GREEK POLITICS AND ALLIED MILITARY POLICY

Domestic and foreign politics now conspired to change the political dynamics in Greece, as these came to affect Greek military policy. Recovered from his wounds, Venizelos publicized his success at Sèvres in the parliament. On September 7, 1920, Venizelos dissolved parliament to hold general elections and began to demobilize the army. The specter of the National Schism returned to haunt Greek politics. In essence, during the middle of World War I, some Greeks, mostly Anglophiles, supported the Allies, and other Greeks supported Germany. Included in the latter category was King Constantine, who had been educated in Germany, while Venizelos was in the former category. While both men advocated the *Megali Idea*, they clashed repeatedly and violently in public and in the parliament. The Allies successfully forced Constantine to abdicate in 1917, followed by self-imposed exile to Switzerland. Constantine's pro-Allied son became King Alexander, and Greece formally joined the Allies against Germany. Venizelos then purged the Greek military establishment of anti-Venizelists and replaced them with his own supporters.

The National Schism continued into the postwar period between Venizelos and the anti-Venizelists. In the 1920 Greek election, the issues that captivated public attention mostly involved wartime legacies, including ending martial law, censorship, and conscription.[72] Then a freak accident occurred on October 2, when King Alexander was bitten by a monkey and infected with a fatal sepsis. As he lay dying, exiled anti-Venizelists, including the politician Dimitrios Gounaris and General Ioannis Metaxas, returned home. Alexander died on October 25, and Venizelos attempted unsuccessfully to place his son Paul on the throne.

Despite the victories in Asia Minor Greek, voters turned against Venizelos and delivered a resounding defeat to his Liberal Party in the national elections of November 14, 1920. A new government formed under the elderly and intemperate, but widely respected, politician Dimitrios Rallis, who held a plebiscite on December 5. Constantine returned home on December 19 and, because the anti-Venizelists had never accepted his resignation, resumed his seat on the throne. This act, however, had dire consequences for Allied support for Greece.

While Greece was caught up in this domestic political crisis, the Allies convened the Second London Conference on November 26, "mainly to decide what should be done about the situation in Greece."[73] The proposed return of the pro-German Constantine, who the Allies saw as a near-war criminal, combined with Venizelos's unbridled aspirations (even though he had lost power) drove the Allies to reverse their policies toward Greece. Previously, on October 5, Venizelos sent a long telegram to Lloyd George stating that he would have to make decisions that conflicted with Sèvres and the wishes of the Allies. These included crushing the Nationalists once and for all, "driving the Turks from Constantinople," and establishing a Greek state in the Pontus, which would be absorbed into Greek territory in Asia Minor.[74] Venizelos appealed for Allied permission to do these things to but, in the end, said he was about to do them anyway. Lloyd George furnished copies of the telegram to the Foreign Office and the War Office, which had both opposed Greek expansion.[75] Likewise, Churchill, Wilson, Milne, and de Robeck all believed that Britain's interests were best served not by the destruction of Turkey but rather by leaving a Turkey strong enough to resist the resurrection of a powerful Russia in the form of a Bolshevik state.[76] Venizelos waited in vain for a reply and fell from power four weeks later.

The British General Staff argued vigorously that Kemalists represented the only real force capable of deterring the Bolsheviks and that the Greeks were too weak to guarantee that. In turn, General Wilson noted that the defeat of the Armenians, the defeat of the anti-Bolshevik White Russians, and the downfall of Venizelos demanded revisions to the Treaty of Sèvres to leave the Turks in a stronger geographical position. Moreover, the French were especially adamant in the initial November 26 meeting at Downing Street that Constantine would impose adversarial policies toward the Allies. Concluding on December 4, the British, French, and Italians sent a declaration to Prime Minister Rallis stating that the restoration of Constantine to the throne created an intolerable and dangerous situation; therefore, "the three Governments reserve to themselves complete liberty in dealing with the situation thus created."[77] In effect, then, the three Allies repudiated the Treaty of Sèvres. They followed this by informing Rallis that financial and military support for Greek military adventures in Asia Minor would be cut off. The most important aspect of this decision was the blocking of Greek credit, which would inevitably lead to financial collapse. Perhaps unwisely, Rallis held his plebiscite the next day.

Greek military policy had already begun to shift in favor of a more aggressive position, in-line with now ex-prime minister Venizelos's ideas. General Paraskevopoulos resigned the day after the new government was formed on November 17, 1920. He was replaced by Lieutenant General Anastasios Papoulas on November 22, and, that day, the General Headquarters was redesignated as the Field Army of Asia Minor (FAAM).[78] Several pro-Venizelos generals and officers resigned. "Moreover, according to pre-election commitments," approximately 1,500 officers, who had been discharged or forced to resign over the past three years were recalled to service with their original ranks.[79] This resulted in the "setting aside of more than 300 capable *Venizelist* officers," which caused immediate and huge disruptions throughout the army.[80] Many of these displaced officers, mostly colonels, formed an anti-government movement simply known as National Defense. By March 1921, almost all the key commands in the army were given to these returned Royalist officers. Importantly for this narrative, the Concise Greek History noted that the sweeping changes in the commands of the Field Army, the army corps, and most of the divisions "resulted in a military leadership composition with no post-Balkan War (1912–13) experience and no familiarity with the conditions of the Asia Minor front."[81]

THE RECONNAISSANCE IN FORCE

The new king, Rallis, and the new foreign minister, Gounaris, were eager to show that they could do far better in Asia Minor than Venizelos had done. After a welcoming ceremony for Constantine in Athens on December 19, 1920, General Papoulas met with Rallis and obtained his support for a "reconnaissance in force" to assess the "combat effectiveness of the Kemalist Army."[82] Such an operation would, reciprocally, prove that the Greek Army could fight successfully and would test whether it actually required full mobilization to defeat the Nationalists. The prime minister approved, and Papoulas returned to Izmir to issue orders on December 24 preparing the Field Army in Asia Minor for active operations. The details are unclear in the Concise Greek History, but Papoulas decided that Bursa and Eskişehir would form the zone of action with a greater number of troops (requiring mobilization of more reserves), under the condition that the operation be completed no later than January 17, 1921. Papoulas ordered the Smyrna Army Corps to prepare the offensive, and, on December 26, he ordered Army Corps A to prepare a supporting attack from Uşak (this was designed to prevent Nationalist forces in the Kütahya and Afyonkarahisar sectors from assisting the forces defending Eskişehir). Papoulas's plan was approved, with the starting date set as January 5, 1921.

In the meantime, Kemal, displeased with the performance of the Western Front Command, relieved Ali Fuat on November 9 by sending him to

Moscow as Turkey's ambassador to the newly proclaimed Soviet state. General Refet (Bele) remained in command of the Southern Front Command. The following day, Minister of War Fevzi (Çakmak) assigned İsmet (İnönü) as the new Western Front commander.[83] As organized, the West Front Command composed the Ertuğrul Group (the 11th and 61st Divisions), the 24th Division, and the 1st Mobile Force.[84] On January 6, 1921, İsmet maintained his headquarters in Eskişehir and, altogether, had 1,098 officers, 19,406 men, and 4,294 animals armed with 45 artillery pieces, 90 heavy machine guns, 23 light machine guns, and 10,283 rifles assigned to his combat units.[85] To the south on January 6, 1921, Refet had moved his headquarters forward to Keçiler, in the center of mass of Colonel Fahrettin's XII Corps units (the 8th and 23rd Divisions and the 1st and 2nd Cavalry Divisions). Fahrettin positioned his headquarters in Konya. Refet also commanded the 57th Division and a provisional division.

Some important organizational changes were afoot in the Nationalist Army.[86] In Ankara, a new 1st Division was being organized and activated under the command of Lieutenant Colonel Kemalettin Sami (Gökçen). And on November 20, Refet's provisional division was redesignated as the 8th Division. Very importantly for the army, in Kayseri, the 7th Mounted Infantry Division was activated by bringing together independent cavalry regiments and moved to Karaman on November 20. In January 1921, this division would be redesignated as the 1st Cavalry Division, signaling a revival of highly mobile cavalry forces. The activation of the 2nd Cavalry Division soon followed. As the Nationalist Army grew, the cavalry force grew to become a cavalry corps of three cavalry divisions. On November 27, the army activated a new 105-mm howitzer battalion. The 24th Division activated an assault battalion and the 61st Division activated an assault company (these were the Turkish version of German *Stosstruppen*, established exclusively for offensive operations).[87] Soldier morale was not forgotten when the army established a Field Postal System on December 21, 1920. These kinds of units (cavalry, assault troops, and heavy artillery) were the tools of offensive tactical operations and reflected the changing – mind-set of the Nationalists.

THE FIRST İNÖNÜ CAMPAIGN

On January 6, 1921, the General Headquarters redesignated the Greek Army's Smyrna Corps as Army Corps C under the command of Major General Konstantinos Petmezas (General Ioannou having left in November).

There were also changes in the designation of Greek Army divisions. The Cydonia Division was incorporated into the Crete Division on January 2, which was then renamed the 5th Division. On the same day, the Archipelago Division was redesignated the 7th Division. Later, on January 14, 1921, the Magnesia Division was redesignated the 11th Division; however, this book will use that unit identification in the First İnönü Campaign narrative. Both the 7th and 10th Division commanders were also replaced in November 1920.

On the morning of January 6, 1921, the Greeks launched their twin offensives, with Army Corps C making the main effort in the north, and Army Corps A conducting the supporting effort in the south. What had been briefed to Rallis as a relatively minor operation looks today, when plotted on a map, as an operational-level encirclement operation, which, if completed, would trap major Nationalist forces in the Kütahya salient (see map 3.2).[88] For the purposes of this book, the area of the northern battles between Army Corps A and the Western Front Command are termed the İnönü front, a small town where the battle would culminate and after which İsmet would derive his last name in 1934. The area of the southern battles between Army Corps A and the Southern Front Command are termed the Southern front. Of concern for the Nationalists were internal uprisings that had broken out in December 1920 (the Demirci Mehmet Efe Rebellion near Isparta) and, in January 1921 (the Çerkez Ethem Rebellion in Kütahya), which drew badly needed strength away from the Greek fronts (see chapter 4).

Army Corps C launched the 3rd and 7th Divisions as its main effort with Colonel Polychrones Karakalos, 7th Division commander, in overall tactical command. The 10th Division contributed an infantry regiment conducting a supporting mission to guard the main effort's left flank while the 3rd Division did not participate in the operation. General Petmezas's divisions hit the outposts of the Nationalist 24th Division's thinly held front lines and easily advanced through them. At the end of the day, the Greeks had pushed the front 20 kilometers southeast. Kemal and Fevzi reacted to the threat by sending reinforcements to İsmet, the new 4th Division from Ankara, and recalling İsmet's 11th Division, which had been suppressing the Çerkez Ethem Rebellion. Fighting a slow withdrawal, the Nationalists held them to a 10-kilometer advance by nightfall on January 7.[89] The next day, the 4th Division had arrived in the town of İnönü, the front was holding along the İnönü-Osmaneli road, and the 11th Division arrived that evening. İsmet arrived at the İnönü railway station

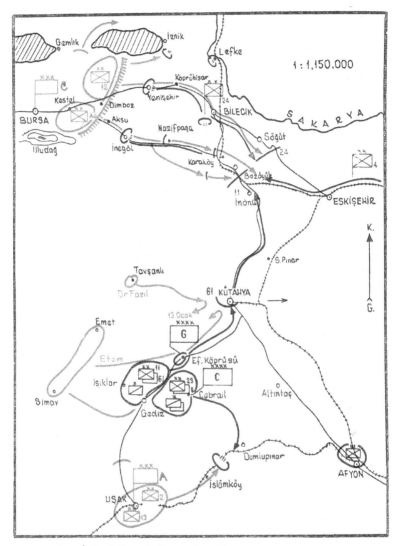

Map 3.2   First İnönü Greek Campaign Plan

The Field Army of Asia Minor's Reconnaissance in Force was designed to test the strength of the Nationalist Army with a two-pronged attack. The northern attacks of Army Corps C were halted by İsmet's strong defense at the İnönü train station, while the southern attacks were voluntarily halted at İslamköy and outside Kütahya. This is the tactical situation on January 10, 1920, after which the FAAM withdrew to its start lines.

Courtesy of the Turkish General Staff Military History and Strategy Institute (ATASE).

on January 9 and met with Colonel Arif, commander of the 11th Division (70th, 126th, and 127th Infantry Regiments) and Lieutenant Colonel Nâzım, commander of the 4th Division (of which only the 58th Infantry Regiment was available).[90]

The Nationalist General Staff had given İsmet permission to abandon Eskişehir if necessary but promised him reinforcements in any event.[91] After discussions reaching into midnight, İsmet decided to conduct a counterattack. He reorganized the 11 infantry battalions and four artillery batteries of the 4th and 11th Divisions as the Left Wing Group (*Sol Kanat Grubu*) and deployed them on a ridgeline northwest of İnönü, with orders to attack the Greek 7th Division the next day. İsmet ordered his exhausted 24th Division to hold the northern flank of the İnönü front for as long as possible. He had about 8,500 men and 28 artillery pieces available to oppose approximately 7,500 to 9,000 men with 72 artillery pieces from the infantry divisions in the Greek main effort.[92] However, İsmet was a very experienced combat commander, and he understood the principles of war in theory and in practice. He employed the 24th Division in an economy of force role, which enabled him to concentrate the Left Wing Group against one-third of Greek Army Corps C. It was masterful display of tactics but very risky if his calculations failed.

On January 10, 1920, the Greek 3rd and 7th Divisions began their attacks, once again "in dense fog at dawn," against the Left Wing Group, which degraded Greek command and control, as well as their artillery support.[93] They made some progress, but, beginning at about 11:00 a.m., İsmet's relentless counterattacks commenced, with the Greek 7th Division recording seven Nationalist assaults between noon and 2:00 p.m. alone.[94] This forced the Greeks to commit their reserves until the Nationalists broke contact late in the day and withdrew to the east. In the meantime, the Nationalist Army released control of the 2nd and 3rd Cavalry Divisions to reinforce İsmet, of which the 2nd Cavalry Division arrived on the left flank of the 11th Division at about 6:00 p.m. In the northern sector of the İnönü front, the battered 24th Division was gradually pushed back under heavy pressure from the Greek 3rd and 10th Divisions. That night, İsmet consolidated his defensive line about five kilometers east of İnönü, with the 24th and 11th Divisions and the 2nd Cavalry Division (from north to south), and the 4th Division in the rear as his tactical reserve.[95]

The Nationalist withdrawal had broken contact between the two armies, allowing the commanders some respite and thinking time. General Petmezas was also considering his options that night and decided that he had achieved his objective of determining the combat effectiveness of the Nationalist Army. Consequently, he decided to return to his original line of departure. On January 11, the 7th Division began to withdraw, reaching their previous initial positions on January 14.[96] Petmezas withdrew the 10th Division on January 12 as well. The Nationalist 3rd Cavalry Division arrived to reinforce İsmet on January 12, and he launched a pursuit forward on the heels of the Greeks. By January 15, his front was again anchored on the Aksu-İznik line, and, on the next day, the Nationalist Army released control of the recently activated 1st Division to the Western Front Command, with the division arriving at the İnönü railway station that day. There was light fighting on the İnönü front for the remainder of January.

In the south, Major General Nider's Army Corps A planned a single thrust from Uşak through Dumlupınar and then north to cut the Eskişehir-Afyonkarahisar railway line.[97] Nider's main effort was composed of the 2nd Division, reinforced with three infantry battalions from the 1st Division.[98] The Greek 13th Division made up the reserve. Opposite them, Refet's Southern Front Command strongly held Dumlupınar with Fahrettin's XII Corps (composed of the 8th and 23rd Divisions) while his 57th Division held the southern sector of his front. On January 6, the Greek 2nd Division began its advance, pushing back light Nationalist resistance, which, by January 8, had carried it forward about 20 kilometers to the village of İslamköy (halfway between Uşak and Dumlupınar).[99] Nider halted his offensive there.

With the outbreak of Greek offensive operations in the south, Kemal and Fevzi determined to reinforce Refet and redirected the 4th Division from the Western Front Command to the Southern Front Command. The division arrived in Afyonkarahisar on January 16 and moved to Dumlupınar the next day. Sensing gathering Nationalist opposition and having completed his mission, General Nider ordered the withdrawal back to the Greek initial positions on January 16.

According to the Concise Greek History, the operations in early January 1921 were successful. "The overall conclusion from the reconnaissance operation was that the Kemalist Army had significantly improved in strength, armament, organization, and discipline."[100] However, the Concise Greek History continued by pointing out that these operations revealed problems in the Greek Army as well, including "many inadequacies in army staff organization, especially on the level of the divisions, the communication and supply of offensive operations." More importantly, however, at least for the Nationalists, the Concise Greek History concluded with an honest appraisal of the general repercussions of the operation, which were boosting Nationalist morale while increasing a favorable public opinion in Europe of the Nationalists and causing intensified distrust in relations between the Allies and Greece.[101] Turkish historians tend to look at First İnönü as a decisive Nationalist victory, as do many western historians.[102]

From a military perspective, however, General Papoulas's objectives were unclear, and there is no evidence of balancing ends, ways, and means at the operational level to achieve a strategic purpose. The Greek Army had been in contact with the Nationalists, both regular and irregular, throughout 1920, and it is hard to imagine that the Greeks needed additional intelligence regarding Nationalist capabilities, although the operation did serve to provide information about the necessity for the Greeks to either mobilize further or to demobilize. It is evident today that Papoulas did not expect the Nationalist reaction to be as prompt or as effective as it was. Shortly following the operation in January, there was a wholesale firing of senior Greek commanders, as well a corresponding political decision to begin further mobilization.[103] On February 11, 1921, Army Corps C commander, Major General Petmezas, transferred command to Major General Aristotelis Vlachopoulos. On February 12, 1921, Army Corps B commander, Major General Mauromichales was relieved and replaced by General Petmezas. Lieutenant General Nider gave up command of Army Corps A and was replaced with Lieutenant General Alexandros Kontoulis on March 12, 1921. In February and March, the commanders of the Greek 2nd, 5th, 7th, 10th 11th, and 13th Divisions were also replaced.[104] On the Nationalist side, İsmet was promoted to major general on March 1, 1921.[105]

CONCLUSION

The Greek government began 1920 in a favorable political and military position. However, as the year ended, the Allies had come to distrust Greek ambitions as dangerously destabilizing in the geopolitical sense. The rise of the new Bolshevik state in Russia revived western European fears of Russian influence penetrating into the Mediterranean. Venizelos's requests and demands gave the Allies second thoughts about the terms of the Treaty of Sèvres and caused the British, the French, and the Italians to reconsider whether the *Megali Idea* was a viable alternative to resurrecting Turkey. Going into 1921, with Venizelos gone and replaced by a government that recapitalized its military investment in Asia Minor, the stage was set for the Greco-Turkish war to enter a decisive phase.

NOTES

1. Sir Henry Wilson to General Sir Henry Rawlinson, Wilson Papers 2/13B/41 (November 23, 1920), quoted in Keith Jeffrey, *The Military Correspondence of Field Marshal Sir Henry Wilson* (Bodley Head: The Army Records Society, 1985), 206.

2. Fromkin, *A Peace to End All Peace*, 403. Maurice Hankey was an influential British civil official who served as the secretary of the cabinet during the Turkish War of Independence. During the planning and execution of the Gallipoli Campaign in 1915, Hankey served as the secretary to the Imperial War Council.

3. Shaw, *From Empire to Republic*, vol. 2, 459.

4. Busch, *Mudros to Lausanne*, 198–200.

5. Shaw, *From Empire to Republic*, vol. 2, 460–462.

6. Llewellyn-Smith, *Ionian Vision*, 182–185.

7. Ibid., 190–193.

8. Ibid., 121.

9. Shaw, *From Empire to Republic*, vol. 3, part 1, 1128.

10. Ibid., 1128.

11. Ibid., 799–801.

12. Ibid., 817.

13. Edmonds, *The Occupation of Constantinople*, 3–6.

14. Shaw, *From Empire to Republic*, vol. 3, part 1, 843–845.

15. These two terms conformed to Venizelos's plan to alter the demographics of the Greek zone by encouraging Pontic Greeks and Armenians to emigrate to the Izmir region and, reciprocally, to encourage Muslims to immigrate out of the region. I am indebted to Professor Konstantinos Travlos for this analysis.

16. For the text of the Treaty of Versailles see The World War I Document Archive, "Peace Treaty of Versailles," https://wwi.lib.byu.edu/index.php/Peace_Treaty_of_Versailles. This is not to say that the Ottomans were kind to their defeated enemies. For example, the terms of the Treaty of Batum (1918) were particularly severe on the defeated Armenians (see Hovannisian, *The First Year*, 28–30.

17. Belen, *Türk Kurtuluş Savaşı*, 209–213.

18. Shaw, *From Empire to Republic*, vol. 3, part 1, 1139–1141.

19. Çiloğlu, *Kurtuluş Savaşı Sözlüğü*, 317.

20. Shaw, *From Empire to Republic*, vol. 3, part 1, 1147–1149.

21. For the complete text of Wilson's award, see Ara Papian and Davit O. Abrahamyan, eds., *Arbitral Award of the President of the United States of America Woodrow Wilson: Full Report of the Committee upon the Arbitration of the Boundary between Turkey and Armenia. Washington, November 22nd, 1920* (Armenia: Modus Vivendi, 2011).

22. Llewellyn-Smith, *Ionian Vision*, 128.

23. Gedeon, Paschalidou, and Dima-Dimitrou, *A Concise History of the Campaign in Asia Minor*, 40.

24. Ibid., 43.

25. Ibid., 48.

26. Shaw, *From Empire to Republic*, vol. 3, part 1, 1174–1175.

27. Fromkin, *A Peace to End All Peace*, 430–431.

28. Gedeon, Paschalidou, and Dima-Dimitrou, *A Concise History of the Campaign in Asia Minor*, 54.

29. Shaw, *From Empire to Republic*, vol. 3, part 1, 1178.

30. Gedeon, Paschalidou, and Dima-Dimitrou, *A Concise History of the Campaign in Asia Minor*, Sketch Map 6.

31. Görgülü, *On Yıllık Harbin Kadrosu*, 255–256.

32. Shaw, *From Empire to Republic*, vol. 3, part 1, 1181.

33. Belen, *Türk Kurtuluş Savaşı*, 189.

34. Gedeon, Paschalidou, and Dima-Dimitrou, *A Concise History of the Campaign in Asia Minor*, 59–61.

35. Gedeon, Paschalidou, and Dima-Dimitrou, *A Concise History of the Campaign in Asia Minor*, 56; and Tefik Ercan, *Türk İstiklâl Hârbi IInci Cilt, Batı Cephesi, 2nci Kısım (4 Eylül 1919–9 Kasım 1920)* (Ankara: Genelkurmay Basımevi, 1999), 254–260.

36. Gedeon, Paschalidou, and Dima-Dimitrou, *A Concise History of the Campaign in Asia Minor*, 56; and Ercan, *Batı Cephesi, 2nci Kısım*, 251–263.

37. Ercan, *Batı Cephesi, 2nci Kısım*, 311–316.

38. Ibid., Kroki 21 (Sketch Map 21, unnumbered page).

39. Shaw, *From Empire to Republic*, vol. 3, part 1, 1182–1183.

40. Ibid., See 1178–1179 for a full translation in English of Paraskevo-poulos's directive.

41. Llewellyn-Smith, *Ionian Vision*, 211–215.

42. Shaw, *From Empire to Republic*, vol. 3, part 1, 1178–1179.

43. Llewellyn-Smith, *Ionian Vision*, 127.

44. Shaw, *From Empire to Republic*, vol. 3, part 1, 1155–1156.

45. Görgülü, *On Yıllık Harbin Kadrosu*, 210–211.

46. Ercan, *Batı Cephesi, 2nci Kısım*, 352–353.

47. Gedeon, Paschalidou, and Dima-Dimitrou, *A Concise History of the Campaign in Asia Minor*, 529.

48. Ercan, *Batı Cephesi, 2nci Kısım*, 367–370.

49. Belen, *Türk Kurtuluş Savaşı*, 192.

50. Ercan, *Batı Cephesi, 2nci Kısım*, Kroki 23 (Sketch Map 23, unnumbered page).

51. Belen, *Türk Kurtuluş Savaşı*, 193.

52. Ökse, Baycan, and Sakaryalı, *Komutanların Biyografileri*, 143–145.

53. Belen, *Türk Kurtuluş Savaşı*, 193.

54. Ercan, *Batı Cephesi, 2nci Kısım*, 384; and Belen, *Türk Kurtuluş Savaşı*, 193.

55. Ökse, Baycan, and Sakaryalı, *Komutanların Biyografileri*, 92–94.

56. Shaw, *From Empire to Republic*, vol. 3, part 1, 1158.

57. Llewellyn-Smith, *Ionian Vision*, 129–130.

58. Gedeon, Paschalidou, and Dima-Dimitrou, *A Concise History of the Campaign in Asia Minor*, 65.

59. Ibid., 66–67.

60. Görgülü, *On Yıllık Harbin Kadrosu*, 256–257.

61. Ökse, Baycan, and Sakaryalı, *Komutanların Biyografileri*, 220–223.

62. Gedeon, Paschalidou, and Dima-Dimitrou, *A Concise History of the Campaign in Asia Minor*, 67.

63. Belen, *Türk Kurtuluş Savaşı*, 215.

64. Gedeon, Paschalidou, and Dima-Dimitrou, *A Concise History of the Campaign in Asia Minor*, 68.

65. Ibid.

66. Gedeon, Paschalidou, and Dima-Dimitrou, *A Concise History of the Campaign in Asia Minor*, 66.

67. Belen, *Türk Kurtuluş Savaşı*, 215

68. Ercan, *Batı Cephesi, 2nci Kısım*, 429–430.

69. Ibid., 431–437; and Kroki 26 (Sketch Map 26)

70. Gedeon, Paschalidou, and Dima-Dimitrou, *A Concise History of the Campaign in Asia Minor*, 72.

71. Ibid., 74.

72. Shaw, *From Empire to Republic*, vol. 3, part 1, 1187.

73. Ibid., 1188.

74. Llewellyn-Smith, *Ionian Vision*, 131. Smith presents the complete text of this telegram in his book.

75. Ibid., 132–161.

76. Churchill, *The Aftermath*, 386–389.

77. Shaw, *From Empire to Republic*, vol. 3, part 1, 1189; Llewellyn-Smith, *Ionian Vision*, 166; and Gedeon, Paschalidou, and Dima-Dimitrou, *A Concise History of the Campaign in Asia Minor*, 81. Both Shaw and Smith provide the text of the declaration in their books.

78. Gedeon, Paschalidou, and Dima-Dimitrou, *A Concise History of the Campaign in Asia Minor*, 77–78.

79. Ibid.

80. Ibid.

81. Ibid., 78. See also Llewellyn-Smith, *Ionian Vision*, 172–178 for a comprehensive appraisal of the resignations and replacements of generals and officers on the army.

82. Gedeon, Paschalidou, and Dima-Dimitrou, *A Concise History of the Campaign in Asia Minor*, 84.

83. Ökse, Baycan, and Sakaryalı, *Komutanların Biyografileri*, 166, 218.

84. Rahmi Apac'ca, Kâmil Önalp, and Selim Turhan, *Türk İstiklâl Hârbi IInci Cilt, Batı Cephesi, 3ncü Kısım (9 Kasım 1920–15 Nisan 1921)* (Ankara: Genelkurmay Basımevi, 1994), Kuruluş 3 (Organizational Chart 3, unnumbered page).

85. Ibid., 39–41.

86. Ibid., 48–53.

87. Doruk Akyüz, "Legacy of the Stormtroop: The Influence of German Assault Troop Doctrines in the Great Offensive," *Salvation and Catastrophe, The Greek-Turkish War, 1919–1922*, edited by Konstantinos Travlos, Latham: Maryland, Lexington Books, 202, 197–230. See Edward J. Erickson, *Palestine: The Ottoman Campaigns of 1914–1918* (Barnsley, UK: Pen and Sword Military, 2016), 98–178 for a comprehensive explanation of the activation and use of Ottoman Army assault troops in World War I.

88. Apac'ca, Önalp, and Turhan, *Batı Cephesi, 3ncü Kısım*, Kroki 18 (Sketch Map 18, unnumbered page).

89. Ibid., 161–186; and Gedeon, Paschalidou, and Dima-Dimitrou, *A Concise History of the Campaign in Asia Minor*, 86–87.

90. Belen, *Türk Kurtuluş Savaşı*, 276–277.

91. Mango, *Atatürk*, 307.

92. Apac'ca, Önalp, and Turhan, *Batı Cephesi, 3ncü Kısım*, 194–195. The Turks assert that the Greeks' main effort involved 17,000 men;

however, the main effort contained only five understrength infantry regiments, each of about 1,500 to 1,800 men.

93. Gedeon, Paschalidou, and Dima-Dimitrou, *A Concise History of the Campaign in Asia Minor*, 89.

94. Ibid.

95. Apac'ca, Önalp, and Turhan, *Batı Cephesi, 3ncü Kısım*, 201–211.

96. Gedeon, Paschalidou, and Dima-Dimitrou, *A Concise History of the Campaign in Asia Minor*, 90.

97. Apac'ca, Önalp, and Turhan, *Batı Cephesi, 3ncü Kısım*, Kroki 18 (Sketch Map 18, unnumbered page).

98. Gedeon, Paschalidou, and Dima-Dimitrou, *A Concise History of the Campaign in Asia Minor*, 91.

99. Belen, *Türk Kurtuluş Savaşı*, 278–280.

100. Gedeon, Paschalidou, and Dima-Dimitrou, *A Concise History of the Campaign in Asia Minor*, 91.

101. Ibid. See also Llewellyn-Smith, *Ionian Vision*, 183; and Mango, *Atatürk*, 307 for commentary on the effects of these operations.

102. For example, see Shaw, *From Empire to Republic*, vol. 3, part 1, 1200.

103. Gedeon, Paschalidou, and Dima-Dimitrou, *A Concise History of the Campaign in Asia Minor*, 521–522.

104. Ibid., 522–523.

105. Ökse, Baycan, and Sakaryalı, *Komutanların Biyografileri*, 216.

FOUR

The Long War against Insurgents

The loss of manpower in Turkey has been appalling,
and too many men are still absent from work and carrying rifles.[1]

Maj. Gen. James G. Harbord, 1919

INTRODUCTION

One of the lesser-known aspects of the Turkish War of Independence in the
English-speaking world is the story of internal uprisings and violent incidents, which the Nationalists had to contend with while fighting on conventional fronts at the same time. The Turkish official military history
Uprisings during the Independence War records 24 acts of rebellion
between May 1919 and March 1923.[2] To this we might add the Urla Incident in January 1919 (see chapter 1) and others. Ismet Görgülü, in his defin-
itive study of Ottoman and Nationalist military organizations, lists 19 acts
of rebellion worthy of assembling detailed Nationalist orders of battle.[3]
Sometimes these rebellions were given a name based on the name of a
leader; sometimes based on a tribe, ethnic group, or region; and sometimes
they were named after a city or town. Some of these uprisings were exclusively domestic, while others were encouraged, instigated, and abetted by
outside influences. In their military histories, the Turks use several words
to delineate the scale and scope of the uprising. From the more serious to
the less serious, these are: *isyan* (rebellion), *ayaklanma* (uprising), *olay*
(incident), and *çarpışması* (clash). In this chapter, I describe the events

using the terms used in the official history. In all cases, these uprisings and rebellions produced a military response from the Nationalist government, which posed a dilemma for Kemal and the military staffs because they forced a diversion of effort and scarce military resources away from the conventional fighting fronts against the Greeks, French, and Armenians.

In this chapter, I have very lightly examined the brutal causalities that instigated these events. Many of the uprisings were the direct consequence of the population engineering and relocation policies of the CUP in 1914–1918, especially in the cases of the Ottoman Greeks and the Circassians. I do not mean to downplay the grievances of the disaffected populations, which were legitimate in many cases, and I am not justifying the tactics used by the forces described herein, which, in many cases, were excessive and draconian. My intent in this chapter is to present the problem as the Nationalists saw it at the time and to briefly present how they dealt with it using military means. This is the story of suppression operations (*Bastırma Harekâtı*), which the Ottomans and the Nationalists used as an inclusive term for what we would today call counterinsurgency operations.

THE END OF THE NATIONAL FORCES

At this point in the narrative, it is important to understand how the National Army and the National Ministry of Defense evolved. In fall 1919, the Representative Committee had established both a National Army (regular formations) and authorized National Forces (irregular volunteer formations, which were already in existence throughout Anatolia) and put Major General Ali Fuat (Cebesoy) in charge of organizing both forces. However, by spring 1920, Ali Fuat was heavily engaged in fighting Greeks and rebels, and he was unable to fulfill this responsibility. In the meantime, Kemal attempted to bring the plethora of National Force irregular formations and militias, many under former officers and some even under known criminals, under the control of the Ankara government. As will be seen, these were vitally important in suppressing the large number of uprisings and incidents occurring in 1919–1920; however, they were not well disciplined and spent much of their time advantaging their sponsors and themselves.[4] Moreover, they sometimes acted on their own initiative and often committed crimes against civilians. In effect, they were both a military asset and a military liability at the same time. Nevertheless, these irregulars were instrumental in the suppression of rebellions but, in several cases, causal to rebellions themselves.

"The first step toward remedying this situation" came on May 16, 1920, when the Grand National Assembly ordered a restructuring of the National Army into two components.[5] The Ministry of National Defense was reorganized under Lieutenant General Mustafa Fevzi (Çakmak), the sultan's former Minister of Defense, who came over to the Nationalists in Ankara on April 27. At the same time, Colonel İsmet (İnönü) was reaffirmed as the chief of the General Staff. On May 26, the Assembly created the Mobile Jandarma (a paramilitary gendarmerie not assigned to a particular city or province and equipped for light combat operations in the field), formed of detachments from some of the National Force infantry and cavalry formations.[6] The Council of Ministers declared martial law on June 6 in the areas under its control, and, on June 26, 1920, the Assembly introduced conscription. Conscripts had the option of joining the Mobile Jandarma or the regular National Army. That month, the Grand National Assembly also put the remaining National Forces under the command of the Ministry of National Defense as mobile forces (*Kuva-yı Seyyare*) and made irregular mobile force soldiers subject to the jurisdictions imposed under military law. The Nationalist government took over funding for the irregular formations and offered to pardon any criminals who were conscripted but who had shown bravery in battle. In effect, the Nationalist government was attempting to take control of the irregular forces.

Naturally, many of the National Force leaders and soldiers resisted their loss of independence and their opportunity to conduct self-serving activities. Throughout 1920, the mobile forces were gradually brought under government control and integrated into the National Army. Some of the most powerful mobile force leaders resisted integration and refused to comply with instructions to demobilize and turn over their weapons, notably Demirci Mehmet Efe and Çerkez Ethem, who would raise rebellions in late 1920. By early 1921, Chief of the General Staff Colonel İsmet had successfully integrated or demobilized the remaining irregular militia groups. Additionally, the government eliminated the mobile Jandarma altogether in January 1921 and absorbed its members into the regular army. According to historian Stanford Shaw, both the Greeks and the British were unaware of this reorganization of the Nationalist military forces, thus leading them to underestimate the capability and capacity of Kemal's regular army in 1921.[7]

THE PONTIC GREEK UPRISINGS (*PONTUS AYAKLANMASI*)
SPRING 1919–FEBRUARY 6, 1923

Almost immediately after the Mudros armistice, the Pontic Greek Orthodox bishop of Trabzon, Metropolitan Chrysanthos (Hrisantos), initially encouraged by British and French armistice control officers, began to stir up unrest in the Black Sea region known as the Pontus. Archbishop Chrysanthos wrote and sent a one-sided memorandum to the Peace Conference in Versailles on January 18, 1919 advocating the establishment of a Greek Pontic State based on political and demographic grounds.[8] Chrysanthos wrongly claimed that more than 600,000 ethnic Greeks lived in the Trabzon, Sivas, Sinop, and the adjacent vilayets (this was an inflated number because he included Greek-speaking Muslims). Additionally, an influx of some 8,000 Greek and 1,200 Armenian refugees into Trabzon in the first few months after Mudros greatly inflamed the situation. During the war, some of these Ottoman Greeks and the Ottoman Armenians had been in rebellion. Notably, the Armenians maintained secret armed revolutionary societies (such as the Armenian Revolutionary Federation) before and during World War I—and some of these refugees still belonged to these societies.[9] Moreover, between November 1918 and March 1919, about 800 armed Greek volunteers landed in Trabzon.[10] In early 1919, the epicenter of organized Ottoman Greek unrest was the Pontus (Pontos), and local Greeks proclaimed a Pontic State there (see map 4.1).[11]

As in mainland Greece, rivalries between factions worked against the aspirations of the Pontic Greeks because there were serious rifts between the supporters of Chrysanthos (who advocated political action) and the supporters of Germanos Karavangelis (who advocated armed resistance).[12] This did not stop Pontic Greeks from organizing various resistance groups. According to the Turkish official military history, by March 1919, armed bands of Pontic Greek bandits (*Rum çeteleri*) began to attack their Muslim neighbors and interfere with the military administration of the region.[13] This is contested by contemporary Greek historians, but the reality is that rogue members of both Christian and Muslim communities preyed on each other, committing crimes against civilians. On May 27, 1919, Archbishop Chrysanthos wrote "an astonishing memorandum on 'The Euxine Pontus Question' to Lloyd George"[14] to secure international support for establishing a Pontic Republic. The archbishop now claimed that there were 850,000 Pontic Greeks, but the Supreme Council at Versailles had, by now, become

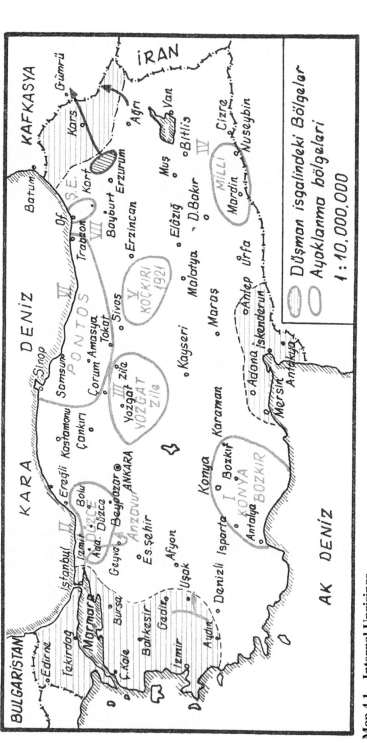

Map 4.1 Internal Uprisings

The dangers posed by internal rebellions to the Nationalist lines of communications are evident on the map. The principal rebellions are shown here: (1) Bozkır (1919) and Konya (1920), (2) 1st and 2nd Düzce (1920), (3) Yozgat (1920), (4) Millî Aşiret (1920), (5) Koçkiri Aşiret (1921), (6) Pontus (1919–1922), and (7) Şeyh Eşraf (1919).

Courtesy of the Turkish General Staff Military History and Strategy Institute (ATASE).

accustomed to exaggerated demographic claims from Ottoman minorities and did nothing.

Abandoned by the West, the Pontic Greeks in the Black Sea coastal region between Trabzon and Hopa would become a serious four-year domestic security problem for the Nationalists.[15] In August 1919, reports of killings and road interdictions inland between Bayburt and Gümüşhane reached both the Ottoman government and the Nationalists.[16] With the Nationalists consolidating in Anatolia, the Ottoman government could do little, and it does not appear that the Nationalists, then busy with unifying the resistance, were able to do much about the problem either. The Turkish official history presents statistics of 11,000 Greeks who were either in rebellion or in bandit gangs by early 1920.[17] This is an impossibly large number given the known Greek population of the Pontus, and it must be noted that in other parts of the official history's chapter on the Pontus uprisings the term *Hıristiyana (Ermeni dahil)* or "Christians (including Armenians)" is used.[18] In any case the outbreaks in the Pontus were the largest and longest-lasting uprisings that the Nationalists dealt with. In the absence of regional rule of law, numbers of local irregular Muslim militia groups armed themselves against their Pontic Greek neighbors.[19]

In June 1920, groups of disaffected Pontic Greeks were strong enough to begin operations that ravaged hundreds of Muslim villages and farms along the coast and hinterlands.[20] In turn, the Nationalists organized the Central Army (Merkez Ordusu) on December 9, 1920 in Amasya under the command of General Nurettin (Sakallı).[21] Nurettin had previously suppressed the Urla Uprising in January 1919 and was known to be tough, capable, and determined to succeed.[22] He was assigned an area of responsibility from Sinop to Trabzon on the Black Sea coast and inland to Çorum-Amasya-Sivas, and given command of the 5th Caucasian Division, the 15th Division, the 14th Cavalry Division (composed of the 27th and 28th Cavalry Brigades), and the 13th Independent Cavalry Brigade.[23] Each of the infantry divisions had an assault battalion and there were three company-sized Nationalist militia groups available (the Erzurum Millî Müfrezesi, the İsa Bey Millî Müfrezesi, and the Çarşamba Müfrezesi) as well. Altogether, Nurettin had around 10,000 men available for combat.

Central Army suppression operations began in early February 1921. This was, obviously, a major effort, and Nurettin was given almost unlimited military and civil authority to stamp out the uprisings. He "carried out his task with exceptional harshness."[24] Nurettin arrested what leaders he could find, as well as Samsun Metropolitan Eftimos and Bishop Platon

Matnoz. His forces swept through the coastal towns and hinterlands, forcibly relocating entire villages of the Pontic Greek population to Sivas and Elaziğ in the interior. Amid these operations (after the Second Battle of İnönü), the 5th Caucasian Division, the 15th Division, and the 14th Cavalry Division were redeployed in May 1921 to reinforce the Western Front Command. The 5th Assault Battalion and the 5th Artillery Regiment remained behind, but these transfers gutted the Central Army. In place of these experienced divisions, the general staff activated two new infantry divisions to bring the Central Army back up to strength, the 10th Division in Samsun (which replaced the 10th Caucasian Division that had been recently inactivated in Istanbul) and the 16th Division in Amasya. Nurettin reorganized his army in June around the two new infantry divisions and the remaining 27th Cavalry Brigade, stationing his army headquarters in Amasya. The Central Army continued to hemorrhage experienced fighting units to the Western Command. The General Staff also ordered the 47th Infantry Regiment to İsmet's Western Front Command and, in July and August 1921, the 48th and 49th Infantry Regiments and the 5th Assault Battalion were sent west as well.[25] To replace these formations, the army further activated the 64th, 65th, and 66th Infantry Regiments. Thus, while nominally maintaining the strength of Nurettin's Central Army, its proficiency levels plummeted, as new and untested formations replaced trained and experienced formations.

The employment of inexperienced and poorly trained soldiers is often a recipe for excesses against civilians, and I believe this was a significant factor in subsequent civilian victimization in central Anatolia. Operations against the rebels in Samsun and nearby Pontic Greek villages resumed in September and yielded the capture of 2,500 rifles and 1,200,000 rounds of ammunition.[26] According to a November report from the Central Army to the Grand National Assembly, Nurettin's men "burned 7,000 homes to the ground, killed 5,000 and wounded 3,000 Pontic Greek civilians, and deported 25,600 to the interior."[27] In August, the Nationalists extended the scope of the Independence Tribunals to include bandits and rebels, convening the infamous Amasya Trials. Many Pontic Greek community leaders, who had been imprisoned, went on trial and were executed. Nurettin's ruthless tactics crushed the major uprisings by the fall of 1921. However, his draconian tactics led to his relief from command on November 8, 1921, and he was put on trial for cruelty and misconduct. After a trial lasting several months, Nurettin was acquitted on the grounds that he had suppressed a savage and bloody uprising and that he had been authorized by the Grand National Assembly to use whatever means necessary.

However, the uprisings in the Black Sea region of eastern Anatolia were not entirely extinguished. The Turkish official history asserts that the Pontic uprisings continued until February 23, 1923 (however, no evidence is presented in that work to support that assertion).[28] With Nurettin gone, command of the remaining formations of the rump Central Army fell to General Kâzim Karabekir of the Eastern Front Command, who was just finishing up his successful campaign against the Republic of Armenia. While that campaign is well documented, information on Karabekir's residual suppression operations is almost nonexistent. In July 1922, Karabekir sent the 53rd Infantry Regiment from Trabzon and the 54th Infantry Regiment from Erzincan to Samsun for further operations against a small uprising.[29] It is unclear who the operation was directed against, and, for all practical purposes, it is fair to say that the Pontic uprisings ended almost entirely in the fall of 1921.

The deployment of Eastern Front Command forces to the west clearly demonstrated that the Nationalists no longer considered internal uprisings in the east a serious a threat. In the winter of 1921/1922, the 16th Division also sent to the Western Front Command, and the Grand National Assembly inactivated the Central Army entirely on February 28, 1922.[30] On October 1, 1922, Karabekir had inactivated his XV Corps headquarters as well.[31] On that date, his Eastern Front Command had been drawn down to the 9th Caucasian Division, the 13th Division, and the 6th Cavalry Division (as well as the Erzurum and Kars Fortresses and border guards).

ALI BATI UPRISING (*ALI BATI AYAKLANMASI*) MAY 11–AUGUST 18, 1919

On May 11, a Kurd named Ali Batı and about 100 supporters seized the town of Nusaybin along the current Turkish-Syrian border in the XIII Corps area. They had been encouraged by rumors that the British were about to establish a Kurdish state.[32] The commander of the 5th Division in nearby Mardin reacted the next day, ordering two infantry battalions and a squadron from the 1st Cavalry Regiment to Nusaybin. A brief firefight ensued, and Ali Batı withdrew to the hills in the north. To assist in ending the incident, the 5th Division commander requested assistance from the 2nd Division, which promptly sent the 3rd Battalion, 6th Infantry Regiment from Midyat.[33] Around 800 soldiers with some mountain howitzers now surrounded the rebels in the village of Mekre. Ali broke out and withdrew to Mizizah where he was again surrounded on June 9. He made a final breakout and escaped to the nearby village of Dirülamı where Major

Pehlivanzade Nuri's 6th Infantry Regiment surrounded the band. After a two-hour struggle on August 18, Nuri's soldiers took the village and killed the remaining rebels.

ALI GALIP INCIDENT (*ALI GALIP OLAYI*) AUGUST 20–SEPTEMBER 15, 1919

A second incident in the XIII Corps area immediately followed the Ali Batı Uprising. After receiving the news of the Erzurum Congress, Elazığ Province governor Ali Galip attempted to halt the dispatch of the Nationalist Malatya delegation for the Sivas Congress.[34] Coordinating with British control officers and local Kurds, Ali Galip sent Damat Ferit a coded telegram on August 20, recommending that Mustafa Kemal be arrested or killed. The Ottoman government authorized Ali Galip to go to Sivas with armed men to break up the congress and arrest Kemal. As Ali Galip was organizing his raid, the Nationalists learned of his plot and dispatched the 15th Infantry Regiment, under its commander Major İlyas, on September 8 to arrest Alli Galip and any foreign officers who were advising him. Assisted by the 12th Infantry Regiment, the Nationalists broke up Ali Galip's Kurdish supporters in Malatya and Elazığ between September 10 and 15. Ali Galip escaped and fled to the protection of the Istanbul government.

THE FIRST STEPPE UPRISING (*BIRINCI BOZKIR AYAKLANMASI*) SEPTEMBER 27–OCTOBER 4, 1919

Bozkır is a town near the central Anatolian city of Konya, and by the summer of 1919, it had become a hotbed of Nationalist activity (*bozkır* translates in English to steppe—many of the inhabitants were Muslim refugees who had been expelled from the broad plains of the Ukraine and the steppes of southern Russia). That summer, Damat Ferit organized an Ottoman Investigation Commission charged with investigating such Nationalist activity (See chapter 2), and the government sent Süleyman Şefik (Söylemezoğlu) Pasha to inspect the Konya-Afyonkarahisar-Antalya region. Konya Province Governor Cemal Bey was an adherent of Damat's government but XII Corps commander in Konya, Colonel Selâhattin, leaned toward the Nationalist cause. Both were closely watched by Allied control officers. Süleyman Şefik arrived in Afyonkarahisar on July 31, inspected his assigned cities, and returned to Istanbul on August 10. His report outlining the loss of control to the Nationalists was deeply troubling to the government, and, consequently, Damat authorized Cemal Bey to take action against them.[35]

In parallel, the ministry of war attempted to replace the XII Corps commander with government loyalist Ali Sait Pasha, but Nationalists in the telegraph offices exposed this maneuver, forcing Ali Sait to flee to Istanbul on September 25.[36] The next day, Governor Cemal Bey issued orders for the forcible arrest of Nationalists in Konya. However, in the meantime, the Nationalists sent Colonel Refet with the 7th Cavalry Regiment to Konya. As Refet took control of the city, Cemal Bey and a handful of supporters escaped and fled to Istanbul. A new governor, Suphi Bey, replaced Cemal and announced that those who supported the Istanbul government would receive amnesty; however, this never came about.

THE SECOND STEPPE UPRISING (*IKINCI BOZKIR AYAKLANMASI*) OCTOBER 20–NOVEMBER 4, 1919

Fighting erupted again on October 20 when some 70 armed and 200 unarmed rebels gathered under tribal leaders in Bozkır. Two days later, after growing to about 600 armed men, the rebels began to cut telegraph lines and block roads. On October 24, newly assigned XII Corps commander, Colonel Fahrettin (Altay) sent Lieutenant Colonel Arif (Karakeçili) with a punitive detachment from the 139th Infantry Regiment to suppress the rebels.[37] A Nationalist militia of about 100 men also organized to assist Arif. Over the next week, Arif swept through rebel villages, killing about 30 rebels and wounding several others. Of note, on October 28–29, the Kızılkuyu Incident (*Kızılkuyu Olayı*) occurred when one of Arif's detachment, commanded by Captain Musa, attacked and captured a handful of rebels inside a mosque. Two further firefights were noted—the Apa Clash (*Apa Çarpışması*) on October 28, 1919 and the Dinek Clash (*Dinek Çarpışması*) on November 1. Arif brought the rebels to heel, surrounded them in Bozkır, and took the leaders prisoner. It appears that due to Allied pressure, neither the Nationalists nor the government punished the leaders or the rebels further.

FIRST ANZAVUR UPRISING (*BIRINCI ANZAVUR AYAKLANMASI*) OCTOBER 25–NOVEMBER 30, 1919

In fall 1919, retired Jandarma lieutenant Ahmet Anzavur was serving as district governor of Izmit but was forced by the Greek occupation to move to Bursa where he led a Nationalist militia. However, his embrace of the

Nationalist cause did not last long. According to one historian, "Ahmet Anzavur represents an older class of provincial notables who led the charge against the Kuva-yı Milliye (National Forces)." [38] After the Sivas Congress, he refused to accept the Representative Committee's demand that he incorporate his militia, which was made mostly of immigrants and marginalized peoples such as North Caucasians, Pomaks, and Bosnians, into the National Forces.[39] Anzavur then became involved in a squabble with the Balıkesir Defense of Rights organization over money, and, on October 25, 1919, he began to raid the villages of the other Nationalist groups, gathering arms and forcibly conscripting men into his personal militia.[40] On November 2, he occupied the village of Susurluk with 50 horsemen and continued to forcibly conscript more men. Over the next few days, the 61st Division commander, Colonel Kâzım (Özalp), got him to halt his illegal activities, but on November 12, Anzavur attacked the army barracks at Susurluk, seizing large quantities of weapons and ammunition. Colonel Kâzım responded by sending his soldiers north from Balıkesir while the 174th Infantry Regiment from his sister 56th Division came south to chase down Anzavur.[41] Kâzım led his men in a clash at Demirkapı (*Demirkapı Çarpışması*) on November 16, pushing the rebels into Susurluk. The two Nationalist Army forces converged and took Susurluk on November 17, pushing the rebels to the west. Kâzım also asked for and received assistance from the powerful National Force leader, Çerkez Ethem, whose highly mobile group of 150 irregular cavalrymen pursued the rebels and joined in the routing of Anzavur's small army on the night of November 19/20.[42] Surrounded again, Anzavur's first uprising ended in the village of Ulubad on November 30, although he escaped and went into hiding.

SHEIKH EŞREF UPRISING (*ŞEYH EŞREF AYAKLANMASI*) OCTOBER 26–DECEMBER 24, 1919

The small town of Hart, 20 kilometers northwest of Bayburt (an eastern Anatolian city) became the point of ignition for the next uprising.[43] Eşref was a sheikh who led a Shiite Alevi religious sect and who resisted invitations to join the Nationalists. On December 9, 1919, Major Nuri, the 28th Infantry Regiment commander, led a 50-man detachment to Hart to apprehend Eşref, but he repelled the attack. Major Nuri was killed in the assault. Following this, the Bayburt Military District commander, Colonel Hasan Lütfi,[44] sent two infantry companies with machine guns from the 17th

Infantry Regiment to suppress the rebellion, but they were also defeated, with many soldiers captured by the rebels.

This defeat caused severe concern in the XV Corps headquarters, and General Karabekir's staff met to discuss an overwhelming response. On December 17, 9th Division commander, Lieutenant Colonel Deli Halit (Karsıalan) (Deli Halit translates to "Crazy Halit"), assembled a strike force in Bayburt composed of two battalions each from the 28th and the 29th Infantry Regiments, four howitzer batteries, and two squadrons of cavalry.[45] Marching to Hart, Halit encircled the town, shelling it with his howitzers, and then assaulted the defenders. The sheik, two of his sons, two of his daughters, and many of his followers were killed, while army casualties were very light.

SECOND ANZAVUR UPRISING (*IKINCI ANZAVUR AYAKLANMASI*) FEBRUARY 16–APRIL 16, 1920

Ahmet Anzavur's second uprising began when brutal Nationalist commander Hamdi Bey attempted to extort money from the town of Biga.[46] Anzavur raised another small army that he called the Forces of the Prophet Muhammad, but which actually was just an assembly of bandit and renegade gangs, and he marched on Biga.[47] On February 16, Anzavur took Biga, killing Hamdi Bey and a number of his supporters. Gathering momentum, Anzavur seized an army weapons depot at Yenice five days later and began to arm his followers. He occupied the port of Bandırma and began to expand his control toward Balıkesir. Alert now to the continuing danger, Kemal ordered XIV Corps commander Major General Yusuf İzzet (Met) to stop Anzavur. The nearest troops belonged to the 172nd Infantry Regiment (56th Division), which sent a detachment north on February 20.[48] Yusuf İzzet ordered his 61st Division to send Lieutenant Colonel Rahmi's 174th Infantry Regiment into action toward Bandırma from Karacabey with a detachment of 220 men armed with machine guns. On February 29, the 61st Division formed the primary tool for the suppression of the rebellion and activated the Pursuit Detachment (*Takip Müfrezesi*) under cavalry Lieutenant Colonel Süleyman Sabri.[49] Sabri's Pursuit Detachment composed 1,500 cavalrymen and infantrymen, two artillery pieces, and nine machine guns. The punitive forces converged on the town of Gönen and fought several battles with Anzavur's men; however, all they accomplished was to push the rebels out of the town.

March 1920 went badly for the Nationalists, who lost several battles with the rebels and were unable to bring Anzavur to a decisive engagement. Yusuf İzzet committed more units and sent two battalions of the 190th Infantry Regiment against the rebels, as well as bringing in several Nationalist irregular militia groups led by retired officers. The most important irregular group was led by former Special Organization (Teşkilat-ı Mahsusa) officer Çerkez Ethem (Ethem the Circassian), who led a highly mobile group of experienced cavalrymen. These overwhelming forces finally trapped Anzavur in Yahyaköy and took the village in a bitter struggle on April 16. Anzavur escaped and fled by ship to Istanbul.[50]

FIRST DÜZCE UPRISING (*BIRINCI DÜZCE AYAKLANMASI*) APRIL 13–MAY 31, 1920

The towns of Düzce and Bolu are roughly halfway between Istanbul and Ankara and became the next in the series of uprisings among the mostly Circassian immigrant tribes of the area. As the government gradually lost control of the countryside, Circassian notables took advantage of the situation by opposing centralized authority, killing a judge and a Jandarma commander, and seizing property and a weapons storage site in Düzce and Bolu on April 13.[51] On April 19, Kemal alerted the 24th Division commander, Staff Lieutenant Colonel Mahmut, to send troops to quell the uprising. Mahmut formed a detachment of two battalions from the 143rd Infantry Regiment with some artillery and cavalry and led it to the town of Hendek the next day. On April 22, Mahmut tried to diffuse the tensions, but he and his chief of staff were ambushed and killed by the rebels. A second smaller detachment (only 60 men) led by Major İbrahim Çolak, accompanied by such well-known personalities as Eşref Kuşçubaşı and Rauf, arrived in nearby Geyve on April 19.[52] They organized a combined force and pushed forward, defeating rebels en route to Mudurnu on May 14, where İbrahim Çolak was able to telegraph Ankara.

Çolak's telegram began the second phase of the Nationalist effort to crush the rebels. In response, the XX Corps commander in Ankara, Major General Ali Fuat, rapidly formulated a plan. He formed a punitive detachment composed of the 1st Battalion, 135th Infantry Regiment, and several irregular Nationalist militia groups under Lieutenant Colonel Arif (Karakeçili). Ali Fuat also ordered the 32nd Infantry Regiment from Zonguldak south and the 58th Infantry Regiment west from Çerkes, converging on the town of Bolu. Arif's detachment pushed east surrounding and eliminating rebels in Beypazarı on April 22/23. He then swung his detachment north and reached

Bolu, where the rebels had concentrated, on May 1. Scattering the rebels in Bolu, Arif pursued them east to Kızılcahamam on May 6. In follow-up operations, Arif was killed in action on May 11/12, as was the commander of the 32nd Infantry Regiment. The Düzce Uprising was proving to be costly and time consuming, as will be seen in the next section, concurrent with combat with Ottoman government forces in Geyve and Adapazarı.

The tactical dilemma for the Nationalists, at this point, was simply that they had too few men to plug the gaps, thus allowing the rebels to escape and regroup. However, once again, the Nationalists called on the irregular cavalry of Çerkez Ethem, who brought his men to Geyve on May 22.[53] Ali Fuat also reinforced the effort by sending in the 24th Assault Battalion and two more regular infantry battalions. Çerkez Ethem's irregulars crushed the rebels in Adapazarı, advancing through Hendek and taking Düzce itself on May 26. Colonel Refet joined the hunt on that day, leading a mixed combat group composed of the 1st Battalion, 135th Infantry, and more irregular Nationalist groups.[54] Major Çolak and Staff Major Nazım took Mudurnu and Bolu on May 27. The survivors were mostly chased down and eliminated in Gerede on May 31, although some escaped to fight again.

DISCIPLINARY FORCE OPERATIONS (*KUVAYI İNZIBATIYE HAREKÂI*) APRIL 18–JULY 25, 1920

The Turkish Nationalists were not the only ones to raise counterrebellion forces. On April 7, Damat Ferit consulted with Admiral Sir John de Robeck to ask for Allied military support against the Nationalists.[55] De Robeck was reluctant to intervene in what he regarded a civil war but agreed to permit the Ottoman government to create loyal military formations. On April 20, the British government ordered de Robeck to provide arms and munitions to regular and irregular forces loyal to the sultan.

With control of the regular army slipping away, Damat Ferit established the provisional Disciplinary Force (*Kuva-yi İnzibatiye*) commanded by Süleyman Şefik Pasha.[56] Activated on April 18, 1920, the Disciplinary Force was essentially an infantry division composed of a division headquarters; the 1st, 2nd, and 3rd Infantry Regiments; and an artillery battalion.[57] The formation fell under the command of the Ottoman ministry of war and deployed into the British Army's perimeter around the town of Izmit. The government hoped to use this force as something of a counterrevolutionary army against the Nationalists. In late April, with military help from British forces, the Disciplinary Force began to attack Nationalist forces. Damat Ferit was also in contact with the renegade Ahmet Anzavur, who Damat offered to make the governor of Afyonkarahisar if Anzavur would lead forces against the Nationalists. Anzavur accepted and joined the Disciplinary Force at Izmir. The government had about 4,000 men in the force, and Anzavur led some of them east on May 8.[58] Reaching the village of Sapanca, he turned to raiding operations, which lasted from May 15 to 18. Although confronted simultaneously with the Düzce Uprising, XX Corps commander Ali Fuat again sent infantry and cavalry units to contain Anzavur's raids. Ali Fuat also backed up his reinforcements with Çerkez Ethem's 700-man irregular cavalry group, which was already en route to Geyve.[59] After three days of continuous combat, Anzavur's raiders were defeated and scattered, with many retreating to Izmit.

After these clashes, the XX Corps concentrated its forces on May 25 in the vicinity of the railway between Geyve and Adapazarı. Lieutenant Colonel Atıf's (Ateşdağlı) 24th Division composed the bulk of the concentration, with the 70th and 143rd Infantry Regiments supported by artillery, and engineers making up the regular forces. In the meantime, the Çerkez Ethem Group briefly rested and recovered in Adapazarı. While the Nationalists concentrated their forces, the Disciplinary Force received orders on June 5 to prepare for offensive operations against them.[60] Disciplinary Force commander Süleyman Şefik Pasha advanced with his three infantry regiments on June 14, and they met the advancing Nationalist XX Corps formations in a series of sharp engagements about 20 kilometers east of Izmit. The Disciplinary Forces' 2nd and 3rd Infantry Regiments skirmished with the Nationalist 143rd Infantry Regiment while the Nationalist 70th Infantry Regiment and Çerkez Ethem's cavalry skirmished with the 1st Infantry Regiment.[61] The next day, the Disciplinary Force, whose morale had collapsed, broke contact and withdrew into the British Army's protective perimeter surrounding Izmit. Süleyman Şefik Pasha withdrew the Disciplinary Force to Istanbul by ship on June 16, but he continued to encourage supporters of the sultan to rise up as late as July 25. Interestingly, Çerkez Ethem's irregular cavalry was becoming something of a highly mobile fire brigade in the National Army's order of battle.

FIRST YOZGAT UPRISING (*BIRINCI YOZGAT AYAKLANMASI*) MAY 15–AUGUST 27, 1920

Yozgat is a town between Ankara and Sivas, and its proximity to the epicenter of the Nationalist movement made it a ripe target for the levying of taxes and for the conscription of men for the Nationalist Army.[62] Although the leaders of the Çapanoğlu clans living around Yozgat initially supported Kemal by sending a delegation to Sivas, heavy-handed tax collection drove them to resist Nationalist authority. Tribal leaders Çapanoğlu Edip and his younger brother Celâl plotted to rebel and started to evict government officials and institutions from the towns under their control.[63] Their plans were discovered, but they ignored subsequent warnings from the Nationalists to cease.[64] Inspired by this, at about the same time and for the same reasons, Kurdish tribesmen in nearby Yıldızeli (many of whom had been forcibly relocated by the CUP) also attempted to break free of Nationalist authority. These tribes formed what they called the Caliphate Army (*Halife Ordusu*) and declared themselves independent.[65] Responding to these outbreaks, the III Corps commander Colonel Selâhattin (Köseoğlu) ordered troops in to restore order. The 5th Caucasian Division at Amasya sent the 2nd Battalion, 10th Infantry Regiment on May 17 to Zile, and the regiment's 3rd Battalion from Tokat to Yıldızeli four days later. Supported by cavalry detachments, these forces, under the command of Major Ali Rıza, conducted combat operations from May 17 to May 25 and cleaned up resistance in the eastern part of the affected area.

However, resistance continued in the western areas around Yozgat, and Colonel Selâhattin met with Colonel İsmet on June 7 to decide on a response.[66] More forces were called in from the 11th Division in Niğde: the 3rd Battalion, 33rd Infantry Regiment from Kayseri and the Kılıç Ali militia. These units were sent in from June 11–14 to clean up resistance southeast of Yozgat, but there was not enough strength to proceed to Yozgat itself. Colonel Refet (Bele) then personally led a punitive force of an infantry battalion and a cavalry regiment from June 15–19 to rout the rebels in Ortaköy. On June 19, Colonel İsmet, the chief of the Nationalist General Staff, sent personal orders to the reliable and capable Çerkez Ethem to advance to Yozgat and end the rebellion. By this time, Çerkez Ethem had reached Ankara, and his irregular force had grown to an astonishing 70 officers, 2,100 infantry, 700 to 1,300 cavalry, 5 artillery pieces, and 8 machine guns, making it larger than most Nationalist divisions.[67] He took Yozgat on June 23 and, over the next four days, eliminated most of the resistance in the vicinity. Several minor operations and raids continued through July to August 27 when the government mistakenly declared the uprising suppressed.

CEMIL ÇETO INCIDENT (*CEMIL ÇETO OLAYI*) MAY 20–JUNE 7, 1920

In the southeastern town of Garzan, Kurdish tribal leader Cemil Çeto fell under the influence of British and French anti-Nationalist propaganda.[68] Refusing to submit to the Nationalist demands for taxes, he declared independence on May 20. Garzan was in the XIII Army Corps area, which alerted 2nd Division commander Lieutenant Colonel Akif (Erdemgil) to send in a punitive force. Akif deployed the 1st Battalion, 1st Infantry Regiment on May 20 to hunt down the rebellious tribesmen. In rapid operations, Major Mehmet Reşit crushed the tribesmen, killing Cemil and his four brothers on June 7.[69]

ZILE UPRISING (*ZILE AYAKLANMASI*) MAY 25–JULY 21, 1920

Zile is a town just south of Amasya in north central Anatolia.[70] Rebellious tribesmen living there were encouraged by the news of the nearby First Yozgat Uprising and quickly rejected the legitimacy of the Nationalist government. They summarily repulsed the Nationalists first attempts at breaking the rebellion using just a few local troops. Unfortunately for the rebels, the 5th Caucasian Division under the command of Lieutenant Colonel Cemil Cahit (Toydemir) maintained his headquarters in Tokat, about 25 kilometers to the east.[71] On June 6, Cemil organized a small punitive expedition composed of two infantry battalions, a cavalry detachment, and some artillery—altogether about 200 men. On June 8, he launched a three-pronged attack to converge on Zile. Cemil led the main effort west from Tokat while the Yıldızeli Detachment advanced from the southeast, and the Çorum Detachment came down from the northwest. There were about 300 armed rebels who attempted unsuccessfully to block the converging Nationalist detachments. On June 9–12, Cemil and his soldiers surrounded Zile and forced its surrender.[72]

BANDIT FAMILY RAIDS (*AYNACIOĞULLARI*) MAY 25, 1920–NOVEMBER 21, 1921

These outbreaks of violence are named after the Aynacıoğulları families of bandits and outlaws, principally the leader Rüştü and his brothers Hasan, Mehmet, and Deli Hacı (Crazy Hacı).[73] Bandit leaders such as Çerkez Musa, Çarkoğlu Mustafa, and others also led gangs in these incidents.[74] The problem spread over a wide area, including Sungurlu, Çorum, Amasya, Tokat, and Yozgat. The bandits included Greeks, Kurds, Circassians, immigrant Muslims from Macedonia, Arabs, and local tribal groups. Their common cause was the freedom to operate outside the restrictions of the rule of law. Some of these gangs numbered as many as 200–300 bandits, and the Turkish official historian General Hamdi Ertuna characterized them collectively as a single uprising and many clashes. Actually, they were episodic, more or less spontaneous, and might really be termed "raids." The Ankara Nationalist government made feeble attempts to restore law and order in the region. Finally, in late September 1921, the government directed the Central Army to deal with the problem, and it sent the punitive Second Mobile Force under the command of recently promoted Lieutenant Colonel İbrahim (Çolak),[75] The Second Mobile Force was a provisional command composed of infantry from the 12th Division, the 27th Cavalry Brigade, the 55th Cavalry Regiment, the 61st Jandarma Cavalry Regiment, and a number of Nationalist militia groups.[76] In October and November 1921, these units swept through the area and pursued the bandits to destruction. Many of the leaders were killed and others arrested and imprisoned.

TRIBAL NATIONALISTS INCIDENT (*MILLÎ AŞIRETI OLAYI*) JUNE 1–SEPTEMBER 8, 1920

Numerous atrocities occurred as the French and Armenians pushed into Cilicia and the southeast in 1919 and early 1920 (see chapter 6). In response, local Nationalist militias organized. In the Urfa-Mardin area, the largest Kurdish tribe organized as the Tribal Nationalists (*Millî Aşiret*) and initially engaged in military actions against the Armenians.[77] Subsequently, troubled by the non-promises to the Kurds at the San Remo Conference (April 19–26, 1920) and disturbed by the approaches of the Nationalist government, the Kurds were a target for Allied anti-Nationalist propaganda. In turn, the *Millî Aşiret* were encouraged to rebel by the French and rose in rebellion against the Nationalists on June 1, 1920.[78]

The XIII Corps headquarters alerted Lieutenant Colonel Mehmet Kenan's (Dalbaşar) 5th Division in Mardin to suppress the rebellious tribesmen.[79] Kenan organized 2,000 soldiers from his 14th, 15th, and 24th Infantry Regiments into punitive expeditions, moving them into position in midsummer.[80] He launched a massive attack on August 24 and trapped most of the rebels in Viranşehir. Two days later, most of the survivors surrendered, but a few hardy individuals escaped and fled into French-controlled Syria on September 7/8.[81]

KULA INCIDENT (*KULA OLAYI*) JUNE 27–28, 1920

The Greek Army began offensive operations aimed at Alaşehir on June 22, 1920, which encouraged the Ottoman Greek inhabitants to rise up five days later in the expectation of rapid liberation.[82] Unfortunately for the

Greek rebels, the Nationalist Army reacted more quickly than expected when the 23rd Division dispatched a battalion of the 159th Infantry Regiment and an assault company from Uşak under Major Şakir to quell the disturbance. Major Şakir secured the town in a single day, but Kula fell to the advancing Greek Army Corps A one week later anyway.[83]

ÇOPUR MUSA INCIDENT (ÇOPUR MUSA [ÇIVRIL] OLAYI) JULY 21–31, 1920

Çopur Musa was a tribal leader cut from the same cloth as Ahmet Anzavur. He initially supported the Nationalists but then turned rogue. On July 21, Çopur and his men seized the village of Çivril (southeast of Uşak). However, a prompt response from the 23rd Division sent Major Ali Rıza and the 2nd Battalion, 33rd Infantry Regiment, supported by the 12th Cavalry Company, against Çopur.[84] Facing regular troops, the resistance collapsed, and Çopur Musa fled to Greece.

SECOND DÜZCE UPRISING (İKİNCİ DÜZCE AYAKLANMASI) JULY 19–SEPTEMBER 23, 1920

Encouraged by Süleyman Şefik Pasha (the leader of the sultan's Disciplinary Force) and instigated by tribal leader Maan Ali, the tribal bands in Hendek rose again in July 1920.[85] The rebellion quickly caught on and spread throughout the Düzce-Bolu region. In addition to the Circassian tribesmen, there were about 1,000 Black Sea Ottoman Greeks who took up arms against the Nationalists.[86] The Greeks were refugees from the CUP's 1914–1918 forcible relocations along the Black Sea coast. Once again, XX Corps commander Major General Ali Fuat was called upon to suppress the rebels by organizing a provisional detachment from the 24th Division.[87] On July 20, the 32nd Infantry Regiment advanced from Bolu toward Düzce but was surrounded and had to break out to retreat back to Bolu. Faced with this repulse, Ali Fuat reorganized his forces into a larger provisional division composed of the 32nd and 70th Infantry Regiments, Cafer Bey's irregular 1st Erzurum National Force, and Major İbrahim Çolak's detachment—all under the command of Major Nazım.[88]

Nazım began serious operations against the rebels on August 8 by sending converging detachments from Bolu, Hendek, Geyve, and Nallıhan toward the rebel epicenter at Düzce.[89] While the geographical centers of resistance fell quickly, the rebels scattered into the countryside, and Nazım had to hunt them down. This caused the campaign against the uprising to last for a total of 66 days before it was judged suppressed.[90]

İNEGÖL INCIDENT (*İNEGÖL OLAYI*)
JULY 20–AUGUST 20, 1920

İnegöl is a town southeast of Bursa near the Sea of Marmara whose population was unhappy with the Nationalists and inclined to support the Ottoman government. When the Greek Army took nearby Bursa on July 8, 1920, they rose in rebellion, expecting to be liberated quickly, but were unaware of Venezilos's efforts to halt the advance (see chapter 3). The Nationalist 56th and 61st Divisions sent in soldiers on July 25, but, even though the rebels were isolated from the Greek Army, the Nationalists were unable to restore control. On August 19, the 11th Division chief of staff Major Hüseyin Rahmi organized a stronger punitive force composed of men from the 126th and 127th Infantry Regiments and led it to İnegöl, where he quickly extinguished the uprising.[91] The Greek Army finally liberated the town in October 1920.[92]

SECOND YOZGAT UPRISING (*İKINCI YOZGAT AYAKLANMASI*)
SEPTEMBER 5–DECEMBER 30, 1920

After the conclusion of the First Yozgat Uprising, some 500 rebels were granted amnesty in exchange for volunteering for service with the Nationalist volunteer Akdağmadeni Regiment. While the regiment was being sent to Ankara, 49 men deserted near Yozgat on the night of September 5/6.[93] The deserters began to riot and cause trouble. More men deserted, and the regiment was disbanded. The uprising spread to Çengelhan and Ortaköy, where rebel groups formed of 120 and 70 men, respectively. The Central Army staff decided to send in Major İbrahim Çolak's detachment, which was now renamed the Second Mobile Force (composed of the 1st Battalion, 21st Mounted Infantry Regiment, and five Nationalist irregular militia groups) to deal with the rebels.[94] Çolak and his men left Ankara and reached Yozgat and Sorgun on September 9, where he split his forces going north to Eymir and east toward Akdağmadeni. On September 23, Çolak sent detachments into the mountains to chase survivors. He took Akdağmadeni on October 6, and then went north to rout rebels in Zile on October 12. The Second Mobile Force was then redirected to fight the Aynacıoğulları; however, minor local operations continued against small parties of surviving Yozgat rebels in the mountains until the end of the year.

KONYA UPRISING (*KONYA AYAKLANMASI*) OCTOBER 2— NOVEMBER 22, 1920

Anti-Nationalist sentiment, fueled by both British and Ottoman government propaganda, reared its head in the provincial city of Konya and its hinterlands in late fall 1920.[95] The Steppe Uprisings had previously erupted near Konya, and there were numerous unpunished rebels still at large and lingering in the area. Moreover, Konya was home to the Mevlevi Order (known in the west as the Whirling Dervishes), who were not well disposed to a renewal of centralized authority under the Nationalists either. This made the area ripe for dissent when the Nationalists attempted to collect taxes and conscript young men.

Led by Delibaş Mehmet, 500 armed rebels occupied the village of Çumra on October 2.[96] Shortly thereafter, they moved into Konya itself. Konya governor Hayder Bay and Çumra Mayor Nadir Bey fled to Niğde and telegraphed XII Corps commander, Colonel Fahrettin (Altay) in Afyonkarahisar, urgently asking him to send forces to suppress the rebellion.[97] Konya was a critical communication and railway center for the Nationalist Southern Front and thus had strategic importance. Nothing reflected this more than the Nationalist response when the request reached Ankara. The Grand National Assembly immediately placed the newly appointed minister of the interior, Colonel Refet (Bele), in command of expeditionary forces to crush the rebels.[98] In the meantime, Colonel Fahrettin had already sent a punitive force from Afyonkarahisar, which merged with another detachment under the highly unusual command of the XII Corps chief veterinarian, Major Sadettin, at the Sarayönü railway station (50 kilometers north of Konya) on October 4. The next day, the Major Sadettin Detachment met the Staff Major Derviş Detachment from the Ertuğrul Group about five kilometers north of Konya.[99] Colonel Refet arrived soon after with a regular cavalry squadron. Altogether, the Nationalists deployed around 400 infantrymen, 300 regular army cavalrymen, several hundred irregular cavalrymen, a half dozen machine guns, and a several small howitzers. They were joined by the Konya Jandarma Battalion, making Refet's command a very substantial force, concentrated rapidly for offensive operations.

On October 6, 1920, Refet's men surrounded Konya, and Major Derviş led the main effort to seize the city. Refet telegraphed this result to Ankara but noted that quite a few rebels had escaped the encirclement and fled to neighboring villages.[100] The chief of the General Staff cabled Refet the next day, urging him to pursue the rebels to destruction. Colonel Refet sent a strong cavalry force of 500 men south along the Karaman railway to Çumra, which fell on October 8. They continued and seized the Akören railway station the next day. Karaman itself fell to a joint attack by the 1st Battalion, 12th Infantry Regiment and the 1st Battalion, 16th Infantry Regiment on October 8. Then, in a remarkably fast pursuit, Refet's men took Dinek and Elmasun on October 11 to encircle the rebellious town of Bozkır on October 16.[101] Turning north, they advanced to Beyşehir, where they met the Demirci Mehmet Efe Detachment of 200 irregular cavalry, which had left Dinar on October 19 to trap the rebels from the west. After trapping a large body of rebels in Beyşehir, the Nationalists pursued the survivors all the way to Antalya on the Mediterranean coast on November 4. Still some rebels escaped their relentless pursuit but were finally brought down in Isparta on November 22.

While the Refet Group was advancing to Konya, another rebel force seized Akşehir in their rear, but Colonel Fahrettin sent Colonel Osman with 820 infantry from the 70th Infantry Regiment and the 1st Battalion, 172nd Infantry Regiment from Afyonkarahisar to crush them.[102] On October 11. Colonel Osman's detachment encircled and retook the town, restoring communication with Refet's forward units, which were then nearing Bozkır.

The suppression of the Konya Uprising was remarkable in several ways. First, the speed of the Nationalist reaction and the scale of the forces committed to the endeavor were exceptionally rapid and strong. This could be termed today as a "must not fail" mission, and every Nationalist commander from the General Staff down to platoon level seemed to understand that. Moreover, the scope of the battle space, some 350 kilometers west to east and 300 kilometers north to south, imposed difficult operational and tactical constraints on both the Nationalists and the rebels. Telegraph stations were available to the Nationalists for communication, but they depended on the initiative and determination of subordinate commanders to carry the war to the enemy. The Nationalist cavalry forces once again proved themselves invaluable in the pursuit phases after October 19.

DEMIRCI MEHMET EFE UPRISING (*DEMIRCI MEHMET EFE AYAKLANMSI*) DECEMBER 11–30, 1920

The Nationalist irregular leaders Demirci Mehmet Efe and his brother Demirci İbrahim Efe finished up operations suppressing the Konya Uprising in the city of İsparta. On November 22, 1920, Southern Front commander Colonel Refet asked Demirci Mehmet Efe and 300 of his men to formally join the National Army as the Mounted Pursuit Force.[103] At first, Demirci Mehmet Efe accepted the offer, but then rejected it at the behest of fellow irregular Çerkez Ethem (who did not want to come under government control). This proved to be deadly advice because Chief of the General Staff İsmet expressed the desire to Refet to use military forces to eliminate the remaining uncooperative Nationalist irregulars using the XII Corps. On December 6, Refet ordered the XII Corps to conduct operations against Demirci Mehmet Efe using the 8th Division and the 1st Cavalry Division.[104] At the time, these divisions were concentrated in reserve (and available for operations) in Afyonkarahisar with the Southern Front and XII Corps headquarters. Colonel Refet exchanged last-minute messages with Demirci Mehmet Efe giving him several opportunities to submit to government control but to no avail.

On December 11, 1920, Refet declared the Demirci brothers and their followers to be in rebellion and ordered the XII Corps to disarm and apprehend them. The 8th Division, reinforced with an additional infantry regiment, and the 1st Cavalry Division, reinforced with the 7th Cavalry Regiment were sent south to Sandıklı that evening under the overall command of Colonel Mehmet Şefik (Aker).[105] On December 15/16, Şefik surrounded the rebels in two villages north of İsparta, again asking Demirci Mehmet Efe to accept government jurisdiction. Demirci Mehmet Efe refused, and Şefik forced the surrender of over 700 irregulars on December 19. Demirci Mehmet Efe and 80 broke out of the trap and fled southeast to the village of Acıpayam. Colonel Refet ordered the regulars of the main force home to Afyonkarahisar and set a Jandarma Pursuit Force under Jandarma Captain Nuri after the rebels. Captain Nuri encircled the rebels in Acıpayam and forced Demirci Mehmet Efe to surrender. He was taken into custody and sent to Afyonkarahisar on December 25.[106] A handful of his men escaped the encirclement but were finally trapped and apprehended in Tavas on December 30.

ÇERKEZ ETHEM UPRISING (*ÇERKEZ ETHEM AYAKLANMASI*) DECEMBER 27, 1920–JANUARY 23, 1921

Çerkez Ethem (or Ethem the Circassian) was a fearless and effective guerrilla fighter who had been of great assistance in suppressing rebellions in Anatolia and confronting Ottoman government forces near Izmit. In summer 1920, he came into conflict with the Nationalist government in Ankara over his belief that he had the right as a local leader to recruit men who might otherwise be conscripted into the National Army. Moreover, Çerkez Ethem and his two brothers, Reşit and Tevfik, were very critical of the Ankara governor, who was a staunch Nationalist. On November 9, 1920, Minister of War Fevzi also became the acting chief of the General Staff (to reduce İsmet's responsibilities) and divided the Western Front in half, with the northern sector as the Western Front Command under Colonel İsmet, and the southern sector as the Southern Front Command commanded by Colonel Refet.[107] Çerkez Ethem's First Mobile Force under İsmet's command. Both front commanders were ordered to bring all National Force formations and irregular militias under formal army control, and both sent messages to Çerkez Ethem, urging him to conform to Ankara's wishes, but to no avail.

Çerkez Ethem was an admirer of İsmet's, but he distrusted Refet and he protested Refet's elevation to front command directly to Kemal and the Assembly. Çerkez Ethem was also not happy with the integration of his group into the National Army as the First Field Force, rejecting that title and proclaiming himself General Mobile Force Commander and Kütahya Area Commander in the third week of November.[108] He was also unhappy with the continuing restrictions on recruiting and collecting taxes and goods from local citizens.[109] Using contemporary vocabulary, it is fair to say that Çerkez Ethem carried a lot of baggage and grievances regarding the relationship between himself and the Nationalist government.

Throughout December, Çerkez Ethem and İsmet traded telegrams with each other as they tried unsuccessfully to negotiate a peaceful solution.[110] This failure forced Çerkez Ethem and his brother Tevfik into open rebellion. At the end of its patience, the General Staff ordered İsmet and Refet to launch a coordinated offensive to force the surrender of the two brothers and recover their weapons for use by the army. Because of an imminent Greek Army offensive, Kemal and Fevzi decided to use over-whelming force to rapidly crush the brothers. The Western Front Com-mand (in Eskişehir) committed the 11th and 61st Divisions and the 1st Cavalry Group while the Southern Front Command (in Afyonkarahisar) committed the 8th and 23rd divisions and the 2nd Cavalry Group.[111] Altogether, excluding the 23rd Division in Dumlupınar, this brought 3,719 infantrymen and 531 cavalrymen supported by 38 machine guns and 16 artillery pieces from the north, and 2,326 infantrymen and 2,174 cavalrymen supported by 34 machine guns and 32 artillery pieces from the south against the brothers and their men.[112] At the point of conver-gence in Kütahya and Gediz, Çerkez Ethem's First Field Force composed the National Army's 159th Infantry Regiment and around 18 assorted irregular militia groups. Excluding the regular infantry regiment, sta-tioned south of Gediz, which refused to cooperate with the rebellious Çerkez Ethem, the brothers could only muster 2,326 men, 8 machine guns, and 4 artillery pieces.

On December 27, İsmet and Refet ordered their divisions forward, com-ing into contact with the so-called rebels on January 4–5 and fighting through to take both Kütahya and Gediz. Many rebels were killed and captured, but Çerkez Ethem and around 600 men escaped to the northeast, and Tevfik escaped to the west. As late as January 2, 1921, İsmet, who was favorably disposed to Çerkez Ethem, attempted to bring Kemal himself into the negotiations to stop the offensive against the two brothers. On January 6, the Greek Army's Reconnaissance in Force toward Eskişehir and Dumlupınar forced the redeployment of the 8th and 11th Divisions and the 1st and 2nd Cavalry Groups.[113] This left the 61st Division (com-posed of the 174th and 190th Infantry Regiments, an artillery battalion, and an assault company), commanded by Lieutenant Colonel İzzettin (Çalışlar) and an independent cavalry brigade commanded by Major İsmail Hakkı in contact with the rebels. Sensing a tactical opportunity Çerkez Ethem launched counterattacks on January 9 against the 1st Cav-alry Brigade, which was screening the front, while the 61st Division was digging in on the ridgeline southwest of Kütahya. The 189th Infantry Reg-iment arrived in town that day to reinforce Lieutenant Colonel İzzettin's tired division. Nevertheless, the next day, the rebels easily brushed aside the cavalry and forced the infantry regiments to withdraw into Kütahya.[114] Çerkez Ethem then conducted two frontal attacks on the town on January 11 and 12, both of which failed.

In the meantime, the Greek Army called off its offensive operations on January 11, 1921 and began to withdraw its forward units. This allowed Colonel Refet's Southern Front to return to the offensive against Çerkez Ethem, and he sent the 8th Division and the 1st, 2nd, and 3rd Cavalry Groups to support the battered 61st Division. On January 14, these forces began a massive counteroffensive, which turned into a pursuit operation the next day. On January 16, the two infantry divisions had recovered Gediz, while the cavalry pursued the rebels west toward Simav, which fell the following day. From there, they pushed the rebels into the Demirci Mountains and on January 23 seized the town of Gördes.[115] Çerkez Ethem, his brothers, and his surviving men retreated into the mountains outside of Akhisar, ultimately abandoning their weapons to find refuge with the Greek Army.

Kemal had all three brothers declared traitors to the nation after a show trial in an Independence Court in May. Later in October 1921, Çerkez Ethem and other Circassians attempted to establish a Circassian national government around Balıkesir and Gönen (which by then lay in the Greek-occupied zone) but enjoyed little success.[116] After the Nationalist victory at Sakarya, Çerkez Ethem and his brothers appealed to Ankara for amnesty, but Kemal refused them. After the war, Çerkez Ethem lived in Europe but later moved to Amman, Jordan, where he died in 1948.[117]

KOÇKIRI UPRISING (*KOÇKIRI AYAKLANMASI*) MARCH 6–JUNE 21, 1921

The town of Koçkırı is just to the northwest of Erzincan in eastern Anatolia, and it was the epicenter of the most serious of the Kurdish uprisings. The Treaty of Sèvres provided for possible Kurdish independence and served to incite the Kurdish tribes. In late November, Kurdish leaders issued a declaration, demanding to know if the Ankara government would honor the Sèvres terms. Kemal delayed responding to buy time for a military response.[118] By December 1920, the Kurdish tribes had built up a large force and gained control of most of Sivas province.[119] Faced with this in the fall of 1920, Nurettin's Central Army could do little except open the armories and provide weapons to those citizens inclined to support the Nationalists. But an early thaw in 1921 enabled the Central Army to take the field against the Kurds by threatening to burn their villages if they did not surrender. In response, the Kurds tried to preempt Nurettin by sending detachments to seize Imranlı and Ümraniye on March 6 and Kemah two days later. On March 10, the Ankara government declared the region in revolt and proclaimed martial law. The rebels mounted a direct assault on Erzincan itself on March 29, but they were beaten back by the well-armed Nationalist militias.[120]

The Central Army's main strike forces, commanded by Lieutenant Colonel Mehmet Hayri, were composed of the 14th Cavalry Division, the 13th, 27th, and 28th Cavalry Brigades, the 5th Assault Battalion, and Nationalist militia groups in Giresun and Erzincan.[121] Unfortunately for the Kurdish tribes, the Nationalists held the cities of Sivas, Zara, Kangal, and Erzincan, which surrounded the Kurds on all sides. This simplified tactical planning for Nurettin because all his forces had to do was execute operations converging on Koçkırı.[122] The Central Army planned to send over 5,000 soldiers armed with 20 machine guns and 13 artillery pieces against the rebels. Moreover, historian Stanford Shaw asserted that the rebellion was weakened further when the Nationalist victory against the Greeks on at Second İnönü on April 1 caused a number of "fence-sitters" to abandon the idea of Kurdish independence.[123] In any case, the Central Army began closely coordinated operations on April 10 against the now discouraged and weakened Kurds.

The 27th Cavalry Brigade drove northeast from Kangal and the 14th Cavalry Division and the 13th and 28th Cavalry Brigades pushed east from Sivas and south from Zara, while the Giresun, Kemah, and Erzincan Nationalist militia detachments pushed west from Erzincan. There were numerous skirmishes and small encirclements as the Central Army compressed the Kurdish rebels day-by-day into an ever-shrinking perimeter. Villages that were taken were burned and their inhabitants resettled. Koçkırı itself was taken by assault on April 15. The major concentrations of Kurdish fighters were broken up by April 18, but large numbers of survivors escaped into the mountains to continue the fight.

The Central Army was forced to reinforce the effort, starting a second phase of the campaign. The infamous irregular leader Osman Ağa (also known as Topal Osman) led the Giresun Detachment in this phase of the operation against the remaining rebels.[124] The reinforcement included the 54th Infantry Regiment, which pursued rebels on May 25 north of Kemah, while the 13th and 28th Cavalry Brigades mounted a combined attack on a group of 500 rebels south of Refahıye on May 27/28.[125] The rebels launched one last attack on Erzincan, which was easily repulsed. The last major rebel band of 500 men, led by Halit and Ali Bey, surrendered on

June 17, but minor mopping-up operations continued until June 21, when the rebellion was declared finished.[126]

CONCLUSION

The uprisings and rebellions varied in purpose, scope, intensity, and duration. They were episodic rather than sustained. Not all were actual threats to the Nationalist movement, but many were. All these uprisings occurred behind the front lines and constituted, at a minimum, a critical threat to Nationalist logistics and lines of communication. As such, they had to be addressed promptly and effectively. But the uprisings were uncoordinated, and only some managed to raise substantial forces. That some overlapped in time and space was coincidental and spontaneous rather than deliberately planned.

In almost every case, the Nationalists easily task organized ad hoc forces led by experienced commanders to crush the rebels in detail. This reflected a legacy capability and capacity remaining from the Ottoman Army's way of war as it had developed in the late nineteenth and early twentieth centuries. The Nationalists' ability to employ highly mobile forces, especially cavalry and fast-marching infantry, effectively demonstrated a high order of tactical proficiency. Like its Ottoman predecessor, the Nationalist Army's ability to form expedient battle groups led by young commanders who were unafraid to use their initiative paid off handsomely during these suppression operations.

NOTES

1. James G. Harbord, *Conditions in the Near East: Report of the American Military Mission to Armenia* (Washington, DC: Government Printing Office, 1920), 22.

2. Hamdi Ertuna, *Türk İstiklâl Hârbi Vnci Cilt, İstiklâl Harbinde Ayaklanmalar (1919–1921)* (Ankara: Genelkurmay Basımevi, 1974), Grafik-1 (Graphic 1, unnumbered page following page 2).

3. Görgülü, *On Yıllık Harbin Kadrosu*, ix–x.

4. Shaw, *From Empire to Republic*, vol. 3, part 1, 985.

5. Ibid.

6. Ibid., 988–989.

7. Ibid., 1256.

8. Veysel Usta, "A Criticism of the Memorandum Submitted to the Paris Conference by Trabzon Metropolitan Hrisantos," *International Periodical for the Languages, Literature and History of Turkish or Turkic*, 6/2 (Spring 2011): 973–984.

9. Ertuna, *İstiklâl Harbinde Ayaklanmalar*, 31.

10. Shaw, *From Empire to Republic*, vol. 2, 585–586; and İsmet Görgülü, *Türk İstiklâl Harbi Haritası (15 Mayıs 1919–24 Temmuz 1923)*, Turkish War Academy Map created by Staff Major İsmet Görgülü, undated. Previously, these Greeks had been organized into a Pontic battalion by the Russians in 1916–1917 in the hopes of raising a division, but the effort failed to attract enough recruits.

11. Belen, *Türk Kurtuluş Savaşı*, 36.

12. Bruce Clark, *Twice a Stranger, The Mass Expulsions that Forged Modern Greece and Turkey* (Cambridge: Harvard University Press, 2006), 111–114.

13. Ertuna, *İstiklâl Harbinde Ayaklanmalar*, 32; and Shaw, *From Empire to Republic*, vol. 2, 587–588.

14. Shaw, *From Empire to Republic*, vol. 2, 594.

15. Ertuna, *İstiklâl Harbinde Ayaklanmalar*, 32.

16. Türkmen, *Mütareke Döneminde Ordunun Durumu*, 197.

17. Çiloğlu, *Kurtuluş Savaşı Sözlüğü*, 293–294; and Ertuna, *İstiklâl Harbinde Ayaklanmalar*, 294.

18. Ertuna, *İstiklâl Harbinde Ayaklanmalar*, 285.

19. Belen, *Türk Kurtuluş Savaşı*, 166.

20. Ertuna, *İstiklâl Harbinde Ayaklanmalar*, 287–289. Based on army reports in the archives, Ertuna asserted that in the Samsun region alone, 699 Turks were killed, 59 were wounded, 40 villages and 27 farms were burned, and 111 villages were plundered. Altogether, according to Ertuna, by 1921, 1,641 Turks died, 323 were wounded, and 3,723 homes were burned.

21. Ertuna, *İstiklâl Harbinde Ayaklanmalar*, 290–292.

22. Ökse, Baycan, and Sakaryalı, *Komutanların Biyografileri*, 30; and Shaw, *From Empire to Republic*, vol. 2, 595.

23. Ertuna, *İstiklâl Harbinde Ayaklanmalar*, 290–292; and Görgülü, *On Yıllık Harbin Kadrosu*, 314–315.

24. Shaw, *From Empire to Republic to Empire*, vol. 2, 596. In the late nineteenth and early twentieth centuries, the Ottomans were well known for their ruthless suppression of rebellions. Readers interested in this may refer to Edward J. Erickson, *Ottomans and Armenians: A Study in*

Counterinsurgency (New York: Palgrave Macmillan, 2013) for a thorough examination of this topic.

25. Ertuna, *İstiklâl Harbinde Ayaklanmalar*, 293.

26. Ertuna, *İstiklâl Harbinde Ayaklanmalar*, 294.

27. Shaw, *From Empire to Republic*, vol. 2, 596. Compare with Karabekir, who reported that between January 1, 1921 and February 6, 1922, the Central Army killed 3,262 Pontic Greek soldiers, captured 2,481, executed 281, and exiled to central Anatolia 24,511 people (see Karabekir, *İstiklâl Harbimiz*, 1002).

28. Ertuna, *İstiklâl Harbinde Ayaklanmalar*, Grafik 1 (following page 2), 325–326.

29. Karabekir, *İstiklâl Harbimiz*, 1002.

30. Shaw, *From Empire to Republic*, vol. 5, 2268.

31. Görgülü, *On Yıllık Harbin Kadrosu*, 223.

32. Ibid., 40–41.

33. Ibid., 42.

34. Ibid., 43–52.

35. Taha Niyazi, "The Bozkır Rebellions in the National Struggle," *Journal of the Institute of Social Sciences*, 16, no. 1 (2004): 173–175.

36. Ertuna, *İstiklâl Harbinde Ayaklanmalar*, 54.

37. Görgülü, *On Yıllık Harbin Kadrosu*, 297.

38. Çiloğlu, *Kurtuluş Savaşı Sözlüğü*, 40–41.

39. Ryan Gingeras, "Notorious Subjects, Invisible Citizens: North Caucasian Resistance to the Turkish National Movement in Northwestern Anatolia, 1919–23," *International Journal of Middle East Studies* 40, no. 1 (2008): 96.

40. Shaw, *From Empire to Republic*, vol. 2, 737–741.

41. Görgülü, *On Yıllık Harbin Kadrosu*, 299.

42. Shaw, *From Empire to Republic*, vol. 2, 739.

43. Çiloğlu, *Kurtuluş Savaşı Sözlüğü*, 41.

44. Ertuna, *İstiklâl Harbinde Ayaklanmalar*, 60–63.

45. Ibid., 65.

46. Gingeras, "Notorious Subjects, Invisible Citizens," 98.

47. Shaw, *From Empire to Republic to Empire*, vol. 2, 739–740.

48. Ertuna, *İstiklâl Harbinde Ayaklanmalar*, 74–76.

49. Ibid., 76–77.

50. Shaw, *From Empire to Republic*, vol. 2, 741.

51. Ertuna, *İstiklâl Harbinde Ayaklanmalar*, 92–93.

52. Ibid., 96.

53. Ibid., 106–107.

54. Görgülü, *On Yıllık Harbin Kadrosu*, 301–302.

55. Shaw, *From Empire to Republic*, vol. 2, 849–851.

56. Shaw, *From Empire to Republic*, vol. 3, part 1, 1156–1157. Professor Shaw called this force the Caliphal Army, but the author prefers Disciplinary Force.

57. Ertuna, *İstiklâl Harbinde Ayaklanmalar*, 119–121.

58. Mango, *Atatürk*, 280.

59. Cebesoy, *Millı Mücadele Hatıraları*, 425–436.

60. Ertuna, *İstiklâl Harbinde Ayaklanmalar*, 131.

61. Ibid., 132–133; and Görgülü, *On Yıllık Harbin Kadrosu*, 303.

62. Shaw, *From Empire to Republic*, vol. 2, 736–737.

63. Demokaan Demirel, "Internal Rebellions during the National Struggle: The Case of Yozgat," *The Journal of International Social Research*, 9, no. 45 (August 2016): 1–8.

64. Belen, *Türk Kurtuluş Savaşı*, 205–206.

65. Ertuna, *İstiklâl Harbinde Ayaklanmalar*, 142–144.

66. Ibid., 148.

67. Ibid., 150–151.

68. Görgülü, *On Yıllık Harbin Kadrosu*, 308.

69. Ertuna, *İstiklâl Harbinde Ayaklanmalar*, 180–181.

70. Görgülü, *Türk İstiklâl Harbi Haritası*, 306.

71. Görgülü, *On Yıllık Harbin Kadrosu*, 307.

72. Ertuna, *İstiklâl Harbinde Ayaklanmalar*, 162–167; and Orhan Yilmaz, *Zile Insyanı* (Ankara: Veni, Vidi, Vici Yayınevi, 2014), 114–127.

73. The largest of these outbreaks (Yozgat) was characterized as an uprising, but the remainder were not identified using the four named categories I have mentioned in the introduction to this chapter. Ertuna's official history simply refers to the incidents and time frame collectively using the bandit family name Aynacıoğulları.

74. Ertuna, *İstiklâl Harbinde Ayaklanmalar*, 167–176.

75. Ökse, Baycan, and Sakaryalı, *Komutanların Biyografileri*, 141–142.

76. Çiloğlu, *Kurtuluş Savaşı Sözlüğü*, 48–49; and Ertuna, *İstiklâl Harbinde Ayaklanmalar*, 173–174.

77. Shaw, *From Empire to Republic*, vol. 2, 897–898.

78. Shaw, *From Empire to Republic*, vol. 3, part 1, 1116.

79. Ertuna, *İstiklâl Harbinde Ayaklanmalar*, 179.

80. Görgülü, *On Yıllık Harbin Kadrosu*, 308.

81. Ertuna, *İstiklâl Harbinde Ayaklanmalar*, 179; and Çiloğlu, *Kurtuluş Savaşı Sözlüğü*, 238–239.

82. Ertuna, *İstiklâl Harbinde Ayaklanmalar*, 185–186.

83. Gedeon, Paschalidou, and Dima-Dimitrou, *A Concise History of the Campaign in Asia Minor*, Sketch Map 5 following page 40.

84. Ertuna, *İstiklâl Harbinde Ayaklanmalar*, 184–185.

85. Çiloğlu, *Kurtuluş Savaşı Sözlüğü*, 98.

86. Ertuna, *İstiklâl Harbinde Ayaklanmalar*, 113–114.

87. Ibid.

88. Görgülü, *On Yıllık Harbin Kadrosu*, 304.

89. Ertuna, *İstiklâl Harbinde Ayaklanmalar*, Kroki 10 (Sketch Map 10) following page 116.

90. Ertuna, *İstiklâl Harbinde Ayaklanmalar*, 118–119.

91. Ibid., 181–183.

92. Shaw, *From Empire to Republic*, vol. 3, part 1, 1188.

93. Ertuna, *İstiklâl Harbinde Ayaklanmalar*, 158–159.

94. Görgülü, *On Yıllık Harbin Kadrosu*, 306.

95. Çiloğlu, *Kurtuluş Savaşı Sözlüğü*, 193.

96. Belen, *Türk Kurtuluş Savaşı*, 223.

97. Ertuna, *İstiklâl Harbinde Ayaklanmalar*, 188–189.

98. Ibid.

99. Ibid., 190.

100. Ibid., 192.

101. Ibid., Kroki 17 (Sketch Map 17) following page 198.

102. Görgülü, *On Yıllık Harbin Kadrosu*, 309.

103. Ertuna, *İstiklâl Harbinde Ayaklanmalar*, 205.

104. Ibid., 206–207.

105. Ibid., 210–211; and Görgülü, *On Yıllık Harbin Kadrosu*, 310.

106. Ertuna, *İstiklâl Harbinde Ayaklanmalar*, 211–212. Demirci Mehmet Efe was released after the war and died in 1959. See Çiloğlu, *Kurtuluş Savaşı Sözlüğü*, 90–91.

107. Apac'ca, Önalp, and Turhan, *Batı Cephesi, 3ncü Kısım*, 44–48. İsmet technically remained the chief of the General Staff until August 5, 1921 when Fevzi became the permanent chief of the General Staff.

108. Ertuna, *İstiklâl Harbinde Ayaklanmalar*, 218–219.

109. Belen, *Türk Kurtuluş Savaşı*, 270–272.

110. Ertuna, *İstiklâl Harbinde Ayaklanmalar*, 228–234.

111. Görgülü, *On Yıllık Harbin Kadrosu*, 311.

112. Ertuna, *İstiklâl Harbinde Ayaklanmalar*, 235–237.

113. Apac'ca, Önalp, and Turhan, *Batı Cephesi, 3ncü Kısım*, 109–110.

114. Ibid., 121–126.

115. Ertuna, *İstiklâl Harbinde Ayaklanmalar*, 250–257.

116. Shaw, *From Empire to Republic*, vol. 3, part 1, 1104–1106.

117. Çiloğlu, *Kurtuluş Savaşı Sözlüğü*, 111–112.

118. Shaw, *From Empire to Republic*, vol. 3, part 1, 1118; and Ertuna, *İstiklâl Harbinde Ayaklanmalar*, 259–263.

119. Shaw, *From Empire to Republic*, vol. 3, part 1, 1116–1117.

120. Ibid., 1118–1119.

121. Görgülü, *On Yıllık Harbin Kadrosu*, 313.

122. Ertuna, *İstiklâl Harbinde Ayaklanmalar*, 270.

123. Shaw, *From Empire to Republic*, vol. 3, part 1, 1119.

124. Ertuna, *İstiklâl Harbinde Ayaklanmalar*, 279

125. Ertuna, *İstiklâl Harbinde Ayaklanmalar*, Kroki 25 (Sketch Map 25), following page 278.

126. Belen, *Türk Kurtuluş Savaşı*, 321.

FIVE

A Short War on the Eastern Front

The Armenian is not guiltless of blood himself; his memory is long and reprisals are due, and will doubtless be made if opportunity offers.[1]

Maj. Gen. James G. Harbord, 1919

INTRODUCTION

The history of the Armenian people's struggle for independence is drenched in blood and controversy, and is today the subject of a heavily politicized literature. Broadly speaking, in the English language, there are two comprehensive scholarly histories of what is termed the eastern front in the War of Independence or the Turkish-Armenian War. Richard Hovannisian's *The Republic of Armenia* (four volumes) presents an Armenian-centric view, while Stanford Shaw's *From Empire to Republic* (five volumes) presents a Turkish-centric view. As one might expect, the narratives reflect the content of the archival material mostly used by the authors—Shaw's on Ottoman and Turkish archives and Hovannisian's on Armenian and Western archives, as well as on Turkish histories. Otherwise, there is almost nothing in print for the English-speaking reader about these events. Even the standard work on the Ottoman wars in Caucasia, Allen and Muratoff's *Caucasian Battlefields*, devotes a scant four pages to the conflict.[2]

When the Ottoman Army lost Erzurum, Trabzon, and Erzincan in 1916, the Russian Army took over these areas. Then, in the aftermath of the Russian Revolutions in 1917 and the collapse of the Russian Army, Armenian

legions and refugee revolutionary formations took over control and absorbed
the Ottoman provinces and what had been Russian Armenia into a de facto
Armenian polity. However, in 1918, Enver Pasha launched a massive offensive to recover these Ottoman territories, which, in turn, destroyed the
nascent Armenian state. After the Mudros armistice the Allies briefly considered an American mandate for a reborn Armenia, but this endeavor collapsed, as did the Italian and British mandates for Azerbaijan. War broke
out episodically in 1919 and early 1920 between the Caucasian states, but
the specter of a Greater Armenia raised in London and codified at Sèvres in
the summer of 1920 drove the Turkish Nationalists to action.

THE WITHDRAWAL FROM BAKU

Article XI of the Mudros armistice agreement required the Ottoman
Army to withdraw its forces from Transcaucasia and Persia to the 1914
prewar borders. However, unlike Palestine, Syria, Mesopotamia, and
Macedonia, the Ottoman armies in Transcaucasia and Persia in 1918 can
only be characterized as victorious armies occupying a vast area. There
were two Ottoman armies in the region; the easternmost in Baku was
called the Army of Islam, under the command of Nuri (Killigil) Pasha; the
westernmost in Kars was called the Ninth Army, under the command of
Yakup Şevki (Şubaşı) Pasha. The Army of Islam was composed of the 5th
Caucasian Division in Baku and the 15th Division, which was engaged in
an assault on the Caspian port of Petrovsk on October 30, 1918. The army
also had under its command the First Azerbaijan Corps of two infantry
divisions of Muslim Azerbaijani soldiers, which would remain behind as
the nucleus of the army of the short-lived Azerbaijan Republic. The Ninth
Army was more substantial and composed of the 11th Caucasian Division
holding Tabriz in northwest Persia, the 9th Caucasian Division in Yerevan,
the 12th Division in Sardarabat (a town west of Yerevan), the 36th Division
in Gümrü, the 3rd Caucasian Division in Asısha (east of Batum), and a
detachment made up of the 177th Infantry Regiment and the 45th Cavalry
Regiment in Batum itself.[3] All of these formations were beyond the 1914
prewar borders and had to be brought home and demobilized.

The Ottoman General Staff sent withdrawal orders to Nuri and Yakup
Şevki on October 27, 1918 (just before the armistice was signed). These
orders included instructions for the 36th Division to inactivate in December and its soldiers to be reassigned to other divisions, and for the 5th

Caucasian and 15th Division to redeploy to Amasya and Samsun respectively.[4] The orders also included instructions to withdraw army stores of rations, fodder, and munitions from the occupied areas as the combat units withdrew. The 15th Division disengaged from the assault on Petrovsk and returned to Baku, while the army's logisticians reserved 30 railway trains to move supplies, artillery, and equipment back to Ottoman territory. Most of the infantry would have to march 350 kilometers by foot back to the pre-1914 frontier. The Ottoman staffs estimated that the army could withdraw from Georgia and Armenia in six weeks (by December 5) but that it would take the formations in Azerbaijan up to two months to withdraw fully (January 1919).[5] The army began to withdraw its forward forces from Baku and Tebriz on November 17 and 18.

THE PROBLEM OF THE THREE PROVINCES

The problem for Ottoman government and then, by default, for the Nationalists was the fate of the three Ottoman provinces lost to the Russians in 1878, which were east of the 1914 frontier: Ardahan, Kars, and Batum. Under the terms of the Treaty of Brest-Litovsk (March 3, 1918), control of these provinces had returned to the Ottoman Empire.[6] But the inhabitants of the three provinces, alarmed when the terms of the Mudros armistice became known, began to agitate and to organize both politically and militarily. In short order, the Kars Muslim Council convened on November 5, 1918, to form a local government for defense. At the end of the month, delegates from the cities of Ardahan, Kars, and Oltu joined Kars delegates at the Kars Great Muslim Congress (November 30–December 2) and formed the Provisional National Government of the Southwest Caucasus.[7] Expecting the situation in the Caucasus to deteriorate further, the British War Cabinet approved the transfer of Major General George Forestier-Walker's 27th Division from Salonika to Batum.[8] HMS *Liverpool* anchored off Batum on December 7 with the British division's advanced party and, on December 18, officers of the British control commission arrived on HMS *Theseus*, coming ashore the next day.[9] Between December 23 and 27, Forestier-Walker's headquarters and his 80th Infantry Brigade disembarked to establish a firm hold on the port. Forestier-Walker then established a military governorship in Batum and the vicinity under his brigade commander, acting Brigadier General W. J. N. Cooke-Collis. Moreover, Forestier-Walker ordered the brigade to send an infantry battalion to occupy Tbilisi (Tiflis). The 81st Infantry Brigade and 82nd Infantry Brigade arrived on December 30 and January 8, respectively, giving Forestier-Walker an entire infantry division.[10]

These unilateral British occupations were regarded as high-handed politics by the Ottomans, the Armenians, and the Georgians—all of whom wanted Batum. Tensions were high when the Ardahan Congress of Caucasian Muslims convened on January 6. On January 7, 1919, Forestier-Walker met with Ottoman Ninth Army commander, Yakup Şevki Pasha, in Kars for discussions regarding the Ottoman withdrawal from the three provinces. The British dictated brutal terms, including the Ottoman Army would totally withdraw from the provinces by January 25, the Ottomans would leave a month's rations for 3,000 men in Kars and Ardahan, a British Army detachment of several hundred soldiers would occupy Kars in cooperation with the Armenians on January 12, and the railways and telegraphs would be turned over intact three days later.[11] Alarmed further by British officers entering the city, a Second Kars Congress convened on January 17, and two days later, delegates added Aras, Nakhichevan, and Batum to the nascent Muslim polity. Yakup Şevki vehemently protested the British and Armenian intrusions but could offer no effective resistance.

In the operational vacuum created by the withdrawal of the Ottoman Army from the Caucasus, confrontations erupted as all parties sought to achieve their objectives. A British expeditionary force from Persia landed and occupied Baku on the Caspian Sea. A revived Armenian Democratic Republic fought with the Georgian Democratic Republic over the Lori district. A Second Congress of Western Armenians met at Yerevan to consider the acquisition of the three Ottoman provinces. The Pontic Greek communities declared their intentions to form an independent republic. Fully understanding the consequences of these events and the inevitability of the withdrawal, Yakup Şevki undertook to secretly evacuate the vast stores of weapons held in Ottoman depots in the areas to be surrendered.[12] Moreover, he laid plans to garrison and patrol the newly established frontier, but he was unable to prevent the occupation of the three provinces by Armenia or to successfully repress the gathering uprisings in his rear areas.

On April 2 and 3, 1919, the Ottoman ministry of war sent orders to Yakup Şevki to inactivate the Ninth Army and transfer command of all remaining army units to the XV Corps, which Major General Kâzım Karabekir had taken command of on March 2.[13] Yakup Şevki boarded a ship for Istanbul on April 14 for the week-long journey to the capital, where he would be assigned to the investigation commissions and detained in Malta by the British in May 1920. On April 6, 1919, British and Armenian forces occupied Kars and the surrounding hinterlands, dissolving the Provisional National Government of the Southwest Caucasus.[14] The Republic of Armenia annexed Kars 13 days later, and, on May 3, Major General Karabekir, who had been in Istanbul for consultations, returned to his headquarters in Erzurum.

TRANSCAUCASIAN POLITICS

As we have seen in the preceding chapters, in summer 1919, Mustafa Kemal and the Nationalists were well under way to establishing a new government to contest the partitioning of Anatolia. The Dashnak Party (the Armenian Revolutionary Federation or ARF) solidified its grip on the Armenian government largely because its opponents, the Hunchaks and Populists, boycotted the June 23 elections. Thus, in summer 1919, the Republic of Armenia was beginning to stabilize as a regional power under aggressive leadership.

There was great confusion among the Allies regarding what might be done with establishing various mandates in the Caucasus and who might administer them, and all sent missions to investigate the situation there. The Americans, who were considering an Armenian mandate, appointed U.S. Army Colonel William N. Haskell as Allied high commissioner in Armenia, and he arrived in the Caucasus on August 2.[15] Haskell was followed by the dispatch of the Harbord Commission (see chapter 3). Italy flirted briefly with a mandate in Azerbaijan, sending a mission to Baku under Colonel Melchiorre Gabba in May 1919 and offering to replace British troops there with Italians.[16] However, because of worrisome Italian encroachments south of Izmir, "Lloyd George was reluctant to offer them encouragement elsewhere. In turn, the cabinet decided to withdraw British forces from the Caucasus to Constantinople to have them ready to counter any move by the Italians."[17] The British 27th Division began to withdraw on August 15. In connection with the troop withdrawal, Britain sent a mission led by Oliver Waldrop, which arrived in Tbilisi in late August before proceeding to Baku. Waldrop's negative recommendations further eroded British resolve to remain in the Caucasus. In the end, none of the Allied powers were willing to stabilize the Caucasus in 1919.[18]

The withdrawal of stabilizing western forces in Caucasia then led to a renewal of the battles between Armenia and Azerbaijan over contested provinces and towns. A bitter conflict grew in the province Nakhichevan between local Muslims, who were cut off from Azerbaijan. The Nationalists could do nothing actively, but they did send Captain Halil and Lieutenant Colonel Kelp Ali Han as military advisors to organize the resistance in July 1919. An interesting aspect of this campaign was the use of armored trains by the Armenians. At the same time, the Azeris worked at seizing control of the largely Armenian province of Karabakh.

The Armenians and Georgians resolved some of their differences diplomatically at a conference in Tbilisi on August 29–30, 1919 with a decision for mixed administration in a neutralized zone. In September, the Ninth Congress of the Armenian Revolutionary Federation met, and Armenia asked Britain for military aid, while Georgia sought the same from Italy. In November, the Georgians signed a transit treaty with Armenia, while the Azeris tried to subjugate Armenian border communities. On December 9, the United States formally withdrew from the Paris Peace Conference, ending any hopes of American involvement in the Caucasus. In mid-January 1920, the Council of Foreign Ministers in Paris recognized the de facto governments of Georgia, Azerbaijan, and Armenia (but not de jure recognition), but then, on January 28, 1920, the United States refused to recognize the three Transcaucasian republics in any form. On another front, trouble was brewing when the Soviet Politburo decided on January 3 to pursue territorial acquisitions in Transcaucasia.

Throughout this period, the Armenian government and the diaspora sought to achieve a Greater Armenia that included not only the three border provinces but Erzurum, Maraş, and Cilicia. On November 21, the British, in the person of Lord Curzon, had told the Armenian delegation in Paris that Cilicia would not be a part of the Armenian state. But then, at the London Conference on February 17, the French noted that they intended to turn Cilicia over to Armenia. This would give Armenia access not only to the Black Sea but also to the Mediterranean Sea. By March 1920, Azerbaijan and Armenia were in an active state of war, and, in April, the final conference of the three Transcaucasian republics failed to resolve existing issues, particularly regarding Batum or the Azeri-Armenian territorial disputes. On April 26, the 11th Soviet Army invaded Azerbaijan, conquering the country in three days. The conquest of Azerbaijan and an active Armenian Bolshevik party in Armenia thoroughly alarmed the Armenian government and led to the declaration of a state of emergency on May 6, 1920. There were many issues with the neighboring Nationalists, which will be covered shortly, but the Armenian Bolsheviks rose in rebellion on May 10. The Soviets did not support the rebels, and the Armenian government mostly crushed them by May 23, 1920. It would reignite in June only to be finally extinguished.

THE MILITARIZATION OF THE TURCO-ARMENIAN FRONTIER

By May 1919, Karabekir's XV Corps had returned to its garrisons behind the 1914 frontier and was reduced under the armistice to a cadre strength of 15,811 men, 6,213 animals, 20,782 rifles, 56 machine guns, and 40 artillery pieces.[19] Through the remainder of the year and into 1920, the Military Bureau (Askerlik Dairesi) worked to reintroduce and reconcile conscription in eastern Anatolia. By March 25, 1920, the Nationalist Army's combat units (infantry, artillery, and cavalry) contained young men from the 1898–1900 year groups, while older men from the 1894–1897 year groups were assigned to combat support units (transportation, logistics, and medical, etc.).[20] Men born in 1891–1893 were assigned to the reserves, and the newly conscripted draft of 1901 was consolidated in recruit depots for training. The XV Corps staff drew up mobilization plans to recall reservists to bring the divisional cadres up to full wartime strength. As previously described, there were large and well-armed groups of Nationalist militias organized and available as well: the I Group near Hopa and the II Group near Rize (together containing 5,000 armed men), the III Group near Trabzon of 2,500 armed men, and the IV Group near Torul of 1,000 armed men.[21] There were also some 3,000 armed irregulars under Muslim tribal leaders such as Osman Ağa Hacı Emin Efendi, who could be counted on to fight the Armenians and Georgians.

On the Armenian side of the border, the government organized a small army of about 8,000 active soldiers, which could be increased to 20,000 men by mobilizing the Armenian committee's irregular militias known as the fedayee (*fedayi*). The fledgling Armenian active army itself evolved from the debris of the largely Armenian 1917 Russian Seventh Corps, led by General Tovmas Nazarbekian (Nazarbekoff), which had become the core of the Armenian Army defeated in 1918 by Enver's offensive.[22] The remnants had survived in the mountains and reformed under Nazarbekian as the Ottoman Army withdrew from Caucasia. Nazarbekian was appointed chair of the Armenian Military Council on March 25, 1919 and appointed lieutenant general on July 15, 1919. He was a graduate of the Moscow Military Academy, was decorated for bravery at Mukden in the Russo-Japanese War, and he was the senior-ranking regular officer in the new Armenian republic. On May 15, 1919, Nazarbekian's army was composed of three small infantry divisions, each of two infantry regiments with two mountain artillery batteries.[23] He also commanded a cavalry brigade of two regiments and an artillery regiment of one field artillery battalion and one mountain artillery battalion. While experienced, the Armenian republic's army was too small and too poorly armed to defend its newly formed homeland against its neighbors.

Armenia was also able to field irregular forces, which were a legacy of the Armenian revolutionary committees, most notably the Dashnaks and Hunchaks, who fought against the Ottomans during World War I. In the war, these men had been organized into quasi-conventional formations known as *druzhiny* (legions) that were led by determined and charismatic leaders (who often assumed a nom de guerre).[24] After the war, these remained a force in being. Dro (the nom de guerre of Drastamat Kanayan) led one group and was instrumental in stabilizing the fight against the Nakhichevan insurgents, now led by Captain Halil, in August 1919. Another well-known and able Dashnak leader, Andranik Ozanian, led another force known as the Special Striking Division[25] of some 3,000 irregulars against the Azeris as well.[26]

The principal shortcoming of the Armenian Army was not a lack of experienced leaders or a shortage of men, but rather a shortage of modern weapons, which were lost during its defeat in 1918. Postwar Armenian leaders in Paris and Kars actively sought military assistance from the Allies. Although the Transcaucasian republics received de facto diplomatic recognition from the Europeans in January 1920, British policy had begun to shift in favor of accommodating the Nationalists rather than favoring Armenia and Georgia. Nevertheless the Allies approved the transfer of arms and equipment to the republics on January 19, 1920. However, two months later, the British in Batum impounded two aircraft purchased by the Armenians for their military. Cash was a problem for the Armenian government, and it launched the Independence Loan campaign on June 19, while the diaspora launched the Gold Fund, both of which were intended to raise badly needed funding to purchase arms and equipment. The single British arms shipment (440 Vickers machine guns, 25,000 rifles, uniforms for 40,000 men, and other equipment) arrived on the SS *Hornsea* at Batum in June 1920.[27] While the Georgians collected 27 percent of the arms and equipment as a transit fee, the reminder reached Armenia in July and August. Subsequently, the Greeks delivered an arms shipment of nearly useless Ross rifles, which ended external support and forced the Armenians to turn to the Russians as their only source for weapons.

Alarmed by Armenian expansion. Mustafa Kemal wrote to Karabekir on February 6, 1920 ordering him to prepare a planning directive for mobilization and offensive operations.[28] Correspondence between them weighing alternatives continued and, on March 14, the brutal suppression of Muslim insurgents in Kars by the Armenian Army accelerated Nationalist war planning. Moreover, when reports of the suppression reached London, it led to a loss of support for Armenia, as well as causing a falling-out between émigré Armenian politicians in the west and the representatives of the Armenian Republic. In March, Dro, now, reinforced by regular Armenian Army battalions, fought a large battle for control of Büyük and Küçük Vedi in Nakhichevan with Captain Halil and his Muslim insurgents.[29] Muslim insurgents also took up arms in Iğdır, and, in Zengibasar province, Captain Muhittin organized three regiments of volunteers, who also joined the fight against Armenian occupation.

Between April 26 and May 9, Karabekir and Kemal engaged in an angry exchange of messages about Karabekir's demands to attack Armenia. Kemal denied his requests. However, the intractable Karabekir kept at it and sent a proposal to Ankara on June 4, asking permission to take Sarıkamış which the Council of Ministers finally approved under the utmost secrecy two days later.[30] The Grand National Assembly considered the question on June 7 and authorized partial mobilization the following day. On June 13, 1920, Karabekir ordered the 9th Caucasian and 12th Divisions to prepare for offensive operations against Sarıkamış, and the 11th Caucasian Division to prepare similar plans against Iğdır. He ordered the 3rd Caucasian Division in Trabzon to prepare to repel a possible amphibious landing by the Allies and the Georgians. The next day, Kemal appointed Karabekir as eastern front commander. Eager to get at the Armenians, Karabekir was disappointed to be immediately restrained by Kemal, who understood the larger geopolitical situation that was unrelated to the three provinces occupied by the Armenians.

KEMAL AND THE BOLSHEVIKS

Historian Michael Reynolds coined the phrase "the geopolitics of inverted alliances" when writing about the turmoil in the postwar Caucasus.[31] How the Nationalists came to a friendly working relationship with their historical enemy Russia is the subject of a large literature, and, unfortunately, only the highlights relating to the narrative of the War of Independence appear here. In 1919, the rump former Russian Empire was beset by the Great Powers, who sought to contain the contagion of Bolshevism by supporting counterrevolutionary leaders and by occupying ports and strategic points. These acts put Vladimir Lenin and the Bolsheviks in the same geopolitical camp as the decaying Ottoman Empire and the resurgent Nationalists. An Anglo-American all-Russian conference in Istanbul failed in late January 1919, setting the stage for continuing tensions between the Bolsheviks and the Great Powers.

On June 7, 1919, Kemal's staff officer for intelligence and political affairs, Major Hüsrev Sami (Gerede), sent a letter to Karabekir suggesting the possibility of a "tactical alliance with the Bolsheviks."[32] Karabekir reacted by warning Kemal not to accept excessive commitments to secure aid. Kemal finalized his thinking on June 23, stating that the Nationalists should be neutral in the contest between the Bolsheviks and the Great Powers, but that contact should be established immediately to determine whether they could supply arms, munitions, and equipment. Minor discussions took place subsequently, but things stood thusly until Kemal was elected president of the Grand National Assembly on April 24, 1920. Two days later, he sent a telegram to Moscow outlining a joint plan against the so-called imperialists. There were four basic parts to Kemal's deal. If the Bolsheviks moved to expel the British and incorporate Georgia into their state, the Nationalists would undertake action against "the imperialist Armenian government, and would ensure that Azerbaijan would become a member of the Bolshevik 'group of states.'"[33] Last, Kemal also requested the immediate dispatch of arms, munitions, equipment, and the first installment of five million gold rubles. On April 27, the Red Army occupied Baku, initiating the beginning of a devil's bargain between Kemal and Lenin.

Kemal's communications with Karabekir then are best seen as operational instructions conducted in parallel with strategic level negotiations with Lenin. Kemal was also trying to balance policy and resources against Greek and Italian encroachments, as well as suppress internal uprisings. It was a delicate balancing of ends, ways, and means, and Kemal was deliberate in his considerations and promises. Moreover, Kemal also had to deal with the public and secret machinations of the Turkish Communist Party, led by Mustafa Suphi, and the aspirations of the former CUP leaders, notably Enver and Cemal—all of whom courted the Bolsheviks and fomented unrest in the Caucasus and Transcaucasus (and, in Enver's case, the Trans-Caspian).[34] On May 6, Kemal appointed a delegation to

Moscow, led by Minister for Foreign Affairs Bekir Sami (Kunduh), In addition to the previous agreements, the Nationalists wanted the Russians to recognize the full sovereignty of the Ankara government and to commit more military aid. En route, the delegation stopped in Erzurum to hear Karabekir's views on the three provinces. While there, they negotiated a deal with Bolshevik foreign affairs commissar Georgy Chicherin (Tchitcherin) on June 4, which reduced the amount of gold to two million rubles but increased the amounts of arms and munitions.[35] In return, the Nationalists promised to conduct plebiscites to determine whether local populations desired to join a Nationalist Turkey or have independence.

Throughout the remainder of June, Chicherin and Bekir Sami exchanged letters and cables with ever-changing terms and conditions, much of which concerned the fate of Armenia. For his part, Bekir Sami sent notes to Armenia demanding that the Armenians accept the borders established by the 1918 Treaty of Batum (which returned the borders to the pre-1878 Russo-Ottoman War) as a starting point for negotiations. This served to inflame Armenian sensibilities because the irredentist territory far exceeded the three contested provinces. Bekir Sami and the Nationalist delegation finally reached Moscow by boat and train on July 18, 1920, and serious negotiations began on July 24. The negotiations were complicated by the continuing advances of the Red Army in the Caucasus, Armenian counter-rebellion operations in Oltu and Nakhichevan, and the conflicting aspirations of a previous Nationalist delegation to Moscow led by Halil (Kut) Pasha. Escorted by Russian soldiers, Halil reached Nakhichevan with the first 500 kilograms of gold at the end of July, where he established contact with Karabekir's men coming from the west to ensure transit to Ankara.[36] In a comic opera farce, Karabekir's soldiers temporarily wore Russian style uniforms and declared themselves the Revolutionary Turkish Eastern Front Red Detachment to alleviate tensions with Armenia. Nevertheless, the Armenian leader Dro intercepted part of the convoy and got away with some of the gold. Uncertain about the safety of transit and to ensure a continuous line of communication to the Nationalists, the Bolsheviks subsequently forced the Armenians to sign a temporary treaty on August 11, which turned over their railroads to the Russians and allowed them to occupy Karabakh, Zangezur, and Nakhichevan. They also forced Dro to return the gold, illustrating how the existence of an independent Armenia was of lesser value to Lenin than the state of Moscow-Ankara relations.

Negotiations continued in Moscow, with Lenin personally intervening to smooth out controversial topics concerning the return of Armenian refugees and the possession of Van and Bitlis. News of the brutal terms to be imposed on the Ottoman Empire by Treaty of Sèvres on August 10, 1920 served to accelerate the Nationalist's desire to reach an agreement. Finally, on August 24, a draft Turco-Russian Treaty of Friendship was initialed, which granted mutual recognition and assured the Russians free access to the Mediterranean. In return, the Russians promised large amounts of money and military assistance to the Nationalists. Russia recognized the boundaries set out by the Nationalist National Pact, but the parties put off finalizing the frontiers in the Caucasus. Neither the Nationalists nor the Russians were entirely happy with the draft, and they continued to argue over the next few weeks about Armenian borders, the exact amount of gold, and the amounts of arms and military equipment to be provided. Moreover, the Russians wanted the Nationalists to include an alliance clause against the western imperialists. However, as we will see, events in fall 1920 invalidated much of the conflicting positions and the Treaty of Moscow, as it came to known, was not actually signed until March 16, 1921.

INTERVENTION IN NAKHICHEVAN

In response to Nationalist military assistance to rebellious Muslims in Zengibasar, the Armenian government instructed Lieutenant Colonel Arsen Shahmazian to launch an offensive into Nakhichevan.[37] Shahmazian attacked on June 18, 1920, with 1,700 infantry, 8 artillery pieces, and 2 armored trains.[38] The Armenians were opposed by Captain Halil's Nationalist Army detachments and Nationalist militias as fighting broke out across the breadth of the province. Although casualties were light, 11th Caucasian Division chief of staff Major Veysel sent two detachments from the 1st Battalion, 18th Infantry Regiment in Doğubayazıt to assist in the fighting on July 1. He also sent the 1st Battalion, 34th Infantry Regiment to Büyük Vedi in northern Nakhichevan and Major Ali Timur to assist Captain Halil. Both forces crossed the Aras River on the bridge at Şahtahtı. With this support, Nationalist militia groups pushed into Armenian territory but were forced back.[39]

Major Timur established his line of defense along the Vedi Çayı Stream on the Yerevan frontier and was attacked by a large Armenian force on July 11. Two days later, he had fallen back to Sadarak. Ali Timur continued his retreat and established a defensive line with his two Nationalist Army battalions, a 600-man Nationalist militia group and an Azerbaijani cavalry regiment between the town of Püsyan on the railway and the Aras River. In support, he had several small mountain howitzers and a small cavalry troop—altogether, 15 officers and 265 trained soldiers. Opposing him, the Armenian Army brought about 2,000 men, eight artillery pieces, and their armored train.[40] At about 10:30 a.m. on July 23, the Armenians began their attack with artillery fire from the armored train and their artillery batteries. Some 1,500 Armenian infantry and 200 cavalry began their assault an hour later, and, by the end of the day, Major Timur was in retreat. Falling back, he held on for two more days but was forced back across the Aras River bridge at Şahtahtı on July 25. Major Timur took his regulars west with him, while the Azeri cavalry and the Nationalist militias withdrew southeast to the city of Nakhichevan.

Major Timur withdrew to the town of Muratlı to reconstitute his tired force, leaving a cavalry screen to guard the bridge. Major Veysel reinforced him with men from the 2nd Battalion, 34th Infantry Regiment. Alerted to the fact that Halil and the gold shipment was approaching from Azerbaijan, Major Timur was ordered to take his detachment to Nakhichevan, and he began a difficult 50-kilometer march southeast. Halil arrived in the city on the night of July 30/31, and Timur's force arrived on August 1. Once there, Halil and Timur's men were combined to form the Nakhichevan Detachment under Halil's command and deployed to defenses to the north of the city. Timur's infantry were put into the line just in time to halt an Armenian attack (who had a force of three infantry regiments at Hok and Şahtahtı), launched using their armored train. The Armenian attacks continued on August 2, but by then, the defenders were too well entrenched. The Armenians followed with a larger attack on August 10, but their offensive operations against Nakhichevan ceased the next day when word of the treaty with the Russians reached them.

INTERVENTION IN OLTU

At the same time as hostilities erupted in Nakhichevan, the Armenian Army opened offensive operations in Kars Province against the Nationalists in villages north of the town Oltu (which is itself about 100 kilometers west of the city of Kars). While Nakhichevan was important emotionally and culturally to the Nationalists, it did not have the strategic importance of the three provinces (Ardahan, Batum, and Kars), which were contiguous to Erzurum and Trabzon provinces. Moreover, there were coal fields near Oltu in the town of Penek, which were important to both sides but to which Armenia laid claim.[41] The Nationalists held Penek with the Oltu Detachment of four Nationalist militia battalions, and Bardız with the 9th Division's 29th Infantry Regiment, artillery, and several companies of Nationalist militia. Against Penek, the Armenians brought their 1st Infantry Regiment, an artillery battery, and a cavalry detachment (altogether about 1,000 men), and against Bardız they brought another force of some 300 irregular fighters.[42]

The Armenian offensive began on the morning of June 19, and they quickly pushed two Nationalist militia battalions off the hills northeast of Penek.[43] At the same time, the provisional forces drove the Nationalist outposts from the hills northeast of Bardız. The next day, the 29th Infantry Regiment commander, Major Ali Rıza, sent reports to 9th Division commander, Lieutenant Colonel Deli Halit (Karsıalan),[44] that his men were in retreat but that he expected he could hold the town. Halit acted immediately and ordered Ali Rıza to send his 1st Battalion to the Oltu Detachment, and he ordered his 1st Battalion, 28th Infantry Regiment to Bardız.[45] In turn, General Karabekir instructed the 3rd Caucasian Division to prepare the 8th Infantry Regiment to reinforce Halit, and he sent the 1st Squadron, 15th Cavalry Regiment to screen the front between the two detachments. On June 21, the Armenians, now reinforced by the 5th Infantry Regiment, took Penek pushing the Nationalists back to positions outside of the town of Tuzla, while in Bardız, Ali Rıza established a strong defense east of the town. By June 29, the 3rd Battalion, 8th Infantry Regiment had reached Tuzla, where it was held in reserve.

In the meantime, the Armenians left a small force screening Tuzla and shifted the 5th Infantry Regiment and several batteries of artillery south to attack Bardız. After positioning their forces, the Armenian attack began at 2:00 a.m. on July 2, 1920, when a cavalry detachment seized a small hill north of town. Ali Rıza blocked this by sending a half company of infantry from his reserves. The main weight of the Armenian attack, about 500 infantrymen, fell on the 1st Battalion, 28th Infantry, while a smaller attack hit the adjacent 1st Battalion, 29th Infantry Regiment. Both Armenian attacks failed, and casualties were light on both sides.[46] The successful defense cheered Lieutenant Colonel Halit, who moved his divisional headquarters to the town of Norşin, just a few kilometers to the west of Bardız. He also ordered his 17th Infantry Regiment and 9th Artillery Regiment to the Bardız front. By mid-August, Halit's 9th Caucasian Division was established, with his weaker left wing centered on Tuzla and his far stronger right wing centered on Bardız. However, Halit's left wing was not so weak that it could not easily repulse an early morning attack by the Armenian 3rd Battalion, 1st Infantry Regiment on Baskot Hill on August 26.[47]

Sensing a tactical opportunity after the failed Armenian attack, on September 1, Halit asked General Karabekir for permission to conduct a counterattack.[48] Karabekir authorized him to begin planning a counterattack against the weaker Armenian 1st Infantry Regiment holding positions northeast of Tuzla. Over the next two weeks, Halit secretly shifted his 29th Infantry Regiment and several artillery batteries from Bardız to Tuzla. Despite darkness and very muddy conditions, Halit launched his main assault group on his left flank (the 29th Infantry Regiment) at 2:30 a.m. on September 13.[49] Halit's principal tactical objective was the seizure of the town of Penek and the hills to its north. He launched a supporting attack on his right with the 8th Infantry Regiment and Nationalist militia. By 6:00 a.m., the Armenians were in full retreat, and by midday Halit's main assault force had pushed well beyond its assigned objectives.[50] The battles ended by September 14, with the Nationalists holding Penek and Bardız.

PREPARATIONS FOR WAR

Major General Kâzım Karabekir was anxious to begin his long-awaited offensive into the three provinces, but he had been restrained for geopolitical reasons by Kemal and the Grand National Assembly.[51] However, in summer 1920, the geopolitical realities of the British withdrawal from the Caucasus, the Treaty of Sèvres, the draft Treaty of Friendship with the Bolsheviks, and Armenian military offensives in Nakhichevan and Oltu drove a reconsideration of Nationalist military policy. Karabekir cabled Kemal on September 15, urgently renewing his request to open an offensive against the Armenians.[52] At Kemal's behest, the Council of Ministers in Ankara approved Karabekir's request on September 20, but there were lingering concerns about becoming overcommitted should the Greeks and the British reengage in the west. These concerns evaporated when the Armenians, who had reinforced the front with the 4th Infantry Regiment, renewed their attacks on Bardız at 4:00 a.m. on September 24. Covered by artillery fire, Armenian infantry broke into the forward trenches of the Nationalist 17th Infantry Regiment but were shortly repelled by counterattacks.[53] The Armenians called off their offensive around midday.

Over the course of the summer, Karabekir refined his plans and reorganized his forces into three tactical groupings. In the north, Karabekir's Left Wing composed Halit's reinforced 9th Caucasian Division; his Center was built around Lieutenant Colonel Osman Nuri's (Koptagel) 12th Division and the 5th and 6th Tribal Cavalry Regiments (*Aşiret Alayı*); and his Right Wing was composed of Lieutenant Colonel Mehmet Ziya's (Yergök) 11th Caucasian Infantry Division.[54] Karabekir's 3rd Caucasian Division, under the command of Colonel Nazif (Kayacık), remained near Trabzon, keeping watch on the Georgian frontier. Karabekir intended to use his Left Wing and Center to converge on the town of Sarıkamış, and he reinforced them with the 15th and 6th Cavalry Regiments, respectively.[55] He positioned his Right Wing on the city of Doğubayazıt with conditional instructions to attack either north toward Iğdır or east toward Nakhichevan, depending on the operational situation. The Nationalists also had about 13 aircraft organized into the 15th Aero Squadron based at the Horasan Flying Station.[56] Between June 22 and July 27, Karabekir moved these forces to assault positions close to the frontiers. These repositionings concentrated the Nationalist Eastern Front Command for offensive operations. Not counting the 3rd Caucasian Division on the Georgian frontier, Karabekir had 1,265 officers, 16,604 infantrymen, 528 cavalrymen, 54 artillery pieces, and 168 machine guns poised for the offensive.[57] On August 22, 1920, Karabekir sent out a 16-paragraph operations order to his divisions with explicit instructions to be ready to seize their assigned objective no later than September 26.

Historian Richard Hovannisian characterized the Armenian Army in September 1920 as being in a state of exhaustion caused by constant alerts; moreover, its ex-Russian Army officer corps had not adjusted to realities of the needs of a small nation-state.[58] General Nazarbekian divided the Armenian Army into two major tactical groupings, a Western Command under Major General Harutium Hovsepian and an Eastern Command under Major General Grigorii Shelkovnikian (Sholkovnikov).[59] These groups exercised command over combinations of the eight regular infantry regiments that Nazarbekian had available in the field army. Additionally, he had a Cavalry Brigade of the 1st and 2nd Cavalry Regiments, five batteries of mountain artillery, four batteries of field artillery, and one battery each of 105-mm and 155-mm howitzers. Unavailable for mobile operations in the field were two regiments of fixed fortress artillery guns (about 40) in the Kars fortress. The army also had the use of several irregular formations, including Dro's Dashnak Detachment (1,500 men), the

General Sahak Detachment (1,500 men), the 1st Militia Regiment (2,000 men), and the Dashnak Guerrilla Regiment (1,000 men). Not counting the problematic irregulars, Nazarbekian had about 12,000 infantry, 1,000 cavalry, 44 artillery pieces, and 250 machine guns available, of which only 2,500 infantry, 400 cavalry, 18 artillery pieces, and 70 machine guns were available for combat in Sarıkamış and its vicinity.[60] The Armenian Army also possessed 10 aircraft organized in two squadrons, but it is unclear exactly where these were located or if the aircraft were operational.[61] General Hovsepian maintained his headquarters in Kars, with the 1st Infantry Regiment near Penek and Bardız, the 4th and 5th Infantry Regiments near Sarıkamış, the 3rd Infantry Regiment near Iğdır, and the Cavalry Brigade in Gümrü (Alexandropol or Gyumri). Hovsepian's deployments had created localized superiorities sufficient for localized tactical offensive operations but, at the operational level, left his forces dangerously spread out over a wide area. Moreover, the operational area occupied by the Armenian Army was effectively a bulge-like salient that was also dangerously vulnerable to concentric assault.

THE SARIKAMIŞ OFFENSIVE

The Nationalist's short war against Armenia occurred as a three-phase campaign, the first of which aimed to seize the town of Sarıkamış, the second to reclaim the town and fortress of Kars, and the third to clear the Armenian Army out of Iğdır and vicinity. On September 26, 1920, Karabekir issued operational orders moving all formations to their assault positions, with the order to begin the offensive at 3:00 a.m. on September 28.[62] Karabekir moved to the field and established his tactical headquarters on Akmezar Dağı (Akmezar Hill) on the front lines between his Left Wing and Center in order to effectively command and control the battle (see map 5.1).

The attacks began on schedule, achieving tactical surprise, and Armenian resistance collapsed within hours across the entire front.[63] The Left Wing and the Center reached their initial objectives in less than one hour, and positive situation reports poured into Karabekir's tactical command post. Casualties were few, and, at 10:00 a.m., Karabekir ordered his attacking formations forward in a pursuit. In the south, the Tribal Cavalry regiments raced north, and the pursuit continued all day ending at about 6:00 p.m. The Center had advanced about 20 kilometers, the Left Wing about 10 kilometers, and the Tribal Cavalry almost 30 kilometers. As darkness fell,

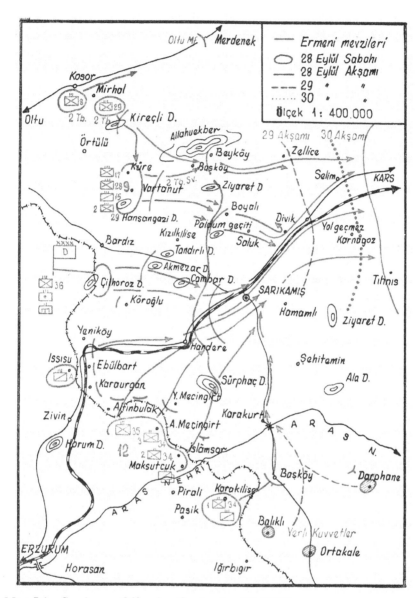

Map 5.1   Sarıkamış Offensive (September 28, 1920)

Sarıkamış was the site of Enver Pasha's great defeat in January 1915. Major General Kâzım Karabekir's Eastern Front Command offensive that began on September 28, 1920, captured the town in two days. The attacks were well organized and surprised the ill-prepared Armenian defenders. The seizure of Sarıkamış positioned the Nationalist XV Corps to advance to Kars.

Courtesy of the Turkish General Staff Military History and Strategy Institute (ATASE).

the Left Wing and the Center rested about 20 from the town of Sarıkamış. That night, Karabekir sent out fresh orders, Halit's Left Wing was ordered to reorient and push northeast to cut off the road from Kars to Sarıkamış, while Osman Nuri's Center and the Tribal Cavalry were ordered to seize the town itself. Karabekir ordered his corps artillery and engineers forward to support the 12th Division if needed for an assault into the town of Sarıkamış, and he prepared to move his tactical headquarters forward as well.[64]

The retreating Armenian regiments were not prepared to offer a determined defense of the town and began to withdraw during the night. They abandoned large stores of provisions, weapons, and munitions, and the Nationalists captured these intact.[65] Meanwhile, General Hovsepian ordered the cavalry brigade south to Kars as a precaution as he struggled to find a defensible position farther to the north. The Nationalist pursuit resumed at dawn on September 29, and the Nationalists pushed forward, occasionally engaging in brief firefights with the retreating Armenians. An Armenian aircraft bombed Halit's 17th and 28th Infantry Regiments at around 10:00 a.m., but they were unable to prevent the Nationalists from reaching the village of Çatak and cutting the Kars-Sarıkamış road at about 11:00 a.m. Halit moved his tactical headquarters there soon after. To the south, by midday, the 12th Division and the Tribal Cavalry closed on Sarıkamış and took the undefended town. Karabekir moved his command post into the town later that evening. He sent a full report to the General Staff in Ankara on the morning of September 30 explaining his success and the locations of his formations. Karabekir also noted that he had rectified the Armenian intrusions of July 24.[66]

The Sarıkamış offensive appears as something of a two-day blitzkrieg, but the Armenians were unprepared, surprised, and wisely decided to withdraw quickly.[67] However, the astonishing success of Karabekir's planning illustrates the high degree of initiative and staff capability that the Nationalist Army inherited from the Ottoman Army. The operation also highlights the high degree of operational and tactical mobility that the Nationalists could accomplish when conducting offensive operations.

THE SEIZURE OF KARS

The Armenian government sent immediate protests to the Russian and British governments and also tried to get the Greeks to renew their attacks in the west.[68] On October 4, 1920, Armenia declared war on the Nationalists and announced full mobilization of all men of military age, in the hope that this would encourage the Allied governments to intervene.[69] The next day, Avetis Aharonian, the Armenian delegate to the Paris Peace Conference, presented a case against the Nationalists to no avail. Unknown to the Armenians, Chief of the General Staff İsmet sent a ciphered telegram to Karabekir informing him of an October 2 decision by the Council of Ministers to seize Kars and destroy the Armenian Army.[70] These events overlapped an Armenian diplomatic effort to negotiate a treaty of friendship with the Russians, and, although the Russians were sympathetic to the plight of the Armenians, Lenin decided on October 13 to occupy Armenia rather than assist them against the Nationalists.[71] Blocked at the strategic level, the Armenians were determined to regain the initiative, and General Hovsepian was ordered to conduct a spoiling attack.[72]

Karabekir began making preparations to continue operations against Kars; however, he was alerted by captured Armenian soldiers of a looming attack on Sarıkamış. In response, Karabekir concentrated Halit's 9th Caucasian Division on the north side of the Kars-Sarıkamış road and Osman Nuri's 12th Division on the south side.[73] To cover the empty terrain on the left flank vacated by Halit (which the prisoners told the Nationalists was nearly empty of Armenian forces), Karabekir formed the provisional Merdenek Detachment. His tribal cavalry forces and militia covered the right flank. Scouts from the Nationalist 15th Cavalry Regiment reported 3,500 enemy troops massing against the left flank on the evening of October 13, 1920. This report corresponded to other reports coming in from Karabekir's forward positions, and he sent out alerts. At 8:00 a.m. on October 14, a large force of several thousand soldiers from three Armenian regiments attacked Halit's defenses, pushing his troops five kilometers to the rear. However, he had the 28th Infantry Regiment in reserve, and he launched counterattacks at 11:00 a.m., which retook his positions. Armenian supporting attacks to the south hit the tribal cavalry positions, and to the north hit the 15th Cavalry Regiment and the Merdenek Detachment.[74] All of these supporting attacks failed completely, and, in the south, Osman Nuri's 34th Infantry Regiment conducted a prompt counterattack that pushed the attackers out of their original positions. By nightfall, the Armenians were retreating to their final defensive positions, which ringed the city of Kars. According to historian Richard Hovannisian, "the confidence of the Armenian general staff was crushed . . . as was the morale of the army, which had retreated in disarray."[75]

Karabekir opined to İsmet that a short delay was necessary but that he was ready to resume offensive operations. On October 20, he sent his draft plan to the chief of staff and, at the same time, ordered the 1884- to 1889-year groups to full mobilization to fill his ranks.[76] Three days later he sent orders to his divisions assigning them tactical objectives. In the same instruction, Karabekir activated a provisional division under Colonel Rüştü (Sakarya) and assigned the 28th Infantry Regiment, several mountain artillery batteries, and a tribal cavalry detachment to him.[77] This gave Karabekir three major maneuver units for planning. Karabekir also assigned the 15th Cavalry Regiment, the 5th Tribal Cavalry Regiment, and a provisional infantry brigade to Lieutenant Colonel Halit. Importantly, Karabekir formed the 1st Provisional Cavalry Brigade, composed of the 7th, 9th, and 11th Cavalry Regiments, and assigned it to Halit as well. The XV Corps operational plan involved disengaging Halit's 9th Caucasian Division from the northern sector and moving it behind the lines to an attack position on the far-right flank. As quietly as possible, Colonel Rüştü's provisional division would take over Halit's former sector. This concentrated Karabekir's two regular divisions and weighted the corps' right wing with almost all the available cavalry under Halit. The plan also used the provisional forces in an economy-of-force mission on the left. Karabekir's intent was to conduct an envelopment from the right by swinging Halit's division, now reinforced with highly mobile cavalry, far to the right, and then north to cut the road from Kars to Tbilisi and isolate the city.[78] At the same time, the 12th Division and the provisional forces would attack to pin the defenders in their forward lines and prevent an escape. Between October 24 and 26, all these forces moved into position.

Kars was a fortress, first for the Ottomans, then for the Russians, and finally for the Armenians. It had fallen to the Turks during Enver's 1918 Caucasian campaign, and then returned to the Armenians as the Ninth Army withdrew to the pre-1914 frontier in 1919. The city was fortified with a ring of 20 concrete, brick, and earth forts, and there were about 40 fixed fortress artillery guns as well. Overall, the fortress was in a poor state of repair, and it was not as strong as it had been in previous conflicts. Defending these forts, the Armenians had the 1st, 4th, 5th, and 7th Infantry Regiments and the Gümrü Volunteer Battalion; the 1st and 2nd Cavalry Regiments; and several regiments of irregular cavalry, as well as four batteries of field artillery and a detachment from the 3rd Infantry Regiment. Karabekir's staff estimated that there were about 25,000 Armenian soldiers, including support troops, defending the fortress. On October 26, 1920, Halit's reinforced division had completed its approach march and stood poised to the east of Kars, while his Nationalist cavalry had driven the Armenian outposts on the hills into the city.

Karabekir's attacks began at 10:00 a.m. on October 27 with a general offensive across the entire front. Rüştü and Osman Nuri's men made contact on the right and in the center and pushed the Armenians off their positions. Halit's right wing conducted assault marches to make contact with the Armenians, and, on his extreme right wing, he sent his cavalry and the 28th Infantry Regiment racing north to cut the railroad to Gümrü (see map 5.2). The cavalry and an infantry detachment cut the railroad and purposefully damaged the track before pulling back when the Armenians sent an armored train south. Halit was unable to advance beyond the railroad and cut the critical highway north out of the city. Despite now being surrounded on three sides, Major General Daniel Pirumian, the Armenian fortress commander, sent encouraging cables to the General Staff expressing his determination to hold the city.[79]

The Nationalists tightened their grip on the city on October 28 and planned the final assault. The next day, the weather turned stormy, with light snow and fog impeding observation and mobility. The Armenians took advantage of the bad weather and began to pull their forces out of the city and retreat to the north.[80] The Nationalists pushed forward and captured most of the forts on the western and southern approaches to the city. Karabekir moved his tactical command post forward to Karakale, adjacent to Osman Nuri's command post. In the ever-optimistic General Pirumian's command post, "there was still no panic or belief that the fortress would fall that day."[81] The final Nationalist assaults began about 6:00 a.m. on October 30. Forward progress was slow, as the Armenians fought desperate rear-guard actions to allow their main forces to retreat. Osman Nuri's 12th Division was particularly hard hit with a counterattack by several infantry regiments supported by artillery and an armored train. Halit's cavalry and infantry advanced beyond the north-south railroad but were unable to completely cut the metaled highway north to Tbilisi. By nightfall, the city was in Nationalist hands, although most of the Armenian garrison escaped to the north.

Karabekir sent a report to İsmet and the General Staff in Ankara at 12:30 p.m. on October 31 announcing the surrender of the fortress by General Pirumian and noting the capture of three Armenian generals (including Pirumian), 50 officers, and 500 men.[82] In fact, over 2,000 Armenian officers and men were captured and sent to prisoner-of-war camps near Erzurum, in which many died during the harsh winter of 1920–1921.[83] Moreover, the Nationalists captured large quantities of arms, munitions,

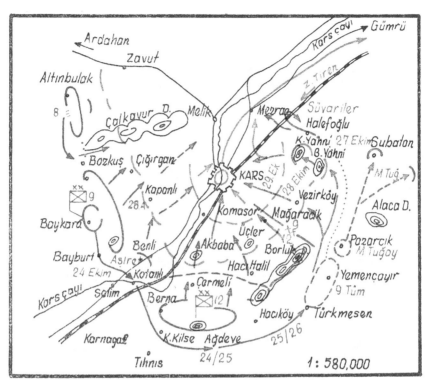

Map 5.2   Encirclement of Kars (October 27, 1920)

The Republic of Armenia declared war on the Nationalists on October 4, 1920, and attempted to secure military aid from Lenin. In the meantime, Karabekir moved his soldiers forward and prepared to seize the fortress city of Kars. On October 24, the Nationalist XV Corps encircled Kars, which surrendered on October 29, while supplementary operations continued in İğdır. The victory over Armenia enabled the Nationalists to move badly needed reinforcements from the XV Corps to the Western Front Command in 1921/1922.

Courtesy of the Turkish General Staff Military History and Strategy Institute (ATASE).

war supplies, locomotives and rail cars, and importantly for the poorly clad Nationalist soldiers, thousands of warm British winter uniforms. İsmet sent an immediate cable in reply containing a directive giving Karabekir authority to pursue the Armenians to destruction. Karabekir replied that he intended to do that along two avenues of approach, the first toward Yerevan, and the second toward Gümrü.[84]

In fact, the aggressive and resourceful Karabekir had already launched Halit's cavalry and infantry in a pursuit toward Gümrü, and, by the end of the day of October 31, Halit was halfway to Gümrü. His operations were characterized by relentlessly outflanking the Armenian rear guards, forcing them into continuous retreat. Osman Nuri's division pushed northeast, guarding Halit's right flank. However, the Armenians regrouped and formed a defensive line that slowed the tired Nationalists, who had been marching and in combat continuously for seven days. Nevertheless, Karabekir kept up the pressure relentlessly, and over the next week, his men pushed north toward the town. He then slowed his advance somewhat and began negotiating an armistice with the Armenians.[85] By November 7, the two Nationalist divisions were poised just a few kilometers west of Gümrü when the armistice negotiations were tentatively completed. Karabekir's advance began the next day, and the town fell, as Halit's 28th Infantry Regiment quickly occupied Gümrü. Not content to take just the town, Karabekir pushed his men 10 kilometers to the northeast to prepare defensive line against possible Armenian counterattacks. More importantly, he also wanted a display of force to encourage the Armenians to accelerate armistice negotiations. The Armenian Army conducted local counterattacks contesting the ground, which failed on November 13, and Karabekir concluded offensive operations the next day.

THE IĞDIR OFFENSIVE

The Right Wing Group, under the command of Lieutenant Colonel Mehmet Ziya, was built around the 11th Caucasian Division, reinforced with tribal cavalry detachments. Mehmet Ziya maintained his headquarters in the city of Doğubayazıt, near the disputed province of Nakhichevan. To maximize the effectiveness of his tribal cavalry, who were notoriously undisciplined and poorly trained, Mehmet Ziya brigaded them with his three regular infantry regiments.[86] The Nationalist Army's infantry divisions were organized with three infantry regiments, supported by the divisional artillery regiment and supporting arms, fighting under the direct command of the division commander. A brigade is a combined arms team, built mostly of infantry but having combat arms and supporting elements directly under the command of the brigade commander, often in an independent role. By reorganizing his infantry regiments as reinforced brigades, Mehmet Ziya enabled the Right Wing Group to maneuver as three independent tactical elements to gain maximum flexibility on the battlefield.

As reorganized, Mehmet Ziya formed three provisional brigades: the 1st Provisional Brigade (the 18th Infantry Regiment, with a machine gun detachment and two artillery batteries, and the 11th and 12th Light Tribal Cavalry Regiments); the 2nd Provisional Brigade (the 17th Infantry Regiment, a Lewis Gun detachment [a type of light British machine gun], a small artillery battery, and the 8th and 13th Light Tribal Cavalry Regiments); and the 3rd Provisional Brigade (the 33rd Infantry Regiment, a Lewis Gun detachment, a half battery of artillery, the 14th Light Tribal Cavalry Regiment, and the Volunteer Tribal Cavalry Group). Mehmet Ziya positioned the 1st Provisional Brigade in Karakilise (20 kilometers west of Doğubayazıt), and the 2nd and 3rd Provisional Brigades just to the north of city. He also exercised tactical control over the Nakhichevan Detachment, operating across the border to his east.

On the night of October 20/21, Karabekir ordered Mehmet Ziya to advance north with a view toward seizing the town of İğdır and pursuing the Armenians as they retreated to the north.[87] Mehmet Ziya moved his three brigades to assault positions over the next two days, and began offensive operations on October 24. The 1st and 2nd Provisional Brigades attacked on two roads, which became twin axes of advance that converged at İğdır itself, and they quickly crushed the weak defenses on the Armenian 2nd Infantry Regiment.[88] By nightfall, the two brigades had penetrated to within three kilometers of İğdır. On Mehmet Ziya's right flank, the 3rd Provisional Brigade advanced unopposed to take the village of Alican on the İğdır-Yerevan road. To avoid encirclement, the Armenians withdrew from İğdır and abandoned the area to the Nationalists. Encouraged by the success at Gümrü and İğdır, Karabekir ordered Mehmet Ziya to attack north with the Nakhichevan Detachment. Led by the detached regular battalions of the 18th and 34th Infantry Regiments, Major Ali Timur began his offensive at 8:00 a.m. on November 7 and, by the end of the day, had taken Hok and Karabağlar.[89] On October 8, he drove north to seize the villages of Norşin and Yenice, establishing a bridgehead across the Arpaçay River and encircling and capturing 180 enemy soldiers, two mountain artillery pieces, and 11 heavy machine guns.[90]

THE ARMISTICE AND THE MOSCOW TREATY

Karabekir issued an appeal from Kars on November 1 for the Armenians to lay down their arms, and the Armenian government subsequently requested a truce, which Karabekir tentatively granted on November 7 before occupying Gümrü.[91] At the same time as Karabekir was attacking from the west and south, the Russian Army and a ragtag host of Azeri, Turk, and Armenian Communist groups entered Armenia from the north and east. The Russians were trying to keep Armenia within their sphere of influence without prejudicing their new friendly relationship with Mustafa Kemal. On November 9, the Turkish Grand National Assembly sent a note to the Armenians offering peace under very moderate terms. However, the armistice agreement previously worked out by Karabekir demanded the surrender of large quantities of weapons and the withdrawal of the Armenian Army behind a line set in the November 7 negotiations. Hoping for a more favorable outcome, the Armenians, according to historian Stanford Shaw, clung to hopes for an Allied intervention and tried to evade the acceptance of a peace treaty with the Nationalists.[92] This accelerated a collapse in the Armenian government between those who wanted to fight on and achieve a compromise with Ankara and those who saw incorporation by the Soviets as the only option. In the meantime, Nationalist operations continued in Nakhichevan, as Ali Timur began another offensive on November 14. He seized the town of Dehne on November 16, Sadarak the next day, and Davalı on the next. On November 17, he had reclaimed the northern provincial towns of Büyük and Küçük Vedi. The Armenians now faced Karabekir's victorious army, which seemed ready to advance and seize Yerevan, and on November 17, they agreed to accept the Nationalist terms before the Russians could move further into Armenia. The next day, the Armenian Army turned over large stocks of weapons and equipment to the Nationalists and withdrew to the agreed line.

Encouraged by these developments, the Nationalists proposed a peace conference be held in Gümrü starting on November 24. The Russians were excluded from the negotiations. Over the next week, the Nationalists and the Armenians completed a peace agreement. On December 3, 1920, they signed the Treaty of Gümrü (the Treaty of Alexandropol).[93] The Nationalists imposed harsh terms on Armenia, which basically ratified their possession of Ardahan, Iğdır, and Kars, while delaying decisions regarding Nakhichevan pending the outcomes of plebiscites.[94] The Nationalists recognized Armenian independence, and, reciprocally, Armenia rejected the Treaty of Sèvres (which had created the stillborn Greater Armenia). Neither side would demand reparations, but the Armenians would demobilize their army and turn their railroads and lines of communication over to the Nationalists. The treaty was supposed to be ratified within 30 days, but, in the meantime, the Russians completed their occupation of Armenia, and the Armenian parliament never ratified the agreement. A new Soviet Socialist Republic of Armenia later repudiated the treaty.

As has been described, the Nationalists and the Russians signed the Treaty of Moscow on March 16, 1921, which adjusted and finalized the international boundaries. The terms that are relevant to this chapter include the Nationalists renouncing all claims to Batum and releasing it to Georgia, recognizing Nakhichevan as an autonomous part of Azerbaijan, and drawing a new borderline giving the Nationalists Artvin, Ardahan, Kars, and Iğdır.[95] Interestingly, the Nationalists conceded Gümrü to Armenia, which was promptly renamed Leninakan.[96] In accordance with the treaty, Karabekir began to withdraw from Gümrü on April 13, 1921. He left infantry and cavalry detachments guarding the new border and pulled the 9th Caucasian and 12th Infantry Division back to Kars, and the 11th Caucasian Division and the Nakhichevan Detachment back to Iğdır and Doğubayazıt. Karabekir activated a new 2nd Infantry Division in April 1921, under the command of Colonel Ziya, and stationed it in Ardahan.[97] He also set Colonel Rüştü to repairing, updating, and fortifying the recovered Kars Fortress.[98]

The 1921 battles in the west forced the Eastern Front Command to undergo further reorganizational changes. On April 4, 1921, the General Staff ordered Karabekir to send most of the 3rd Caucasian Division and large quantities of rifles and munitions to the Western Front Command.[99] The General Staff followed this by ordering the remainder of the division west. In April, the General Staff also consolidated the 15th, 16th, 17th, and 18th Cavalry Regiments into a newly activated 6th Cavalry Division under the command of Colonel Sami Sabit (Karaman). In Trabzon, the army reactivated the 13th Division, under the command of Lieutenant Colonel Seyfi (Düzgören) in May 1921. Desperate for fresh troops, on July 30, the General Staff ordered Karabekir to send the experienced 12th Division west as well. To make up for the loss of manpower, the General Staff ordered the men of the 1901-year group to the colors for conscription. By August 4, the regiments of the 12th Division were on trains bound for the west, but in Erzincan, some of the units were temporarily assigned to the Central Army to quell uprisings, and it took 48 days for the entire division to arrive in Ankara. The General Staff also ordered two batteries of 105-mm howitzers from the 20th Artillery Regiment from Kars to the west on September 6.

Because of unrest in the southern part of his area of responsibility (particularly around the city of Van), Karabekir sent a request on July 4, 1921 to the General Staff asking permission to activate the 7th Cavalry Division from unassigned cavalry detachments and the Van Tribal Cavalry Brigade.[100] This was duly approved, and, in September, Karabekir activated the 7th Cavalry Division under the command of Lieutenant Colonel Sabri by consolidating a dozen different tribal regiments with some regular cavalry detachments into three brigades. It was stationed it Karaköse—east of Iğdır. Karabekir activated the Van Tribal Cavalry Brigade under the command of Staff Lieutenant Colonel Veysel (Ünüvar), using five tribal cavalry regiments and, about the same time, he reorganized the 6th Cavalry Division into a two-brigade division (the 11th and 12th Cavalry Brigades).

Karabekir had become essentially a theater commander, and, on January 1, 1922, the General Staff reactivated the IX Corps headquarters, under the command of Rüştü Pasha, as the Eastern Front's primary tactical unit, as well as a number of border regiments to separate tactical from administrative frontier duties.[101] However, to provide formations and men for the border regiments, both the newly formed 2nd Division and the 7th Cavalry Division were inactivated. In spring 1922, the 11th Caucasian Division and an infantry regiment from the 13th Division were also sent west from Erzincan. In the summer, several smaller units were sent west, requiring further reorganization, and the 9th Caucasian Division was renamed the 9th Division. On October 1, 1922, the XV Corps headquarters was inactivated, leaving Karabekir's Eastern Front Command with the IX Corps, composed of the 9th and 13th Divisions, the 6th Cavalry Division, the Tribal Cavalry Division, the Erzurum and Kars Fortress Commands, and the Border Commission.[102] On that date, the Eastern Front Command was composed of 1,438 officers, 28,076 soldiers, 146 artillery pieces, 140 heavy machine guns, and 38 light machine guns.[103] This total was considerably higher than the 18,491 men Karabekir had commanded in September 1920, but his area of operations was much larger and included fortresses and frontier duties.

CONCLUSION

The war in the east was episodic, short, and produced few casualties. At the end of it, because of the Allied withdrawals and Russian intervention, the Armenians were left in an untenable and uncomfortable position. The Nationalists emerged with most of what they wanted, and, equally importantly, after the peace accords, they were left with excess force capacity in the east. This enabled them to transfer badly needed trained men and equipment to the Western Front Command to confront the Greeks. The battles in the east displayed the strengths of the Ottoman and Nationalist armed forces—resiliency, initiative, and high levels of mobility. Kara-bekir's forces showed a gift for concentration and maneuver, which enabled them to execute complex and difficult offensive operations successfully and rapidly. The ability of the Nationalists to task organize into combined arms teams quickly and effectively was also on display in the Caucasus.

NOTES

1. Harbord, *Conditions in the Near East*, 18.
2. Allen and Muratoff, *Caucasian Battlefields*, 497–500.
3. Bıyıklıoğlu, *Mondros Mütarekesi ve Tatbikatı*, Kroki 7 (Sketch Map 7) following page 176.
4. Bıyıklıoğlu, *Mondros Mütarekesi ve Tatbikatı*, 154.
5. Ibid., 155.
6. Bıyıklıoğlu, *Mondros Mütarekesi ve Tatbikatı*, 156–157.
7. Shaw, *From Empire to Republic*, vol. 3, part 1, 925.
8. Busch, *Mudros to Lausanne*, 112; and Falls and Becke, *Military Operations Macedonia*, 307–308.
9. Bıyıklıoğlu, *Mondros Mütarekesi ve Tatbikatı*, 161.
10. Hovannisian, *The First Year*, 61.
11. Bıyıklıoğlu, *Mondros Mütarekesi ve Tatbikatı*, 163–164. See also Yel, *Yakup Şevki Paşa*, 121–129.
12. Bıyıklıoğlu, *Mondros Mütarekesi ve Tatbikatı*, 167.
13. Ibid., 170; and Ökse, Baycan, and Sakaryalı, *Komutanların Biyo-grafileri*, 178.
14. Hovannisian, *The First Year*, 237–239; and Shaw, *From Empire to Republic*, vol. 3, part 1, 926–928.
15. Hovannisian, *The First Year*, 238–240.
16. Jamil Hasanli, *Foreign Policy of the Republic of Azerbaijan: The Difficult Road to Western Integration, 1919–1920* (London: Routledge, 2016), 258–261.
17. "Minutes, Council of Four, Paris Conference" (May 5, 1919), quoted in Busch, *Mudros to Lausanne*, 155.
18. A fundamental problem for the Allies was the positions taken by White Russian General Anton Denikin. As long as the allies were commit-ted to Denikin, they could not support the Caucasian Republics, since Denikin had clearly stated that he would never accept an independent Georgia or Azerbaijan. He was more willing to discuss the existence of an

independent Armenia. As a result, both the U.K. War Office and the French in general opposed any closer support or ties to states they expected to be restored to Russia. Email with Dr. Konstantinos Travlos, December 6, 2019.

19. Hüsamettin Tugaç, *Türk İstiklâl Hârbi: IIIncü Cilt, Doğu Cephesi (1919–1921)* (Ankara: Genelkurmay Basımevi, 1965), 45.

20. Ibid., 51.

21. Timur, Atakan, Berktay, and Ertekin, *İdari Faaliyetler*, 87.

22. Allen and Muratoff, *Caucasian Battlefields*, 275–276.

23. Tugaç, *Doğu Cephesi*, 46–47.

24. Erickson, *Ottomans and Armenians*, 148, 153, 167.

25. Hovannisian, *The First Year*, 190–192.

26. Tugaç, *Doğu Cephesi*, Kroki 5 (Sketch Map 5), following page 48.

27. Richard G. Hovannisian, *The Republic of Armenia: From London to Sèvres, February–August 1920*, vol. 3 (Los Angeles: University of California Press, 1996), 347–352.

28. Tugaç, *Doğu Cephesi*, 56–58.

29. Ibid., 66–67.

30. Ibid., 81–84.

31. Michael A. Reynolds, *Shattering Empires: The Clash and Collapse of the Ottoman and Russian Empires, 1908–1918* (Cambridge: Cambridge University Press, 2011), 255.

32. Mango, *Atatürk*, 226–227. Mango presents an excellent summary of the content of the letter.

33. Ibid., 278.

34. See Shaw, *From Empire to Republic*, vol. 3, part 2, 1455–1487; and Mango, *Atatürk*, 287–297 for more comprehensive narratives of these personalities and events.

35. Shaw, *From Empire to Republic*, vol. 3, part 2, 1464–1465.

36. Ibid., 1476–1477.

37. Hovannisian, *From London to Sèvres*, 293-294.

38. Tugaç, *Doğu Cephesi*, 101–103. Tugaç asserted that an Armenian officer named "General Skobof" led this attack but did not provide a first name. I believe that Arsen Shahmazian used the name Skobof as a *nom de guerre*.

39. Hovannisian, *From London to Sèvres*, 293–296.

40. Tugaç, *Doğu Cephesi*, 104–106.

41. Hovannisian, *From London to Sèvres*, 296.

42. Tugaç, *Doğu Cephesi*, 117–118.

43. Hovannisian, *From London to Sèvres*, 298–299.

44. Görgülü, *On Yıllık Harbin Kadrosu*, 217.

45. Tugaç, *Doğu Cephesi*, 120.

46. Hovannisian, *From London to Sèvres*, 310–312.

47. Richard G. Hovannisian, *The Republic of Armenia: Between Crescent and Sickle: Partition and Sovietization*, vol. 4 (Los Angeles: University of California Press, 1996), 108–111.

48. Tugaç, *Doğu Cephesi*, 126.

49. Ibid., 129.

50. Hovannisian, *Between Crescent and Sickle*, 188.

51. Ibid., 181.

52. Tugaç, *Doğu Cephesi*, 138. See also Belen, *Türk Kurtuluş Savaşı*, 242–243.

53. Tugaç, *Doğu Cephesi*, 147. See also Shaw, *From Empire to Republic*, vol. 3, part 2, 1488. Professor Shaw asserted that the Armenians "captured Bardiz for a short time and ravag[ed] the city" but the Turkish official military history does not mention this.

54. Görgülü, *On Yıllık Harbin Kadrosu*, 217–218.

55. Tugaç, *Doğu Cephesi*, 141.

56. Saim Besbelli and İhsan Göymen, *Türk İstiklâl Hârbi Vnci Cilt, Deniz Cephesi ve Hava Harekâtı* (Ankara: Genelkurmay Basımevi, 1964), 125–131. The authors stated that the Turks had about 10 Russian type aircraft and several German Albatross aircraft.

57. "Eastern Front Strength Returns, September 1920," in Tugaç, *Doğu Cephesi*, Ek 9 (Document 9), following page 298.

58. Hovannisian, *Between Crescent and Sickle*, 184–185

59. Tugaç, *Doğu Cephesi*, 142–143.

60. Ibid., 142–144.

61. Belen, *Türk Kurtuluş Savaşı*, 244.

62. Tugaç, *Doğu Cephesi*, 153–155. The author detailed Karabekir's operational order.

63. Hovannisian, *Between Crescent and Sickle*, 194–195

64. Tugaç, *Doğu Cephesi*, 162–164.

65. Hovannisian, *Between Crescent and Sickle*, 196.

66. Tugaç, *Doğu Cephesi*, 168.

67. Hovannisian, *Between Crescent and Sickle*, 197–198.

68. Ibid., 204–205.

69. Shaw, *From Empire to Republic*, vol. 3, part 2, 1489.

70. Ciphered telegram to Eastern Front Commander from Council of Ministers, 7-10-1336 (1920), *Kar'a Taarruz İçin Bakanlar Kurulu Kararı*, quoted in Tugaç, *Doğu Cephesi*, Ek: 11 (Document 11) 303.

71. Shaw, *From Empire to Republic*, vol. 3, part 2, 1491–1493.

72. Hovannisian, *Between Crescent and Sickle*, 242.

73. Tugaç, *Doğu Cephesi*, 175.

74. Ibid., 173–176.

75. Hovannisian, *Between Crescent and Sickle*, 244.

76. Tugaç, *Doğu Cephesi*, 182.

77. Ibid., 191–193.

78. Belen, *Türk Kurtuluş Savaşı*, 250–293.

79. Hovannisian, *Between Crescent and Sickle*, 251.

80. Tugaç, *Doğu Cephesi*, 196.

81. Hovannisian, *Between Crescent and Sickle*, 256.

82. Tugaç, *Doğu Cephesi*, 203.

83. Hovannisian, *Between Crescent and Sickle*, 259

84. Ibid., 204.

85. Shaw, *From Empire to Republic*, vol. 3, part 2, 1501; and Hovannisian, *Between Crescent and Sickle*, 266–272.

86. Tugaç, *Doğu Cephesi*, 139–140.

87. Ibid., 210.

88. Ibid., Kroki 34 (Sketch Map 34), following page 210.

89. Belen, *Türk Kurtuluş Savaşı*, 252.

90. Tugaç, *Doğu Cephesi*, 211–212.

91. Shaw, *From Empire to Republic*, vol. 3, part 2, 1498.

92. Ibid., 1500; and Hovannisian, *Between Crescent and Sickle*, 278–282.

93. Tugaç, *Doğu Cephesi*, 225–226.

94. See Shaw, *From Empire to Republic*, vol. 3, part 2, 1501–1152 for the clauses and terms, as well as an excellent explanation of why the treaty was not ratified.

95. Shaw, *From Empire to Republic*, vol. 3, part 2, 1549–1561.

96. Tugaç, *Doğu Cephesi*, 245–250.

97. Ibid., Kroki 42 (Sketch Map 42), following page 248.

98. Görgülü, *On Yıllık Harbin Kadrosu*, 222.

99. Tugaç, *Doğu Cephesi*, 250.

100. Ibid., 254–255.

101. Ibid., 261.

102. Görgülü, *On Yıllık Harbin Kadrosu*, 223.

103. Tugaç, *Doğu Cephesi*, 266–268.

SIX

The Franco-Turkish War

The French Government, having accepted responsibility for the protection of the Armenian people, the British Government will consent to the immediate dispatch of French troops via Alexandretta and Mersina for this purpose.[1]

Philip Kerr to Lloyd George, 1919

INTRODUCTION

Wartime agreements such as the Sykes-Picot agreement in 1916, allotted substantial parts of Ottoman territory to French occupation, including modern Lebanon and Syria. However, the British and Indian armies essentially won the war in the Middle East against the Ottomans with very little help from the French. Thus, the French were latecomers to the actual occupation of their share of the Ottoman Empire. The area known as Cilicia (a name originating in ancient times) included what is now south-central Turkey, including Adana, Iskenderun (Alexandretta), Maraş, Mersin, and Urfa. Unlike Palestine, Syria, and Mesopotamia, Cilicia had not been conquered during the war, but, under the terms of the Mudros armistice, the Ottomans agreed to withdraw their army from Cilicia. From the Ottoman perspective, withdrawal did not translate into occupation, but the Allies exceeded what they had agreed to and occupied the area in late 1918. In turn, the Ottomans obstructed and contested the occupation, and complicating this situation, the Armenian delegation at the Paris Peace Conference convinced the French to support their aspirational claims to Cilicia. These conflicting claims led to the short Franco-Turkish War.

THE OTTOMAN WITHDRAWAL AND PROGRESSIVE OCCUPATION

The Allied occupation of Cilicia and what is now southeast Turkey was initially the responsibility of General Sir Edmund Allenby, commander of the British Egyptian Expeditionary Force.[2] Allenby's specified tasks, under the terms of the armistice, were the occupation of strategic points (clause 7) and the withdrawal of Ottoman troops from Cilicia, except those necessary to maintain order (clause 16), as will be determined under clause 5 (immediate demobilization). In Allenby's area of responsibility, the key strategic points were the two railroad tunnel complexes at Pozantı and Amanus. Initially Allenby's opposite numbers were Second Army commander, Major General Nihat (Anılmış) Pasha, in Cilicia and Sixth Army commander, Major General Ali İnsan (Sabis) Pasha, in upper Mesopotamia. Because his operational force was already on the ground in Cilicia and Syria, Allenby assigned the mission to Lieutenant General Sir Henry G. Chauvel, the commander of the Desert Mounted Corps with its headquarters in Homs.[3]

As previously presented, the Ottoman General Staff inactivated the Yildirim Army Group and the Ottoman Seventh Army on November 4, 1918 and assigned the remaining army formations to the Ottoman Second Army headquarters in Adana. The earliest confrontations began on November 3, when French torpedo boats appeared in the Iskenderun (Alexandretta) harbor, which generated a spate of cables between the army and the government about how to implement the clauses of the armistice concerning the occupation of strategic points.[4] Mustafa Kemal, then in command of the Second Army, received clear instructions from the General Staff to allow British and French officers free use of the port and a road through the former front lines from Aleppo to Iskenderun. Kemal began to withdraw his army from Iskenderun and Antakya (Antioch) on November 9 but turned over control of the army to Nihat Pasha on November 10. Nihat continued the withdrawal from Adana Province and the key railroad tunnel complexes at Pozantı (west to Konya through the Toros Mountains) and Amanus (east toward Mosul through the Amanus Mountains). Under protest, Nihat allowed Allied officers to come ashore in Iskenderun.

A conference was arranged between Nihat and Allenby's representative, British Brigadier General Goland V. Clarke at Raco on November 12, 1918, at which Clarke demanded a timetable of occupations and permissions.[5]

Clarke demanded that the Ottoman Army withdraw west of the Ceyhan River by December 1 and north of a line drawn between Islahiye-Misis. By December 5, they would withdraw west of the Seyhan River and withdraw west of Pozantı by December 14. Moreover, he insisted that Nihat's army demobilize and turn over weapons as prescribed by the armistice agreement and return all prisoners of war held in the area. Last, he told Nihat that as of 6:00 p.m. that day, the British Army would consider the Aleppo-Katma-Iskenderun road open to the Allies. The Ottomans had no choice but to accept these terms. On November 23/24, Nihat's chief of staff reported to the British headquarters that the withdrawals were going smoothly and that Nihat expected to complete them on time; that the army had no heavy artillery, as all had been lost in Palestine; that the infantry divisions were being reduced to the cadre strength permitted by the Allies; that he was transporting his sick on the railroads; and that he expected returning demobilized soldiers from the Ottoman Sixth Army in Mesopotamia to transit his roads en route home.

Under the armistice terms, the Ottomans brought in a mere 26 artillery pieces of mixed types and 47 machine guns to Katma to turn over to the British on December 4. The demobilization continued, and by December 14, the III Corps headquarters departed for Sivas, the XV Corps headquarters departed for Erzurum, and the 44th Division inactivated.[6] This left the Second Army with two corps headquarters (XII and XX Corps) and five reduced-scale infantry divisions. The Second Army headquarters was inactivated on December 15 and, under the prewar inspectorate system, reconstituted as the Second Army Inspectorate.[7] While on the surface the demobilization appeared to be proceeding smoothly, Allenby was unhappy with Nihat, who was "a master of the arts of obstruction and procrastination" and tried to evade the terms of the armistice by leaving soldiers behind "in the guise of gendarmerie."[8] According to the British official history, Allenby had even greater difficulties with Ali İnsan, who was actively anti-British and anti-Armenian.

Allenby ordered detachments from the British 5th Cavalry Division to occupy Gaziantepe (Aintab), Iskenderun, Islahiye, Maraş, Arab Punar, and Jerablus on the Euphrates. As a result of his distrust of the Ottomans, Allenby reinforced the Desert Mounted Corps with the 28th Indian Infantry Brigade and ordered the infantry to occupy Kilis, Birecik, Urfa, and Maraş.[9] The British and Indians occupied Kilis and Gaziantepe on December 24,[10] but logistical difficulties delayed the occupation of Maraş and Birecik until February 1919 and Urfa until March 1919.[11] Due to political understandings with France, Allenby divided the "Occupied Enemy Territory Administration" (commonly recorded then as OETA) into two parts, western Cilicia composed of the Ottoman vilayet of Adana under French administration and the area of Cilicia to the east of the Adana vilayet under the control of the Desert Mounted Corps.[12]

The French had very few forces available at the end of the war in the Eastern Mediterranean and planned to shift General Jules C. Hamelin's Troupes Françaises du Levant from Syria into Cilicia.[13] To make up the shortfalls of men, France planned to employ the La Légion d'Orient, a brigade-sized formation of about four thousand Armenian soldiers, then stationed in Beirut. The Armenians were volunteers, organized in battalions and led by French officers. They were poorly trained and famously prone to indiscipline.[14] Altogether, Hamelin had some 7,000 soldiers available for occupation duty. There were geopolitical dimensions to this because at the end of the war, the Armenian legation in Paris was beginning to push for the creation of an independent Armenia. The Armenian 4th Battalion, under the command of Lieutenant Colonel Louis Romieu, occupied Dörtyol on December 11, commandeering 12 houses.[15] The Ottoman Army abandoned Adana on December 13, and, four days later, 1,500 French Algerian soldiers and the Armenian 1st, 2nd, and 3rd Battalions landed at the port of Mersin, immediately occupying Tarsus, Adana, and Misis. In addition to the Ottoman Army withdrawal, the local Jandarma had left the area as well, leaving the area vulnerable to civilian victimization. On December 17, the French and Armenians pushed farther inland, occupying additional areas.

In the British zone, beset with claims from Armenians, the British established a Reparations Committee in Aleppo with representatives in Gaziantepe and Maraş.[16] Attempts were made to evict squatters from Armenian homes abandoned during the wartime relocations, but these efforts were resisted by former Ottoman officials and CUP adherents. Displaced Armenians flocked to the committee offices, attempting to receive some sort of monetary compensation, and the British were overwhelmed with claims. The British dispatched the 19th Indian Infantry Brigade and 13th Cavalry Brigade to keep order in Gaziantepe and Maraş respectively. The Desert Mounted Corps was inactivated on June 7, 1919, and administration of occupied territory was taken over by Northforce, under the command of Major General George Barrow, composed of the 4th and 5th Cavalry Divisions and two divisions of infantry.[17] Northforce continued the occupation of southeast Anatolia with the 5th Cavalry Division and also "took over the administration of the Baghdad Railway from Constantinople to the railhead east of Nusaybin in Mesopotamia."[18]

In the French zone, the French General Staff appointed Colonel Edouard Brémond on January 30, 1919, as chief administrator of Cilicia, which he exercised from the city of Adana (Brémond would serve there until September 4, 1920). The French occupation regime has been characterized as excessively harsh, including such measures as surrendering personal weapons, selling property and goods at far below market value, removing all symbols of Ottoman sovereignty, and restrictions on movement and gathering in public.[19] Also in February, the La Légion d'Orient was renamed the Légion Arménienne. Unfortunately, problems with collective discipline began with the Armenian battalions immediately upon their deployment into Cilicia, and there were many well-documented instances of civilian victimization of all kinds at their hands.[20] Unruly Armenian soldiers even clashed with French Algerian soldiers, and the Armenian 4th Battalion was dissolved in February 1919. However, the criminality of this handful of Armenian soldiers was only part of Muslim unrest in Cilicia; it was the return of displaced Ottoman Armenians and the immigration of Ottoman Armenians from the western provinces of the empire that drove many Muslims into the arms of the Nationalists.

THE ARMENIANS AND THE FRENCH

Colonel Brémond was not the instigator of the Armenian repopulation of Cilicia, but he was favorably inclined to the Armenians and did not stand in the way of efforts to repatriate displaced persons or reacquire lost property.[21] Moreover, Allenby was inclined to repatriate displaced Armenians from the Aleppo area and the concentration camps in the Euphrates Valley because he saw them as an impediment to turning over Syria and Palestine to the Arabs, then envisioned by the Allies.[22] Spring 1919 "swelled the stream of Armenians into Cilicia to a raging torrent."[23] Cilicia was the only region "to which Armenians repatriated in large numbers."[24] By the end of the year, Brémond estimated that 120,000 Armenians had resettled in Cilicia. Historian Stanford Shaw noted of that total, 70,000 settled in Adana, 12,000 in Dörtyol, 8,000 in Hacın (Saimbeyli after October 1920), and the remainder elsewhere in Cilicia. Shaw also noted that in addition to these numbers, some 50,000 Armenians from Istanbul and the western provinces immigrated to Gaziantepe, Maraş, and Zeytun, "all for the purpose of establishing an Armenian state in Cilicia under the permanent protection of France."[25] Although the British and French believed that these mass movements of people would not cause significant disruption, the opposite became the norm. Making things worse, Brémond had no funding available to assist the influx of hundreds of thousands of impoverished refugees entering an occupation zone with a collapsed economy.

While Colonel Brémond had no money to spend on caring for the Armenians, he had plenty of weapons to give them.[26] These came from the stocks of confiscated arms as well as from former Ottoman Army stocks turned in under the terms of the armistice.[27] Altogether, by mid-1919, the French armed irregular Armenian bands with military-grade weapons. With 2,000 men in Gaziantepe and another 2,000 in Maraş (these totals include the men of the Armenian Legion), 1,500 in Hacın, 1,000 in Urfa, 500 in Zeytun, 350 in Şar, 300 in Kozan, 1,000 in Adana and Mersin, and 1,000 in Osmaniye and Bahçe—altogether, 10,500 men.[28] Moreover, soldiers of the Armenian Legion chose desertion in increasing numbers rather than submit to the discipline (and punishment for crimes) imposed by the French Army, further swelling the number of armed men in irregular Armenian bands. In summer 1919, a wave of widespread violence against unprotected local Turks and Muslims by irregular Armenian bands swept through Cilicia.[29] The failure of the French to prevent anti-Muslim violence served as a powerful instrument for the formation and increased recruitment of irregular Turkish Nationalist militias.

THE BRITISH WITHDRAWAL AND THE RISE OF NATIONALIST RESISTANCE

General Allenby was unhappy with his instructions from London regarding the turnover of large areas conquered by his army, but he was determined to implement the Anglo-French agreements. London had already instructed Allenby to hand over Syria, Lebanon, and Cilicia to the French by November 1, 1919.[30] As such, Allenby regarded the British occupation of these areas as temporary, and he was agreeable to the French reinforcing their forces in Cilicia.[31] Because of the disintegration of the Armenian Legion, the French sent the 412th Infantry Regiment to reinforce Colonel Brémond in midsummer 1919. The French high command planned other changes for the region as well, including the dispatch of four infantry divisions as an army of occupation. On October 9, France activated the Army of the Levant under the command of General Henri

Gouraud, who was also given the title of French high commissioner for Syria and Cilicia.[32]

Allenby's staff prepared a timetable and plan for the final withdrawals of British forces from the areas to be handed over to the French. The British withdrew its northernmost garrisons, such as Urfa, first and progressively withdrew toward the sea. Colonel Brémond had few troops available to fill in behind the departing British to ensure security for the Armenians, but he and the Adana military commander, Colonel Marie de Piépape, sent some small detachments to Gaziantepe and Maraş. According to historian Richard Hovannisian, "Unlike the departing British battalions, the French had neither airplanes nor armored cars, heavy artillery nor automatic weapons, wireless transmitters nor swift courier service."[33] The French intended to rectify this by deploying the 156th Division from Istanbul to Cilicia, but most of its heavy equipment went to Beirut rather than Adana. In December 1919, the 156th Division was renamed the Division of Cilicia and, in January 1920, renamed again as the 1st Division of the Army of the Levant. Major General Julien Dufieux commanded this division, which composed two brigades: the 1st Brigade, composing the 412th Infantry Regiment, the Armenian Legion, and the 18th Regiment of Senegalese Tirailleurs, and the 2nd Brigade, composed of the 17th and 18th Regiments of Algerian Tirailleurs.[34] The 412th Infantry Regiment was, thus, the only metropolitan regiment in Dufieux's division (the other being French colonial regiments).

A 2nd French Infantry Division composed the garrison in Syria and Lebanon, giving Gouraud only about 20,000 soldiers to cover his entire area of responsibility and to replace the 48,000 British and Indian soldiers withdrawn in fall 1919. In addition to shortfalls in manpower, the basic tactical problem for the French Army in Cilicia was its geography.[35] The area to the south of the Taurus Mountains around Adana enjoyed good road networks and was close to ports on the Mediterranean. However, the area east of the Amanus Mountain chain, accessed by a single railroad tunnel and poor secondary roads, was at the extreme limit of French operational reach. Distance and communications worked against the French and multiplied the ease with which the Nationalists could organize and arm militia groups.

Nationalist resistance to the haphazard and heavy-handed occupation of southeast Anatolia and Cilicia began immediately, as foreign armies flowed into the Ottoman provinces. As discussed previously, irregular Nationalist militias quickly coalesced around determined men, who were

often former officers or respected local leaders. By February 1919, irregu-
lar militia groups emerged in the major cities and towns of Anatolia, and
Cilicia was no exception. The decisions taken at the Sivas Congress on
September 11, 1919, regarding the formation of the National Army and its
integration with the National Forces, energized and altered the nature of
resistance in Cilicia.[36] As discussed in chapter 2, the Ottoman Army's XIII
Corps in Diyarbakir responded to Ali Fuat's call to arms and joined the
Nationalists in mid-September. This enabled Mustafa Kemal to issue
orders to the XIII Corps on October 26 to help the local National Forces
fight the French occupation of Gaziantepe, Urfa, and Maraş.[37]

On November 1, 1919, Kemal appointed an artillery officer named
Major Kozanoğlu Doğan (Kemal Doğan) as the Commander of Nationalist
Forces in Cilicia.[38] Major Doğan organized two strongly led and
well-organized subordinate militia organizations in southern Anatolia: the
Western Adana Nationalist Force led by Captain Ali Ratip (also known as
Tekelioğlu Sinan Pasha)[39] and the Eastern Adana Nationalist Force led by
Captain Osman Nuri (Tufan).[40] The Western Adana Nationalist Force had
Nationalist militia detachments in Mersin-Silifke, Tarsus, Kavaklıhan,
Pozantı, Kozan, and Kadirli; and the Eastern Adana Nationalist Force had
Nationalist militia groups in Hacın, Ceyhan, Osmaniye-Bahçe-Islahiye,
Dörtyol, Karahan, and Belen.[41] In this way, the irregular militias came
under the aegis of the Nationalist Forces, giving Kemal a powerful tool of
resistance to oppose the occupation of southeast Anatolia.

The Maraş Defense of Rights Society met at the Ulu Cami mosque to
organize resistance on November 29, as well as to solicit more weapons
from the regular formations of the Nationalist Army.[42] This soon became
publicly known and, in turn, alarmed repatriated Armenians also began to
acquire arms. Responding to the unrest, and likely sensing opportunity,
the Nationalists sent Captain Ali Saip (Ursavaş) and an ex-army officer
named Kılıç Ali to Urfa to organize the Nationalist militia there. [43] They
arrived on December 19, and they brought a machine gun platoon with
them. Moreover, Colonel Hüseyin Selahattin (Çolak), commander of the
III Corps in Sivas, had already prepositioned 800 military rifles in Elbi-
stan, 70 kilometers north of Maraş.[44] On December 23, Kılıç Ali led a
group of Nationalist irregulars from the village of Pazarcık in ambushing
and destroying a French column coming to Urfa from Gaziantepe. Colonel
Selahattin sent word to Kemal on January 4, 1920 that the prepositioned
rifles were in the hands of Kılıç Ali and that he was sending more machine
guns to the group.[45] The Nationalists were now poised to test French

resolve with fighting strength. Historian Robert Zeidner has suggested that Kemal picked Maraş for its geographically exposed position away from the main French force and sent Kılıç Ali there to generate an incident.[46] Three days later, a French column "ravaged a village near Maraş, burning 35 homes, killing 23 people and making off with 2,500 animals, before itself being attacked by Kılıç Ali and suffering heavy losses before arriving at Maraş."[47] Photographs of the dead and destroyed homes were sent to Kemal on January 13.[48] Making things worse, a contingent of the Armenian Legion bivouacked in the village of Araptar on the night of January 12 and committed a large number of outrages against the Muslim villagers, thereby further inflaming tensions between the French and the Turks.

The French, who were now strung out along the lines of communication or garrisoning cities and major towns, were at a severe disadvantage as they confronted what amounted to a guerrilla war. Aware of these problems and faced with the geographic isolation of the area, on January 6, Major General Dufieux ordered his deputy in Gaziantepe, Brigadier-General Louis Albert Querette, to move his headquarters and brigade of 1,500 soldiers to Maraş.[49] Quérette arrived there on January 13 to find heavily armed groups of Armenians facing off with similar groups of heavily armed Muslims, both of which had fortified their neighborhoods.[50] Dufieux ordered reinforcements to join Quérette, who, by January 17, had more than 2,000 French and Algerian soldiers in the city.[51] Altogether, he had an infantry regiment, four artillery batteries, two cavalry detachments, four armored cars, eight Nordenfelt "pompoms," and 2,000 armed Armenian volunteers, giving Quérette some 4,500 to 5,000 men.[52]

THE SIEGE OF MARAŞ AND OTHER FRENCH DISASTERS

On January 19, 1919, Quérette sent an infantry battalion and a cavalry detachment to open the road to Pazarcık. Alerted to this, Kılıç Ali used the local telephone system to organize an ambush at the Aksu Bridge, which turned the French back.[53] Effectively cut off from his higher headquarters in Adana, Quérette brought the Muslim civil, religious, and community leaders of Maraş into his headquarters on January 21 in an attempt to calm the situation but ended by threatening reprisals.[54] Immediately after the talks terminated, gunfire erupted throughout the city—the 22-day siege of Maraş had begun. In response, French artillery began to pound away at Muslim and Turkish neighborhoods, destroying many houses. The previously well-organized Nationalist and Armenian defense groups joined the fight, and the city was soon in ruins. Kılıç Ali's irregulars surrounded the city, cutting it off completely. Colonel Selahattin, the III Corps commander in Sivas, connected by telegraph with Kılıç Ali, received news of the outbreak and immediately sent trained officers to assist the local Nationalists. General Dufieux, having not provided Quérette with radios, did not learn of the siege until January 28 when a survivor of one of Kılıç Ali's ambushes reached Adana.[55]

By the end of January, Quérette was beginning to run short of food and rations for his soldiers and for the Armenian civilians trapped in the city.[56] They were also running short of artillery shells and machine gun ammunition. The Nationalists were not alone in the struggle against occupation and Captain Ali Saip gathered several hundred Kurdish and Arab tribesmen to threaten the French garrison in Urfa, further tying up the ability of the French to relieve Quérette. It was not until January 31 that Dufieux received "first-hand accounts of the critical situation in Maraş" after which he decided to send a relief column under Lieutenant Colonel Robert Normand to break the siege.[57]

Normand was reinforced with artillery and aircraft sent from Beirut by General Gouraud, and he led his force north from the village of İslahiye. Normand's force composed an infantry regiment, four artillery batteries, cavalry, and substantial amount of food and ammunition.[58] Morale among the beleaguered French defenders was buoyed when a lone French airplane, sent by Normand, appeared over the city on February 6. It took Normand several days to fight his way through the 70 kilometers to Maraş, but on February 7, he reached the southern suburbs of Maraş and opened an intense artillery bombardment of the Nationalist positions. That evening, Normand finally broke through the Nationalist lines. Although the relief was successful in the short run, Normand had sustained casualties in his relief march, and he was now in the same situation as Quérette—isolated and with limited supplies. Over the next two days, Normand and Quérette had bitter discussions about what to do next.[59] In the end, Normand, who was convinced that Urfa was about to explode in revolt, persuaded Quérette that the sensible course of action was to withdraw to İslahiye, where they could connect with the main French army. Normand was also very concerned about the bitterly cold weather and the fact that the French had rapidly diminishing supplies of food, fodder, and fuel, and he carried instructions from Dufieux that the safety of the force was the primary objective (rather than the security of the Armenian inhabitants of the city).[60] Ironically, at the same time, the Nationalists also ran low on supplies of food and ammunition, and they sent a delegate to Quérette's headquarters to negotiate a truce; however, the French had already made their decision.

Quérette ordered a withdrawal, which began at 3:00 a.m. on February 11, accompanied by the explosions of the French munitions dumps. The Nationalists contested the withdrawal with ambushes along the roads and by fortifying the Aksu Bridge. A French battalion, led by Major Bernard, fought its way across the bridge on February 12 but at the cost of some 50 dead.[61] The Armenian civilian population was caught in Quérette's tragic withdrawal, and thousands attempted to flee by following the rear of the French column. Hundreds were cut down by Nationalist fire as they vacated their fortified neighborhoods and churches.[62] American historian Richard Hovannisian characterized the flight of some 4,000 to 5,000 Armenians as a "death march" lasting three days in bitter winter weather, at the end of which, only 1,500 struggled into İslahiye.[63] About 8,500 Armenians remained in the city and were interned by the Nationalists without reprisals. French casualties during the siege and withdrawal totaled about 160 killed, 170 missing, 280 wounded, and 300 severely frostbitten (most of which seemed to be Senegalese and Algerians). The Nationalists reported 200 dead and 500 wounded.[64]

Driving the French from the city of Maraş was a momentous victory for the Nationalists, marking the end of French attempts to maintain long-term control of Cilicia. It also encouraged Anatolia-wide support for the Nationalists and brought Armenian aspirations for the inclusion of Cilicia in a Greater Armenia to a halt. The French vigorously protested the attacks on their soldiers, as did the Armenian delegation protest the massacres of Armenian civilians. The European newspapers bestowed the name Maraş Massacre and covered the gory details using greatly inflated numbers, which were later revised downward.[65]

The initial success of isolating Maraş led to further Nationalist efforts against occupation. Five hundred armed Armenians, who had been terrorizing the locals, were surrounded in the village of Haçın (85 kilometers northwest of Maraş) by Major Kemal Doğan on February 3 and held there until they broke out in October.[66] Captain Ali Saip isolated Major G. Hauger's French garrison of 700 soldiers in Urfa on February 9 in a siege lasting two months.[67] Like Quérette in Maraş, Hauger had no radios, and Saip cut the telegraph lines. At the end, the starving French surrendered but were allowed to depart Urfa. However, on the road out, they were ambushed and wiped out on April 11 by a large band of Kurdish tribesmen.[68]

There were outbreaks of anti-French and anti-Armenian resistance throughout Cilicia. In the city of Gaziantepe, the Nationalist Antep Defense of Rights group watched Colonel Normand (who had survived the withdrawal from Maraş) lead most of the French garrison out of the city to reinforce Urfa on April 1 and took advantage of the opportunity to rise in rebellion. The well-armed Nationalists quickly fortified their own Turkish quarter of the city and began to attack the Armenian quarter and the remaining French garrison.[69] The French Army and the Armenians rapidly isolated the Nationalists in what became known as the siege of Gaziantepe, which lasted for the next 10 months. Elsewhere in Cilicia, Emin Aslan (Karataş) raised a nationalist militia in Konya and led it to attack the port of Mersin in mid-February; however, his guerrillas could not hold the port (see map 6.1). From March through August 1920, the Nationalists fought numerous firefights and small battles with the French and Armenians.[70]

Perhaps the most important loss for the French in this period was their failure to retain control of the strategically important railroad tunnel complex through the Taurus Mountains at Pozantı (which allowed French reinforcements and supplies to travel by rail from Istanbul to Adana). The complex was guarded by a large French garrison of over 1,000 soldiers under the command of Major Pierre Mesnil. On April 1, 1920, Mustafa Kemal ordered Lieutenant Colonel Mümtaz, the commander of the 11th Division in Niğde, to support an effort to reclaim the tunnels.[71] In turn, Mümtaz ordered the 33rd, 126th, and 136th Infantry Regiments to provide infantry detachments with machine guns for the operation. The local Nationalist militias had about 500 armed men and 3,000 unarmed men available. On April 8–9, the Nationalists, under the overall command of Captain Ali Ratip (Tekelioğlu Sinan) began to cut off the roads and bridges to Pozantı.

The French sent a regimental force of 3,000 men with artillery and armored cars to relieve Mesnil and his 2nd Battalion, 412th Infantry Regiment in Pozantı on April 11. But the Nationalist militias successfully blocked them at Kavaklıhan (10 kilometers north of Tarsus) the next day, forcing the French relief column to retreat.[72] The French launched a second relief attempt on May 19–21, but Ali Ratip had used the interval to fortify the Kavaklıhan position and to station regular soldiers on the flanks. The French attacked with infantry and artillery on May 21, but their attacks failed when Ali Ratip launched enveloping attacks. The Nationalists pursued them into Tarsus. In a final desperate attempt to relieve Mesnil,

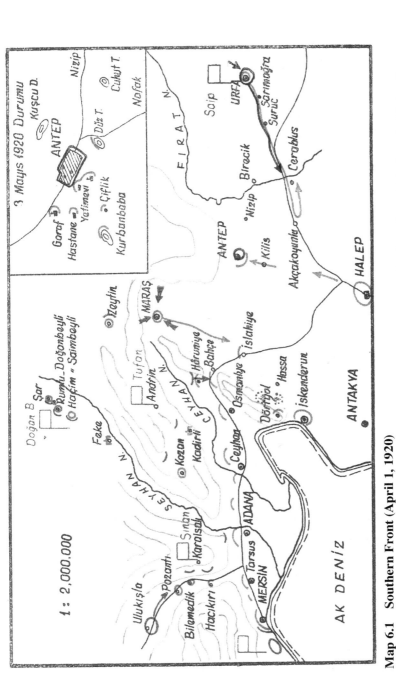

Map 6.1 Southern Front (April 1, 1920)

The fighting on the southeastern front was a mix of conventional and unconventional combat, which, from the Nationalist perspective, was an economy of force measure. The Nationalist campaign was designed to exhaust the French into abandoning
Cilicia rather than defeating them militarily. The compartmentalized geography of Cilicia, especially the Amanus range,
imposed severe operational limitations on the French, making the war unwinnable. On this map, Gaziantepe is shown as Antep.

Courtesy of the Turkish General Staff Military History and Strategy Institute (ATASE).

General Dufieux took personal command of the relief and attempted to push through behind an armored train on May 25.[73] However, the Nationalists had torn up the railway, and this attempt also failed.

Now isolated for several months and running low on supplies, Major Mesnil held what one historian has called "a veritable Dien Bien Phu in miniature"—a main bastion surrounded by small outposts that were gradually being overrun by the Nationalists.[74] Facing a hopeless situation, Mesnil laid plans to evacuate the tunnel complex and attempt a breakout to safety. On the night of May 25, 1920, General Dufieux ordered him to attempt a withdrawal on the mountain paths leading to Mersin. Mesnil led his men south as ordered, leaving his sick and wounded behind who could not make the treacherous journey. The next night, over 50 kilometers from Pozantı, Mesnil's overextended and exhausted column was ambushed in a narrow defile. Asked to surrender to what he erroneously believed to be a much larger force, Mesnil surrendered to a small force of Nationalist militia.[75]

THE CEASE-FIRE AND OPERATIONAL REORGANIZATION

As the French position in Cilicia collapsed in spring 1920, General Gouraud asked the ministry of war for reinforcements. He also began to shift Major General Marie de Lamothe's 2nd Division of the Army of the Levant from the Bekaa Valley to the port of Iskenderun on February 11, 1920.[76] De Lamothe's division was then stationed between Aleppo and İslahiye, putting de Lamothe in a position to relieve Dufieux of responsibility for operations east of the Amanus ranges. On May 1, the French high command moved a division from Istanbul to Iskenderun, which became Gouraud's 4th Division, commanded by Major General Fernand Goubeau. Meanwhile in Beirut General Mariano Goybet organized the 3rd Division, finally giving Gouraud four complete infantry divisions and 80,000 men to deal with the Nationalists and the Syrian Arabs. Thereafter in Cilicia, Gouraud's operational posture deployed Dufieux's 1st Division in the Adana-Amanus sector and de Lamothe's 2nd Division east of the Amanus range (which ran north-south).

Gouraud continually needed more men to contain the Nationalists, and he asked the General Staff for permission to reconstitute the Armenian Legion, which had been significantly reduced by desertions and casualties. The French General Staff responded that it was not in the interests of

France to retain the Armenian Legion, and it was ordered disbanded on August 1, 1920.[77] However, Colonel Brémond organized many of the discharged legionnaires as an Armenian gendarmerie, under the command of John Aram Shishmanian, and they carried on with criminal behavior until the final French withdrawal.[78]

Despite these increases in manpower, Gouraud desired an operational pause to restore morale and to complete his reorganizations geographically. At higher levels, there had already been numerous discussions between Kemal and the French regarding either a cease-fire or a mutually acceptable ending to the conflict in Cilicia.[79] Negotiations were long and tumultuous, but, in the end, the French agreed on May 23 to withdraw their forces south of the Mersin-Tarsus-Adana-İslahiye rail line and to bring de Lamothe's forces out of Gaziantepe.[80] Unknown to the French negotiators, east of the Amanus range, the newly arrived General de Lamothe delivered a serious defeat to the Nationalists at Akbaba on May 22, inflicting some 1,500 casualties on them. The cease-fire was scheduled to go into effect at midnight May 29/30 and to last for 20 days, during which prisoners would be exchanged, and after which both parties could request an extension.

Both sides endeavored to carry out the agreed-upon terms explicitly and honorably. While there were violations, the French withdrew to the agreed-upon line, and de Lamothe withdrew beyond the range of his artillery from Gaziantepe. Thousands of Armenians fled with the withdrawing French forces behind the agreed-upon line. However, according to Turkish sources, Armenians deliberately sought to violate the cease-fire hoping to cause its collapse. These violations, in combination with the landing of French reinforcements at Zonguldak on the Black Sea on June 8, enraged Kemal; on June 17, he denounced the cease-fire, which expired two days later.[81]

Now convinced that the fighting in Cilicia would continue Kemal and İsmet made major structural changes on June 26, 1920 to the operational posture of the Nationalist war effort in southeast Anatolia by activating two fronts and a corps headquarters.[82] Kemal appointed Colonel Mehmet Selahattin (Adil) as commander of the Adana Front and the new II Corps. Under his command, he had the 9th (to be activated in September) and 41st Divisions, and the Adana-Kavaklıhan, Tarsus, Mersin, Seyhan, Kıyı, and Çakıt Nationalist militia groups.[83] East of the Amanus range, Kemal appointed Brigadier General Nihat Pasha (Anılmış) as the Elcezire Front commander and placed Colonel Ahmet Cevdet's XIII Corps under his command.[84] Colonel Cevdet's headquarters was in

Diyarbakir, and his corps was composed of the 2nd and 5th Divisions. Thus, in the same manner as Gouraud had divided responsibility for the defense of Cilicia geographically along the Amanus Mountain range, so too did the Nationalists follow suit.

THE RESUMPTION OF HOSTILITIES

Summer 1920 went badly for the French in Cilicia, as the Nationalists resumed offensive operations. In the west, Selahattin's 139th Infantry Regiment and Nationalist militias attacked Tarsus on July 15, driving the French out of the town a week later and capturing many abandoned supplies.[85] Kemal and Fevzi travelled to Pozantı on August 5 to coordinate guerrilla operations.[86] Kemal ordered the II Corps to continue its offensive in early August, with Selahattin's forces advancing to the northern hills overlooking Adana.

In the east, the Nationalists maintained their grip on the Turkish quarter of Gaziantepe, but de Lamothe isolated them after the cease-fire ended. Nihat was determined to relieve the town and launched a night attack on Gaziantepe with the 9th Infantry Regiment, supported by artillery on July 29.[87] The French took up defensive positions on the hills to the northwest but continued to isolate the town. Determined to take the town, Nihat reinforced the effort with the 24th Infantry Regiment, a dozen Nationalist militia groups, and several tribal militias—altogether, around 500 regular soldiers and 2,000 militia under the command of Major Fikri. These forces surrounded Gaziantepe over the first two weeks of August. Major Fikri launched a night attack on August 18/19, and, by morning, Nationalist militias entered parts of the town.[88] However, there were not enough artillery munitions available to dislodge the French, who were running very short of food and fodder. On August 21, the French, under Colonel Charles Joseph Edouard Andréa and Lieutenant Colonel Maurice Abadi, conducted a violent counterattack supported by heavy artillery and armored cars.[89] The battle raged for three days, and the French renewed the siege. While the Nationalists were unable to dislodge the French force of 3,000 soldiers and 16 artillery pieces, the French were isolated because the Nationalists blockaded the roads from Kilis.

On September 20, the French sent a reinforced battalion south from Gaziantepe to clear the roads, but it was stopped at the Nafak defile by the 1st Battalion, 9th Infantry Regiment. Both sides saw the retention of

Gaziantepe as the tactical key to the eastern sector. Chief of Staff İsmet sent orders to Nihat demanding that he take control of the town; however, both sides were exhausted by the battles for Gaziantepe.

The intensity of Nationalist resistance over the summer months troubled Gouraud who, in addition to facing the Nationalists in Cilicia, faced a significant Arab nationalist movement in Syria, which forced him to divide his forces in different directions. When the cease-fire with Kemal ended Gouraud was tied up in the reoccupation of Damascus—operations that consumed his attention for the remainder of the summer. On September 18, a discouraged Gouraud met with Dufieux and Brémond and told them he intended to withdraw entirely from Cilicia. In preparation for withdrawal, the French began transferring civil administration back to the Turks and removing Armenian administrators who had filled positions in the interim. "Thus, the shooting phase of the war appeared at an end."[90] However, in France on September 24, Georges Leygues became both premier and foreign minister, and he immediately stopped Gouraud's planned abandonment of Cilicia. Moreover, in October, the government ordered Gouraud to resume offensive operations to reclaim Cilicia.

THE STRUGGLE FOR GAZIANTEPE

As subsequent events demonstrate, the provincial capital of Gaziantepe came to be seen as the decisive point for control of Cilicia by both sides. On November 9, 1920, critical operational circumstances forced Kemal to undertake massive changes in the command structure of the Nationalist armies. Kemal reassigned Chief of Staff İsmet as the Western Front commander and Interior Minister Refet as the Southern Front commander. In the southeast, Kemal was determined to hold Gaziantepe, and he ordered Colonel Selahattin's II Corps headquarters to the Gaziantepe sector. To accommodate this and to ensure that the front north of Adana remained intact, Kemal detached the 41st Division from the II Corps and transferred it to Refet's XII Corps.[91] He also transferred control of the area west of the Seyhan River, to be held by the 41st Division, to the XII Corps as well. This greatly increased the length of the division's defensive sector, thereby weakening it. Finally. Kemal ordered Nihat to send the 5th Division (XIII Corps) from Urfa to Gaziantepe, where it would fall under Selahattin's command.[92] Together, these reorganizational changes led to a single senior Nationalist commander focused on Gaziantepe.

The French were also reorganizing as a result of the directives from Paris; however, Gouraud was preoccupied with the restoration of authority in Syria, and he placed Major General Noel M. A. Garnier-Duplessis in command of Cicilian offensive operations.[93] Gouraud assigned Dufieux's 1st Division (Adana), de Lamothe's 2nd Division (Aleppo), Goubeau's 4th Division (Iskenderun), artillery, and cavalry to Garnier-Duplessis, effectively making him an army corps commander. French intelligence provided Garnier-Duplessis with an accurate picture of the Nationalist deployments, and he determined to take advantage of them. He ordered Dufieux and de Lamothe to maintain their positions and reinforced Goubeau's 4th Division. Then he launched Goubeau from Iskenderun on "a massive search and destroy" mission to reclaim Pozantı.[94] To Goubeau's south, Garnier-Duplessis ordered Dufieux to send a column, under Colonel Gracy de La Hayrie, to relieve Tarsus and Mersin. On November 20, Goubeau's division encountered the Nationalist 41st Division at Kurttepe, 20 kilometers northwest of Adana, and was stopped there in a three-day battle. However, in the end, the weakened 41st Division could not maintain the line and withdrew into the Taurus Mountain range, thereby losing the territorial gains made by the Nationalists over the summer.

Garnier-Duplessis ordered Dufieux to push to the east, clearing Nationalist resistance to unblock the roads, and join de Lamothe at Gaziantepe. Dufieux left his main base at Ceyhan and, on October 10, immediately had to fight a three-day battle to clear the road 30 kilometers east at Kovanbaşı. He resumed his advance on November 1, but his division was slowed by ambushes and road interdiction. On November 8, Dufieux reached the village of Kanlıgeçit, 30 kilometers west of Bahçe, where he fought another three-day battle, breaking through to shift south east to take İslahiye on the night of November 10/11.[95]

The Nationalist 5th Division reached the Gaziantepe battle area on November 15, joining the 9th Division, while Colonel Selahattin's II Corps headquarters arrived six days later to assume control. On November 19, Garnier-Duplessis ordered Goubeau to take his division from Kilis to Gaziantepe, and it arrived there on November 21, bringing the total of French forces in the town to over 12,000 soldiers altogether, organized in 13 infantry battalions, 13 field artillery batteries, two 105-mm/155-mm howitzer batteries, and an aircraft detachment.[96] It was a powerful force, and Goubeau launched a massive attack toward the east on November 24 that reached Birecik on the Euphrates River in two days. The 5th Division was unable to hold him and withdrew to the north.[97]

Selahattin withdrew the 9th Division to the hills on the north of Gazian-tepe, established defensive positions, and ordered the 5th Division to join him there. The French launched a spoiling attack on the 9th Division on December 1 but withdrew back into the city the next day. With the arrival of winter, Garnier-Duplessis ordered Goubeau to withdraw his division and, by December 18, most of the 4th Division had gone. Lieutenant Colo-nel Abadi remained in command of the French force of some 6,500 men composed of four infantry regiments, three artillery batteries, and a detachment of tanks.[98] Observing the withdrawal, Selahattin decided to attack south with both divisions on December 19, but Abadi's counterat-tacks three days later restored the situation.

There were still Nationalists holding out in the center of Gaziantepe, but they were dangerously short of food and ammunition. On December 26, Selahattin noted that the French were in a similar condition because they dispatched a large convoy of empty trucks guarded by an entire infan-try battalion on the road south to Kilis.[99] He decided to risk another attack to relieve the Nationalists, and the next day, he sent the 9th Division around the west side of the city to envelop the French force. At 5:00 a.m. on December 27, the 9th and 5th Divisions launched concentric attacks to cut off the French. The battle raged for several days, but Selahattin was unable to completely isolate the French.

Operations continued in January 1921, with a French attack north from the Akçakoyunlu railway station on 18th, which was defeated by the 9th Division halfway to Gaziantepe. On January 25, Selahattin launched another attack using both his divisions and several Nationalist militia groups, but this failed against a well-organized French defense on the hills north of the city. Selahattin attempted a final night attack on January 30/31, which also failed.[100] Now convinced that relief of the city was impossible, on the night of February 4/5, Selahattin ordered the defenders to prepare to break out. The remaining 400 soldiers and a few officers prepared to escape on the night of February 6/7, but only about 50 made it successfully to the safety of the Nationalist lines the next night, with the French capturing the rest.[101]

Garnier-Duplessis made a ceremonial entry into the Turkish quarter of the city on February 9, 1921 formally ending the siege of Gaziantepe. The city of Gaziantepe had a population of 80,000 inhabitants at the beginning of the siege, but only 20,000 remained in the destroyed city on February 9. The French commander made every effort to feed the starving residents and to offer them medical treatment, but there was never enough, and the survivors lived in pitiable conditions until the French departed in the fall of 1921.[102]

After the Battle of Second İnönü (March 26–31, 1921) the Nationalists were forced to give up conventional operations in Cilicia. With the war against the Greeks going badly in the west, the Nationalist ministry of war notified Colonel Selahattin on April 25 to begin the redeployment of his II Corps to the Western Command.[103] By mid-July, most of the 5th and 9th Divisions and the corps headquarters had reached Akşehir to join the fight against the Greeks. In many ways, Gaziantepe was a sort of Verdun for the French and the Nationalists, but it proved to be a hollow victory for France, as guerrilla war continued unabated throughout Cilicia in the spring and early summer of 1921.

THE END OF THE FRENCH OCCUPATION

While these battles were unfolding in Cilicia, British and French decision-makers in London and Paris were at loggerheads regarding Middle Eastern policy. One historian noted that it was obvious, as early as November 1920, that the costs of trying to contain the Nationalists in Cilicia outweighed the benefits to France.[104] Despite this Georges Leygues wanted to maintain the French position in Cilicia but failed to gain support in parliament. The British had abandoned all support for the Armenians, and France was left with the entire expense of feeding and housing a quarter million Armenians in Cilicia. A crop failure in the Adana province exaggerated the problem locally, and, in Paris, the French faced a difficult choice between supporting the Armenians or supporting the Poles in their struggle with the Red Army. In the end, the French notified the British on January 7, 1921 that they would soon have to evacuate Cilicia.[105] The Leygues government collapsed on January 16, and Leygues was succeeded by Aristide Briand. These issues coincided with a general unhappiness with the Treaty of Sèvres by all its signatories except Greece. A second London conference was convened, to which the Nationalists sent Bekir Sami. In early March, Briand gave up all pretensions to retain Cilicia, and he reached an agreement with Bekir Sami to end the war against the Nationalists on March 9. Three days later, the French government instructed Garnier-Duplessis to cease all offensive operations in Cilicia.

Overall, the Franco-Turkish Agreement favored the French. The agreement stipulated that prisoners held by each side would be exchanged, the inhabitants of Cilicia would turn in their weapons, a French-commanded police force would be established, Armenians would administer areas with Armenian majorities, and France acquired substantial economic benefits, including the right to operate coal and mineral mines.[106] Needless to say, Kemal and the Grand Nationalist Assembly rejected the agreement, mainly because it resembled the despised capitulations, and they forced Bekir Sami to resign as foreign minister on May 8, 1921. To conciliate Bekir Sami, the assembly sent him back to Paris to attempt to renegotiate a treaty, but these efforts came to naught.

In parallel, removed from politics in the theater of war, discussions continued between Kemal and Gouraud. This led to negotiations in Ankara between Robert de Caix, the secretary general for the French High Commission in Syria, and Kemal beginning on May 14. After a week of difficult negotiations, they agreed to a 20-day cease-fire, effective at midnight May 30, 1921. Over this period, the French would withdraw from Gaziantepe, Urfa, Sis, Pozantı, and Maraş, and, in return, the Nationalists would refrain from attacking the French.[107] The cease-fire was unevenly applied and was broken with regularity, but hostilities gradually drew down to almost nothing. Peace negotiations continued in Paris but moved to Ankara in late summer. Neither Kemal nor the French government was particularly pleased with the draft agreements, but Nationalist military successes against the Greeks encouraged the French to finally settle. On October 20, 1921, Kemal and French representative Henri Franklin-Bouillon signed the Treaty of Ankara, which formally ended the Franco-Turkish War. There were a number of clauses, but the most relevant to this narrative are: the French withdrew from Cilicia, while Nationalists conceded the French occupation of the district of Iskenderun-Antakya (which they would maintain until 1939), and prisoners of war would be exchanged.[108] More important to the Nationalist cause was the informal agreement by the French to leave all confiscated weapons behind and intact upon withdrawal and to ship new supplies of weapons from Syria to the Nationalists.[109]

The French Army began its withdrawal on November 4, 1921, and they were completely out by the end of the year.[110] The real losers were, of course, the Armenians who had pinned their hopes on French protection and support. The Nationalists made proclamations guaranteeing the safety of Armenians and Christians who wished to remain in Turkish Cilicia. However, most were terrified, and few chose to stay. About 30,000 Armenians, Greeks, and anti-Nationalist Turks left the Adana district in

November and December, but 10,000 Armenians remained at the port of Mersin and another 7,000 at Dörtyol under the watchful eye of French troops. The French Army evacuated Kilis on December 7, Adana on December 20, Osmaniye on December 24, Gaziantepe on Christmas Day, Tarsus on December 27, Mersin on January 3, and Dörtyol on January 4.[111] Almost all the remaining Armenians left with them as the French occupation of Cilicia came to an end.[112] Reliable estimates of the number of persons evacuated from the French occupation are not available, but a quarter of a million is not unreasonable.[113]

CONCLUSION

The Franco-Turkish War was neither long nor particularly costly in military casualties, which have been estimated at 8,000 dead for both sides combined.[114] However, the number of civilian casualties was, likely, quite high, given such factors as the nature of combat in built-up areas, the frequency of civilian victimization, insufficient food and medical aid, and winter weather. The French spent an inordinate amount of money trying to maintain the occupation of Cilicia and, at the same time, provide food and shelter for several hundred thousand refugees and repatriated Armenians. The Nationalists fought the war as an economy of force measure and never invested much in Cilicia that was not already there at the end of World War I. Their integration of regular and irregular forces was very effective, as was the Nationalists' use of guerrilla warfare, which was particularly damaging to the French lines of communication.

For Kemal and the ministry of war, the Franco-Turkish War was a strategic distraction that by itself was not serious. However, when combined with simultaneous insurrections throughout Anatolia, the war in Caucasia against the fledgling Republic of Armenia, and the war in the west against the Greeks—it was a very serious problem. A military victory against France was never possible, but Kemal understood and pursued a Fabian strategy, which conserved his core strength while exhausting his enemies. In the end, the Nationalist strategy against France worked because the French had not the resources to wage an endless war in Cilicia for undetermined objectives, inevitably forcing them to the negotiating table. Kemal and the new Nationalist government achieved a decisive victory at low cost, which enabled them to concentrate their strength in the west, as well as secure badly needed military assistance against the Greeks.

NOTES

1. Philip Kerr to Lloyd George, Lloyd George Papers, F/511/40 (Sept. 12, 1919), U.K. National Archives, quoted in Robert F. Zeidner, *The Tricolor over the Taurus: The French in Cilicia and Vicinity, 1918–1922* (Ankara: Turkish Historical Society, 2005), 30.

2. Cyril Falls and A. F. Becke, *Military Operations, Egypt & Palestine: From June 1917 to the End of the War* (London: Her Majesty's Stationery Office, 1930), 622.

3. R. M. P. Preston, *The Desert Mounted Corps* (New York: Houghton Mifflin Company, 1921), 296.

4. Bıyıklıoğlu, *Mondros Mütarekesi ve Tatbikatı*, 58–59.

5. Ibid., 64.

6. Ibid., 66–68.

7. Türkmen, *Mütareke Döneminde Ordunun Durumu*, 45–53.

8. Falls and Becke, *Military Operations, Egypt & Palestine*, 622.

9. Ibid., 623; and İsmail Özçelik, *Milli Mücadele'de Güney Cephesi: Urfa (30 Ekim 1918–11 Temmuz 1920)* (Ankara: Kültür Bakanlığı, 1992), 49–53.

10. The city was formerly known as Antep or Aintep. However, after heroic resistance during the ten-month siege, the city was renamed Gaziantepe in 1921. *Gazi* is an Ottoman honorific meaning "heroic warrior"; thus, today, it is the "Heroic Warrior City of Antep."

11. Shaw, *From Empire to Republic*, vol. 2, 861–863. According to Professor Shaw, "The sources vary widely regarding the exact dates on which these occupations took place."

12. Falls and Becke, *Military Operations, Egypt & Palestine*, 623.

13. Le Ministère de la Guerre, *Les Armées Françaises dans la Grande Guerre, Tome IX–Ier Volume, Les Fronts Secondaires* (Paris: Imprimerie, 1936), 165–169.

14. Zeidner, *The Tricolor over the Taurus*, 67–69.

15. Bıyıklıoğlu, *Mondros Mütarekesi ve Tatbikatı*, 70.

16. Preston, *The Desert Mounted Corps*, 298.

17. Ibid., 302.

18. Ibid., 872.

19. Shaw, *From Empire to Republic*, vol. 2, 865–872.

20. See "The Armenian Legion" in Shaw, *From Empire to Republic*, vol. 2, 876–884 for a comprehensive treatment of this subject. See also Maxim Gauin, "Imperialism, Revolution and Nationalism: The Relations

between the French Republic and the Armenian Committees, from 1918 to 1923" (unpublished PhD diss., Middle Eastern Technical University, Ankara, Turkey, 2019), 101–107.

21. Gauin, "Imperialism, Revolution and Nationalism," 100, 119.

22. Zeidner, *The Tricolor over the Taurus*, 95.

23. Ibid.

24. Richard G. Hovannisian, *The Republic of Armenia: From Versailles to London, 1919–1920*, vol. 2 (Los Angeles: University of California Press, 1982), 416. Professor Hovannisian stated that 150,000 Armenians had returned to Cilicia by 1920.

25. Shaw, *From Empire to Republic*, vol. 2, 886.

26. Ahmet Hulki Saral, Atike Kaptan, and Alev Keskin, *Türk İstiklâl Harbi, IV'üncü Cilt Güney Cephesi* (Ankara: Genelkurmay Basımevi, 2009), 19, 54.

27. Shaw, *From Empire to Republic*, vol. 2, 870, 893.

28. Saral, Kaptan, and Keskin, "Armenian Forces," Tablo 1 (Table 1), in *Güney Cephesi*, 49.

29. Zeidner, *The Tricolor over the Taurus*, 114–119, 246.

30. Le Ministère de la Guerre, *Les Armées Françaises*, 162.

31. Hovannisian, *From Versailles to London*, 412.

32. Ibid., 414–415.

33. Ibid., 415.

34. Zeidner, *The Tricolor over the Taurus*, 139. See also Konstantinos Travlos and Onur Buyuran, "Orders of Battle of the Turkish War of Independence" (unpublished manuscript), 28–30. Their information is compiled from Eric de Fluerian, "Levant avril 1917–juin 1941: Participation des Regiments de Tiraillerus," Les tirailleurs D'hier et d'aujourd'hui, Oct. 3, 2014, http://www.les-tirailleurs.fr/documents/ed0688be-301e-4890 -a43d-0cb494906bb1/afficher; the part of the French Official military history Armée Française du Levant, *Histoire militaire du Moyen-Orient: Conflits du Moyen-Orient des origines à nos jours*, Mar. 9, 2014, https:// histoiremilitairedumoyenorient.wordpress.com/category/armee-francaise -du-levant/; and Mümtaz Ulusoy, *İstiklal Harbi'nde 2nci Kolordu (1918– 1921)* (Ankara: Genelkurmay Basımevi, 2006).

35. Zeidner, *The Tricolor over the Taurus*, 175–177.

36. Saral, Kaptan, and Keskin, *Güney Cephesi*, 75–77.

37. Yaşar Akbıyık, *Milli Mücadelede Güney Cephesi (Maraş)* (Ankara: Kültür Bakanlığı Yayınları, 1990), 14–15; and Shaw, *From Empire to Republic*, vol. 2, 890–891.

38. Akbıyık, *Milli Mücadelede Güney Cephesi (Maraş)*, 89.

39. Çiloğlu, *Kurtuluş Savaşı Sözlüğü*, 319.

40. Görgülü, *On Yıllık Harbin Kadrosu*, 227–230.

41. Saral, Kaptan, and Keskin, *Güney Cephesi*, 78–84.

42. Shaw, *From Empire to Republic*, vol. 2, 892–893.

43. Ibid., 894.

44. Özçelik, *Urfa*, 167–182.

45. Zeidner, *The Tricolor over the Taurus*, 176.

46. Ibid., 177.

47. Shaw, *From Empire to Republic*, vol. 2, 897.

48. Saral, Kaptan, and Keskin, *Güney Cephesi*, 94.

49. Ibid., 91. I am indebted to Dr. Maxime Gauin for Quérette's first name, which does not appear anywhere in the extant literature in either English or Turkish.

50. Zeidner, *The Tricolor over the Taurus*, 179.

51. Hovannisian, *From London to Sèvres*, 38.

52. Saral, Kaptan, and Keskin, *Güney Cephesi*, 97.

53. Ibid., 95–96.

54. Zeidner, *The Tricolor over the Taurus*, 180; and Hovannisian, *From London to Sèvres*, 39.

55. Zeidner, *The Tricolor over the Taurus*, 181.

56. Saral, Kaptan, and Keskin, *Güney Cephesi*, 104–105.

57. Hovannisian, *From London to Sèvres*, 40.

58. Saral, Kaptan, and Keskin, *Güney Cephesi*, 105–106.

59. Ibid., 107–108.

60. Hovannisian, *From London to Sèvres*, 40.

61. Shaw, *From Republic to Empire*, vol. 2, 954–959.

62. Hovannisian, *From London to Sèvres*, 41.

63. Ibid. See also Shaw, *From Empire to Republic*, vol. 2, 904–905, which presents the same horrific numbers.

64. Saral, Kaptan, and Keskin, *Güney Cephesi*, 110.

65. Hovannisian, *From London to Sèvres*, 46–48.

66. Shaw, *From Empire to Republic to Empire*, vol. 2, 908–909.

67. Saral, Kaptan, and Keskin, *Güney Cephesi*, 115–120.

68. Shaw, *From Republic to Empire*, vol. 2, 908; Saral, Kaptan, and Keskin, *Güney Cephesi*, 120–130; and Zeidner, *The Tricolor over the Taurus*, 209–211.

69. Shaw, *From Empire to Republic*, vol. 3, part 2, 1392–1396.

70. See Saral, Kaptan, and Keskin, *Güney Cephesi*, 120–150.

71. Ibid., 151.

72. Ibid., 153–155.

73. Zeidner, *The Tricolor over the Taurus*, 213–214.

74. Ibid., 215.

75. Saral, Kaptan, and Keskin, *Güney Cephesi*, 157–158; Zeidner, *The Tricolor over the Taurus*, 215.

76. Zeidner, *The Tricolor over the Taurus*, 217–218.

77. Shaw, *From Empire to Republic*, vol. 2, 888–889.

78. Yücel Güçlü, *Armenians and the Allies in Cilicia, 1914–1923* (Salt Lake City: University of Utah Press, 2009), 128.

79. See Zeidner, *The Tricolor over the Taurus*, 220–240 for the details of this long process.

80. Ibid., 237.

81. See Ulusoy, *İstiklâl Harbi'nde*. Kemal's directives ending the cease-fire are presented on pages 19–20.

82. Saral, Kaptan, and Keskin, *Güney Cephesi*, 173–174.

83. Görgülü, *On Yıllık Harbin Kadrosu*, 231–232.

84. Ibid., 241–242.

85. Saral, Kaptan, and Keskin, *Güney Cephesi*, 194–196.

86. Mango, *Atatürk*, 296.

87. Saral, Kaptan, and Keskin, *Güney Cephesi*, 230–231.

88. Ibid., 234–237 and Kroki 26 (Sketch Map 26 following page 237).

89. See also Kevork Baboian, *The Heroic Battle of Aintab*, trans. Ümit Kurt (London: Gomidas Institute, 2017), xx.

90. Zeidner, *The Tricolor over the Taurus*, 255.

91. Ibid., 243.

92. Saral, Kaptan, and Keskin, *Güney Cephesi*, 242–243. Interestingly, Kemal instructed Nihat to continue to be responsible for the logistical support of the division.

93. Zeidner, *The Tricolor over the Taurus*, 256.

94. Ibid., 257.

95. Saral, Kaptan, and Keskin, *Güney Cephesi*, Kroki 24 (Sketch Map 24 following page 247).

96. Ibid., 245.

97. Belen, *Türk Kurtuluş Savaşı*, 261.

98. Saral, Kaptan, and Keskin, *Güney Cephesi*, 250.

99. Ibid., 251–253.

100. Ibid., Kroki 32–34 (Sketch Maps 32–34 following pages 252, 254, and 255); and Ulusoy, *İstiklâl Harbi'nde*, 69–84.

101. Belen, *Türk Kurtuluş Savaşı*, 264; and Saral, Kaptan, and Keskin, *Güney Cephesi*, 266–267.

102. Shaw, *From Empire to Republic*, vol. 3, part 2, 1398–1401.

103. Saral, Kaptan, and Keskin, *Güney Cephesi*, 273–274.

104. Yücel Güçlü, "The Struggle for Mastery in Cilicia: Turkey, France and the Ankara Agreement of 1921," *The International History Review*, 23, no. 3: 589–591. See also Alex Weisiger, *Logics of War: Explanations for Limited and Unlimited Conflicts* (Ithaca; London: Cornell University Press, 2013), 178–202. Weisiger's chapter titled "The Limits on Leaders: The Falklands War and the Franco-Turkish War" contains very perceptive observations and correlations.

105. Zeidner, *The Tricolor over the Taurus*, 263–265.

106. Shaw, *From Empire to Republic*, vol. 3, part 1, 1247.

107. Ibid., 1403–1405

108. Saral, Kaptan, and Keskin, *Güney Cephesi*, 275–282; and Güçlü, *Armenians and the Allies in Cilicia*, 140–142.

109. Shaw, *From Empire to Republic*, vol. 3, part 1, 1415–1416.

110. Özçelik, *Urfa*, 261–270.

111. Shaw, *From Empire to Republic*, vol. 3, part 1, 1431.

112. Güçlü, *Armenians and the Allies in Cilicia*, 153–156.

113. At Lausanne in 1923, Armenian National Delegation representative Gabriel Noradounghian presented the delegation's official estimates of the number of Armenian refugees as 345,000 Turkish-Armenians in the Caucasus (distinct from Russian-Armenian refugees); 140,000 in Syria; 120,000 in Greece and the Aegean Islands; 40,000 in Bulgaria; 50,000 in Iran; and 110,000 orphans under the care of relief agencies. See Güçlü, *Armenians and the Allies in Cilicia*, 170.

114. Turgut Özakman, *Vahidettin, M. Kemal ve Milli Mücadele: Yalanlar, Yanlışlar, Yutturmacalar* (Istanbul: Bilgi Yayınevi, 1997), 44.

SEVEN

Second İnönü and Kütahya-Eskişehir

The Turks are very dangerous, because they are very fierce and unget-at-able. If the Greeks try to conquer Turkey they will be ruined.[1]

Winston S. Churchill, 1921

INTRODUCTION

By the end of January 1921, the Greek Reconnaissance in Force was completed and the army returned to its original lines. A massive change in the Greek command structure followed in February. The Greeks were now faced with both political and military decisions regarding whether to pursue offensive operations in western Anatolia. If so, to what end?

In the fall of 1920, Kemal unleashed Karabekir on the Armenians, rapidly reestablishing the eastern border and securing a favorable peace treaty in December. In the southeast, the Nationalists waged a war against the French for control of Cilicia and suppressed a series of Anatolia-wide insurrections. These operations were successful, but they prevailed largely because they were conducted against militarily or politically weak adversaries. The first real test of the revived Nationalist army came in early 1921, when the long-awaited Greek offensive erupted toward Kütahya and Eskişehir.

STRATEGIC DECISIONS AND OPERATIONAL PLANNING

In early February 1921, Greek prime minister Nikolaos Kalogeropoulos, who had been in office for just one week, left Athens for what would become the Third London Conference (February 21–March 12, 1921). On March 1, Colonel Ptolemaios Sarrigiannis and Ambassador to Great Britain Lysimachos Kautantzoglou met privately with Lloyd George's secretary and advisors to discuss future offensive operations in Anatolia. They were warmly received and left with what they believed was a "blank check" to proceed.[2] The next day, the French informed the Greek delegation that they were about to conclude an agreement with the Nationalists to abandon their occupation of Cilicia (which would enable Kemal to concentrate forces against Greece). Furthermore, Lloyd George's office informed Minister of Military Affairs Demetrios Gounares, who had arrived in London on March 9, that the prime minister had no objections to the resumption of offensive operations. Now facing increasing Nationalist strength and with the private encouragement of the British prime minister, Prime Minister Kalogeropoulos cabled the Ministry of Military Affairs to resume formal planning of an offensive campaign in western Anatolia.[3]

After the January Reconnaissance in Force, the Field Army of Asia Minor (FAAM) tentatively continued its operational planning for renewing the offensive. Colonel Konstantinos Pallis, the army's chief of staff formulated a plan for operations in the spring of 1921 (when the roads would be more trafficable), with the goal of occupying the key transportation axis of Eskişehir and Afyonkarahisar.[4] In early February, the FAAM shifted forces to support their planning and requested reinforcements from mainland Greece. The final plan envisioned two axes of advance converging on the city of Kütahya and, on March 12, the FAAM sent its operations order to the subordinate commanders. In the north, the entire Army Corps C would advance toward Eskişehir, while in the south, Army Corps A would advance through the pass at Dumlupınar to Afyonkarahisar. Once resupplied, both corps would advance together and seize the vital communication hubs of Afyonkarahisar and Kütahya. Army Corps B would maintain the sector between Army Corps C and Army Corps A.

Like many army-level plans, the FAAM's plan, in isolation, was sound at the operational level. However, "there was no clear connection between the success of the operation and a diplomatic result that would resolve the war in favor of Greece."[5] In effect, the offensive lacked a purpose to fulfill strategic goals such as the destruction of the enemy army or the seizure of key terrain, without which the enemy could continue the war (i.e., the ground to be gained by the Greeks would not cripple the Nationalist strategic position). Altogether the FAAM planned to use 61,476 men from Army Corps A and C in the offensive, while the remaining 46,747 men, mainly of Army B Corps and reserve and rear formations, would hold the occupation line. The weaker Army Corps A, under Lieutenant General Alexandros Kontoulis, of 21,677 men, with the 2nd and 13th (minus one regiment) Divisions, would attack against Dumlupınar and Kütahya. The stronger C Corps under Major General Aristoteles Vlachopoulos, composed of 39,799 men with the 3rd, 7th, and 10th Divisions, would strike at Eskişehir, following the same axis of advance as it did previously in the campaign that led to the Battle of First İnönü. The average size of the Greek divisions was about 9,000 men, with the combat strength being around 5,000 men, while the average manpower of a Nationalist division was 3,000 to 5,000 men, with a combat strength of half that.[6] Importantly, Greek operations were to be conducted before the completion of the new round of mobilizations that had been requested by the military high command.

In early February in Ankara, Mustafa Kemal and Chief of the General Staff Major General Fevzi had successfully concluded counterinsurgency operations to suppress the Çerkez Ethem Uprising. This had been a major effort for Refet's Southern Front and had drawn most of available Nationalist cavalry to the Kütahya area. In February, Kemal and Fevzi redesignated the cavalry groups as cavalry divisions. On March 10, İsmet's Western Front Command, composed of the 1st, 11th, 24th, and 61st Divisions, and the 3rd Cavalry Division;[7] Refet's Southern Front Command, composed of Colonel Fahrettin's XII Corps, made up of the 8th, 23rd, and 57th Divisions, while Refet maintained direct command of the 4th, 8th, 41st Divisions as well as the 1st and 2nd Cavalry Divisions.[8] Tactically, İsmet's smaller force had a much narrower sector, and he maintained his headquarters 30 kilometers west of Eskişehir. To İsmet's north, Colonel Halit's Kocaeli Corps held the ground with the 7th Division at Geyve and a provisional infantry division at Hendek. To İsmet's south, Refet's front was much longer, and Refet trusted Fahrettin's XII Corps (flanked on his north by the 1st Cavalry and 4th Division, and by the 2nd Cavalry Division to his south) to guard the vital Dumlupınar-Afyonkarahisar axis. Refet maintained his headquarters in the city of Konya, over 100 kilometers to the rear of Fahrettin's corps headquarters in Afyonkarahisar.

Kemal and Fevzi expected the Greeks to resume offensive operations when the spring weather arrived; they warned the front commanders of this and ordered them to maintain adequate reserves. At the operational level, the Nationalists' plan was straightforward in that it concentrated forces on the two main avenues of approach to Eskişehir and Afyonkara-hisar.[9] In the third week of March, at the tactical level, İsmet had more time to fortify his line and he had more defensible terrain, while Refet was still redeploying the XII Corps from the most recent rounds of counterin-surgency operations. On March 16, 1921, Kemal's ambassador in Moscow signed the Treaty of Moscow (sometimes called the Turkish-Soviet Treaty of Friendship). This was an important political accomplishment for Kemal because it ended the diplomatic isolation of the Nationalist government with international recognition of the new Turkish state and continued the flow of weapons to Kemal's army. Against this success, the Greeks launched their offensive campaign on March 23 aimed at Eskişehir and Afyonkara-hisar (see map 7.1).

THE SECOND İNÖNÜ CAMPAIGN

The campaign began with twin Greek offensives on the morning of March 23, 1921. In the north, Major General Vlachopoulos's Army Corps C attacked on a narrow front with the 10th, 3rd, and 7th Divisions (from north to south), and they quickly burst through İsmet's cavalry screen. By nightfall, the Greeks had advanced 20 kilometers, while İsmet sent the 1st Division forward to establish a main line of defense. The Greeks resumed their advance at 8:00 a.m. the next day, and, on Army Corps C's north flank, the FAAM's 11th Division launched a supporting attack on the Kocaeli Group designed to prevent it from sending reinforcements to İsmet.[10] Over the course of March 24, the Greeks advanced east another 10 kilometers, but İsmet withdrew his battered forces that night behind a strong defensive line composed of the fresh 1st Cavalry Division, the 24th and 61st Divisions, and three infantry battalions the Kocaeli Group (which had successfully stopped the Greek supporting attack) managed to send south.[11] İsmet built his main line of resistance just to the east of the Izmit-Eskişehir railway, 10 kilometers northwest of his headquarters at the İnönü railway station, and he kept the fresh 11th Division there in hand as an immediate reserve as well. On March 25, bitter fighting raged as Vlacho-poulos's 3rd and 7th Divisions assaulted the Nationalist lines only to be driven back by fierce counterattacks.

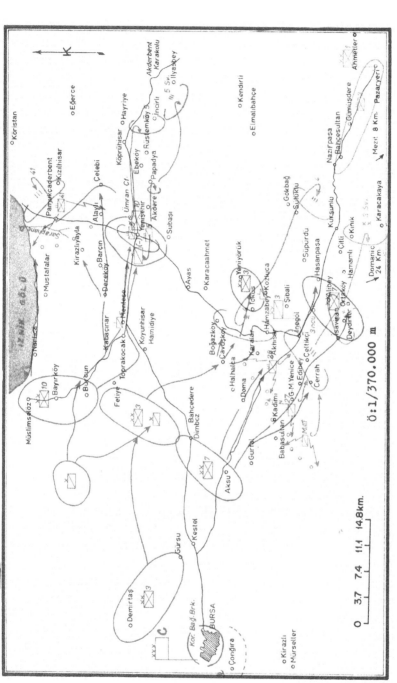

Map 7.1 Greek Northern Advance (March 23, 1921)

Greek Army Corps C's axis of advance in the Kütahya-Eskişehir Campaign led directly through the First İnönü battlefield to Eskişehir. The objective of the FAAM's campaign was geographically focused on the seizure of the cities and transportation nodes of Kütahya-Eskişehir.

Courtesy of the Turkish General Staff Military History and Strategy Institute (ATASE).

On March 26, uncertain about the forces confronting Army Corps C, Vlachopoulos ordered air reconnaissance and concentrated his forces (the Concise Greek History asserted that İsmet had much better intelligence than Vlachopoulos).[12] Fighting continued that day, with the Greeks making small advances. The Kocaeli Group commander, Colonel Halit, understanding the necessity to assist İsmet, sent two artillery batteries and a howitzer battery south to reinforce the 61st Division.[13] As dawn broke on March 27, Vlachopoulos, who had moved his headquarters forward to the village of Pazaryeri from Bursa, launched a three-division attack across the entire front. His main effort was a concentration of his 7th and 10th Divisions against İsmet's 24th Division (holding his center and flanked on the south by the 11th Division and on the north by the 61st Division).[14] The Nationalists were unable to hold the Greeks and were pushed back again, causing great confusion in the retreating regiments. Fortunately for the Nationalists, a series of parallel ridges behind them enabled them to fall back. To restore cohesive command and control, İsmet reorganized his forces that night by forming the provisional Right Wing Group from the retreating regiments of the 24th Division.

The morning of March 28 brought further concentrated attacks by the Greek 3rd and 10th Divisions against the Nationalist main line of resistance, while Greek cavalry guarded both flanks of Army C Corps. On his right, Vlachopoulos launched the 7th Division, which immediately found a thinly guarded gap between İsmet's Right Wing Group and the 3rd Cavalry Division, collapsing the Nationalist center and coming to within 10 kilometers of the İnönü Station. The fighting raged, hand to hand in many places, but died down by 7:00 p.m.[15] As darkness fell, İsmet's artillery pounded the Greeks. The next day was largely one of attritional combat from the Greek perspective, as Vlachopoulos adjusted his lines but did not mount major attacks.[16] İsmet reinforced his lines with an assault battalion and the regiments of the newly arriving 5th Caucasian Division; he also conducted a spoiling attack on his left with the 3rd Cavalry Division. The front was now stabilized, and his confidence grew when Fevzi notified him that the 8th Division was entrained as a reinforcement.[17]

The culmination of Army Corps C's northern offensive began on the morning of March 30 with coordinated attacks from all three Greek divisions, following a 10-minute artillery bombardment against the well-fortified Nationalist positions. The Greeks made small gains on İsmet's left but were repulsed everywhere else. As darkness fell, Vlachopoulos, who had committed all his reserves, decided to make one final attack the next morning.[18] On the morning of March 31, many of the Greek regiments found themselves facing fierce Nationalist resistance, did not attack with vigor, and were easily repulsed. Recognizing that his exhausted army could not continue the attack, Vlachopoulos asked for permission to withdraw back to Bursa.[19] As the tempo of the Greek attacks died down, İsmet launched a half-dozen counterattacks probing the Greek lines. A major Nationalist counterattack at 2:00 p.m. by the 4th Division nearly destroyed the Greek 28th Infantry Regiment. According to one scholar, İsmet "concentrated half of his artillery firepower on the Greek regiment and then assaulted it with seven battalions (about 1400–3000 men). The Greek's 10th Division artillery failed to provide any support. The regimental commander, Colonel Christos Christou, and most officers fell in the battle, and the regiment disintegrated and was routed."[20] Vlachopoulos began his withdrawal at 7:00 p.m. and had largely broken contact by dawn.

İsmet launched a major counterattack on the morning of April 1, 1921, with his 1st and 4th Divisions against the Greek 10th Division pushing his main line forward six kilometers. He also sent the 1st Cavalry Division to reinforce the 3rd Cavalry Division, and launched them on an encirclement movement attempting to envelop Vlachopoulos's right flank (held by his 7th Division). The two cavalry divisions swept north from İnönü Station but were stopped by well-led Greek rear guards after an advance of some 20 kilometers. The next day the Greeks again broke contact and withdrew to the northwest. On April 3, İsmet organized a pursuit of the rapidly withdrawing Greeks, pushing the limit of advance about 30 kilometers forward (see map 7.2). The Nationalists continually tried to outflank the Greeks but could not move fast enough to accomplish this. Finally, on April 4, Vlachopoulos reconstituted a unified defensive line from Kazancı (30 kilometers east of Bursa) to a midpoint on the shore of the Lake Iznik, while İsmet moved his headquarters forward to Kurşunlü. The next day, İsmet closed on the Greek lines with three cavalry divisions pushing through the town of İnegöl on his left and infantry regiments pushing through Yenişehir on his right. For the next two days, small firefights broke out when Greek infantry conducted counterattacks, which took back some ground, but by April 8, the campaign in the north was finished, with Army Corps C back where it started.

THE FIRST BATTLE OF DUMLUPINAR

The Çerkez Ethem Uprising had completely occupied Refet's Southern Front Command until late in January, but as the spring campaign season approached, Refet had reassumed a defensive posture, with Colonel

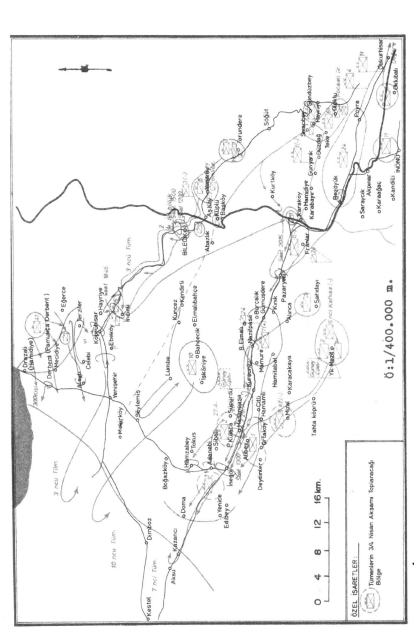

Map 7.2 İsmet's Pursuit (April 3, 1921)

Reinforced with additional troops, İsmet once again stopped the Greeks near the İnönü train station and launched a pursuit of the defeated Greeks. By early April 1921, he had driven Army Corps C back to its starting lines and restored the operational situation.

Courtesy of the Turkish General Staff Military History and Strategy Institute (ATASE).

Fahrettin's XII Corps guarding the rail line approach from Uşak to Afyon-karahisar. Fahrettin's main defensive position blocked the pass through the mountains west of Dumlupınar, which was held by the 23rd Division, with the 57th Division in immediate tactical reserve. On the FAAM's southern axis of advance, Lieutenant General Alexandros Kontoulis's Army Corps A launched its attack simultaneously with Army Corps C on the morning of March 23, 1921. Kontoulis's 2nd and 13th Divisions advanced abreast from Uşak, quickly pushing aside the Nationalist outposts. Fahrettin moved the 57th Division forward on the left of the 23rd Division, while Refet sent the 8th Division forward to a position on its right, thus putting three Nationalist infantry divisions in the defensive line. The next morning the Greek 2nd Division followed the rail line northeast, while the 13th Division advanced directly east. Fahrettin did not oppose the advance and began to withdraw; by evening the Greek 2nd Division had pushed 10 kilometers beyond the village of Dumlupınar. The Nationalists kept up their withdrawal, and, by midnight March 25/26, they had fallen back to the Oren Lake, just 20 kilometers west of Afyonkarahisar.[21]

General Kontoulis brought both of his frontline divisions abreast, and at 7:00 a.m. on March 27 attacked Fahrettin's thinly held lines. Kontoulis's subsequent attacks the next day were successful and brought the 5/42 Evzone Regiment of Colonel Nicholaos Plasteras into Afyonkarahisar at 3:00 p.m.[22] Fighting for the city raged, but the Greeks could not be stopped. Earlier that day, Refet sent a warning to Colonel Fahrettin that the General Headquarters viewed the Western Front Command's ongoing battle at İnönü as the operational priority and to expect orders to send reinforcements to İsmet.[23] Whether this triggered Fahrettin's decision to abandon Afyonkarahisar is unclear from the Turkish narrative; in any case, the XII Corps withdrew to the east. The fall of the city dealt Refet an intractable tactical problem with the question of which way to retreat—north toward Kütahya or east toward Konya. Now, with Fahrettin retreating toward Konya, Refet took his headquarters north, thus splitting his army. Army Corps A continued its steady advance beyond the city, pushing 10 kilometers east toward Konya and 30 kilometers north toward Kütahya on March 29.

Major General Refet moved his Southern Front Command headquarters north ahead of the Greeks, establishing his command post in the village of İhsaniye, with the 2nd Cavalry Division and the 8th Division holding the line. Colonel Fahrettin moved his XII Corps headquarters east to the railway station at Çay where he concentrated the 23rd, 41st, and 57th

Divisions with some miscellaneous corps and labor battalions. The Southern Front Command was now broken into two parts and geographically separated by Army Corps A in Afyonkarahisar. At 3:00 p.m. on March 30, Fahrettin launched the 23rd Division west toward Afyonkarahisar in a movement to contact. The next day, Fahrettin gained contact with Kontoulis's 13th Division, and he brought up the 41st and 57th Divisions. While Fahrettin was trying to restore the situation in Afyonkarahisar, the General Staff ordered Southern Front Commander Refet to prepare to send the 8th Division and the 2nd Cavalry Division north to reinforce the Western Front Command. This would leave him with only the 4th Cavalry Brigade to screen the Greeks, and at 9:30 p.m. on March 31, Refet withdrew his headquarters farther north to Alayunt on the Afyonkarahisar-Kütahya rail line.

At the strategic level, the situation for the Nationalists was not as bleak as the operational situation facing Major General Refet. On April 1, İsmet sent Kemal a message from the newly recaptured hill named Metristepe (which later became famous in Turkey) informing Ankara that he had beaten the Greeks and they were retreating.[24] In a remarkable demonstration of strategic agility, Kemal and Fevzi ordered İsmet to disengage the 4th and 11th Divisions and send them south to Refet.[25] These divisions were rushed to the İnönü train station where they loaded and departed on April 3. Further, they ordered Halit's Kocaeli Group to send 2,300 trained infantrymen south as well. Colonel Mehmet Arif's (Ayıcı) 11th Division was very powerful, containing 173 officers, 3,106 soldiers, 8 howitzers, and 800 draft animals.[26] The next day, Refet ordered Fahrettin to press the enemy hard from the east to keep Kontoulis focused on the XII Corps rather than the Nationalist's gathering strength north of Afyonkarahisar. On April 3, Kemal and Fevzi ordered İsmet to detach the 1st and 2nd Cavalry Divisions from his pursuit and send them south to reinforce Refet. They also ordered the first regiment of the 5th Caucasian Division then arriving from the east, the 10th Caucasian Infantry Regiment, to Refet's front as well. That night, Fevzi sent Refet an order to prepare to attack with all available forces.[27]

As he made his final preparations for the offensive, Refet reported that his logistical situation was excellent and he had two weeks of rations for 16,000 men and fodder for 5,000 animals in his storehouses. On April 4, Refet pushed the 11th Division and the 4th Cavalry Brigade south to make contact with the Greek 2nd Division. Over the next three days, he also deployed both incoming cavalry divisions on his far-right flank

(50 kilometers west of the Afyonkarahisar-Kütahya rail line) and brought the 4th Division into attack positions. Lacking another corps commander and corps headquarters, Refet organized these formations into the Northern Attack group under his personal command. Meanwhile, because of the withdrawal of Army Corps C to Bursa, on April 3, the FAAM ordered General Kontoulis to revert to a defensive posture and prepare to hold Afyonkarahisar and Dumlupınar.[28] However, Kontoulis's intelligence had picked up the Nationalist troop concentrations, and he became concerned about being encircled if he attempted to retain Afyonkarahisar. The next day, Kontoulis sent a cable to the FAAM asking for freedom of action should the situation turn for the worse, as well as the authority to abandon Afyonkarahisar. He met with his two division commanders and informed that that he intended to withdraw if his request was approved. Over the next two days, Kontoulis traded cables with his higher headquarters but moved his own headquarters back to Uşak on April 6. The next day, sanctioned by the FAAM, Army Corps A began its withdrawal from Afyonkarahisar.

Refet's Southern Front Command began its offensive on April 8, beginning what the Turks would call the Battles of Aslıhanlar and First Dumlupınar.[29] Refet's basic tactical plan hinged on his Northern Attack Group and the XII Corps holding the Greeks in place while his cavalry divisions swept in from the north to cut the Greek lines of communication at Dumlupınar. The campaign would be won by maneuver designed to encircle Army Corps A. General Kontoulis was already withdrawing but had left well-led and well-organized rear-guard detachments to slow the enemy and allow his divisions to escape the trap. By day's end, Fahrettin's XII Corps took Afyonkarahisar, pushing its cavalry screen 20 kilometers west of the city, while the Northern Attack Group drove south but was stopped by determined defenders at Küçük Aslıhanlar (just north of the Uşak-Afyonkarahisar rail line).[30] For the next two days, Kontoulis held the Nationalists at bay with his 2nd Division while skillfully disengaging and withdrawing his 13th Division. Now aware of the Nationalist cavalry divisions bearing farther west along the rail line to Uşak, he sent the 33rd Infantry Regiment southwest to block them. On April 12, Kontoulis withdrew both divisions to defensive positions on the high ground west of Dumlupınar, with the 2nd Division north of the rail line and the 13th Division to its south.

Kontoulis was in a dangerously vulnerable tactical position. While having a strong defensive front facing east, his flanks were entirely exposed, and Refet was preparing to encircle Army Corps A with fast-moving cavalry.

Refet launched his final attacks on April 13 using eight small infantry divisions against Kontoulis's two large infantry divisions while Refet's 1st and 2nd Cavalry Divisions attempted to cut the rail line from the north, and the 4th Cavalry Brigade and two tribal cavalry regiments attempted the same maneuver from the south. For the Greeks, this was a desperate moment but Kontoulis's soldiers fought well, and he maintained excellent command and control of his corps. The next day, Kontoulis broke contact and withdrew his divisions back to their original positions around Uşak.

Like İsmet at Metristepe, Refet sent a proclamation to Ankara on April 11 that he had won a great victory, but this was premature. In the end, much to Kemal's disappointment, Refet failed to deliver a battle of annihilation. The premier biographer of Atatürk, Andrew Mango, asserted that "İsmet's generalship was certainly better than that of Refet," but he continued and noted that Ankara guessed correctly that İsmet would be attacked and detached some of Refet's forces to reinforce İsmet.[31] İsmet certainly operated under conditions of more certainty than did Refet. Second, İnönü was a pitched battle, and it was a more clear-cut victory, but it was far more costly, with 5,000 Nationalists killed, while Refet only lost around 500 killed in the south. The Turks celebrate what would later become First Dumlupınar as a victory, but it was incomplete because Refet failed to trap Kontoulis's army corps. Aslıhanlar, on the other hand, must be judged as a Greek victory, since they held the numerically superior Nationalists long enough to withdraw their forces from encirclement. Operationally, the Nationalists were blessed with interior lines of communication, which enabled them to shift centrally positioned forces north and south rapidly. This benefited both Nationalist commanders but served, more importantly, to demonstrate the brilliant level of command that Kemal had developed over his career. İnönü-Dumlupınar showcased Kemal's ability to take risks and move troops between tactical sectors–a skill he had developed at Gallipoli, in the Caucasus, and in the retreat through Syria during World War I.

STRATEGIC AND OPERATIONAL RESET

The Concise Greek History asserted, "The operations of March 1921 not only failed to provide a Greek solution to the Asia Minor problem, but acted adversely to the Greek cause."[32] In its reports to the General Staff and the ministry of war, the FAAM noted that the Nationalists were cheered by their victories, but, more importantly, the Nationalist Army had made significant progress in composition and organization. Moreover, the FAAM warned the government that reinforcements were urgently needed if major operations were to continue. On April 28, 1921, newly sworn in prime minister Demetrios Gounares arrived in Izmir for briefings. The staff told him that the Nationalists had 88,000 men with 250 artillery pieces and 316 machine guns available but could only deploy 70,000 men and 200 artillery pieces against the FAAM, which could, in turn, deploy 100,000 men and 238 artillery pieces.[33] This numerical superiority gave the Greeks sufficient forces to defeat the Nationalists. However, operationally the Greeks faced the problem of concentration because their forces were dispersed in two large groups (in Bursa and Uşak) separated by a mountain range, which made unified action difficult. Understanding the need for more forces, the Greeks detached the 11th Division from British control on May 18, as well as completed the mobilization started in March. The Nationalists enjoyed the reciprocal—what is called the central position—enabling them to concentrate or amass forces at will (in military doctrinal terms the Greeks were operating on exterior lines of communication, while the Nationalists operated on interior lines of communication). Mindful of these challenges, the Greek government decided to continue offensive operations with a view toward the destruction of the Nationalist Army, and King Constantine arrived in Smyrna on June 12, taking the role of nominal commander in chief of the FAAM.

On June 16, the commander of the FAAM, General Papoulas, his deputy chief of staff Colonel Ptolemaios Sarrigiannis (who had returned from London), met with King Constantine at his palace in Kordelio. Also present was the new chief of the Army Staff Service, Major General Victor Dousmanes, as well as the government liaison Major General Xenophon Strategos. Dousmanes and Strategos, together with Metaxas, had been part of the General Headquarters under then-Prince Constantine of the Greek field army in the Balkan Wars. Colonel Sarrigiannis presented the operational plan, which was agreeable to all present: encirclement from Army Corps C in the north meeting Army Corps A from the south near Kütahya, with Army Corps B making a frontal attack to fix the enemy in place while they were encircled. It was a classic maneuverist approach leading to a battle of annihilation, and it used the entire force. To bring their forces in Asia Minor up to strength, the government mobilized three classes of reserves on March 16, 1921 (1913b, 1914, and 1915) and, on April 28 mobilized four more classes of reserves (1903, 1904, 1912, 1913a)—altogether, some 58,000 men.[34] The Greeks also conscripted 12,000 Ottoman Greeks living in the areas occupied by the FAAM in the 1910–1921 classes. The logisticians provided 1,000 heavy and 500 light trucks, as well as 250 ambulances by the end of June. The overall strength of the FAAM grew to over 200,000 men with over 300 artillery pieces.

On July 17, Papoulas undertook a massive operational reorganization of the FAAM to achieve more effective command and control by activating two principal maneuver groups.[35] The Northern Field Army Section, under the command of Major General Georgios Polymenakos, was composed of the Army Corps C (7th and 10th Divisions) and the provisional Northern Group of Divisions (3rd and 11th Divisions) under the command of Major General Nikolaos Trikoupes. The Southern Field Army Section, under direct command of the Army HQ, was composed of Army Corps A (1st and 2nd Divisions), Army Corps B (5th and 13th Divisions), and the provisional Southern Group of Divisions (4th and 12th Divisions) under the command of Major General Demetrios Gidas. The Greek 9th Division remained independent under FAAM control and acted as the link between the field army sections. Both field army sections were well supported with army and corps artillery, as well as with robust aviation sections, with the Southern Field Army Section of the FAAM designated as the main effort (with 7 out of 11 infantry divisions). This command architecture employed 10 of 11 infantry divisions organized into five army corps or corps-equivalent formations, thus more effectively achieving unity of command than previously employed by the FAAM. However, the group commanders were not provided with additional staff officers (thereby forcing them to use their own divisional staffs for higher-level command functions). The objective of the offensive was the destruction of the bulk of the Nationalists' western armies and the denial of the communication hubs of Eskişehir and Kütahya. A military planning assumption behind the success of this plan was that the Nationalists would fight for Kütahya. If successful, this operation would lead to the termination of the conflict because the Nationalists could not recover from such physical and geographical losses.

The Nationalists were also reorganizing their command architecture to achieve more effective command and control. With the threat of internal uprisings receding, the Nationalist acting chief of the General Staff Fevzi sent orders to Refet on May 3, 1921 to merge his Southern Front Command into İsmet's Western Front Command, thereby achieving unity of command in the Nationalists' western armies.[36] Fevzi set June 15 as the effective date of implementation (Refet resumed his post as minister of the interior at the end of June). In the Western Front Command, the use of the term "army corps" was changed to the term "group" (e.g., the XII Corps became the

XII Group). It is unclear why the Nationalists did this, although the Ottoman Army had previously used ad hoc task-organized groups with great
success at Gallipoli and in Palestine.[37] Other organizational changes
included the completion of the transfer to the west of the 5th Caucasian
Division and the 5th Division, as well as the activation of the 6th Division
and a provisional infantry division in İsmet's Western Front Command. To
fill out the casualty-diminished rolls, Fevzi ordered the Central Army to
send 2,454 officers and 55,537 men to İsmet and mobilize the remaining
reservists of the classes of 1881–1888 and 1894–1900.[38] To improve tactical proficiency, specialized schools were opened to train officers and technical specialists in the most up-to-date methods.

On June 15, 1921, İsmet's Western Front Command had swelled to a
theater-level command that included four corps-sized groups: the I Group
commanded by Colonel İzzettin, composed of the 1st, 11th, 23rd, and 61st
Divisions and the 3rd Cavalry Division; the III Group commanded by Colonel Arif, composed of 4th, 24th, and 41st Divisions and the 1st Cavalry
Division; the IV Group commanded by Colonel Kemalettin Sami, composed of the 5th Caucasian Division, the 7th and 8th Divisions, and the 2nd
Cavalry Division; and the XII Group commanded by Colonel Halit, composed of the 57th Division, the Provisional Division, and the 4th Cavalry
Brigade. İsmet retained direct command of the 3rd Caucasian Division, the
6th and 16th Divisions, and the 14th Cavalry Division.[39] The Nationalists
were aware of the impending Greek offensive but were unsure exactly when
it would begin or where the main blows would fall. Tactically, İsmet
deployed his command with a thinly held outpost line of cavalry and infantry detachment on the line of contact between the armies. His main line of
resistance was composed of regimental strong points on high ground, with
reserves positioned to counterattack, but importantly this positioned the
bulk of his army to the east of Kütahya (making it much less vulnerable to
Greek encirclement).

Throughout the month of June 1921, the Greeks repositioned their forces,
and there was desultory fighting east of Bursa and north of Uşak as the
attacking formations moved into their assigned positions. Estimates on
strength vary considerably, but, overall, the FAAM likely had about 126,000
men, 410 artillery pieces, and 4,000 machine guns opposed by some 122,000
Nationalists armed with 160 artillery pieces and 700 machine guns.[40] According to the records of the Nationalist General Staff, in the main battle area
available for combat (not counting forces on the far flanks and forces assigned
to interior duties), Papoulas had 57,000 riflemen, 750 heavy machine guns,

2,204 light machine guns, and 195 artillery pieces, while İsmet had 47,000 riflemen, 326 heavy machine guns, 210 light machine guns, and 137 artillery pieces.[41] Papoulas oversaw two major army-level "Field Army Sections," while İsmet oversaw four corps-level "Groups." The Greek divisions, thanks to mobilization, had now reached their on-paper combat strength with about 9,000 infantrymen, 72 heavy and 288 light machine guns, and 12 artillery pieces. The Nationalist infantry divisions generally fielded around 3,000 rifles, 40 to 50 mixed machine guns, and 10 to 12 artillery pieces. The Nationalist cavalry divisions typically had 700 to 1,000 cavalrymen, a dozen machine guns, and two to five artillery pieces. Only in cavalry did the Nationalists enjoy a superiority of five cavalry divisions (some 5,000 cavalrymen) to the FAAM's single cavalry brigade of fewer than 1,000 cavalrymen.

At this point in the war, the Greeks were much better armed and equipped than the Nationalists. This began to change in the summer of 1921, when the Russians began to ship weapons to the Nationalists under the agreements made during the Treaty of Moscow in March. The first major shipments of weapons arrived on March 30, 1921. Overall totals included 100 artillery pieces, 15 four-gun batteries of 105-mm mountain howitzers, 100,000 rifles, 24 aircraft, five batteries of anti-aircraft guns, wireless and telephone equipment, uniforms, millions of rounds of small arms ammunition and thousands of artillery shells, and hundreds of heavy and light machine guns.[42] This equipment had either been captured from the Germans and Austro-Hungarians at the end of the war or taken from Allied stocks abandoned at ports such as Murmansk and Archangel.

THE KÜTAHYA-ESKİŞEHIR CAMPAIGN

At 6:00 a.m. on July 10, 1921, Major General Nikolaos Trikoupes's Northern Group of Divisions began its advance toward İnegöl.[43] The 3rd Division seized the town immediately, while the untested 11th Division marched on its right flank. For the next three days, the Greeks advanced 40 kilometers against light Nationalist resistance from the 3rd Cavalry Division. Opposing Trikoupes's advance, İsmet's I Group moved its 11th and 61st Divisions forward to the Metris Tepe-Çıplak Tepe ridge line. On Trikoupes's left, the 7th and 10th Divisions of Army Corps C had begun moving directly south from Bursa over 100 kilometers on July 8. Army Corps C also made contact with the outposts of İsmet's III Group on July 10. In the southern sector, Army Corps B and A had worked their way forward to positions north of Dumlupınar and launched attacks there on

July 11.[44] On the FAAM's extreme right flank, the Southern Group pushed toward Afyonkarahisar, while the Greek 9th Division pushed against the Nationalist 1st Cavalry Division in Gediz. Unsure of the exact Greek intentions, İsmet did not make any major changes in his dispositions and kept his headquarters in the north at Eskişehir, while General Papoulas moved the FAAM headquarters forward to Dumlupınar.

On July 12, the Greek attacks in the south began in earnest with Army Corps A and B attacking the IV and XII Groups from the south, while the Southern Group supported the main effort and closed on Afyonkarahisar. In the north, Army Corps C and the Northern Group continued probing attacks. İsmet abandoned resistance against the Greek main effort and delayed with the 2nd Cavalry Division while he established a defensive line farther north at Kütahya. General Papoulas launched his main effort on July 13 with Army Corps A and B attacking abreast.[45] The point of attack was the seam between İsmet's IV and XII Groups, which would rupture the Nationalist's defense. That day, the Southern Group's 4th Division seized Afyonkarahisar, which had been abandoned by the XII Group. To the far north, Army Corps C launched a powerful attack, which drove the I Group's cavalry detachments back to the main line of resistance, and the Northern Group continued to exert pressure east. Now aware of the threat from the Greek main effort in the south, İsmet moved his Western Front Command headquarters southeast to the small village of Seyitgazi.

On July 14, the Greek Northern Group established contact with the I Group's defensive lines on the road to Eskişehir, while Army Corps C pushed relentlessly toward Kütahya. Now alerted to Army Corps C's strong threat to his center, İsmet activated the V Group, commanded by the capable Colonel Fahrettin (Altay), whose skillful command of the XII Corps had been instrumental in Refet's Dumlupınar campaign.[46] This shortened the front of Colonel Arif's III Group and focused him on the defense of the city of Kütahya against the independent Greek 9th Division. İsmet assigned the 14th Cavalry Division and the 15th Division to Fahrettin's command. As we will see in the later campaigns, İsmet's confidence in Fahrettin was not misplaced. This restructuring of the Nationalist command architecture now placed corps-level headquarters against their Greek counterparts. In the south, the Greeks pushed north, and General Papoulas moved the FAAM headquarters from Dumlupınar to the village of Belcemeşe on the railway, 30 kilometers north of Afyonkarahisar.[47] The Greek 12th Division also moved north from Belcemeşe that day, and it would appear that General Papoulas removed the division from the

Southern Group and placed that division under the command Army Corps A.[48] This added additional weight to the FAAM's main effort that came at a critical moment.

The next day, Army Corps B and A made significant progress in forcing the IV and XII Groups north to the point that İsmet felt forced to move his headquarters back to the village of Karacahisar just outside of Eskişehir.[49] Moreover, well-conducted attacks by Army Corps C relentless drove Fahrettin's newly activated V Group to the east. On July 16, the FAAM continued its relentless attacks, further compressing the Western Front Command into a dangerous salient west and south of Kütahya.[50] The situation confronting İsmet was now critical, and he had only bad choices—abandon Kütahya and probably Eskişehir or lose his entire army in an encirclement. On July 17, İsmet met with his commanders at his headquarters, and he informed them that the army could no longer hold its current positions. To save the army, İsmet decided to retreat to the Sakarya River line, and he ordered a rear-guard action designed to hold the Greeks, while the main bodies of troops could break contact and retreat.[51] Papoulas's Northern Group occupied the railway station at İnönü that day, and the 9th and 10th Divisions occupied Kütahya, which had been abandoned by the III Group.[52]

For General Papoulas and the FAAM, the culminating point in the offensive came on July 18, 1921 when İsmet withdrew most of the III and IV Groups to the east of the battle front. Papoulas moved his own headquarters to Kütahya that day, placing himself farther from the decisive point, which can be identified as his far-right wing (had he been closer, he might have been able to push the three divisions of Army Corps A north in time to cut off İsmet's retreat). In any case, İsmet brought Fahrettin's V Group southeast in time to assist the XII Group in stopping Army Corps A's advance. İsmet moved his front headquarters east along the railway to Ankara to the village of Ağapınar.[53] July 18 was arguably the most dangerous day for the Nationalists because the tactical situation was so chaotic that a single collapse would have led to a cascade failure of the entire scheme of retreat. The next day, İsmet abandoned Eskişehir but organized a strong withdrawal with the I, III, V, IV, and XII groups in-line from north to south.[54] Army Corps C seized Eskişehir and the FAAM advanced, with its divisions harrying the retreating Nationalists and moving the 12th Division north to the left flank of Army Corps B.[55] On July 20, İsmet conducted a tactical counterattack with the III Group, attempting to reclaim Eskişehir, but the city was irretrievably lost. İsmet withdrew the Western

Front Command headquarters to Karatokat in the center of mass of his forces, while his V Group conducted successful counterattacks to block the attacks of Army Corps A.[56]

İsmet wanted to launch an operational-level counteroffensive, and, after meeting with his commanders (and cabling Kemal in Ankara), he ordered his staff to begin planning a counteroffensive to begin no later than July 21, 1921.[57] Planning proceeded while the Western Front Command withdrew, but İsmet decided to try a small encirclement of what he believed to be the exhausted Greek forces around Eskişehir, composed of Army Corps C and the 12th Division. İsmet estimated that the Greeks were tired from 10 days of continuous combat and prolonged marching and were running low on munitions and supplies. In its final form, İsmet planned a northern envelopment by the I Group's 1st Division and the reinforced 1st Cavalry Division to Eskişehir, while the IV Group conducted a breakthrough in the center using the 5th, 23rd, and 61st Divisions, with the 3rd Caucasian and 7th Divisions exploited the breach to an objective south of the city.[58] Fahrettin's V Group would conduct a supporting attack on the right flank of the FAAM.

On the night of July 20, the Western Front Command notified I Group commander Colonel İzzettin to attack the next morning and, at 8:30 a.m. on July 21, İsmet telephoned IV Group commander Colonel Kemalettin Sami to begin his attack as well.[59] The I and IV Groups made initial gains of about five kilometers but were driven back to their lines by Greek counterattacks, while the V Group made no gains at all. The repulse of the Nationalists was due to the prompt movement of reserves to reinforce the front lines and to counterattack the enemy. The FAAM headquarters in Kütahya, 100 kilometers west of the front lines, only learned of the Nationalist counteroffensive in the afternoon.[60] İsmet called off his failed counteroffensive that night and ordered his commanders to continue the retreat the following morning.[61] The absence of intervention by the FAAM meant that no immediate pursuit was ordered, and the Nationalists were allowed to retreat without pressure.

In fact, General Papoulas had already issued orders at 4:40 a.m. on July 22 for the FAAM to continue offensive operations in pursuit of the enemy, but this was negated by İsmet's counteroffensive.[62] The Nationalist counteroffensive was a failure, but it did slow the Greek advance significantly; moreover, it caused General Papoulas to reconsider his plans. On July 23, General Papoulas suspended offensive operations in order to conduct rest and reconstitution of combat forces and reorganizations of the lines of communication (supply).[63] Overall casualties in the FAAM were large, amounting to over 8,000 killed and wounded, while the Nationalists lost about the same but also sustained major numbers of desertions—as many as 30,000.[64] The Nationalists also lost large amounts of supplies stored in the warehouses of Eskişehir, as well as 55 machine guns and 18 artillery pieces in the retreat.[65] However, the Nationalist army had survived to fight another day. The Greek victory was geographic rather than the destruction of the Nationalist Army and, in turn, cannot be called decisive. The victory was very important, however, for future Greek operations in Asia Minor because the FAAM captured the rail lines intact (a major failure on the part of the Nationalists), which allowed lines of communication to be established northeast from Eskişehir to Bursa and west from Kütahya-Afyonkarahisar-Uşak to Izmir.

Modern Greek Brigadier General Vasileios Loumiotes (retired) has calculated that of the 10 divisions participating in the campaign, during the crucial period July 14–16, only two really took the brunt of the fighting—the 1st and 5th divisions. The 2nd Division conducted some secondary operations on July 16, while the 7th, 9th, and 10th divisions mostly fought Nationalist rear guards. The 3rd, 11th, 12th, and 13th divisions did not engage in serious fighting—that is to say, Papoulas was able to concentrate the largest army in modern and ancient Greek history in one theater and failed to use it effectively. Essentially, Papoulas had a good plan, though the topography and transportation network largely imposed a certain course of action if one aimed to take two objectives and provided ideal conditions for a Cannae-like encirclement at the same time. The forces available were adequate for the task. But when it came to executing the plan, it seems Papoulas and his staff were unable to coordinate their subordinates, to impose their will on them, or to back them up when they, in turn, attempted to impose their will on recalcitrant lower-level commanders. As a result, three army corps, two army sections, and the 11 divisions fought largely individual and isolated battles rather than mutually supporting each other in a cohesive campaign.[66]

THE RETREAT TO THE SAKARYA RIVER

The Nationalists withdrew about 10 kilometers on July 22, while İsmet moved his headquarters east to the village of Sarıköy on the railway to Ankara (a position 55 kilometers east of Eskişehir and 180 kilometers west of Ankara). He directed his staff to plan for a defensive line to be established there by the evening of July 23. The proposed line would have the I Group north of the Sakarya River and the III and XII Group to the south of the river. The IV Group would be positioned in immediate tactical reserve in the center of the position.[67] İsmet's V Group, now reinforced with more cavalry, was charged with delaying the Greeks with rear guards while the main body of the Western Front Command withdrew. The FAAM briefly maintained contact but allowed the retreating Nationalists to withdraw unhindered.[68] By the evening of July 23, İsmet's army had gained the proposed defensive position; however, unsure as to the Greek intentions, he directed his staff to begin planning to fall back 10 kilometers to another defensive line.[69] On July 24, İsmet moved his headquarters east to the village of Bicer.[70]

On July 25, 1921, İsmet moved his Western Front Command headquarters to the village of Polatlı, about 85 kilometers southwest of Ankara. The Western Front Command headquarters would not move east again. With the ending of the Greek offensive, the front in western Anatolia briefly stabilized. The Nationalists had held off the Greeks in the Kocaeli Peninsula in the north, while the Nationalist 6th Division held the Greeks on the road to İsparta, and a provisional division held the line east of Afyonkarahisar. İsmet deployed the 2nd Cavalry Division to Aziziye to maintain communication between these southern forces and his main body of combat groups on the Sakarya. Fortunately for the Nationalists, the incoming (from Cilicia) II Corps headquarters reached the city Akşehir (roughly halfway between Afyonkarahisar and Konya) on July 25 and began to assume control over the southern wing of İsmet's far-flung command.[71] As noted in chapter 6, Kemal had ordered the II Corps headquarters and the 9th Division from the Southern Front Command (against the French) to reinforce the Western Front Command on April 25.[72]

The political consequences of the Nationalist defeat were significant. Ankara itself was threatened by the Greek offensive, and the population was "in a panic" and the government "in an uproar."[73] On July 22, the Council of Ministers decided to abandon Ankara and move the government to Kayseri.[74] However, Fevzi informed the National Assembly that it had been decided to defend Ankara—causing enormous disruption and debate. On July 24, Kemal intervened and convinced enough members to reverse the decision to evacuate the capital. In the end, the government moved its offices and documents to Kayseri, but the assembly remained in Ankara. Kemal went to İsmet's headquarters at Polatlı on July 26 for updated briefings. In a secret session of the assembly, Kemal blamed the disastrous defeat on İsmet. Kemal went on to assert that "he was ready to take on the authority of a commander-in-chief for a period of time like three months, during which he would have absolute power to mobilize the nation's resources for its defense."[75] The next day, the assembly voted in secret (169 to 13), and then unanimously in public (184 to 0) to appoint Mustafa Kemal as commander in chief (*baş kumandan*). Almost as important as this momentous decision, Kemal then rearranged the senior leadership of what might be called his war cabinet. On August 5, İsmet resigned his position as chief of the General Staff because it was impossible for him to perform those duties in addition to those of the commander of the Western Front Command. Kemal then appointed Fevzi as the permanent chief of the General Staff and Refet as the minister of war.[76] At the strategic level, gathering these capable individuals in key positions to manage the Nationalist's war effort proved decisive.

CONCLUSION

The Nationalists survived the Kütahya-Eskişehir Campaign by the narrowest of margins. Problems with Greek corps and the army section commander's execution of Papoulas's plan were as important in saving İsmet's army as were İsmet's decisions and actions themselves. In fairness to İsmet, although he was a very experienced commander, he was "double-hatted" as chief of the general staff, in addition to his role as a field army commander. It is also worth noting that this campaign was his first experience in what amounted to a theater command and that he faced a multidirectional offensive by an entire enemy field army. His previous experience at First and Second İnönü had been against an army corps attacking on a single axis of advance. That İsmet was able to maintain his army in being was a considerable achievement. The next year would see him grow into a mature and capable theater commander.

NOTES

1. Churchill, *The Aftermath*, 391.
2. Gedeon, Paschalidou, and Dima-Dimitrou, *A Concise History of the Campaign in Asia Minor*, 95. The phrase "blank check" refers to Germany's famous promise to back Austria-Hungary against the Serbs in July 1914 under any and all circumstances, including going to war.

3. Gedeon, Paschalidou, and Dima-Dimitrou, *A Concise History of the Campaign in Asia Minor*, 95–96.

4. A full discussion, in Greek, of the debates around the planning of the operation can be found in Vasileios Loumiotes (Λουμιώτης, Βασίλειος), "Η Ανώτατη Διεύθυνση των Επιχειρήσεων της Στρατιάς Μικράς Ασίας του Δεκέμβριου 1920 και του Μάρτιου 1921 (The Higher Direction of the Operations of the Field Army of Asia Minor in December 1920 and March 1921)," *Στρατηγειν*, 1 (Summer 2019): 33–78. I would like to thank Dr. Konstantinos Travlos for his help in accessing the information in this article. According to Loumiotes, the convoluted story of how the final plan of operations was decided shows the serious problems at the level of high command of the Greek war effort. These saw a lack of clear chain of command; disagreements between Pallis and Sarrigiannis; and interventions by the Army Staff Service chief, Major General Konstantinos Gouveles, with Papoulas being essentially a passive receiver of recommendations. The main point is that an initial plan, possibly by Sarrigiannis, for operations on converging axes of advance (Uşak to Kütahya and Bursa to Eskisehir and then from both to Afyonkarahisar), was replaced by one on divergent axes of advance (Bursa to Eskisehir and Uşak to Afyonkarahisar), probably suggested by Gouveles to Pallis when Sarrigiannis was in London. Papoulas does not seem to have given input in either case. Importantly, Gouveles considered necessary the reinforcement of the army in Asia Minor with 30,000 men via a new mobilization before the operations began. Gounares, for political reasons, declared mobilization but demanded that the operations be conducted before they were completed. Gouveles was the first chief of the Army Staff Service (the precursor of the Greek Army General Staff) to attempt to establish the primacy of his office over that of operational commanders. Failing to do that, he resigned in February 1921.

5. Gedeon, Paschalidou, and Dima-Dimitrou, *A Concise History of the Campaign in Asia Minor*, 102–104.

6. For a summary of the manpower situation and sources of both forces see Loumiotes, "The Higher Direction," 33–78.

7. Görgülü, *On Yıllık Harbin Kadrosu*, 263–265.

8. Apac'ca, Önalp, and Turhan, *Batı Cephesi, 3ncü Kısım*, Kuruluş 4 and 4a (Charts 4 and 4a following page 612).

9. Ibid., 300–301.

10. Apac'ca, Önalp, and Turhan, *Batı Cephesi, 3ncü Kısım*, 308–317; and Gedeon, Paschalidou, Dima-Dimitrou, *A Concise History of the*

Campaign in Asia Minor, 105–112. See also Kaymakam Salahaddin, "Ikinci İnönü Meydan Muharebesi," *Askeri Mecmua*, 31 (September 1, 1933): 5–160.

11. During this advance, the axis of movements of the 3rd and 10th Divisions, by corps command were to cross over at Bilecik, an order that the commander of the 3rd Division, Major General Nikolaos Trikoupis found perplexing. See Nikolaos Trikoupis (Τρικούπης, Νικόλαος), *Διοίκησης Μεγάλων Μονάδων εν Πολεμώ 1918–1922 (Command of Major Units during War 1918–1922)*, Eleftheris Skepsis 2001[1935], 117. I am indebted to Dr. Konstantinos Travlos for bringing this to my attention.

12. Gedeon, Paschalidou, and Dima-Dimitrou, *A Concise History of the Campaign in Asia Minor*, 112.

13. Apac'ca, Önalp, and Turhan, *Batı Cephesi, 3ncü Kısım*, 336.

14. Ibid., Kroki 42 (Sketch Map 42 following page 612).

15. The ferocity of the Greek attacked can be judged by the fact that the 2/39 Evzone Regiment of the 3rd Division saw three commanding officers wounded or killed. See Trikoupis, *Command of Major Units in War*, 127. It would lose a fourth over the next few days.

16. Gedeon, Paschalidou, and Dima-Dimitrou, *A Concise History of the Campaign in Asia Minor*, 115–118.

17. Apac'ca, Önalp, and Turhan, *Batı Cephesi, 3ncü Kısım*, 408.

18. Gedeon, Paschalidou, and Dima-Dimitrou, *A Concise History of the Campaign in Asia Minor*, 118; and Apac'ca, Önalp, and Turhan, *Batı Cephesi, 3ncü Kısım*, 396–413, Kroki 50 (Sketch Map 50 following page 612).

19. Gedeon, Paschalidou, and Dima-Dimitrou, *A Concise History of the Campaign in Asia Minor*, 121.

20. Summary provided by Dr. Konstantinos Travlos based on a series of blog posts by Vasileios Loumiotes at http://belisarius21.wordpress.com/. These, in turn, are based on the third volume of the Greek Army General Staff, Directorate of Army History multivolume official military history of the campaign, *Επιθετικαί Επιχειρήσεις Δεκεμβρίου 1920–Μαρτίου 1921 (Offensive Operations December 1920–March 1921)*, Directorate of Army History 1963 (republished in 1986).

21. Apac'ca, Önalp, and Turhan, *Batı Cephesi, 3ncü Kısım*, 396–413, Kroki 38 (Sketch map 38).

22. Gedeon, Paschalidou, and Dima-Dimitrou, *A Concise History of the Campaign in Asia Minor*, 129–130.

23. Apac'ca, Önalp, and Turhan, *Batı Cephesi, 3ncü Kısım*, 391–392.

24. Belen, *Türk Kurtuluş Savaşı*, 314.

25. Apac'ca, Önalp, and Turhan, *Batı Cephesi, 3ncü Kısım*, 468–469.

26. Ibid.

27. Ibid., 501.

28. Gedeon, Paschalidou, and Dima-Dimitrou, *A Concise History of the Campaign in Asia Minor*, 133.

29. Görgülü, *On Yıllık Harbin Kadrosu*, 267–268.

30. Apac'ca, Önalp, and Turhan, *Batı Cephesi, 3ncü Kısım*, Kroki 63 (Sketch Map 63 following page 612).

31. Mango, *Atatürk*, 311.

32. Gedeon, Paschalidou, and Dima-Dimitrou, *A Concise History of the Campaign in Asia Minor*, 147.

33. Ibid.

34. The Ottomans and Nationalists identified conscription year cohorts by the date of birth, while the Greeks identified the cohorts by the year in which the men became eligible for conscription. Occasionally, the Greeks apportioned part of a year group, for example, 1913a.

35. Gedeon, Paschalidou, and Dima-Dimitrou, *A Concise History of the Campaign in Asia Minor*, 151–152.

36. Hakkı Alpay, Şadi Sükan, and Kâmil Önalp, *Türk İstiklâl Harbi IInci Cilt Batı Cephesi 4ncü Kısım, Kütahya, Eskişehir Muharebeleri (15 Mayıs 1921–25 Temmuz 1921)* (Ankara: Genelkurmay Basımevi, 1974), 51.

37. See Edward J. Erickson, *Gallipoli: The Ottoman Campaign* (Barnsley, UK: Pen and Sword Military, 2010); and Erickson, *Palestine, The Ottoman Campaigns* for information about why and how the army formed temporary groups to hold key terrain or conduct complex offensive operations.

38. Alpay, Sükan, and Önalp, *Kütahya, Eskişehir Muharebeleri*, 57.

39. Ibid., Kuruluş 3 (Organizational Chart 3 following page 96).

40. Mango, *Atatürk*, 315.

41. Alpay, Sükan, and Önalp, *Kütahya, Eskişehir Muharebeleri*, 124.

42. Timur, Atakan, Berktay, and Ertekin, *İdari Faaliyetler*, 266–269. The official history of Nationalist logistics presents a comprehensive listing of weapons received from the Soviets. See also Mango, *Atatürk*, 310, which gives much lower numbers of weapons received from the Soviets; for example, 43,000 rifles and 100 field artillery guns.

43. Gedeon, Paschalidou, and Dima-Dimitrou, *A Concise History of the Campaign in Asia Minor*, 164.

44. Alpay, Sükan, and Önalp, *Kütahya, Eskişehir Muharebeleri*, Kroki 19 (Sketch Map 19 following page 192).

45. Ibid., Kroki 22 (Sketch Map 22 following page 232).

46. Görgülü, *On Yıllık Harbin Kadrosu*, 275.

47. Alpay, Sükan, and Önalp, *Kütahya, Eskişehir Muharebeleri*, Kroki 23 (Sketch Map 23 following page 256).

48. Gedeon, Paschalidou, and Dima-Dimitrou, *A Concise History of the Campaign in Asia Minor*, 190.

49. Alpay, Sükan, and Önalp, *Kütahya, Eskişehir Muharebeleri*, Kroki 24 (Sketch Map 24 following page 280).

50. Ibid., Kroki 25 (Sketch Map 25 following page 312).

51. Shaw, *From Empire to Republic*, vol. 3, part 1, 1325.

52. Alpay, Sükan, and Önalp, *Kütahya, Eskişehir Muharebeleri*, Kroki 27 (Sketch Map 27 following page 350).

53. Ibid., Kroki 28 (Sketch Map 28 following page 382).

54. Ibid., Kroki 29 (Sketch Map 29 following page 398).

55. Gedeon, Paschalidou, and Dima-Dimitrou, *A Concise History of the Campaign in Asia Minor*, 203–206. See also Alpay, Sükan, and Önalp, *Kütahya, Eskişehir Muharebeleri*, Kroki 30 and 34 (Sketch Maps 30 and 34 following pages 430 and 512, respectively).

56. Alpay, Sükan, and Önalp, *Kütahya, Eskişehir Muharebeleri*, Kroki 30 (Sketch Map 30 following page 430).

57. Alpay, Sükan, and Önalp, *Kütahya, Eskişehir Muharebeleri*, 441; Gedeon, Paschalidou, and Dima-Dimitrou, *A Concise History of the Campaign in Asia Minor*, 204; Mango, *Atatürk*, 315; and Shaw, *From Empire to Republic*, vol. 3, part 1, 1325.

58. Alpay, Sükan, and Önalp, *Kütahya, Eskişehir Muharebeleri*, Kroki 31 (Sketch Map 31 following page 468).

59. Ibid., 445–455.

60. Gedeon, Paschalidou, and Dima-Dimitrou, *A Concise History of the Campaign in Asia Minor*, 212.

61. Belen, *Türk Kurtuluş Savaşı*, 333–334.

62. Gedeon, Paschalidou, and Dima-Dimitrou, *A Concise History of the Campaign in Asia Minor*, 213.

63. Ibid., 214.

64. Mango, *Atatürk*, 316.

65. Alpay, Sükan, and Önalp, *Kütahya, Eskişehir Muharebeleri*, 537.

66. I am indebted to Professor Konstantinos Travlos for this analysis. Further, Professor Travlos asserted, "To be frank the corps commanders were abysmal. Loumiotes and his group think that if Paraskevopoulos and Pangalos were in command, under the same conditions they would ha[ve]

won, because Pangalos had no tolerance for insubordination. Loumiotes has shown that during the attempt of the 5th Division to break Nationalist positions around Çaüş Çiftlik, the units of the 13th Division were ordered to take Akçal Dag. Plasteras' 5/42 Evzone Regiment was given the task of attacking first, Plasteras refused to execute the order, and neither his divisional or corps commanders intervened." Konstantinos Travlos, email to author, November 18, 2019.

67. Alpay, Sükan, and Önalp, *Kütahya, Eskişehir Muharebeleri*, 489–509, Kroki 33 (Sketch Map 33 following page 500).

68. Gedeon, Paschalidou, and Dima-Dimitrou, *A Concise History of the Campaign in Asia Minor*, 216.

69. See Fahri Aykut, *İstiklâl Savaşı'nda Kütahya ve Eskişehir Muharebeleri* (Ankara: Genelkurmay Basımevi, 2006), 148–158 for a series of messages between Kemal and İsmet and İsmet and his subordinates regarding the withdrawal.

70. Alpay, Sükan, and Önalp, *Kütahya, Eskişehir Muharebeleri*, 510–525, Kroki 35 (Sketch Map 35 following page 544).

71. Ibid., 544.

72. Saral, Kaptan, and Keskin, *Güney Cephesi*, 273–274.

73. Mango, *Atatürk*, 316.

74. Shaw, *From Empire to Republic*, vol. 3, part 1, 1335.

75. Ibid., 1336.

76. Ökse, Baycan, and Sakaryalı, *Komutanların Biyografileri*, 57, 99.

EIGHT

The Culminating Point at Sakarya

The enemy not having shown a disposition to negotiate and accept peace, I asked the Army Command if it considers the annihilation of the enemy . . . is imminent.[1]

Prime Minister Demetrios Gounares, July 26, 1921

INTRODUCTION

While the Kütahya-Eskişehir Campaign was a great geographical victory for the Greeks, it failed to achieve a decisive result over the Nationalist Army.[2] The Nationalists had lost important terrain and lines of communication, but their army remained a powerful instrument with which to continue the war. It had been defeated, but the damage was repairable. As a result, the Greeks faced a strategic quandary. The Greek politicians and the generals convened a council of war at Kütahya on July 27, 1921 to discuss and determine the way ahead for the FAAM. The outcome was a decision to renew offensive operations, with a view toward the destruction of the Nationalist Army and the occupation of Ankara. However, the balancing of operational ends, ways, and means in terms of how exactly the FAAM might achieve this result was problematic in the extreme. Nevertheless, this led to an underresourced campaign that floundered on the banks of the Sakarya River (called the Sangarios River by the Greeks).

THE COUNCIL OF WAR

On July 27, Greek prime minister Demetrios Gounares arrived in Küta-hya to examine the military situation.[3] The next day, Gounares conducted a council of war with Minister of the Army Nikolaos Theotokes, FAAM commander General Papoulas, and his chief of staff Colonel Konstantinos Pallis. Reflecting the army concerns about logistics, the chief of the Army Staff Service, Lieutenant General Victor Dousmanes, and the government liaison with the FAAM, Major General Xenophon Strategos also attended. Gounares asked his commanders whether the Nationalist Army had been annihilated to the extent that he could declare that the war had been won. He continued by suggesting that, if so, Greece might impose a unilateral peace settlement on the Nationalists leading to a semiformal peace and demobilization. The generals quickly disabused him of these ideas because the Nationalist armies remained intact and in being. Gounares then asked about the viability of continuing offensive operations, which, according to the Concise Greek History, after discussions led to "unanimous agreement to continue offensive operations toward Ankara."[4] Historian Michael Llewellyn-Smith, however, presents a picture of a much more contentious meeting, with the final decision only reached reluctantly.[5] Llewellyn-Smith asserted that at the meeting, Gounaris and Theotokes, supported by Strat-egos, prevailed over the military leaders.

Within General Papoulas's staff, there were differences of opinion about what could be accomplished and what could not be accomplished. The doubts of the FAAM were expressed in a memorandum to the council that highlighted logistics difficulties and outlined a series of assumptions that had to be overcome in order to achieve success.[6] The English-language translation of the memorandum uses the word "if" four times, establishing that the FAAM staff considered the operation contingent on at least four conditions—any one of which would cause failure. These doubts notwith-standing, all agreed that failure would be catastrophic.

The FAAM plan of operations sought to achieve an annihilation of the main Nationalist Army west of the Sakarya River. The basic Greek plan envisioned a screening force in the north, which would fix as many Nation-alist forces as possible, while the army conducted the main effort in the south from Eskişehir and Afyonkarahisar toward Ankara.[7] Army Corps C and B held the front lines from north to south (respectively), while Army Corps A was in reserve in Eskişehir. Army Corps C would attack east to fix as many Nationalist forces as possible, while Army Corps A and B would attack southeast to seize objectives south of the upper Sakarya and Gök rivers. The Greeks thought that, the Nationalists would have to fight in order to save its position and defend Ankara from a flank attack from Army Corps A and B. In terms of the principles of war, Papoulas's plan depended on concentration by maneuvering overwhelming forces against İsmet's left flank. While the operation looked like an encirclement on the map, Papoulas was positioning his army with the intent of forcing İsmet into an attritional battle, which would "dissolve," "remove," or "crush" the Nationalist Army.[8]

PREPARATIONS

The FAAM dissolved the provisional army sections and combat groups fielded at the end of its previous operations and reorganized its forces: Army Corps A, composed of the 1st, 2nd, and 12th Divisions under Major General Kontoulis; Army Corps B under Lieutenant General Prince Andreas Vasilopais, composed of the 5th, 9th and 13th Divisions; and Army Corps C. composed of the 3rd, 7th, and 10th Divisions under Major General Polymenakos. On his right flank, General Papoulas established a Southern Group of Divisions under Major General Trikoupes with the 4th Division at Afyonkarahisar, and Papoulas placed the remaining 11th Division directly under the FAAM headquarters guarding his army's left flank. To support the operation. Papoulas established the General Supply Center of Eskişehir, which enjoyed excellent rail communication with Bursa and Izmir. The field army also had 600 three-ton heavy trucks and 240 one-ton light trucks; however, the 11 infantry divisions remained reliant on animal-drawn wagons and pack animals for supply.[9]

On August 7, Papoulas issued his orders for operations against Ankara, which was composed of two phases in its final form. The first phase called for flanking and enveloping İsmet's defensive positions, which were west of the Sakarya River around Polatlı and north of the Gök River. The second phase would consist of a simultaneous main attack by all three army corps with the objective of the "annihilation and dispersal" of İsmet's army.[10] Unfortunately, the wide-flanking maneuver from the south extended the logistic lines of the FAAM by 138 kilometers through the poorly serviced (by roads) region south of the Sakarya River. It also meant that on the wide plains to the southwest of Ankara, enemy scouts would quickly locate the massive columns of two army corps marching east.[11] Altogether, the Greeks committed nine out of 11 infantry divisions in Asia Minor to the offensive, with an available strength of about 110,000 men. Of this total, Papoulas fielded an offensive combat strength of 77,060 infantrymen, 1,380 cavalrymen, 684 machine guns, and 296 artillery pieces.[12]

İsmet's Western Front Command occupied an L-shaped defensive position, with one leg running north-south behind the upper Sakarya River and the other leg running from the west to east along the Gök River. However, by mid-August only the upper Sakarya River line was manned and prepared for battle. Watching the front against the Greeks about 50 kilometers east of Eskişehir, İsmet deployed two cavalry groups in a north-south line of outposts.[13] The I Group, composed of the 1st Cavalry Division, the 1st Division, and a combat group from the 41st Division, patrolled astride the Eskişehir-Polatlı rail line, and the V Group, composed of the 14th Cavalry Division and the 4th Cavalry Brigade, patrolled the ground south to the Afyonkarahisar-Akşehir rail line.[14] Their mission was to slow a Greek offensive and to identify the main effort. On the upper Sakarya defensive line, İsmet deployed from north to south the III Group, composed of the 15th and 24th Divisions, and the XII Group, composed of 8th, 11th, and 57th Divisions and the 20th Cavalry Regiment. Behind the main lines, İsmet maintained the IV Group in reserve, composed of the 5th Caucasian Division and the 4th, 7th, 23rd, and 61st Divisions. On his southern flank, İsmet maintained the 6th Division and a provisional division east of Ayfonkarahisar. Additionally, the II Corps and 9th Division had arrived in Akşehir, and the 5th Division was due to arrive shortly. Altogether, İsmet had about 96,000 soldiers (not including his southern-flank formations), comprising 82,966 infantrymen, 3,342 cavalrymen, 742 machine guns, and 168 artillery pieces.[15]

SAKARYA—THE GREEK FIRST PHASE

There was minor tactical activity from July 25 to August 3 as General Papoulas moved his forces forward to make contact with the Nationalists' outpost line.[16] These movements caused İsmet to make significant repositioning decisions on July 29–31, moving the 3rd Cavalry Division and the 41st Division behind the Sakarya River to his northern (or right) flank. İsmet also formed and repositioned a Reserve Group (the 4th and 23rd Divisions) 30 kilometers north toward Ankara. These redeployments on his right or northern flank, which were designed to place major Nationalist forces in front of Ankara, indicate that İsmet misunderstood where Papoulas intended to strike. However, as more intelligence reached him, İsmet sent the 15th Division to Haymana on the Gök River line on August 2. On August 3, İsmet withdrew the 3rd Caucasian Division behind the Sakarya River. Between then and August 5, Army Corps C and B closed on the I and V Group's cavalry outposts.[17] Between August 6 and 12, minor skirmishing occurred on the line of contact.

General Papoulas began his offensive movement on August 13, 1921, with all army corps and groups pushing east to drive the Nationalist outpost line back toward the Sakarya River. In incremental attacks, the three Greek army corps advanced about 20 kilometers every day for seven days, fighting several small battles along the way.[18] The Nationalist I and V Groups fell back fighting rear-guard actions designed to slow the Greek advance (see map 8.1). As the Greeks advanced, İsmet had a clearer idea about their intentions and, on August 14, he brought the Reserve Group back south to the center of his position. Dilatory and inconclusive fighting erupted on the Kocaeli and Afyonkarahisar fronts.[19] On August 15, İsmet brought the II Group (formerly the II Corps), composed of the 5th and 9th Divisions, north from Akşehir to a position behind the withdrawing V Group.[20] İsmet was also concerned with such tactical matters as increasing the effectiveness of artillery support for his infantry, and he urged his subordinate group commanders to not change the partnering of artillery formations with infantry formations as frequently as had been done in the past.[21] The next day, İsmet moved the II Group north to the Gök River, while the V Group fell back on its southern flank. He also dissolved the Reserve Group and returned its divisions to their original commands.

On August 17, 1921, Kemal went to İsmet's headquarters at Polatlı and took personal command of the army in the field. However, İsmet was in the process of pulling his Western Front Command headquarters back to the small village of Alagöz. According to Andrew Mango, Kemal was housebound with a broken rib suffered earlier, and Mango casts him as determined but stricken with occasional bouts of despair.[22] On the same day, İsmet pulled the II Group and its two infantry divisions behind the Gök River. The FAAM now closed on the upper Sakarya River and drew within 20 kilometers of the Gök River. By August 20, Papoulas had concentrated most of his three army corps against the Gök River line, with Army Corps C (3rd and 10th Divisions), Army Corps A (1st, 2nd, and 12th Divisions), and Army Corps B (5th, 9th, and 13th Divisions) on a

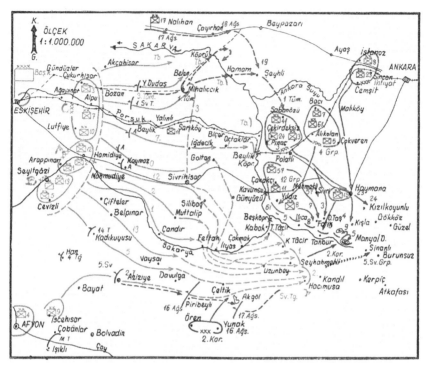

Map 8.1   Movement to Contact (August 14–17, 1921)
In early August 1921, the FAAM was not in contact with the main strength of the Western Front Command, which maintained only an outpost line against the Greeks. On August 13, General Papoulas began a movement to contact to the Sakarya River. Unfortunately for the Greeks, the long march to the east gave İsmet plenty of time to react and form a strong defensive position.
Courtesy of the Turkish General Staff Military History and Strategy Institute (ATASE).

50-kilometer wide front.[23] Army Group C detached the 7th Division to hold the wide upper Sakarya River sector to the north of General Polymenakos's two remaining divisions. The FAAM's Cavalry Brigade guarded Army Corps B's right flank opposite the Nationalist V Group. However, after a week of intense marching, Papoulas's infantry were in no condition to immediately assault the Nationalist defensive positions. Moreover, the slower moving ammunition and supply trains needed more time to catch up with the combat formations.[24] Thus, the FAAM sat along the Gök River for an additional three days.

Unfortunately for General Papoulas and the FAAM, İsmet used the three days well by restructuring and repositioning his army. İsmet detached the 8th and 57th Divisions from the XII Group (which now faced only the Greek 7th Division on the upper Sakarya), sending the former to the III Group and the latter into army reserve.[25] He also rushed the I Group on a 50-kilometer, 12-hour forced march from the north to Haymana and allocated the 23rd and 24th Divisions to it.[26] İsmet left a Provisional Group under Colonel Kâzım, along with three infantry divisions and a cavalry division to secure his northern sector. İsmet placed the I Group in army reserve 15 kilometers north of the Gök River line. By August 22, İsmet had established a solid defensive line on the high ground north of the Gök, composed of (from west to east) the IV Group (5th Caucasian Division and 61st Division in the line), III Group (8th and 15th Divisions in line and 7th Division in immediate reserve), and II Group (5th and 9th Divisions in line and 4th Division in immediate reserve). Holding his left flank south of the Gök River, the V Group (14th Cavalry Division and the 4th Cavalry Brigade) stood on the defense. In general army reserve to the north of the river line, İsmet had the two divisions of the I Group—the 3rd Caucasian Division, the 57th Division, and the 2nd and 3rd Cavalry Divisions. While the Nationalist infantry divisions were 60 to 70 percent smaller than their Greek counterparts, these allocations gave İsmet six infantry divisions holding the Gök River line, with two infantry divisions in immediate reserve under group command, and four infantry divisions and two cavalry divisions available in general army reserve. Given that the V Group would tie up at least one Greek infantry division, General Papoulas now had seven infantry divisions facing six entrenched Nationalist infantry divisions on the Gök River—and these were supported by six more infantry divisions in reserve.

İsmet had won the positional battle largely because time was always on the side of the Western Front Command. His army enjoyed interior lines of communication, which enabled him to shift formations rapidly to bring them into battle positions and to maintain his reserves fresh and ready to fight. Papoulas and the FAAM were penalized by extended exterior lines of communication, which caused a 10-day period of marching and resting the tired Greek divisions before they were ready to attack. Once again, the problem of not fully concentrating the operational force for offensive operations would afflict the Greeks. Going into this battle, the Greeks committed about 70 percent of their available forces, while the Turks concentrated 85 percent.[27] This created an unfavorable tactical ratio in the main battle area of 1.2 attackers to one defender, which was exacerbated by the fact that the Nationalists were entrenched on high ground behind a river. Finally, the Greeks had lost the element of surprise, and the entire FAAM knew it.

What effect did the presence of Mustafa Kemal and Fevzi have on İsmet's decisions and on his Western Front Headquarters?[28] The Turkish official history records continuous dialogue between the three men in the six days before the main Greek attack. Unquestionably Kemal adjusted some of İsmet's deployments—particularly regarding the flanking Kocaeli and Afyonkarahisar fronts. Thus, Kemal's involvement enabled İsmet to focus almost exclusively on the impending battle in the decisive central front. It is also true that conversations with Kemal and Fevzi served to clarify İsmet's understanding of Papoulas's intentions. By August 20, Kemal and İsmet agreed that the Greek intentions were to assault the left flank of the Western Front Command, and they made last-minute adjustments to the army's dispositions.[29] The next day, İsmet sent orders to his group commanders that he expected the Greeks to attack the army's left wing within two days and alerted them to stand ready to receive their assaults.

SAKARYA—THE GREEK SECOND PHASE

General Papoulas moved his army headquarters forward to Uzunbey and opened his attack on August 23 by moving his three corps forward to assault positions (called the "jump-off base" in the Concise Greek History).[30] This put Army Corps C on the west bank of the lower Gök River. It put Army Corps A across the upper Gök on the west bank of the Katranji Dere (a small stream) but, more importantly enabled its 1st Division to seize Mangal Dağ, a small mountain in the II Group's sector, with almost no opposition. The Concise Greek History asserted that the Nationalist 5th Division commander evacuated Mangal Dağ with the approval of the II Group chief of staff, leading to the relief of the division commander.[31] However, Turkish histories record that 5th Division commander, Lieutenant Colonel Mehmet Kenan (Dalbaşar), remained in command until September 29 when he took command of the 41st Division and was promoted to colonel the following year.[32] Despite this success, Papoulas remained concerned that his assault troops were not fully prepared for a major offensive, and he issued orders at 11:30 p.m. on August 23 to delay the attack for 24 hours (until August 24, which conflicted with his previous orders to begin the main attacks at dawn on August 23).[33]

As the F.A.A.M. repositioned its heavy artillery on the morning of August 24 (see map 8.2), an intelligence report based on aerial reconnaissance came into the headquarters at 12:30 p.m. confirming that the Nationalists were moving to the east and had withdrawn from the northern sector of the front. Hoping to seize an unexpected opportunity, Papoulas ordered his Army Corps A and C to attack immediately, while Army Corps B would continue preparations. Unfortunately for the Greeks, the aviators had apparently observed Nationalist reserves moving to the east, and the report was false. İsmet was actually moving his reserve I Group and the 3rd Caucasian Division to the southeast to block a Greek encirclement.[34] As a result, Papoulas rushed the attack with unready forces on August 24, using only two of his three army corps.

Major General Kontoulis, Army Group A commander, had contrary reports from his own frontline troops that the enemy was not withdrawing and asked for a delay. Papoulas overruled him, and Army Corps A launched the 1st and 2nd Divisions across the Katranji Dere to capture the village of Tamburoğlu and the Türbe Tepe hill. Kontoulis ordered his 12th Division to follow behind the attacking divisions which engaged Colonel Selahattin's II Group. The Greek 2nd Division hit Selahattin's 9th Division, but because its artillery was not in position, on Mangal Tepe, the 1st Division postponed the attack. The unsupported 2nd Division crossed the Katranji Dere stream, taking Tamburoğlu but, as darkness fell, stopped about a half kilometer from Türbe Tepe.[35] That night, İsmet ordered Major General Yusef İzzet's (Met) III Group to assume control of the high ground north of Tamburoğlu. At first light on August 25, the Greek 2nd Division seized Türbe Tepe despite heavy enemy artillery fire, while 1st Division launched its delayed attack but also seized its objective. Coincidentally, Nationalist Chief of the General Staff General Fevzi was visiting the front at that moment and ordered Selahattin to conduct an immediate counterattack to reclaim Türbe Tepe. The II Group conducted counterattacks with the 3rd Caucasian Division but had insufficient force to do more than push the 1st Division back to Mangal Dağ. Reacting to his own aerial reconnaissance at 10:00 a.m., İsmet ordered the IV and XII Groups to conduct demonstration attacks, while the III Group launched an attack with the 57th Division to recapture Türbe Tepe.[36] He also ordered Colonel Izzettin's I Group, then arriving from reserve on the left (southern) flank of Selahattin's II Corps, to launch a supporting attack. Finally, because of the threat to his left flank, İsmet released the 2nd and 3rd Cavalry Divisions from army reserve and allocated them to the II Group. The Nationalist

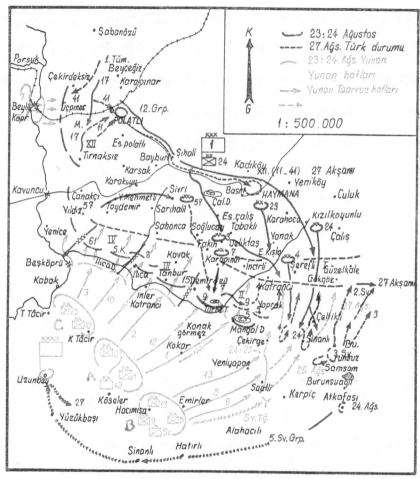

Map 8.2 Tactical Pause (August 23–27, 1921)

When the Greek divisions arrived on the Gök River line, they were exhausted, low on supplies, and in need of a period of rest and resupply before launching the main attacks. This tactical pause proved providential for İsmet because it gave the Nationalists the time to reposition their reserves and develop a very strong defensive line. In particular, İsmet was able to move the cavalry-heavy V Group to his far-left flank.

Courtesy of the Turkish General Staff Military History and Strategy Institute (ATASE).

counterattacks reached their peak at about 3:30 p.m., when the Greek 2nd Division was forced to withdraw from Türbe Tepe. To the east, Izzettin's 23rd and 24th Divisions conducted an attack to recapture Mangal Dağ, but this failed in the face of the Greek 1st Division's defense, which was well supported by artillery fire.[37]

To the north, Lieutenant General Polymenakos's Army Corps C received Papoulas's order to attack immediately at 1:00 p.m. on August 24. He ordered his 3rd and 10th Divisions to attack across the Gök River at 2:00 p.m. to capture the Yıldız Dağ and the Toydemir village as a salient. The Greek divisions launched the attacks on time but ran into heavy artillery fire and the outposts of Colonel Kemalettin Sami's IV Group, which deployed the 5th Caucasian and the 11th and 61st Divisions. The Greek attacks dwindled as night fell, with the enemy still in possession of the high ground. Polymenakos renewed his attacks the next morning. capturing the Yıldız peaks but bogging down by nightfall. That night, he ordered the 10th Division to shift its axis of attack east toward the village of Sabanca. To the south on that day, V Group commander Colonel Fahrettin noticed an absence of Greek formations to his front and decided to conduct a large raid into the Greek rear areas, and he ordered his 14th Cavalry Division and the 4th Cavalry Brigade to prepare to move to Uzunbey.[38]

On Army Corps C's far-left flank, its 7th Division, operating in a nearly independent mode, launched an attack on August 24 across the upper Sakarya River, following the rail line toward Polatlı. Unfortunately for the Nationalists, İsmet had chosen the rail line itself as the boundary between Colonel Kâzım 's Provisional Group and Colonel Halit's XII Group, thus complicating the defense.[39] The Greeks attacked the 47th Infantry Regiment (from Kâzım's 41st Division) at the Beylik Bridge (Beylikköprü) and quickly forced the Nationalists to retreat. İsmet immediately released the 48th Infantry Regiment from army reserve, which was rushed to the high ground south of the rail line, while Kâzım ordered the 1st Division south to defend the high ground north of the rail line.[40] Rather than vigorously counterattacking, the two Nationalist commanders independently reinforced their defensive positions; losing the opportunity to throw the Greeks back from the bridge. Later in the day, Halit ordered the 11th Division north to buttress the left flank of the 48th Infantry Regiment. However, it was too late to stop the Greeks from establishing a bridgehead extending seven kilometers east of the river.[41] İsmet maintained the group boundary along the rail line, thus continuing the error by failing to establish unitary command opposing the Greek 7th Division. By midnight August 24/25, situation reports to İsmet's headquarters indicated strong enemy attacks at the Beylik bridgehead and across the Gök River, as well as a significant massing of the Greek Army on left flanks of the Western Front Command.[42]

On August 26, Army Corps C captured Toydemir and Sabanca. Papoulas then ordered Polymenakos to continue his attacks toward Eskiçalış, which would force Yusef İzzet's 8th and 7th Divisions to abandon the Tamburoğlu defensive position.[43] Despite the danger to his right flank, Yusuf İzzet counterattacked, employing only the 7th Division against the Greek 1st and 2nd Divisions. Although the counterattacks failed, they bought enough time for the 57th Division to dig in completely on the Türbe Tepe. However, İzzet had no choice but to withdraw the battered 7th Division.[44]

Army Corps B's 13th and 5th Divisions attacked the I Group's 9th, 23rd, and 24th Divisions at 6:00 a.m. on August 26, relentlessly pushing them back throughout the day. However, directly behind the II Group Colonel Selahattin's I Group rushed to create a defensive line to fall back on with the 4th and 5th Divisions along the Güzelkale (Kale Gözü) Ridge. Army Corps B's 9th Division and the cavalry brigade remained unengaged all day but guarded the attack's right flank against the Nationalist 2nd and 3rd Cavalry Divisions. That night, İzzettin's divisions fell back to join the II Group on the new defensive line. General Papoulas renewed his attacks on August 27, with all his divisions conducting frontal attacks against the Nationalists but resulting in almost no gains across the FAAM's front that day. To the south, Papoulas ordered the cavalry brigade and the 9th Division to the army's far right flank. This enabled Fahrettin's V Group to push west to a position deep behind Greek Army's rear to harass its lines of communication with localized raiding. The absence of enemy resistance to the V Group lent enough confidence to İsmet to order Colonel Fahrettin to execute the cavalry raid he had been planning. İsmet also belatedly cleaned up the command arrangements opposing the enemy's Beylik bridgehead by withdrawing Colonel Selahattin's II Group headquarters to the town of Maymana (in the II Group's sector) and turning the area over to Colonel Kâzım's Provisional Group, thus establishing unity of command against the Greek 7th Division.

Early in the morning on August 27, Colonel Fahrettin led the 14th Cavalry Division and the 4th Cavalry Brigade northwest from the village of Sinanlı toward Uzunbey. It is unclear today whether the Nationalists knew that General Papoulas maintained his FAAM headquarters in Uzunbey, but Fahrettin certainly knew that there were Greek aviation squadrons and field hospitals there.[45] The Nationalists' main effort was aimed directly at the village, but it was held up by a determined defense on the heights east of Uzunbey from an infantry battalion of the 9th Division. The 14th Cavalry Division conducted a dismounted attack while the 4th Cavalry Brigade attacked on the left flank into the village itself. The FAAM headquarters staff was completely surprised, but quick-thinking staff officers organized a defense from headquarters clerks and lightly wounded men from the field hospitals, who repelled the cavalry brigade. During the fight, the Greeks ordered the aircraft to take off and the headquarters equipment and communication gear to be destroyed. This proved unfortunately premature when the enemy attacks slackened and were then abandoned. General Papoulas moved the FAAM headquarters north to the village of Kavuncu köprü. Fahrettin ordered a withdrawal, and he and his men were back in friendly territory at 10:00 that night. In the northern sector, the Greek 7th Division's attacks to enlarge the Beylik bridgehead made minor gains, while Army Corps A and C's attacks fell short but pushed the enemy back several kilometers. In the center, Army Corps A's attacks gained about five kilometers of ground from the Nationalists.

Although General Papoulas ordered a continuation of the offensive, the FAAM's operations on August 28 were disjointed.[46] From the army's left flank to its right flank, the 7th Division's attacks against the Provisional Group at the Beylik bridgehead were soundly repulsed, both divisions of Army Group C attacked the IV Group but were repelled, Army Corps A did not attack at all, and Army Corps B attacked the II and XII Groups but were repelled as well. The 9th Division held off an attack by the Nationalists' 2nd and 3rd Cavalry Divisions on the army's far right flank, while İsmet's V Group remained well behind the rear of Army Corps B, and Lieutenant Colonel Ahmet Zeki's Provisional Division drove even deeper into the enemy's rear at Erenköy (see map 8.3a). Lieutenant General Kontoulis's inaction is explained by stating that Army Corps A's reserve—the 12th Division—was late in assembling for the attack.[47] In any case, three of seven Greek divisions did not attack that day.

General Papoulas issued a contradictory series of orders on the morning of August 30, but at 10:00 a.m. ordered Army Corps A to continue its attack toward Yapan Hamam. He also ordered Army Corps C to attack north. Army Corps B had been ordered to move east but the new orders specified an attack the Güzelkale position, which was held by the Nationalist 7th Division but nearly surrounded (see map 8.3b).[48] While the corps was making preparations, the hard-fighting 5th Division, commanded by

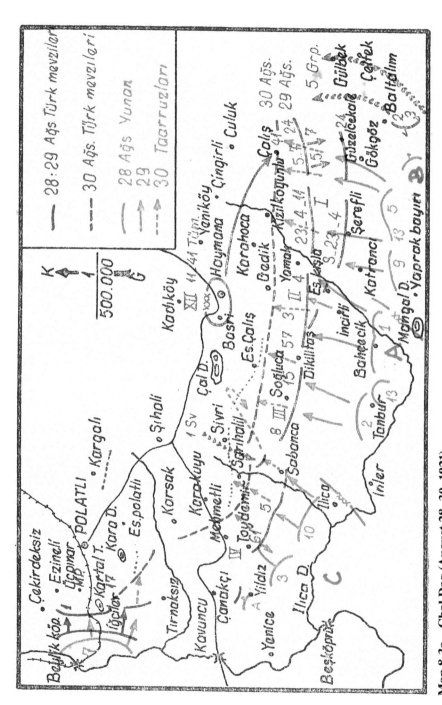

Map 8.3a Chal Dag (August 28–30, 1921)
Courtesy of the Turkish General Staff Military History and Strategy Institute (ATASE).

218

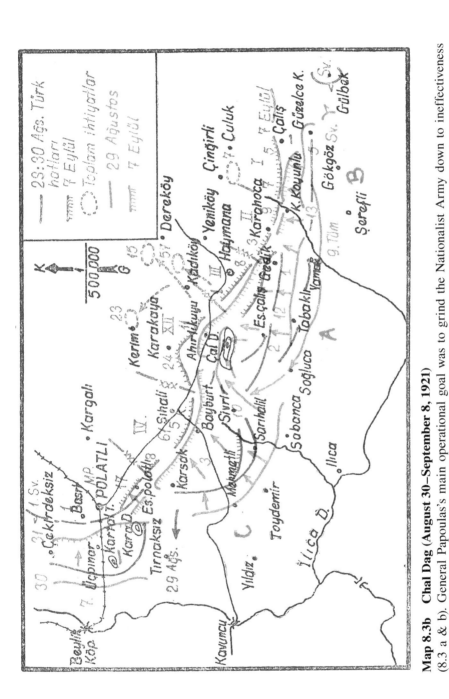

Map 8.3b Chal Dag (August 30–September 8, 1921)
(8.3 a & b). General Papoulas's main operational goal was to grind the Nationalist Army down to ineffectiveness through direct offensive combat. In theory, his operational maneuver brought his three army corps into a concentration against a portion of İsmet's army. However, the long approach march and tactical pause brought the FAAM into an attritional battle favoring the Nationalists.

Courtesy of the Turkish General Staff Military History and Strategy Institute (ATASE).

Colonel Ioannes X. Trivilas, launched twin assaults and, after an all-day battle, seized the Güzelkale ridge and the high ground known as the Uludağ at 8:00 p.m. Army Corps A continued preparations but did not conduct significant operations. On its left, Army Corps C's 28th Infantry Regiment (10th Division) made good progress and swept up to capture one peak of the Çal dağı (Chal Dag); however, since Army Corps A's 2nd Division did not advance, a gap appeared between the divisions and a Nationalist counterattack drove the 28th Infantry Regiment to the western part of the Çal dağı. This began a series of battles that would prove to be the culmination of the Greek offensive.

In the Beylik bridgehead, the veteran 7th Division (formerly the Archipelago Division), under the command of Colonel Andreas Plates, attacked early in the morning and was successful in pushing the enemy back, substantially widening its bridgehead.[49] While Papoulas conducted these operations, İsmet ordered Fahrettin's V Group northeast to the army's left flank and, while marching, the V Group conducted probing nuisance raids against the rear of the Greek 9th Division. Nevertheless, at dusk, Fahrettin joined the 2nd and 3rd Cavalry Divisions guarding the Western Front Command's left flank. Effectively this massed 80 percent of the Nationalist cavalry on İsmet's left and ended any hope the Greeks might have had about enveloping the Nationalist army.

REACHING THE GREEK CULMINATION POINT

The Western Front Command entered a period of "extreme danger" on August 30 because its reserves had been used up and the Greeks continued to attack.[50] However, the Greeks were now confronted with a positional battle in mountainous terrain, which favored the defenders tactically and logistically. Moreover, the FAAM was approaching the limits of its capacity to conduct offensive operations due to casualties, diminishing supplies, and exhaustion. Even so, these events were in the future, and August 30 was an important day logistically for the Greeks because the efforts of the 7th Division expanding its bridgehead enabled the FAAM's supply wagons and trucks to begin using the Beylik Bridge over the upper Sakarya River. The 7th Division also made contact with the 3rd Division, reestablishing contact with Major General Polymenakos's Army Corps C, which also meant that the Greek lines of communication from Eskişehir to the FAAM could flow unimpeded.[51] The week-long battle for the bridgehead had been costly for the 7th Division, which lost 277 killed and 1,696 wounded. General Papoulas's three army corps all attacked directly north, pushing the Nationalists back another 10 kilometers; however, on his extreme right flank, İsmet's cavalry blocked the 9th Division from further progress to the east.

The key terrain tactically speaking lay in İsmet's III Group sector and was a series of peaks and ridges known as the Çal dağı ve Ardıç dağı (Chal Dag and Ardiz Dag). The Çal dağı lay to the west and is kidney shaped with a peak of 1,140 meters; the Ardıç dağı lies to its southeast and is also kidney shaped, with a higher peak 1,755 meters. The saddle in between has an elevation of about 980 meters. While the Çal dağı-Ardıç dağı massif is key terrain tactically, it is not key terrain operationally because a series of equally high peaks and ridges lie directly behind it to the north. Papoulas ordered Army Corps A to seize this key tactical terrain on August 30, but it did not attempt to do so. On August 31, the 10th Division attacked again and gained some ground on the northern face of Çal dağı and held it against several counterattacks. The 2nd Division tried unsuccessfully to capture the saddle but did make contact with the Nationalist 28th Infantry Regiment. In the meantime, İsmet reinforced Major General Yusuf İzzet's III Group by subordinating Colonel Kemalettin Sami's 15th Division and part of the 1st Cavalry Division to his command, temporarily naming the consolidated command the Çal Mıntıkası (Chal Zone).[52] This placed the key tactical terrain in the hands of a single commander (which was a tactic frequently used by the Ottoman Army in World War I).[53]

Army Corps A launched a full-blown attack at 4:30 a.m. on September 1, with the Greek 2nd, 12th, and 1st Divisions in-line facing the III Group's 23rd, 8th, and 57th Divisions on Çal dağı and the II Group's 3rd Caucasian Division on Ardıç dağı.[54] The fighting was fierce and frequently hand to hand as the Greeks struggled to capture the heights above them. A battalion of the Nationalist 176th Infantry Regiment (57th Division) was caught by surprise and surrendered its commander, many officers, and 355 men.[55] By 10:00 a.m., the Greek 1st Division captured the Ardıç dağı but was thrown back by violent counterattacks. In late afternoon, the 1st Division stormed the ridge with a bayonet attack, completing its capture. The 2nd Division began its attacks at 6:30 a.m. against Çal dağı, and the 12th Division attacked the Çal dağı-Ardıç dağı saddle. Despite fighting the entire day, neither the 2nd nor the 12th division was successful in capturing their assigned objectives. To their northwest, Army Corps C unsuccessfully attacked the IV

Group's 5th Caucasian Division. Army Corps A blamed its failures on the inactivity of Army Corps C, but it is fair to argue that the two corps headquarters, which were supposed to coordinate their operations failed to do so.[56] To their southeast, Army Group B's three divisions pushed the I Group's 4th and 11th Divisions north a few kilometers, while on the F.A.A.M.'s far-left flank, the hard-fighting 7th Division continued to attack east, finishing the day on the outskirts of Polatlı. In response to these attacks, İsmet reinforced the Çal Zone group with the 24th Division.[57]

The advance echelons of the FAAM were about 70 kilometers from Ankara, but it had not yet dissolved, removed, or crushed the Nationalist Army as directed, and General Papoulas renewed his offensive on September 2, 1921. Army Corps C's now-weakened 7th Division unsuccessfully attacked Polatlı, while its 3rd Division conducted a disastrous attack against the IV Group's 61st and 5th Caucasian Divisions. In its only success, the 10th Division attacked Yusef İzzet's 24th Division, overrunning the northwestern spur of the Çal dağı. Army Corps A renewed its attacks on the eastern Çal dağı with the 2nd Division, but the division delayed its assault while the 12th Division prepared to assault the saddle. The Greek attack finally began at 5:15 p.m. with the 2nd Division conducting a "dashing attack" that overran the 15th Division, capturing Height 1,140 in the Çal dağı and the saddle at 10:00 p.m.[58] Belatedly, the 12th Division came forward to occupy the saddle. However, these successes came too late to prevent Army Corps C from withdrawing its unsupported 10th Division back to its starting line. It appears that Army Corps B did not conduct attacks on September 2, but the reasons are unclear today.[59]

İsmet observed in his orders to the Western Front Command at 1:30 a.m. on September 1 that the Greek attacks were losing momentum in his center. This enabled him to more clearly calibrate his defense, and he assigned the Çal Mıntıkası (15th and 24th Divisions) to defend the Çal dağı and the III Group (8th and 57th Divisions) to assume control of the Ardıç dağı and the approaches to Haymana.[60] It is unclear if Yusuf İzzet commanded one or both groups. In any case, İsmet ordered them to entrench themselves and defend their ground. He sent the 11th Division to reinforce the III Group and instructed the 23rd Division to prepare to go into army reserve.

The battles for the Çal dağı-Ardıç dağı massif were the last major offensive attacks by the Greeks east of the Sakarya River, and Greek casualties over the four-day battle were heavy. The FAAM lost 49 officers and 613 men killed, 145 officers and 3,434 wounded, and 72 men missing (4,313 total) the bulk of whom obviously came from the 10th and 2nd Divisions.[61] As the Greek soldiers on the Çal dağı-Ardıç dağı massif looked to the north, they could easily observe Yusuf İzzet's 24th Division digging in on the next series of ridges, which were even higher than the Ardıç dağı.[62]

The Nationalist 15th Division bore the brunt of the fighting for Çal dağı and suffered enormous losses from the 220 officers 5295 enlisted men (5,515 total assigned strength) it began the campaign with. The division lost in officers 11 killed, 48 wounded, 5 missing, and 1 taken prisoner, and in enlisted men 196 killed, 1,288 wounded, 847 missing, and 8 taken prisoner (2,404 total), amounting to a 44 percent casualty rate.[63] However, it is worth considering that the division's initial rifle strength was 2,725 officers and men, from which we can infer that its 38th, 45th, and 56th Infantry Regiments must have been nearly wiped out on the Çal dağı.[64] The division commander Colonel Şükrü Naili (Gökberk) survived and continued on to a distinguished career in the Turkish Army.[65]

THE SUSPENSION OF GREEK OFFENSIVE OPERATIONS

On September 3, the six infantry divisions of Army Corps A and C conducted frontal attacks, but these were half-hearted, and no ground was captured except in the 2nd and 10th Division's sectors (where minor gains were achieved). General Papoulas also detached the 9th Division from Army Corps B and reallocated it to Army Corps A. The division moved to a reserve position behind the 1st Division that night. İsmet believed that the Greek offensive was finished, and he made no major corrections to his army that day. However, he was concerned about the condition of his divisions in the Çal dağı sector, and he was determined to relieve them. He sent Colonel Halit's XII Group headquarters, which had been in reserve status, west toward Haymana and ordered Halit to take over command of the Çal dağı sector.

According to the Concise Greek History, "The constant, and dedicated enemy resistance contesting every meter of ground, the significant reduction in strength due to losses, the inability to replace them, as well as the problem of supply, finally provoked serious concern."[66] On September 4, General Papoulas ordered his slow-moving supply columns to begin the laborious process to withdraw the army's supplies and munitions to the railhead located behind the Beylik Bridge over the Sakarya River. Greek army railway engineers had been able to repair the rail line to Sazilar about five kilometers east of the Beylik Bridge. Logistics were a great concern to

Papoulas and his staff because nearly half his trucks were immobilized by breakdowns and a lack of spare parts.[67] Recognizing the vulnerability of an operational withdrawal, Papoulas ordered the FAAM to "widen the bridgehead" to secure a safer retirement in recrossing the rivers.[68] Army Corps C and A were ordered to attack to capture favorable high ground, which would protect the withdrawal, and to assist Army Corps C. Papoulas allocated the reasonably fresh 9th Division to the effort. Army Corps C launched unsuccessful attacks at about noon while Army Corps A continued preparations and did not attack. Unimpeded by the Greeks, on September 3, İsmet moved the XII Group headquarters into position to control the Çal dağı sector.[69]

More relevant to the ending of the campaign, General Papoulas had the staff of the FAAM prepare a detailed report on September 4 for Minister of the Army Nikolaos Theotokes at the Bursa headquarters. The report was a mixed bag in the sense that it touted the fact that the army retained the initiative, maintained superior morale, and had captured large areas of Nationalist territory. However, it also compared the relative combat strengths and baldly stated the obvious—"that progressive reduction of combat strength would make further offensive operations impossible."[70] The report referred to the memorandum submitted to the Council of War on July 28 noting that the conditions set for victory had not been achieved nor were they likely to be achieved, as the Nationalists were getting stronger by the day, and bad weather was approaching. General Papoulas ended by requesting the government decide what to do.

While General Papoulas was finalizing his report, Minister Theotokes in Bursa was informed that Army Corps A had not participated in the attacks or captured its objectives, and he asked the extent to which its orders had not been executed in whole or in part. Papuolas's answer only addressed Army Corps C, unsettling the Minister of War. This came on top of an earlier admonitory order from Theotokes regarding the FAAM's failure to send situation reports to the king and the government. Papoulas took all this as criticism and raised the issue that the government should relieve him if it had lost confidence in his ability to command the army. In the end, Papoulas was not relieved of his command, and, on September 5, Major General Xenophon Strategos delivered the FAAM's report to Minister Theotokes, who sent the report on to Athens.

On September 5, Papoulas continued his attacks, with Army Corps C's 9th and 10th Divisions capturing the positions of the IV Group's 5th Caucasian and 61st Divisions. While the center groups were fighting off the

Greek attacks, İsmet ordered his 2nd and 3rd Cavalry Divisions to conduct a deep raid behind the right flank of Army Corps B, which remained in its positions. The cavalry swept south and west about 20 kilometers and returned to friendly lines.[71] Army Corps A again failed to attack, and Papoulas ended his efforts to "widen the bridgehead." He broke contact with the Western Front Command and fell back to defensible positions.

General Papoulas ordered his army to assume a defensive posture on September 6 while he waited for instructions from the government. There was minor skirmishing that day as the three Greek army corps sought to straighten their lines. Additionally, the FAAM made a concerted effort to create the tactical reserves necessary for defensive operations. Over the next two days, Army Corps C lengthened its lines and pulled the 3rd Division back into reserve, Army Corps A withdrew the 11th Division from the front lines into reserve, and, on the right flank, Army Corps B withdrew the 5th Division into a reserve position. While the Greeks were repositioning, İsmet sent the 2nd Cavalry Division on another raid deep in Army Corps C's rear area, coming within 10 kilometers of the FAAM's headquarters at Kavuncu köprü, and he also ordered the IV, V, and XII Groups to prepare to conduct counterattacks. The next day was quiet, with the exception of local counterattacks by the IV Group, which were repulsed by Army Corps C.

The Greek campaign to end the war through the destruction of the Nationalist Army was over, and failure left the FAAM in the dangerous and vulnerable position of occupying a salient that could be outflanked and isolated. General Papoulas had great difficulty in getting his army corps commanders to coordinate operations and in getting them to execute his orders explicitly in a timely manner. This led the FAAM's failure to achieve the synergistic and simultaneous advantage of employing the entire army in a continuous battle. It led to tactical pauses, which allowed the Nationalists to recover and reposition reserves. Compounding this, Papoulas's subordinates often left entire infantry divisions out of the fight or without meaningful missions. This was particularly true of Lieutenant General Kontoulis and the 12th Division and Lieutenant General Polymenakos and the 9th Division. The Cavalry Brigade under FAAM control proved nearly useless. Certain divisions fought exceptionally well, including the 7th, 1st, 5th, and 10th Divisions. Overall, Papoulas failed to concentrate his army at a decisive point, and the overall operational concept itself remains much in doubt.

The command team of Kemal, Fevzi, and İsmet turned in a respectable performance, albeit they enjoyed a significant advantage in having interior

lines of communication and shorter supply lines. İsmet displayed a growing ability to command a theater-level army and proved very proficient in
his handling of reserves. Criticisms of the Nationalist effort include the
loss of the Beylik Bridge, the initial failure to station more men on the
nearly unassailable Çal dağı-Ardıç dağı massif, and the unexplainable
failure to exploit the FAAM's exposed right flank with the massive Nationalist cavalry force assembled there.

THE WESTERN FRONT COMMAND'S COUNTEROFFENSIVE

Nationalist air reconnaissance reported masses of vehicles moving
west over the Beylik Bridge at 8:30 a.m. on September 7. Combined with
reports from his group commanders, İsmet recognized that the Greeks
were conducting an operational withdrawal. He was determined to gain
the initiative, and he ordered his groups to conduct local probing attacks
to test the Greek lines. Throughout the day, except for the Provisional
Group, his commanders relentlessly probed the enemy. İsmet also
directed the Western Front Command staff to prepare plans for a counteroffensive once the Greek withdrawal began. General Papoulas continued the withdrawal of his supply trains and moved his headquarters to
Kavuncu köprü on the Sakarya River, colocating with the headquarters
of the 7th Division.

September 8 passed relatively quietly while the Greeks continued to
consolidate their positions and create reserves. Papoulas pushed a few
infantry battalions forward on the west bank of the Sakarya River, north
of the Beylik Bridge, as a caution against a flanking attack on the bridge.
İsmet ordered a day of preparation and refitting, and small counterattacks
were limited to the IV Group in the center and the I Group on the left
flank. He also ordered his I, IV, and XII Groups to consolidate their heavy
artillery at Karapınar.[72] Throughout the night of 8/9 September İsmet sent
out a flurry of orders with a view toward crushing the Greek center while
enveloping Papoulas's right flank. He also moved the 7th, 15th, and 23rd
Divisions and the heavy artillery battalions from reserve to positions
around Polatlı, and he assigned deep objectives to the Provisional and IV
Groups.[73] İsmet assigned the recapture of the Çal dağı to the XII Group,
the Ardıç dağı and the village of Yamak (five kilometers behind the Greek
front line) to the II Group, while the I Group conducted supporting attacks
on the Greek right flank. He tasked the V Group, now composed of three
cavalry divisions and an independent cavalry brigade, to envelop the Greek

Army Corps B. The Western Front Command's operational main effort was designated as the Right Wing Force (the Provisional and IV Groups)— its objective aimed at the Beylik bridgehead, and İsmet reckoned it would take two days of battle to achieve this result.

Early on September 9, Fahrettin, whose V Group now controlled almost all of the Nationalist cavalry, moved the 2nd Cavalry Division deep into the rear behind Army Corps C while the 3rd Cavalry Division moved south (see map 8.4). İsmet ordered his other group commanders to move

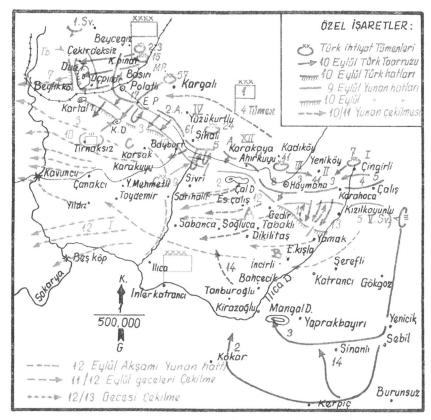

Map 8.4   Nationalist Counteroffensive (September 9–12, 1921)
İsmet's transition of the battered Western Front Command from a defensive posture to an offensive posture was a remarkable achievement that reflected the operational agility of the Nationalist Army. However, the steady hand of General Papoulas in managing the retreat saved the FAAM from encirclement.
Courtesy of the Turkish General Staff Military History and Strategy Institute (ATASE).

their infantry into assembly positions for the assaults. Meanwhile, Papoulas telegraphed Army Corps C and B to be prepared for major enemy attacks in their sectors. At 8:00 a.m., İsmet's Provisional Group (the 7th, 8th, 23rd, and 57th Divisions), supported by the army's heavy artillery, attacked the Greek 7th Division's thin lines. The attacks proceeded slowly, and a second artillery preparation fire enabled the Nationalists to capture the ridge line called Dua Tepe.[74] A prompt reaction by Army Corps C sent the reserve 3rd Division forward to assist the 7th Division, but by day's end, the Provisional Group had captured key high ground. The IV Group's 5th Caucasian and 61st Divisions attacked at the same time as the Provisional Group took its objectives before being forced back by the counterattacks of the Greek 9th Division.[75]

In İsmet's center, the XII Group's 11th Division and the 34th Infantry Regiment (24th Division) began an assault about 8:00 a.m. on the Çal dağı, which was held by the Greek 1st Division. The III Group's 3rd and 41st Divisions also assaulted the Greek 1st Division's positions on the western Ardıç dağı while the II Group's 3rd Caucasian Division assaulted the eastern Ardıç dağı. The II Group's 7th Division ruptured the Greek front, enabling the Nationalist 5th and 9th Divisions to break through to Yamak. To their left, the I Group's 4th Division drove forward to protect the flank but was forced to retreat in the face of counterattacks by the Greek 10th Division. Moreover, heavy and vigorous counterattacks by the Greek 1st Division and part of the 5th Division from Army Corps B in the late afternoon forced the II Group to abandon Yamak and retreat as well.[76] Army Corps B commander Lieutenant General Polymenakos, on his own initiative, had begun to move his supply wagons and noncombatant elements to the west in preparation for a retreat, but Papoulas reversed his orders, directing Army Corps B to conduct a diversionary attack. This left Polymenakos vulnerable to envelopment by Nationalist cavalry.

As night fell, İsmet had not achieved his principal objectives, but he prepared to continue his counteroffensive and moved his Western Front Command headquarters to Polatlı. Belatedly Papoulas ordered Army Corps C to recapture the Dua Tepe ridge and Army Corps A to hold the Çal dağı at all costs. Papoulas also authorized Army Corps B, on his endangered right flank, to withdraw. Late that night, Papoulas received the prime minister's response to Minister of War Theotokes, which granted the FAAM the freedom of action to continue the offensive or withdraw. However, Papoulas had already decided to suspend offensive operations.

The Western Front Command renewed its assaults on September 10, which proved to be disastrous for the FAAM Army Corps C's 7th Division, which had launched an unsuccessful counterattack at 7:00 a.m., supported by artillery against the Dua Tepe ridge. Opposite the Beylik bridgehead, İsmet's Provisional and IV Groups attacked several times, but well-organized Greek counterattacks drove them back with small gains and heavy losses. The XII Group made a determined assault to capture the Çal dağı, which also failed, as did the III and II Groups attacks on the Ardıç dağı. Overall, the Western Front Command's attacks failed completely; however, in the south it made great gains. Faced with envelopment, Army Corps B broke contact with the I Group and withdrew the 13th Division from the far-right flank into Army Corps A's sector (with its sister 5th Division). Simultaneously, Lieutenant General Polymenakos withdrew the Cavalry Brigade, deploying it to block Fahrettin's 2nd and 3rd Cavalry Divisions, which were driving north in an effort to encircle Army Corps B. Polymenakos's timely actions saved his corps from destruction.[77]

On the evening of September 11, General Papoulas decided to withdraw to a more defensible line, and he ordered Army Corps C to stand fast and Army Corps A to abandon the Çal dağı-Ardıç dağı massif and form a continuous line south of Army Corps C.[78] He ordered Army Corps B to maintain its withdrawal, with a view to establish a defensive line on the north-south along the Sapanca Dere, anchored on its right by the Gök River and the town of Ilica. While these orders were going out to the Greek corps commanders, İsmet ordered his group commanders to continue the counteroffensive.

Nationalist attacks began again as early as 2:00 a.m. on September 11, with the 1st and 57th Divisions conducting night assaults against Army Corps C's 3rd and 7th Divisions on the Kartal Tepe ridge. Reinforcing the attack, with its 15th Division the I Group captured the ridge in the late afternoon, but Greek counterattacks restored the line. A supporting attack by the 17th Division on the Kara Dağ was also repulsed. To their south, the IV Group launched four unsuccessful attacks between 2:00 p.m. and 5:30 p.m. against the 10th Division's positions south of Eskipolatlı. Army Group A abandoned the Çal dağı-Ardıç dağı massif on the night of September 10/11, which the XII, III, and II Groups discovered at dawn while rushing forward to occupy the vacant peaks and ridges. With the retreat of Army Corps B, İsmet pulled the I Group headquarters into reserve and relocated its divisions to the II Group, which pushed west against the

Greek right flank. Colonel Fahrettin's 2nd and 3rd Cavalry Divisions swept west to the outskirts of Ilica on the Gök River.[79]

With the initiative clearly in İsmet's hands, General Papoulas decided to withdraw west of the Sakarya and issued orders at 1:30 p.m. on September 12 to begin pulling back that night. The FAAM planned to withdraw Army Corps B starting at 6:30 p.m. using the Tepeköy and Kavuncu bridges and, from there, establish defensive line on the heights above the west back with 5th and 13th Divisions.[80] Army Corps A would start its withdrawal at 7:00 p.m. using the Kavuncu and Beş Köprü bridges, with its 12th Division occupying the high ground south of Army Corps B (the 1st and 2nd Divisions would occupy reserve positions behind the 12th Division). This plan reversed the previous deployment by positioning Army Corps B in the Greek center and Army Corps A on the right flank. Army Corps C also began moving at 6:00 p.m. toward the Kara Elias and Tepeköy bridges, with the 10th and 9th Divisions crossing in the night. The 7th Division would conduct a demonstration at the Beylik bridgehead at midnight to cover the withdrawal of its sister divisions but would follow them starting at 1:30 a.m. on September 13 over the Beylik and Kara Elias bridges.

The withdrawal of the FAAM west of the Sakarya River was complicated, but it was conducted successfully, with the Western Front Command advancing west and trying to maintain contact with the enemy on September 13. However, the Nationalists were unable to either stop the Greek withdrawal or to envelop it from the south. The final elements of the 7th Division made it across the river in the early hours of September 13. The FAAM's withdrawal to the west of the Sakarya was completed, and, according to the Concise Greek History, all of its armament and equipment was successfully evacuated as well.[81] After crossing the Sakarya River, Greek engineers dismantled and evacuated its temporary bridges and destroyed the remaining permanent bridges (except for one remaining at Fethioğlu). By midday on September 13, the Western Front Command had closed on and occupied the east bank of the Sakarya River.[82] İsmet sent a report to Kemal on September 13 proclaiming that the campaign, which had started on August 23, was over and that his counteroffensive had pushed the enemy back across the Sakarya River. He noted that his army would pursue the Greeks, and he gave the campaign a name—the Battle of Sakarya.[83] Kemal immediately forwarded the message to the Grand National Assembly, noting that İsmet's assessment was correct.

THE REORGANIZATION OF THE WESTERN FRONT COMMAND

On September 13, Kemal sent orders to İsmet affirming that the command architecture of the Western Front Command was ill-suited to a pursuit operation, and Kemal ordered the establishment of conventional permanent army corps headquarters instead of the combat groups.[84] Kemal specified the activation of five army corps, each composed of 3 divisions for a total of 15 divisions in İsmet's army while retaining one legacy group of 2 divisions to maintain the northern Kocaeli Front. Since there were currently 21 infantry divisions serving on the Western Front and many of them were severely understrength; Kemal proposed to inactivate the 5th, 9th, and 24th Divisions and reassign their surviving regiments to other divisions. He also noted that he was assigning XII Group commander Colonel Halit and the 17th Division to the Kocaeli Group. Kemal also specified which commanders would command corps in the Western Front Command: I Corps, Colonel İzzettin; II Corps, Colonel Selahattin; III Corps, Colonel Kâzım; IV Corps, Colonel Kemalettin; and V Corps, Colonel Fahrettin. Apparently unhappy with the performance of III Group commander Yusuf İzzet and 1st Cavalry Division commander Süleyman Sırrı, Kemal invited them to Ankara to take a seat in the Grand National Assembly rather than return them to command in the reorganized army.

At 10:10 p.m. on September 13, İsmet sent a 45-paragraph order to his subordinates explaining these changes and ordering them into effect the next day.[85] While this reorganization would delay the pursuit for four days, it was overdue and would clean up the *ad* hoc attachments and detachments of formations in place at the end of the Battle of Sakarya. İsmet officially moved his front headquarters to Polatlı, and he made the following organizational allocations: I Corps—15th, 23rd, and 57th Divisions; II Corps—3rd Caucasian, 4th, and 7th Divisions; III Corps—1st and 41st Divisions and 1st Cavalry Division; IV Corps—5th Caucasian, 11th, and 61st Divisions; and V Corps—2nd, 3rd, and 14th Cavalry Divisions. He announced the inactivation of the 5th, 9th, and 24th Divisions, the 48th and 49th Infantry Regiments, and the 3rd Battalion, 57th Regiment. The 4th Cavalry Brigade does not appear in subsequent orders of battle so it appears that it was inactivated at about this time as well. İsmet kept his eye on logistics and ordered the inactivated XII Group to send its transportation and communication assets (animals, wagons, and telephone and telegraph equipment) to the Line of Communication Command on September 14 and its artillery to the adjacent corps on September

15. He also ordered the III Group's 8th Division to join the Line of Communication Command and to hand over some of its weapons, animals, and equipment for the training of new soldiers. Finally, İsmet allocated the 22nd Cavalry Regiment to the Kocaeli Group.

From the scope of the changes, it is obvious that Kemal, Fevzi, and İsmet must have had numerous discussions that resulted in concrete recommendations and decisions before September 13; however, when these occurred is unclear. What is important for the narrative is that Kemal had found his tactical command team in the war against the Greeks. These six corps and group commanders would remain in command for the duration of the war. Kemal would activate just one additional corps headquarters in 1922, and he would assign Şükrü Naili, the able and heroic commander of the 15th Division on the Çal dağı, to corps command. Many military historians would agree that in the modern age, corps-level command posts are the hardest to fill with capable men. The position requires officers to move from direct command to indirect command, and qualities such as personal bravery become less important than the ability to supervise subordinates through written orders. In these men, Kemal and İsmet had proven and combat tested commanders who could transition quickly from the operational defense to the operational offense.

The Greek Concise History records the fighting on September 15 and as "particularly intense."[86] Although occupied with repositioning its new army corps, the Western Front Command maintained constant pressure on the enemy. The III Corps' 1st Cavalry Division captured the Kartal Tepe on September 15, and the I Corps' 57th Division established a bridgehead on the west bank of the Sakarya but was driven back across the river by fierce counterattacks. Nevertheless, at day's end on September 16, General Papoulas decided to withdraw to a new line to the west beginning on the evening of September 17. He was concerned about the Nationalist V Corps (three cavalry divisions) which was moving directly south of Army Corps A. By September 15, İsmet deployed (from north to south) the Kocaeli Group, III Corps, I Corps, and IV Corps against the Greek main line of resistance. İsmet held the II Corps in reserve. The three cavalry divisions of the V Corps had crossed the upper Sakarya River to join the Lieutenant Colonel Ahmet Zeki's Provisional Infantry Division, which İsmet then allocated to Fahrettin's command, thereby threatening the Greek right flank with a powerful combined arms force.

On September 15, all of İsmet's corps then in contact conducted frontal attacks but were repelled by counterattacks. The V Corps pushed even farther to the west while Ahmet Zeki's Provisional Division launched an attack on the Greek 12th Division, which was also repulsed.[87] İsmet then reversed his decision regarding the 8th Division and allocated it to the V Corps (giving it a second infantry component), but the Greek Cavalry Brigade blocked the northern advance of Fahrettin's 3rd Cavalry Division. At the end of the day, the FAAM successfully broke contact and withdrew to its new defensive line about 10 kilometers west of the Sakarya River (see map 8.5). The next day, the FAAM received reinforcements in the form of Lieutenant General Georgios Leonardopoulos's Independent Division, which had arrived in Eskişehir from the island of Chios and which

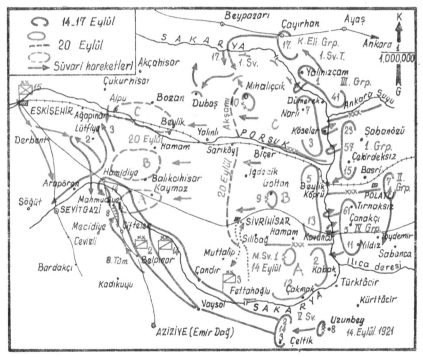

Map 8.5   The Greek Retreat to Eskişehir (September 14–20, 1921)
The danger posed to the FAAM by Fahrettin's V Cavalry Group is obvious from this map. However, rather than panicking, General Papoulas remained in control and skillfully withdrew his army. He left well-led rearguard detachments to slow the Nationalists and maneuvered on his right flank to block the V Cavalry Group.

Courtesy of the Turkish General Staff Military History and Strategy Institute (ATASE).

Papoulas quickly deployed south to Derbent.[88] Meanwhile, Papoulas abandoned his defensive line and withdrew another 10 kilometers into hasty positions. İsmet's V Corps penetrated deep into the Greek rear near Çifteler, capturing supply wagons, cutting telegraph lines, and disrupting the Greek lines of communication in Army Corps A's sector.[89]

Thus, as September 17 ended, İsmet considered that the time was ripe to launch his pursuit operation with the objective of destroying the FAAM. He certainly enjoyed a positional advantage and his army had seized the initiative from the Greeks. Moreover, in addition to the tactical disarray of Papoulas's army, İsmet had received intelligence reports concerning the strategic disarray caused by the uncertain outlook of the political-military decision-making process between Athens-Bursa-Eskişehir (where Papoulas had now moved his headquarters) regarding the Asia Minor theater.[90]

THE NATIONALIST PURSUIT

At 10:15 a.m. on September 18, İsmet ordered a pursuit of the enemy, directing the four infantry corps and the Kocaeli Group to push west with their cavalry detachments leading to find gaps in the Greek withdrawal.[91] He also ordered the V Corps to continue its pursuit northeast. The FAAM held a defensive position, with Army Corps C and B holding a north-south line and Army Corps A behind Army Corps B. The Greek line that day was composed of Army Corps C in the north holding the Kartal Tepe, with the 3rd Division and the 7th Division in reserve. Army Corps B held the Porsuk-Kınık line with the 5th, 8th, and 12th Divisions. On his endangered southern flank, Papoulas's Army Corps A was grouped in a compressed mass (the 9th, 10th, and 11th Divisions) behind Army Corps A's 12th Division, which held the front lines. On the Greek's southern (right) flank, the 1st Division and the Cavalry Brigade blocked Fahrettin's cavalry. On September 19, the V Corps drove north with its three cavalry divisions, ending with the 14th Cavalry Division on the Sarı Kovanca Dağ, within 10 kilometers of the Eskişehir-Beylik Bridge rail line. General Kontoulis reacted swiftly on September 20 by withdrawing the 2nd and 9th Divisions west to Balçikhisar and the 1st Division and the Cavalry Brigade to the Çerkes Çal heights east of Mahmudiye to maintain blocking the V Corps.[92] At the day's end, the situation facing the FAAM was monumentally bleak, although the 2nd Division had reached Hamidiye.

The most pressing tactical concern for General Papoulas on September 20 was the advance of Fahrettin's V Corps, which threatened to cut off the FAAM from its supply base in Eskişehir. Papoulas withdrew the 3rd Division from Army Corps C and used it to drive the Nationalist cavalry off from the Sarı Kovanca Dağ. He also ordered the Independent Division east to the Malyabaşı Tepe to block Fahrettin's fast-moving cavalry, which was maneuvering and looking for an open flank. General Kontoulis moved the 10th Division to the Orta Tepe heights, the 9th Division to Mahmudiye, and the 1st Division and Cavalry Brigade to the Çerkes Çal heights.[93] The 2nd Division remained in Hamidiye. These maneuvers saved the FAAM, and Fahrettin's V Corps was now blocked from advancing north. In turn, Fahrettin withdrew the 14th Cavalry Division from the front and replaced it with infantry. In the meantime, İsmet's infantry corps maintained relentless pressure on Army Corps C and B, forcing them back and into an ever-compressed perimeter.[94] At 12:30 p.m., the minister of war in Bursa sent instructions to the FAAM ordering that, despite the losses in the campaign, Eskişehir must be held at all costs.[95] Later in the day, Papoulas issued orders to his corps commanders fixing the timing of the army's withdrawal into a defensive position east of Eskişehir.[96]

The Greek retreat that began the next day (September 21) can be described as chaotic, as Army Corps C and B abandoned the Kartal Tepe-Kınık line and withdrew to the Don Tepe-Uzunburun-Çerkes Çal line. Except for the Kocaeli Group, which relentlessly pushed forward, İsmet's infantry corps followed but could not stop the retiring Greek divisions. The Nationalist advance was also slowed by the deliberate destruction of eight kilometers of rail track east of the Sakarya and 130 kilometers of rail track west of the river by the FAAM's army engineers.[97] Lieutenant General Kontoulis now had his Army Corps A headquarters in Eskişehir with General Papoulas, and they coordinated a counterattack on the V Corps with the Independent Division, attacking east toward Seyitgazi and the 2nd Division attacking west toward Çiçegiz, almost isolating the Nationalist 8th Division.[98] This forced the V Corps to retreat south, eliminating almost all the gains it had made since September 17. With the width of the front compressing by the day, İsmet was able to withdraw the II and IV Corps into reserve. By the end of the day, the FAAM occupied an L-shaped position, with Army Corps C and B holding the Don Tepe-Uzunburun-Çerkes Çal line (the north-to-south leg) and Army Corps A holding the east-to-west leg.

According to General Papoulas's plan for the defensive area east of Eskişehir, Army Corps C and B would hold the defensive lines while Army Corps A, the Independent Division, and the Cavalry Brigade would assemble in the vicinity of the city as the army's reserve. On September 22. Papoulas put the final withdrawal into motion to achieve this, and he felt confident enough to detach the 9th and 10th Divisions from Army Corps A and return them to their parent Army Corps B and C respectively.[99] The 7th and 5th Divisions held the front while the FAAM began its withdrawal that day with little intervention from the Western Front Command.

On September 22, the FAAM occupied its defensive zone, with Army Corps C holding the line from Dağcılar to Aziz Kışlı, with the 3rd and 10th Divisions and the 7th Division in corps reserve. Army Corps B occupied the front from Aziz Kışlı to Cevizli on the Eskişehir-Afyonkarahisar rail line, with the 9th and 5th Divisions in the line and the 13th Division in corps reserve. İsmet's army gained contact but did not attack, leaving Papoulas's outlying formations to withdraw unimpeded into army reserve.[100] However, İsmet continued to threaten the FAAM with the V Corps on the Greek right flank and the 1st Cavalry Division on the Greek left flank.[101] The next day passed quietly, giving Army Corps C and B time to examine their defensive positions closely. However, Lieutenant General Polymenakos believed that the ground to his rear presented a better position without jeopardizing the defense of Eskişehir, and he asked the FAAM for permission to withdraw further. Papoulas examined the request and, using Orta Tepe (just northeast of Hamidiye) as the army pivot point, approved an Army Corps C withdrawal to the Dede Tepe-Sidikli Kaya-Kovanca Dağ-Orta Tepe line.[102] This change made Army Corps C's exposed left flank much less vulnerable than the original line had provided. General Polymenakos began a deliberate withdrawal, and Army Corps Army C successfully occupied its new positions on September 27.

Appraisals of command and control in this period are mixed. İsmet had performed exceptionally well during the pitched defensive Battle of Sakarya, but his performance during the counteroffensive was less than stellar. The Western Front Command repeatedly squandered the positional and mobility advantages of the V Corps. Opportunity to trap decisively the FAAM certainly presented itself to the Nationalists on September 18, and perhaps even earlier on September 15. On the other side, the potential for the catastrophic annihilation of his army weighed heavily on the mind of General Papoulas as he wrestled with the decision to somehow continue the offensive after his decision to withdraw. In the profession of arms, a retreat under enemy pressure is considered exceptionally difficult because command and control tends to break down quickly, leading to the disintegration of the withdrawing force. General Papoulas kept his army intact and conducted what might be described as a brilliant retreat to Eskişehir under difficult and demanding conditions. The same might be said for Army Corps A commander Lieutenant General Kontoulis during the retreat as well. His repeated and what might be called "just-in-time'" deployments to block Fahrettin's fast-moving V Corps was noteworthy.

The narrative has excluded the extended operations conducted on the northern and southern flanks of the main armies. While these operations were locally important, they were not decisive factors in the outcome of the campaign. In the north, between Geyve (near Lake İznik) and Bilecik, a provisional infantry and cavalry force battled the Greek 11th Division. Combat was intermittent and casualties generally light. Neither side made any gains against the other. In the south, the Nationalist 6th Division, under the command of Lieutenant Colonel Nazmi (Solok) coming from the south and a provisional force coming west from Akşehir, waged continuous operations against the Southern Group of Divisions commanded by Major General Nikolaos Trikoupes, who held Afyonkarahisar with the Greek 4th Division. Both the Nationalists and the Greeks operated in an independent mode, and heavy combat occurred intermittently as the action seesawed around the hinterlands of the city, but the Greeks always remained firmly in control of Ayfonkarahisar. These peripheral operations tied up two of the FAAM's 12 infantry divisions in holding operations with no strategic purpose or operational gain. Reciprocally, in an economy of force effort, the Western Front Command employed only one infantry division and several provisional and militia formations in these peripheral operations. Overall, the extended operations near Lake İznik and the city of Afyonkarahisar on the flanks of the main battle area clearly favored the Nationalists.

CONCLUSION

By September 26, what the Turks call the Battle of Sakarya had concluded. It was actually a campaign and ought to be thought of as the Sakarya Campaign because the Greeks planned it to lead to a strategic outcome resulting in war termination. Moreover, it was composed of four distinct parts—the Greek movement to contact, the pitched Battle of Sakarya, the Nationalist counteroffensive, and the Nationalist pursuit. The decisive phase was, of course, the pitched Battle of Sakarya. In the words of Michael Llewellyn-Smith, "This was a watershed in the Asia Minor policy of the Gounaris government. The Greek army had shot its bolt. The retreat from Sakarya marked the end of the Greek hopes of imposing a settlement on Turkey by force of arms."[103]

While there were periods of bitter hand-to-hand fighting, at the tactical level, much of the tactical conduct of operations was characterized by maneuver. This was possible because, unlike the static trench lines of World War I, there were gaps in the defenses and open flanks. At the operational level, the campaign must be viewed as maneuver oriented, resulting from the fact that both armies presented open flanks. This was especially true in the Greek movement to contact, the Nationalist counteroffensive, and the Nationalist pursuit. However, the decisive pitched Battle of Sakarya was decided by repeated and brutal frontal assaults that quickly exhausted the combatants. Equally important to the outcome of the campaign was logistics, which clearly favored the Nationalists in the decisive phase, as they withdrew toward their supply bases and penalized the Greeks who moved ever farther away from theirs.

It was an exceptionally long and costly campaign, with most of the losses coming from the fierce battles on the massifs north of the Gök River. Casualties were about even, with the Western Front Command losing 3,700 killed and 18,000 wounded and the FAAM losing 4,000 killed and 19,000 wounded. However, the retreating Greeks lost many of the wounded to capture as they pulled back (perhaps as many as 15,000). Mustafa Kemal called Sakarya an "officer's battle," as the army lost 300 officers killed and 1,000 wounded out of a total of 5,000 present. Although General Papoulas was defeated in the field, İsmet had not defeated him intellectually or spiritually. He would shift his army's center of gravity south to Afyonkarahisar to try to regain the initiative before winter set in.

NOTES

1. Demetrios Gounaris to Athens (July 26, 1921), quoted in Llewellyn-Smith, *Ionian Vision*, 230.

2. For further commentary on this campaign, see Edward J. Erickson, "Decisive Battles of the Asia Minor Campaign," in *Salvation and Catastrophe: The Greek-Turkish War, 1919–1922*, ed. Konstantinos Travlos (Lanham, Maryland: Lexington Books, 2020), 173–196.

3. Gedeon, Paschalidou, and Dima-Dimitrou, *A Concise History of the Campaign in Asia Minor*, 216.

4. Ibid.

5. Llewellyn-Smith, *Ionian Vision*, 228–232.

6. Gedeon, Paschalidou, and Dima-Dimitrou, *A Concise History of the Campaign in Asia Minor*, 217. The F. A. A. M. memorandum is presented on this page and contains many assumptions that the army had to overcome to achieve success, such as the capture of intact bridges, roads, and railway lines.

7. Belen, *Türk Kurtuluş Savaşı*, 347–351; and Gedeon, Paschalidou, and Dima-Dimitrou, *A Concise History of the Campaign in Asia Minor*, 227–228.

8. These are the three words used in the FAAM memorandum to describe the end state of the Nationalist Army after the successful termination of the operation. See Gedeon, Paschalidou, and Dima-Dimitrou, *A Concise History of the Campaign in Asia Minor*, 217

9. Gedeon, Paschalidou, and Dima-Dimitrou, *A Concise History of the Campaign in Asia Minor*, 224–225.

10. Ibid., 228.

11. See the fifth sketch map at Mikrasiatiki Ekstrateia, He Apofaseis gia Epihirises pros Agyara [Asia Minor Campaign, The Decision for Operations towards Ankara], http://mikrasiatikhekstrateia.gr/epixeiriseis/augoustos21 /apofasi_epixeiriseon_pros_Agkura, accessed on 4/6/2021.

12. Gedeon, Paschalidou, and Dima-Dimitrou, *A Concise History of the Campaign in Asia Minor*, 219.

13. Kâmil Önalp, *Türk İstiklâl Harbi Batı Cephesi: Sakarya Meydan Muharebesinden Önceki Olaylar ve Mevzi İlerisindeki Harakât (25 Temmuz–22 Ağustos 1921), Türk İstiklâl Harbi IInci Cilt Batı Cephesi 5nci Kısım Inci Kitap* (Ankara: Genelkurmay Basımevi, 1972), 81–82.

14. The V Group is sometimes referred to as the V Cavalry Group. In 1922, it was renamed the V Cavalry Corps, but in late summer 1921, the proper nomenclature was V Group.

15. Önalp, *Sakarya Meydan Muharebesi*, 309. For Greek estimates of Nationalist strength, see Gedeon, Paschalidou, and Dima-Dimitrou, *A Concise History of the Campaign in Asia Minor*, 220–221. Numbers regarding the strength of the Nationalist Army vary considerably; for example, see Peter Kincaid Jensen, "The Greco-Turkish War, 1920–1922," *The International Journal of Middle East Studies* 10 (1979): 560. Jensen asserted that İsmet had "only about 25,000 Turks."

16. Önalp, *Sakarya Meydan Muharebesi*, 81–105, Kroki 4 (Sketch Map 4 following page 88).

17. Ibid., 135–142, Kroki 11 (Sketch Map 11 following page 120).

18. Gedeon, Paschalidou, and Dima-Dimitrou, *A Concise History of the Campaign in Asia Minor*, 236–263 and Sketch Map 35 (following page 200).

19. Önalp, *Sakarya Meydan Muharebesi*, 220–235.

20. Ibid., Kroki 28 (Sketch Map 28 following page 232).

21. Ibid., 240.

22. Mango, *Atatürk*, 318–319.

23. Gedeon, Paschalidou, and Dima-Dimitrou, *A Concise History of the Campaign in Asia Minor*, 234–240 and Sketch Map 37 (following page 236).

24. Dionysis Tsirigotis, "The Impact of the Excess of the Culminating Point of Attack in the Greek Military Strategy on the Outcome of the Greek Campaign in Asia Minor (August 1921–August 1922)," *Defensor Pacis* 24 (June 2009): 156–157. The author makes the point that the mechanical reliability of the army's motor transport was degraded significantly by the poor condition of the roads, and the farther the army advanced (from the positions of August 10, 1921), the greater the loss of logistical capability.

25. Görgülü, *On Yıllık Harbin Kadrosu*, 278–283.

26. İzzetin Çalışlar, *İstiklâl Savaşı Hatıraları Sakarya Meydan Muharebesi'nde 1nci Grup* (Ankara: Genelkurmay Basımevi, 2006), 13; and Önalp, *Sakarya Meydan Muharebesi*, 297.

27. Using the yardstick of 9,000 men in Greek divisions and 4,400 in Nationalist divisions (from Önalp, *Sakarya Meydan*, 311 (Ek-3)). Papoulas brought about 63,000 men against İsmet's 26,400 defenders and 26,400 reserves (52,800 men altogether). This gave Papoulas a superiority of only 1.2 to 1.

28. As an American, the author is reminded of Union commander in chief General Ulysses S. Grant joining General George Meade's Army of the Potomac headquarters in 1864 during the American Civil War.

29. Önalp, *Sakarya Meydan Muharebesi*, 260.

30. Gedeon, Paschalidou, and Dima-Dimitrou, *A Concise History of the Campaign in Asia Minor*, 236–268 and Sketch Map 37 (following page 236).

31. Ibid., 239.

32. Ökse, Baycan, and Sakaryalı, *Komutanların Biyografileri*, 196–197.

33. Gedeon, Paschalidou, and Dima-Dimitrou, *A Concise History of the Campaign in Asia Minor*, 240.

34. Ahmet Timural, Rauf Atakan, and Alişan Berktay, *Türk İstiklâl Harbi: IInci Cilt Batı Cephesi 5nci Kısım 2nci Kitap, Sakarya Meydan*

Muharebesi (23 Ağustos–13 Eylül 1921) ve Sonraki Harekât (14 Eylül–10 Ekim 1921) (Ankara: Genelkurmay Basımevi, 1973), 7.

35. Gedeon, Paschalidou, and Dima-Dimitrou, *A Concise History of the Campaign in Asia Minor*, 243–244.

36. Timural, Atakan, and Berktay, *Sakarya Meydan Muharebesi*, 16–18.

37. Gedeon, Paschalidou, and Dima-Dimitrou, *A Concise History of the Campaign in Asia Minor*, 245–246 and Timural, Atakan, and Berktay, *Sakarya Meydan Muharebesi*, Kroki 3a (Sketch Map 3a following page 18).

38. Timural, Atakan, and Berktay, *Sakarya Meydan Muharebesi*, 27.

39. Ibid., Kroki 3a (Sketch Map 3a following page 18).

40. Ibid., 19–22.

41. Gedeon, Paschalidou, and Dima-Dimitrou, *A Concise History of the Campaign in Asia Minor*, 264–267.

42. Timural, Atakan, and Berktay, *Sakarya Meydan Muharebesi*, Kroki 4b (Sketch Map 4b following page 28).

43. Gedeon, Paschalidou, and Dima-Dimitrou, *A Concise History of the Campaign in Asia Minor*, 252–253.

44. Timural, Atakan, and Berktay, *Sakarya Meydan Muharebesi*, Kroki 5c (Sketch Map 5c following page 44).

45. Gedeon, Paschalidou, and Dima-Dimitrou, *A Concise History of the Campaign in Asia Minor*, 249–250. See Timural, Atakan, and Berktay, *Sakarya Meydan Muharebesi*, Kroki 10 (Sketch Map 10 following page 76) for Fahrettin's routes.

46. Gedeon, Paschalidou, and Dima-Dimitrou, *A Concise History of the Campaign in Asia Minor*, 270; and Timural, Atakan, and Berktay, *Sakarya Meydan Muharebesi*, Kroki 11 (Sketch Map 11 following page 92).

47. Gedeon, Paschalidou, and Dima-Dimitrou, *A Concise History of the Campaign in Asia Minor*, 270.

48. Ibid., 262.

49. Timural, Atakan, and Berktay, *Sakarya Meydan Muharebesi*, Kroki 12 (Sketch Map 12 following page 108).

50. Ibid., 115.

51. Gedeon, Paschalidou, and Dima-Dimitrou, *A Concise History of the Campaign in Asia Minor*, 269.

52. Timural, Atakan, and Berktay, *Sakarya Meydan Muharebesi*, 101–105; and Gedeon, Paschalidou, and Dima-Dimitrou, *A Concise History of the Campaign in Asia Minor*, 274–275.

53. See Erickson, *Gallipoli, The Ottoman Campaign*, 55–56, 156–157 for examples of this tactic in the First World War.

54. Timural, Atakan, and Berktay, *Sakarya Meydan Muharebesi*, Kroki 15 (Sketch Map 15 following page 136).

55. Gedeon, Paschalidou, and Dima-Dimitrou, *A Concise History of the Campaign in Asia Minor*, 275.

56. This conclusion was reached after a conversation between the author and Assistant Professor of International Relations Konstantinos Travlos, November 30 2019. Travlos based his arguments on the work of Vasileios Loumiotes. In general, Greek corps commanders in the June–August 1921 operations failed to coordinate their efforts. This frequently left enterprising divisional commanders to take local action to coordinate their operations, as was the case during the Battle of Akchal Dag-Chavus Chiflik during the operations against Kütahya.

57. Timural, Atakan, and Berktay, *Sakarya Meydan Muharebesi*, 132.

58. Gedeon, Paschalidou, and Dima-Dimitrou, *A Concise History of the Campaign in Asia Minor*, 276–277.

59. Army Corps B is only mentioned once in the relevant pages (274–279) from the *Greek Concise History*. However, see Timural, Atakan, and Berktay, *Sakarya Meydan Muharebesi*, Kroki 17 (Sketch Map 17 following page 140).

60. Ibid., 141–142.

61. Gedeon, Paschalidou, and Dima-Dimitrou, *A Concise History of the Campaign in Asia Minor*, 278.

62. Timural, Atakan, and Berktay, *Sakarya Meydan Muharebesi*, Kroki 17 (Sketch Map 17 following page 140).

63. Timural, Atakan, and Berktay, *Sakarya Meydan Muharebesi*, 133.

64. Önalp, *Sakarya Meydan Muharebesi*, Table of Strength Returns 5 August 1921, Ek 3 (Document 3 following page 310).

65. Ökse, Baycan, and Sakaryalı, *Komutanların Biyografileri*, 92–94.

66. Gedeon, Paschalidou, and Dima-Dimitrou, *A Concise History of the Campaign in Asia Minor*, 282.

67. Ibid., 282.

68. Gedeon, Paschalidou, and Dima-Dimitrou, *A Concise History of the Campaign in Asia Minor*, 282–284.

69. Timural, Atakan, and Berktay, *Sakarya Meydan Muharebesi*, Kroki 20 (Sketch Map 20 following page 164).

70. Gedeon, Paschalidou, and Dima-Dimitrou, *A Concise History of the Campaign in Asia Minor*, 281.

71. Timural, Atakan, and Berktay, *Sakarya Meydan Muharebesi*, Kroki 22 (Sketch Map 22 following page 168).

72. Ibid., 206.

73. Ibid., 208.

74. Gedeon, Paschalidou, and Dima-Dimitrou, *A Concise History of the Campaign in Asia Minor*, 293–294.

75. Timural, Atakan, and Berktay, *Sakarya Meydan Muharebesi*, Kroki 35 (Sketch Map 35 following page 218).

76. Gedeon, Paschalidou, and Dima-Dimitrou, *A Concise History of the Campaign in Asia Minor*, 289–291.

77. Timural, Atakan, and Berktay, *Sakarya Meydan Muharebesi*, Kroki 36 (Sketch Map 36 following page 230).

78. Gedeon, Paschalidou, and Dima-Dimitrou, *A Concise History of the Campaign in Asia Minor*, 297.

79. Timural, Atakan, and Berktay, *Sakarya Meydan Muharebesi*, Kroki 38 (Sketch Map 38 following page 232).

80. Gedeon, Paschalidou, and Dima-Dimitrou, *A Concise History of the Campaign in Asia Minor*, 298.

81. Ibid., 299.

82. Timural, Atakan, and Berktay, *Sakarya Meydan Muharebesi*, 265–266.

83. İsmet to Mustafa Kemal, September 13, 1921, reproduced in Timural, Atakan, and Berktay, *Sakarya Meydan Muharebesi*, 269.

84. Mustafa Kemal to İsmet, September 13, 1921, reproduced in Timural, Atakan, and Berktay, *Sakarya Meydan Muharebesi*, 269–271.

85. Ibid., 271–273.

86. Gedeon, Paschalidou, and Dima-Dimitrou, *A Concise History of the Campaign in Asia Minor*, 301.

87. Timural, Atakan, and Berktay, *Sakarya Meydan Muharebesi*, Kroki 48 (Sketch Map 48 following page 300).

88. Gedeon, Paschalidou, and Dima-Dimitrou, *A Concise History of the Campaign in Asia Minor*, 303.

89. Ibid., 303; and Timural, Atakan, and Berktay, *Sakarya Meydan Muharebesi*, Kroki 50 (Sketch Map 50 following page 306).

90. Timural, Atakan, and Berktay, *Sakarya Meydan Muharebesi*, 310.

91. Ibid., 310.

92. Ibid., Kroki 53 (Sketch map 53 following page 312).

93. Gedeon, Paschalidou, and Dima-Dimitrou, *A Concise History of the Campaign in Asia Minor*, 304.

94. Timural, Atakan, and Berktay, *Sakarya Meydan Muharebesi*, Kroki 54 (Sketch Map 54 following page 312).

95. See page 326 for these orders.

96. Gedeon, Paschalidou, and Dima-Dimitrou, *A Concise History of the Campaign in Asia Minor*, 304.

97. Ibid., 306.

98. Ibid., 304.

99. Ibid., 305.

100. Timural, Atakan, and Berktay, *Sakarya Meydan Muharebesi*, Kroki 57 (Sketch Map 57 following page 332).

101. Ibid., Kroki 60 (Sketch map 60 following page 344).

102. Gedeon, Paschalidou, and Dima-Dimitrou, *A Concise History of the Campaign in Asia Minor*, 306.

103. Llewellyn-Smith, *Ionian Vision*, 234.

NINE

Operational and Strategic Pause

Something must be done quickly to remove us from the nightmare of Asia Minor.[1]

Prince Andreas to Metaxas, January 1, 1922

INTRODUCTION

The resiliency of the Nationalists had upset the Greek plans for a low-cost occupation of Asia Minor. İsmet's Western Front Command and Papoulas's FAAM fought an extended campaign followed by a positional battle for Afyonkarahisar, at the end of which, both armies were exhausted. As a result, and with the Anatolian winter setting in, both armies went into a period of reconstitution, training, and reorganization. This might well be termed an "operational pause," during which neither side conducted major operations (as had also been the case in 1920). At the strategic level, this is best described as a "strategic pause," as the Greeks wrestled with the dilemma of a war that had led them into a quagmire from which there seemed to be no satisfactory exit. While the Greeks argued, Mustafa Kemal used the time well to mobilize the country for total war. More importantly for the Nationalists, the team of Kemal, Fevzi, used the time to create an army capable of operational-level maneuver warfare.

THE BATTLE FOR AFYONKARAHISAR

With his army stalled by General Papoulas's defensive zone east of Eskişehir, İsmet determined September 24 to regain the initiative by launching a coordinated series of offensive operations. He planned to envelop the FAAM's left flank with the Kocaeli Group and its right flank with the V Corps. Simultaneously, his II Corps in reserve would conduct a three-day march south to positions east of Afyonkarahisar and, in conjunction with the 6th Division, attempt to seize the city.[2] It was a very ambitious plan. However, Greek aviation detachments observed the southern shift of Nationalist forces, and Papoulas ordered Army Corps A to send the 2nd Division south to the Hamamaltı train station on the Eskişehir-Afyonkarahisar rail line, and he gave the 1st Division a warning order to prepare to move south as well.[3] The next day, İsmet moved his II Corps south of the Sakarya River, maintaining pressure on the Greek left with the Kocaeli Group and holding the remainder of the line with cavalry outposts. But as the left wing of the FAAM retracted west, İsmet recognized that the opportunity to envelop the main body of the FAAM had passed, and he decided to employ the V Corps in the plan to capture Afyonkarahisar. Orders moving the V Corps to Seydiler and Selimye (35 kilometers northeast of Afyonkarahisar) went out to Fahrettin.

On September 27, Papoulas completed the withdrawal of Army Corps C to better positions on his left flank, and he decided to deploy the entire Army Corps A to the Afyonkarahisar front.[4] As a result, he ordered the 1st Division to march south from Derbent, and when the 2nd Division arrived at the Hamamaltı train station, Papoulas allocated it to the Southern Group of Divisions commanded by Major General Nikolaos Trikoupes. Meanwhile the advance elements of the Western Front Command's V Corps reached Seydiler and Selimye and moved to the outskirts of Ayfonkarahisar that evening, joining the 6th Division and the Sinan Bey Müfrezesi in launching probing attacks on the Greek 4th Division in the city. The next day, Trikoupes expanded the 2nd Division's sector from the train station to connect with the 4th Division in Afyonkarahisar and ordered the division to prepare defensive positions. The FAAM also began to move the 12th Division south to join its sister divisions. While the Greeks were digging in, Fahrettin pushed his cavalry divisions west toward the rail line, and Sinan Bey Müfrezesi repeated its probing attacks. On September 28, the Greek 1st Division had moved south to Akin (halfway to Hamamaltı) while the Nationalists did little else but conduct minor probes in their sectors.

On September 29, the Greek 1st Division occupied the sector to the north of the 2nd Division while the 12th Division arrived in Akin.[5] The V Corps divisions pushed forward to establish contact with the 1st and 2nd Divisions, and Fahrettin deployed his 8th Division on his left, making the connection with Sinan Bey Müfrezesi. From the southwest to the north, the Nationalists ringed Afyonkarahisar with the 6th Division, Sinan Bey Müfrezesi, the 8th Division, and the 14th, 3rd, and 2nd Cavalry Divisions (Fahrettin's 1st Cavalry Division manned his right flank, connecting with the adjacent I Corps). İsmet also finally deployed the II Corps to reserve positions immediately behind Fahrettin's lines.

Commander in Chief Mustafa Kemal issued orders to begin offensive operations on September 30 with the V Corps attacking that day and the II Corps attacking on October 1.[6] Fahrettin's 14th Cavalry and 8th Infantry Divisions launched their assaults at 10:00 a.m. and the remaining cavalry divisions, as well as the Sinan Bey Müfrezesi attacked shortly thereafter. The 6th Division was unready and did not participate in the attacks. Nationalist cavalry and the army's provisional detachments were very lightly armed and had almost no artillery. As a result, the poorly supported Nationalist assaults were handily repulsed. At noon, October 1, Lieutenant General Kontoulis arrived with the Army Corps A headquarters to take command of the battle from Trikoupes (dissolving the Southern Group of Divisions), and his 12th Division arrived on the northern flank of the 1st Division. The Greeks now had a united army corps under an active commander on the Afyonkarahisar front, and Kontoulis immediately began planning to take the offensive.[7]

On October 2, Kontoulis established the 12th Division in defensive positions north of the 1st Division along the rail line. Unfortunately for the Nationalists, the II Corps and the 6th Division remained unready. Nevertheless, the V Corps cavalry divisions all attacked and were repulsed again.[8] This turn of events encouraged Kontoulis, who decided to counterattack the next day. Kontoulis's counterattack began late in the day on October 3, with the 1st, 2nd, and 4th Divisions attacking to seize the high ground occupied by the V Corps. These attacks were generally successful, causing the Western Front Command offensive to stall in its tracks.[9] A Nationalist assault from the south on Afyonkarahisar by the 6th Division was beaten back by Greek 4th Division reserve. These successes enabled Kontoulis to pull the 12th Division into corps reserve in the city. The next day also went to the Greeks, as they captured more high ground along their front. At 11:00 p.m. on October 2, İsmet finally ordered his II Corps to join the fight on October 3. His plan involved the V Corps sliding to the north while the II Corps occupied the front, taking the places of the 14th Cavalry and 8th Divisions. Once in place, both corps and the 6th Division would launch an encirclement of the Greek forces in Afyonkarahisar.[10]

Colonel Selahattin's II Corps brought three fresh infantry divisions to the fight (the 3rd Caucasian, 4th, and 7th Divisions), and İsmet launched his long-awaited offensive at 8:00 a.m. on October 3 in very foggy, wet, and muddy conditions. While some ground was gained in the II Corps sector, Greek counterattacks blunted the Nationalists assaults. The next day, with the careful commitment of the 12th Division, Kontoulis conducted corps-wide counterattacks and took most of the high ground to the east of the rail way.[11] In the south, the Nationalist 6th Division lost all its gains. General Papoulas decided to resolve the situation around Afyonkarahisar by withdrawing Army Corps B's 5th and 13th Divisions to Seyitgazi and to attack the Nationalist V Corps right flank with these formations.

A confusion of combat occurred on October 5 as the V and II Corps attacked and counterattacked, and, reciprocally, Army Corps A attacked and counterattacked in return.[12] The battered Nationalist 6th Division was unable to participate and remained on the defensive. As a result of Papoulas's decision on October 4, the 13th Division reached the Akin staging area on October 5 and the 5th Division a day later. General Kontoulis continued his attacks on October 6 with the 2nd Division, which failed, but he was able to bring his 12th Division back into reserve.[13] Prince Andreas, commander of Army Corps B, had relinquished command and returned to Izmir on leave on October 1, and, in his stead, Papoulas appointed Major General Trikoupes to command the corps.[14] General Papoulas also detached the 9th Division from Army Corps B, allocating it Army Corps C, which was left with the mission of defending the FAAM's Eskişehir base. In the far north, İsmet's Kocaeli Group launched its 1st Cavalry Division in unsuccessful flank attacks on Army Corps C. Otherwise, the northern front was mostly quiet.

On the morning of October 8, Trikoupes swung his 5th Division east and formed a defensive line north of Army Corps A's right flank while his 13th Division continued marching south to a position behind the 1st Division. The Nationalist V and II Corps stood on the defensive while the battered 6th Division abandoned its long-held position south of Afyonkarahisar and withdrew to the east.[15] İsmet ordered his III Corps south, but it was too late to retrieve the battle. The next day, Trikoupes attacked with the fresh 5th Division supported by Kontoulis's 1st and 2nd Divisions. Bitter fighting raged throughout the day, but V and II Corps counterattacks drove them back. On October 9, Trikoupes and Kontoulis attacked again across their combined front; the 5th Division made gains in the V Corps sector, but Nationalist counterattacks repulsed the rest. Unable to contest the Greeks with the forces at hand, İsmet conceded making the decision to withdraw.

On October 10, the Western Front Command withdrew its forces from close contact around Afyonkarahisar. İsmet moved the fresh I Corps into the line against Army Corps B, while the V Corps withdrew its battered 2nd, 3rd, and 14th Cavalry Divisions and the 8th Division behind the lines held by the II Corps.[16] Over the remainder of October, İsmet moved the V Corps to positions at Sütlaç, south of Afyonkarahisar, and the Kocaeli Group north toward Lake İznik.[17] On November 6, the Western Front Command redeployed the 1st Cavalry Division from the northern flank of Kocaeli Group and brought it south to the army's center. These deployments gave İsmet strong cavalry formations north and south of Afyonkarahisar.

The battle for Afyonkarahisar was over, with the Greeks victorious. In a reversal of roles, the Nationalists were operating without railroads and on external lines of communication, while the FAAM enjoyed railroads and interior lines of communication. This enabled General Papoulas to make timely decisions and deploy his divisions rapidly to decisive points. For his part, İsmet failed to concentrate the Western Front Command in real time, and, consequently, only part of his army engaged the enemy. By the time the V Corps reached the Afyonkarahisar battle zone, Papoulas had reinforced the orphan 4th Division with an entire army corps. Understandably, İsmet's army was exhausted by weeks of herd fighting, but his decision to commit the mostly cavalry V Corps to an assault on entrenched infantry is hard to fathom. In the end, the Western Front Command did not control the battle as effectively as the FAAM.

REORGANIZATION OF THE ARMIES

On October 1921, General Papoulas withdrew the headquarters of the FAAM to Izmir and divided the operational forces into a Northern Group under the command of Army Corps C commander Lieutenant General Polymenakos in Eskişehir with (from north to south) the independent 11th Division and Army Corps C's 3rd, 10th, and 7th Divisions in-line and the

9th Division in corps reserve.[18] The allocation of the Independent Division in reserve in Seyitgazi is unclear.[19] In Afyonkarahisar, Papoulas established a Southern Group under the command of Army Corps A commander Lieutenant General Kontoulis, with Major General Trikoupes Army Corps B subordinate to him. From north to south, Army Corps B deployed the 13th and 5th Divisions in-line northeast of Afyonkarahisar, and Army Corps A deployed the 12th and 4th Divisions east and south of the city, with the 1st and 2nd Divisions held in Southern Group reserve.[20]

As a result of several Nationalist attacks in the Afyonkarahisar sector, the FAAM developed a contingency plan on October 16 to conduct a preemptive counteroffensive. However, due to the exhausted condition of the army, the FAAM decided "to move its center of gravity farther south" instead.[21] General Papoulas allocated and moved the Cavalry Brigade and the 9th Division on October 29 into Kontoulis's Southern Group sector. On November 2, the FAAM expanded the independent Cavalry Brigade to a full Cavalry Division by consolidating the brigade with several independent cavalry regiments. When it became known to Greek intelligence that the enemy had formed a field army in the Afyonkarahisar sector in mid-November, General Papoulas sent the 7th Division to the Southern Group as well. By the end of the year, the operational center of gravity of the FAAM was in Kontoulis's Southern Group, which was composed of eight infantry divisions and one cavalry division, while Polymenakos's Northern Group was composed of four infantry divisions. According to the Concise Greek History, this transferring of forces unbalanced the FAAM, resulting in a loss of operational flexibility.[22]

The Nationalists also undertook a major reorganization of their western armies in October.[23] Encouraged by their success in driving the Greeks back to Eskişehir, Kemal and Fevzi were determined to create a command architecture that would accommodate the conduct of operational-level offensive operations. The reactivation of army headquarters was the first step toward this goal. On October 15, 1921, Kemal activated the First Army headquarters under the command of Major General Ali İnsan (Sabis), who had returned from detention on Malta on July 25.[24] Kemal allocated to the new First Army the II Corps (3rd Caucasian, 4th, and 7th Divisions), the V Corps (2nd, 3rd, and 14th Cavalry Divisions), and the independent 6th and 8th Divisions (as well as a number of provisional infantry detachments). Furthermore, he assigned Ali İnsan the Afyonkarahisar sector of the front, while the Western Front Command retained direct command of the I, III, IV Corps and the Kocaeli Group. On November 1, Kemal allocated the I and IV Corps to the First Army as well.[25] The overall personnel and equipment strength returns of the Western Front Command on November 15, 1921 showed 6,629 officers, 133,079 enlisted men, 50,056 animals, 6,666 motorized trucks, 47 motorized staff cars, 66,732 rifles, 518 light machine guns, 576 heavy machine guns, and 230 artillery pieces.[26] However, the personnel strength in the combat formations was wildly unbalanced, with infantry divisions having from 550 to 7,000 men and cavalry divisions fielding from 1,500 to 3,500 men.

WESTERN FRONT PLANNING AND REORGANIZATION

The Nationalists began planning an operational-level offensive that would end the war when Kemal sent İsmet a directive on November 15 and asked him to consider Chief of Staff Fevzi's *Sad Taarruz Planı* (the Main Assault Plan).[27] Conceptually, Fevzi's plan called for shifting the entire army south and fixing the Army Corps A and B in Afyonkarahisar, with direct attacks by eight unidentified infantry divisions. Simultaneously, I and IV would envelop the city from the south and west while the 1st Cavalry Division enveloped it from the north. The pincers would converge at Altıntaş-Döger. On the far-left flank, the V Corps would penetrate and seize Uşak, preventing reinforcements from reaching the pocket. It was an exceptionally high-risk concept because it left only a few cavalry regiments in the north opposing Army Corps C.[28]

İsmet's staff examined the proposal and liked the concept but returned a more refined plan. Ismet's plan was not quite as risky and proposed leaving three infantry divisions in the north to fix Army Corps C in Eskişehir, while the II Corps and the 8th Division would fix the Greeks in Afyonkarahisar with direct attacks as the III and IV Corps swept north to meet the 1st Cavalry Division in the Altıntaş-Döger area.[29] The V Corps would screen the far-left flank and cut the railroad at Uşak. İsmet also asked Ali İnsan's staff for a proposal, which it forwarded as well. Ali İnsan's First Army staff produced a plan that was, in retrospect, the most realistic. The plans from Ankara and Polatlı headquarters envisioned the main effort coming from the south of the city of Afyonkarahisar, which meant deploying large masses of men. Ali İnsan's plan envisioned the I, II, and IV Corps attacking north of the city and linking up with the V Corps attacking northwest from the south. Only two divisions would conduct an attack to fix the enemy in the city. Two army corps—the Kocaeli Group and the III Corps—would fix Army Corps C at Eskişehir.[30] Colonel İzzettin, the I

Corps commander, also produced a plan similar to the Western Front Command's. There was certainly no shortage of concepts, and the range of plans, from the national general staff down to corps level, demonstrates the aggressive view of the Nationalist commanders who recognized the imperative of decisive offensive operations. Importantly, every Nationalist commander supported a southern offensive against the Afyonkarahisar salient, which, in addition to its obvious geographic vulnerability, was masked from a flanking counterattack from Greek Army Corps C by the Turkmen Mountains.

Ali İnsan followed up with logistical estimates that at least 100,000 men and 20,000 animals would be required to execute such an operation with appropriate supplies and lines of communication. But with winter setting in, it was obvious that the magnitude of the concept exceeded the means at hand, and planning was put aside. Local operations, however, continued, and, to the south of Afyonkarahisar, the 6th Division and the V Corps' cavalry divisions attacked west to Banaz and Çivril, temporarily cutting the Uşak-Afyonkarahisar railroad.

In the meantime, İsmet recognized the need for greater command and control to manage the multiple avenues of advance required by a major operational offensive, and he asked Kemal on November 18 for permission to establish a second army-level headquarters.[31] Kemal approved the request on November 19, 1921 and activated the Second Army headquarters under the command of Brigadier General Yakup Şevki (Subaşı) in the town of Bolvadin.[32] Initially the Second Army would comprise of the II Corps; the independent 8th, 16th, and 17th Divisions; and the 1st Cavalry Division. Ali İnsan's First Army was composed of the I and IV Corps, the newly redesignated V Cavalry Corps, and the independent 6th and 14th Divisions. İsmet continued in command of the Western Front Command, now composed of both field armies, the III Corps, and Kocaeli Group. With the danger to Ankara removed, İsmet moved his headquarters from Polatlı southwest to Sivrihisar.

From November 20–25, the V Cavalry Corps attacked to capture the Şeyhelvan Dağı seizing the heights and advancing toward Çivril. The 3rd and 14th Cavalry Divisions took the heights but were stopped from taking Çivril by the counterattacks of the Greek 2nd Division.[33] By December 10, the Nationalists had extended the front below Afyonkarahisar by moving the 14th Cavalry Division west to Çal, 80 kilometers south of Uşak, forcing General Kontoulis to deploy the 2nd Division south of the city in response. Thus, by mid-December 1921 the Nationalists had achieved the geographical preconditions necessary for the execution of the Main Assault Plan with strong cavalry forces north and south of Afyonkarahisar, which now had an exposed extended southern flank. The Greeks were not unaware of their vulnerability, and Major General Trikoupes forwarded a staff study on January 5, 1922 to the FAAM outlining the vulnerability of the Afyonkarahisar salient and offering some ideas on counteroffensives should the Nationalists attack the city.[34] This led to General Papoulas directing coordinated planning by the Northern and Southern Groups as contingencies against a Western Front Command offensive.

THE WINTER OF DISENCHANTMENT

British historian Michael Llewellyn-Smith used the phrase "winter disenchantment" to describe the effects of the intersection of Great Power politics, domestic politics in Greece, and the terrible realities of the military situation in Asia Minor on Greek decision-making in 1921/1922.[35] While many factors were involved, Llewellyn-Smith described a "Council of Lieutenant-Generals" held in Izmir in early October 1921, attended by Prince Andreas (Lieutenant General Vasilopais), who had just relinquished command of Army Corps B. At the conference, Andreas said that he thought the Nationalists would launch an offensive in the early spring. He followed this with a compelling analysis of the military dilemma— the front was too long, and there were too few troops available to hold the line. He felt this would lead to disaster, and the epigraph at the head of this chapter expressed his personal recommendation, "Something must be done quickly to remove us from the nightmare of Asia Minor."[36] However, without political support and clarity of a strategic objective, there was little the generals could do.

Allied support for the Greek occupation of a large part of western Asia Minor had been steadily decreasing throughout 1921, and the defeat of the FAAM accelerated this trend. This was a terrible problem for the Greek government, and it sought a diplomatic solution. In mid-October, Prime Minister Gounares and Foreign Minister Georgios Baltatzes met in Paris with French Prime Minister Aristide Briand, who promised to stop the flow of military aid to Kemal.[37] They then travelled to London for discussions with British Foreign Secretary Lord George Curzon. These discussions resulted in a reaffirmation of the Curzon Plan, acknowledging that the Treaty of Sèvres was a dead issue and that Greek autonomy in Asia Minor had to be implemented with the cooperation of the Ottoman sultan.[38] The

Greek Army would remain in Asia Minor until a joint western-supervised gendarmerie could be established. Gounares cabled Athens on October 29, arguing that the Curzon Plan should be accepted because the British desired a quick peace and the preservation of ties to the other Powers. The Greek cabinet accepted the plan, and, four days later, the Greek delegation met with British prime minister Lloyd George. Although he was pro-Greek, Lloyd George faced opposition in his cabinet and in the army general staff, which preferred a strong and unitary Turkish state, rather than Greece, as a stable polity to act as a buffer keeping the Soviets from the Mediterranean. To the delegation's disappointment, Lloyd George could offer no financial support. While he was in London, Gounares tried unsuccessfully to arrange loans with British banks, but these fell through.[39]

Gounares made several additional overtures to the British government, stressing that without military and financial support, the war effort would collapse, and Greece would be compelled to withdraw completely from Asia Minor, but these entreaties fell on deaf ears. Gounares sent a final request to Curzon, and he returned to Athens on March 6, determined to order an evacuation of Asia Minor. His government fell four days later, a successor government failed to form, and Gounares returned to power. He then decided to wait for Curzon's reply, which was delivered to the Greek *chargé d'affaires* in London on March 18. Curzon downplayed the Greek dilemma and urged Gounares to defer a decision until an Allied conference would be held in Paris. Gounares decided to delay a decision to withdraw the army from Asia Minor.

On March 21, the foreign ministers of Britain, France, and Italy met in Paris to discuss the terms of a peace.[40] The French tried unsuccessfully to arrange a three-month cease-fire, and then followed this up with detailed recommendations for a peace treaty, including a withdrawal timetable for the Greek Army to leave Asia Minor. The sultan's rump government attempted to join the conference, but its requests were ignored. The Nationalists sent a diplomatic note of April 17 suggesting a cease-fire beginning with an immediate Greek withdrawal from the Eskişehir-Afyonkarahisar line, followed by complete withdrawal from Anatolia within four months. Of course, this was not acceptable to either the Allies or to the Greeks, who made a counteroffer, which Ankara rejected. Peace negotiations stalled, and, in the middle of May, following the Nationalist rejection, the Greek government judged "that there remained only one solution to the Asia Minor question: the occupation of Constantinople by the Greek forces of Thrace."[41] The political decision-makers in Athens believed that such dramatic action would somehow force the Nationalists to make peace and prompt the Allies to implement the terms of the Treaty of Sèvres. The General Staff went to work planning for the occupation but considered the Field Army of Thrace's two infantry divisions insufficient for screening both the Bulgarian border and occupying eastern Thrace and Istanbul.

By this time, Greece was in desperate economic straits. The government was deeply in debt, and the near-total mobilization of military age men badly crippled the existing economy. Moreover, the cost of the war and the continuing occupation of Asia Minor had drained the treasury. Gounares sought the advice of his military advisor, Major General Xenophon Strategos, who told him to abandon Asia Minor if the economic situation could not be resolved.[42] The Greeks were saved by the ingenious ideas of Minister of Finance Petros Protopapadakis, who proposed a compulsory domestic loan. The minister's idea was to cut each currency bill literally in half—there were three billion drachmas in circulation in the spring of 1922. The parliament enacted legislation on April 5, 1922, after which the drachmas actually were cut in half. The half bearing the portrait of Georgios Staurou would have one half the printed value, and the other half represented one bond on deposit at the National Bank with an interest of 6.5 percent. "By this simple, innovative, and rapid method a domestic loan was secured, the proceeds of which strengthened the government's economic position by the sum of 1.5 billion drachmae."[43] Surely the people of Greece felt otherwise.

There were other issues in Greece gathering momentum as the military situation grew darker. A nationalist organization, which was composed mostly of Venizelists who were out of power after the November 1920 elections, established the *Amyna* or National Defense Movement. Initially, they sought to restore Venizelos to power by any means necessary, including a coup, and to restore active British support for Greek operations in Asia Minor. These efforts came to nothing, but the failure of the FAAM's summer and fall offensive reenergized the organization. As *Amyna* gathered strength, its objectives changed to support the idea that Asia Minor, including Istanbul (Constantinople) and Izmir (Smyrna), should become a Greek autonomous zone defended by a volunteer army.[44] In January and February 1922 *Amyna* became a real force in Greek politics, to the extent that it contacted Allied governments and formally approached General Papoulas for support. Papoulas was frustrated by Gounares repeatedly ignoring his warnings and recommendations regarding the dangerously vulnerable position of the FAAM. As a result, Papoulas considered the

Amyna proposals, and he sent a message informing Athens that he supported them. On March 16, 1922, Minister of the Army Theotokes replied to Papoulas, rejecting the idea of an autonomous zone and asking for all Greeks to support the Athens government. Unhappy with this result, Papoulas submitted his resignation on March 21, and the government brought him back to Athens where he presented his ideas to the prime minister and the cabinet on March 29.[45] Papoulas again asked for the establishment of an autonomous zone and suggested that the government replace him as commander of the FAAM if this were not done. He returned to Izmir and submitted a memorandum on April 4 recommending that his army be authorized to pull back from Eskişehir and Afyonkarahisar to a more defensible operational perimeter. When this was denied, General Papoulas submitted his resignation on May 25, and it was accepted on June 3, 1922.[46] He was replaced by Lieutenant General Georgios Chatzanestes, who had been the commander of the Field Army in Thrace.[47] Llewellyn-Smith presented Papoulas as more or less having been duped by *Amyna* resulting in his fall from grace. He continued with "the ineffective diplomacy of the Powers reduced the government to impotence, Papoulas' stand and the government's hostility reduced the *Amyna* to confusion and despair."[48] The replacement of Papoulas by Chatzanestes would prove disastrous.

While Greek politics were in such turmoil over strategic end states, there was strategic clarity in the Nationalists' position. For Kemal's part, he played a game of wait and see because he recognized that time was on the side of the Nationalists. Every day that passed, the Greeks grew weaker militarily and more fragmented politically. Equally as important for Greece, Allied support for their cause was evaporating among the European Powers. Well-negotiated Nationalist treaties with the Soviets, the Caucasian republics, the French, and the Italians further isolated Greece. Kemal deliberately dragged out the cease-fire negotiations until his armies were ready to force a conclusion to the war by military means.[49]

NATIONALIST MOBILIZATION

In terms of preparing to inflict a catastrophic defeat on the Greeks in western Anatolia, diplomacy played a key role in Nationalist success. The Moscow Agreement with the Soviets of March 16, 1921 paved the way for the shipment of large quantities of badly needed arms and military equipment. Equally important were the Kars Agreement of October 13, 1921 with

Soviet Armenia and the Ankara Agreement of October 20 with France, which enabled the Nationalists to shift now-excess forces from the Eastern and Southern Front Commands to İsmet's Western Front Command.[50]

On October 31, 1921, the Grand National Assembly extended Kemal's appointment as commander in chief for an additional three months. [51] In November Ali Fethi (Okyar) returned from imprisonment on Malta, and Kemal appointed him minister of the interior. This released Refet (Bele) to concentrate exclusively on his duties as minister of national defense.[52] Rauf (Orbay) also returned from Malta with Ali Fethi and, with Kemal's encouragement, entered the national assembly. These appointments gave Kemal control over the economy and, equally importantly, ensured that he had a well-known and respected advocate and friend in the assembly. Effectively, Kemal now had complete authority over the national war effort, and he took immediate and far-reaching actions.

The actions taken by Kemal in the winter of 1921/1922 as commander in chief form an important part of the contemporary Turkish historical narrative. Famously, Kemal rushed Soviet gold and weapons, which were now arriving in shipments every two weeks, to the embattled front using oxcarts and the labor of peasant women.[53] In addition to the Soviet shipments, as the French evacuated Cilicia, they left behind 10,000 rifles and tons of equipment, munitions, and uniforms, which were transferred to the Nationalists and shipped west. Included in the French transfers were 10 much-need aircraft, 4 of which went to the western front, and 6 of which remained in Adana for pilot training.[54] With peace treaties signed, both the French and Italians signed armaments contracts with the Nationalists. The Nationalists purchased 1,500 light machine guns from the French and procured 50 fighter aircraft.[55] The French set up an ammunition factory at Adana, and French equipment flowed in through the port of Mersin, including 400 three-ton Berliet trucks. The Nationalists purchased an additional 150 Fiat trucks from Italy, which arrived in the port of Antalya. The Greek Navy could only watch these transfers, since the cargo ships were French and Italian, and the Allies had refused to recognize a state of war, denying Greece the rights of a belligerent on the sea.

Refet purchased tons of grain and flour with Soviet gold and stockpiled it in the army's warehouses, and he set the army's engineers to repairing the railways, bridges, and roads. The government requisitioned supplies, including underwear, oxen, and carts, and 40 percent of all leather, cloth, flour, and candle production for the army. Refet established a domestic network of dozens of small factories throughout Anatolia (employing even more women), which produced artillery shells, bayonets, ammunition, uniforms, and even new artillery breech blocks to replace those confiscated by the Allies in 1919/1920. In effect, Kemal ordered the total mobilization of the impoverished Turkish nation, and the modern Turkish narrative asserts that, in response, the people heroically threw their collective will and toil into the war effort.

Of course, there was resistance, not the least of which came from the Grand National Assembly and from Eastern Front commander Major General Kâzım Karabekir, who tried unsuccessfully to persuade Kemal to set up a senate. After a difficult vote, the assembly passed another three-month extension for Kemal. "Matters came to a head in May 1922," when the assembly again tried to limit Kemal's powers, but another extension passed with a vote of 177 to 11, with 15 abstentions.[56] Another crisis erupted on July when the assembly again attempted to limit Kemal, but Rauf's intervention carried the day. On July 12, Fevzi resigned his post as prime minister, retaining his portfolio as minister of war, and Rauf was elected as the new prime minister. Rauf succeeded in taming the opposition, and when the vote to extend Kemal's powers came up on July 20, 1922 Rauf succeeded in passing it with an indefinite time limit.

The long summer and fall campaigns had drained the army of strength, and Kemal set about restoring its rolls. Between October 1921 and June 1922, the army added 2,739 officers (with new commissions and promotions). On February 16, 1922, Kemal persuaded the national assembly to order full mobilization of the classes of 1881–1900 and to order the class of 1901 to the colors as well. Deserters, who had become a major drain on the field army, were rounded up and returned to duty. Altogether, between October 1921 and June 1922, an additional 120,442 men were brought to active service.[57] By the time of the summer campaign season, the personnel division of the General Staff was able to bring the personnel strength of the army's infantry divisions up to a standardized strength of 7,000 to 7,500 men and 5 to 15 artillery pieces.[58] This was still well below the Greek standard of about 10,000 men in each infantry division, but the Nationalists now had 19 infantry and 4 cavalry divisions in the Western Front Command. Moreover, the Eastern Front Command dispatched the 12th Division to the west, and the General Staff activated a new 16th Division. Altogether, including the east, south, and central fronts, the Nationalist Army in January 1922 was composed of 23 infantry and 5 cavalry divisions and 1 cavalry brigade.[59]

İsmet, who was a highly trained General Staff officer, likely spent much of his time building and training a theater-level army headquarters staff. This was necessary because the activation of two field-army headquarters transitioned the Western Front Command from a headquarters conducting tactical-level operations to an operational-level headquarters conducting campaign planning and operations. Fortunately for the Nationalists, the army had an abundance of trained General Staff officers with years of experience in combat during the Balkan Wars and World War I. İsmet organized his headquarters in the German Army-style, with 17 staff divisions (*Şube* meaning branch or division), of which the "first among equals" was the First Division (Operations), closely followed by the Second Division (Intelligence).[60] As his chief of operations, İsmet selected Staff Major Şemsettin (Taner), and as his chief of intelligence, he selected Staff Major Mehmet Şükrü (Ögel).[61] Other staff divisions included logistics, personnel, medical, veterinary, transportation, and postal services. Additionally, there were artillery, engineer, and machine gun inspectorates to coordinate and supervise specialized arms training. An artillery school was set up at Konya to teach artillery officers the latest techniques in the planning and conduct of indirect fire, as well as machine gun and engineer schools. In the army's rear areas, seven regimental infantry training depots and one artillery and one machine gun depot were established to train the influx of conscripts and mobilized reservists.[62] Of note, the Nationalist infantry regiments were trained in modern German-style assault troop (storm troop) tactics.[63]

THE WAR CONTINUES

Throughout the winter, Kemal fended off repeated queries from his political opponents in the Grand National Assembly who wanted to know why he had not taken the offensive against the Greeks. The simple answer is that he was busy rebuilding and reorganizing his army. While he was willing to consider planning an operational-level offensive, the army was not ready to conduct an operational-level offensive. Kemal gave instructions to İsmet not to conduct offensive operations and to conserve his forces. On March 21, the army organized a VI Corps headquarters under the command of Major General Kâzım (İnanç).[64] Overall, the late winter and early spring were quiet, but on April 12, Ali İnsan launched an unauthorized attack with his 6th and 8th Divisions against the Greek 4th Division's positions on the high ground southwest of Afyonkarahisar.[65]

The two-day assault resulted in minor gains for the First Army, but the attacks served to alert the FAAM to its vulnerable southwestern flank. In preparation for the coming offensive, İsmet relocated his Western Front Command headquarters to near Akşehir (about 100 kilometers southeast of Afyonkarahisar). He also removed the V Cavalry Corps from Ali İnsan's First Army into Western Front Command reserve near Akşehir. On April 30, the Western Front Command activated a Provisional Cavalry Division from independent detachments and squadrons and sent it to Adapazarı and allocated the 16th and 17th Divisions to the recently activated VI Corps.[66] On May 17, Kemal and İsmet made their final selection for corps command in the west by appointing Colonel Ali Hikmet (Ayerdem) to replace Major General Selahattin in command of the army's II Corps.[67] Selahattin was transferred to join Fevzi in the Ministry of Defense as undersecretary.[68]

However, everything was not as smooth as Kemal might have wanted, and an unanticipated problem arose in the person of Major General Ali İnsan, the recently appointed commander of the First Army. Ali İnsan was something of a conniver, and General Allenby had a difficult time with him in Mesopotamia immediately after the war. He often caused problems—for example, military pay was usually in arrears, and, when it arrived, Ali İnsan appropriated the Second Army payroll and distributed it to his own men.[69] He was critical of his superiors, İsmet especially, who had been an army corps commander when Ali İnsan was a field army commander. He conducted unauthorized small-scale operations southwest of Afyonkarahisar and tried to rally support against Kemal, Fevzi, and İsmet. As a result of Ali İnsan's high-handed behavior, İsmet asked Kemal to relieve him.[70] On July 18, 1922, Kemal and Fevzi relieved Ali İnsan and sent him to Konya to await court-martial.[71] Command of the First Army was offered to Ali Fuat, who refused, and then to Refet, who also refused; neither man would serve under İsmet.[72] Finally they transferred Central Army commander Major General Nurettin (Sakallı), who took command of the First Army on June 30, 1922.[73]

In Ankara, Kemal and Fevzi reached a decision on June 16 that the army was at last ready to renew offensive operations. On July 2, Kemal directed İsmet to submit his plans for an operational-level "Great Offensive." İsmet replied immediately on July 3, endorsing a double envelopment of Army Corps A and B in Afyonkarahisar.[74] The Western Front Command envisioned the First Army as the main effort coming from the south (west of the city), combined with the II Corps coming from the east (north of the city).[75] However, over the next few days, İsmet, Nurettin, and Yakup Şevki exchanged their thoughts and concerns about the plan with Kemal and Fevzi. All were concerned about the maintenance of an operational reserve and about the logistical support required.[76] Nevertheless, the strategic and operational leadership of the army unanimously supported a campaign of annihilation conducted through a double envelopment. The mature Nationalist campaign plan dramatically shows the effect of this combined thinking on the operation (see map 9.1).

The Greeks were not idle during this period, as Lieutenant General Georgios Chatzanestes assumed command of the FAAM on June 5, 1922. He insisted on retaining command of the Greek forces in Thrace, and he has been characterized as "eccentric, high-strung, excitable, and widely thought to be mentally unbalanced."[77] Major General Konstantinos Demetrakopoulos took command of the Field Army in Thrace, which was then redesignated Army Corps D and placed under command of the FAAM.[78] Chatzanestes believed that the FAAM should withdraw to a shorter line of defense, which was unpopular with the Athens government. He was also apparently unpopular with many of the senior leadership within the FAAM, as Lieutenant-General Kontoulis (Army Corps A), Lieutenant General Polymenakos (Army Corps C), and Major General Konstantinos Pallis (FAAM chief of staff) requested reassignment to mainland Greece.[79] On June 5, Major General Petros Soumilas replaced Polymenakos as Army Corps C commander. More critically for the Afyonkarahisar front, on June 15, Major General Trikoupes replaced Kontoulis in command of Army Corps A, and Major General Kimon Digenis replaced Trikoupes as Army Corps B commander. In turn, the 2nd Division commander Major General Georgios Valetas replaced Pallis as the FAAM chief of staff, and Army Corps D was placed under the command of the FAAM.

After taking command, Chatzanestes reversed the operational planning of the FAAM, which had been oriented toward operational counteroffensives, by ordering his staff to study a deliberate withdrawal to two lines of defense (Chatzanestes had not decided which line offered the best advantage to his army). On June 8, Chatzanestes went on a 15-day inspection tour of his army, which had a significant impact on the future of not only the FAAM but of Greece itself. Travelling from Uşak-Bursa-Eskişehir-Kütahya-Afyonkarahisar-Izmir-Mudanya, Chatzanestes visited every division, and he took the time ask his commanders what they thought of the situation. Initially, he was appalled by what he found, and was famously quoted as saying to his corps commanders, "How can you sleep at night

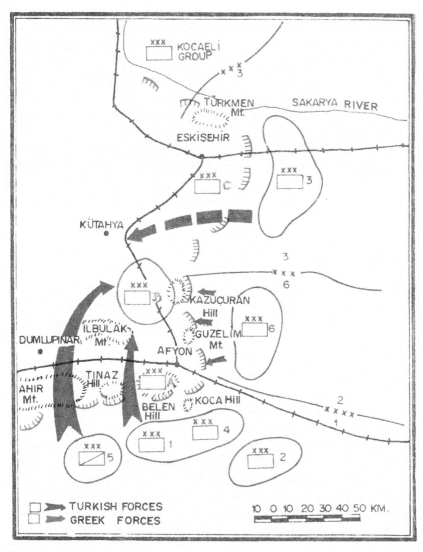

Map 9.1   The Nationalist Plan

The acute vulnerability of the FAAM salient around Afyonkarahisar is obvious from this map. Army Corps A and B (two-thirds of the Greek Army in Asia Minor) were dangerously exposed to encirclement by the Nationalists. The buildup of the Nationalists' two infantry corps and the cavalry corps on the lines south of the city shows the concentration for the main effort.

Courtesy of the Turkish General Staff Military History and Strategy Institute (ATASE).

with positions such as this?"[80] In reply, his commanders "were determined and dedicated to defending their positions. As a result of this inspection the commander in chief formed the impression that, although there had been great progress in the defensive organization of the front, insistence on the occupation of such an extended line, with such a limited force, amounted to a criminal act." This opinion conformed to his previous beliefs, but, unbelievably, Chatzanestes estimated that he could safely dispatch troops from the FAAM to Army Corps D in Thrace. He was apparently swayed by the strong assurances of his subordinate commanders and by the army's opinion that Nationalist morale was low. In any event, Chatzanestes was so focused on Istanbul that he needed very little encouragement to proceed.

On June 30, Major General Aristotelis Vlachopoulos assumed command of Army Corps D and was ordered by the FAAM to form two new infantry divisions from his own units and from units to be sent from Asia Minor. The FAAM ordered three infantry regiments, two Evzone battalions, one cavalry, and one pack artillery battalion to Thrace, which became Division A (Division B was formed from regiments already in Thrace).[81] The FAAM also prepared to send two additional infantry regiments, but these orders were rescinded. Overall, the FAAM lost 11 infantry battalions and 5 artillery batteries (4 and 3 of which, respectively, came from the soon-to-be-attacked Army Corps A and B).[82] On July 23, Chatzanestes returned to the mainland for consultations with the prime minister and minister of the army. At the meeting, the details for the occupation of eastern Thrace and Istanbul were worked out, and July 29 was established as the starting date for the operation. After the discussions, Chatzanestes returned to Tekirdağ in Thrace to direct the operation.[83] On July 26, Athens sent Chatzanestes a diplomatic note to be delivered to the Allied high commissioners in Istanbul, more or less warning them of Greek intentions.[84]

The Allies did not stand idle while the Greeks moved troops into Eastern Thrace. Warned by French general Charles Charpy that Chatzanestes intended to occupy the capital, the British commander, Major General Timothy Harrington, occupied the Çatalca Lines with his forces. By August 1, Harrington had troops manning the old Ottoman fortifications, including the 3rd Hussars and the XIXth Brigade, Royal Artillery, under the command of Colonel W. B. Emery.[85] Reinforced by French infantry regiments and artillery, the Allies remained in the lines, restoring the trenches and re-laying barbed wire, until the crisis ended. The French and the British had differing views on the way forward, but the popular press and Lloyd George favored the Greeks. In any event, on July 26, Army Corps D advanced the Edirne Division and Division A and occupied positions about 10 kilometers west of the Çatalca Lines on July 30. However, faced with uncertainty from Athens, a flurry of diplomatic exchanges followed, in which the British ambassador asked the Greeks to delay their occupation. Chatzanestes, who was now faced with attacking the Allies, then suspended the operation.

Chatzanestes did not remain in Thrace and returned to Izmir.[86] Regarding the forces, the equivalent of an entire infantry division was sent from the FAAM to Thrace, and the Concise Greek History of the campaign asserts that "the absence of these forces from the battlefield had no significant consequences."[87] This assertion is arguable but it is true that only a regimental-equivalent had been redeployed from the FAAM's vulnerable southern flank. However, the occupation of Istanbul certainly removed Chatzanestes from his own army headquarters in Asia Minor at a critical time.

After his return to the FAAM headquarters in Izmir, General Chatzanestes threw himself into the staff studies of preparing successive lines of withdrawal for his army. However, he did not receive meaningful guidance from Athens, and these studies remained paper proposals rather than operational decisions of fact. From August 19 to 24, 1922, the Nationalists probed the Greek front lines in a number of places but mostly in the Army Corps C sector, attempting to lure Chatzanestes into committing his reserves.[88] Increasing amounts of information about the Nationalists' intentions came into Greek corps and army headquarters from Greek aviation reconnaissance flights, as well as from deserters. On August 20, the FAAM sent a warning for the army to be on alert and enjoining commanders at every level to maintain adequate reserves. As late as August 24, the Greek frontline regiments were preparing for an enemy offensive, as every division in Army Corps A and B noticed increased Nationalist activity leaving no doubt of impending attacks.[89]

CONCLUSION

The Greek government was politically unready to either advance or withdraw from Asia Minor. Its hopes for a satisfactory way out from what Llewellyn-Smith called "a maze with no exit" rested on Allied intervention of some sort.[90] At the strategic level, the Greeks had spent their time over the summer focusing on the seizure of Eastern Thrace and Istanbul, thus avoiding a difficult decision about Asia Minor. The government believed that the occupation of Istanbul might tip the balance in its favor and encourage the Allies to intervene or force a peace with the Nationalists. This proved to be time poorly spent and, unfortunately for Chatzanestes and the FAAM, their time in Asia Minor had run out.

NOTES

1. Prince Andreas to Ioannis Metaxas (January 1, 1922), Ioannis Metaxas, *Diary*, vol. 3 (Athens: Icarus Publications, 1964), app. 13, quoted in Llewellyn-Smith, *Ionian Vision*, 244–245.

2. Timural, Atakan, and Berktay, *Sakarya Meydan Muharebesi*, Kroki 65 (Sketch Map 65 following page 354).

3. Gedeon, Paschalidou, and Dima-Dimitrou, *A Concise History of the Campaign in Asia Minor*, 309.

4. Ibid.

5. Timural, Atakan, and Berktay, *Sakarya Meydan Muharebesi*, Kroki 76 (Sketch Map 76 following page 372).

6. Ibid., 380.

7. Gedeon, Paschalidou, and Dima-Dimitrou, *A Concise History of the Campaign in Asia Minor*, 310.

8. Timural, Atakan, and Berktay, *Sakarya Meydan Muharebesi*, Kroki 82 (Sketch Map 82 following page 396).

9. Gedeon, Paschalidou, and Dima-Dimitrou, *A Concise History of the Campaign in Asia Minor*, 310–311; and Timural, Atakan, and Berktay, *Sakarya Meydan Muharebesi*, Kroki 83 (Sketch Map 83 following page 400).

10. Timural, Atakan, and Berktay, *Sakarya Meydan Muharebesi*, Kroki 84 (Sketch Map 84 following page 404).

11. Ibid., Kroki 86 (Sketch map 86 following page 410).

12. Gedeon, Paschalidou, and Dima-Dimitrou, *A Concise History of the Campaign in Asia Minor*, 311; and Timural, Atakan, and Berktay, *Sakarya Meydan Muharebesi*, 419–421.

13. Timural, Atakan, and Berktay, *Sakarya Meydan Muharebesi*, Kroki 88 (Sketch Map 88 following page 426).

14. Gedeon, Paschalidou, and Dima-Dimitrou, *A Concise History of the Campaign in Asia Minor*, 312.

15. Timural, Atakan, and Berktay, *Sakarya Meydan Muharebesi*, Kroki 89 (Sketch Map 89 following page 430).

16. Ibid., 226–229, Kroki 91 (Sketch Map 91 following page 442); and Gedeon, Paschalidou, and Dima-Dimitrou, *A Concise History of the Campaign in Asia Minor*, 312.

17. Şükrü Erkal, *Türk İstiklâl Harbi IInci Cilt Batı Cephesi 6ncı Kısım Inci Kitap, Büyük Taarruza Hazırlık ve Büyük Taarruz (10 Ekim 1921–31 Temmuz 1922)* (Ankara: Genelkurmay Basımevi, 1967), Kroki 9 and 11b (Sketch Maps 9 and 11b both following page 72).

18. Gedeon, Paschalidou, and Dima-Dimitrou, *A Concise History of the Campaign in Asia Minor*, 321.

19. See also Ali Soysal, *On Binlerin Yürüyüşü Bir Yunan Tümeni'nin Kaçış Öyküsü* (Istanbul: Tarihçi Kitabevi, 2014), 69–72.

20. Ibid.

21. Ibid., 322.

22. Ibid., 323.

23. Erkal, *Büyük Taarruza Hazırlık ve Büyük Taarruz*, 18–24.

24. Ökse, Baycan, and Sakaryalı, *Komutanların Biyografileri*, 174–176. Ali İnsan had previously served as the Ottoman Sixth Army commander in Mesopotamia and was detained by the British and imprisoned on Malta in March 1919.

25. Changes in Western Front Organization by Month (chart), Erkal, *Büyük Taarruza Hazırlık ve Büyük Taarruz*, 26–27, Kuruluş çizelge-2b (Tabular Chart-2b, pages 26-27).

26. Ibid., 24.

27. Ibid., 50–52.

28. Ibid. See Kroki 5 (Sketch Map 5 following page 52) for an excellent map of the General Staff plan.

29. Ibid. See Kroki 4 (Sketch Map 4 following page 51) for the Western Front Command plan.

30. Ibid. See Kroki 6 (Sketch Map 6 following page 56) for an excellent map of the First Army plan.

31. Ibid., 60.

32. Ökse, Baycan, and Sakaryalı, *Komutanların Biyografileri*, 71–73; and Erkal, *Büyük Taarruza Hazırlık ve Büyük Taarruz*, 61.

33. Gedeon, Paschalidou, and Dima-Dimitrou, *A Concise History of the Campaign in Asia Minor*, 323; and Erkal, *Büyük Taarruza Hazırlık ve Büyük Taarruz*, Kroki 13 (Sketch Map 13 following page 72).

34. Gedeon, Paschalidou, and Dima-Dimitrou, *A Concise History of the Campaign in Asia Minor*, 325. Later, according to Professor Konstantinos Travlos, he would tell Chatzanestes that the front was fine and could be held. Trikoupis left that detail out of his military memoirs

35. Llewellyn-Smith, *Ionian Vision*, 236–265.

36. Prince Andreas to Ioannis Metaxas (Jan. 1, 1922), Metaxas, *Diary*, app. 13, quoted in Llewellyn-Smith, *Ionian Vision*, 244–245.

37. Gedeon, Paschalidou, and Dima-Dimitrou, *A Concise History of the Campaign in Asia Minor*, 325–357.

38. Llewellyn-Smith, *Ionian Vision*, 241–242.

39. Ibid., see 243–244 for details concerning the collapse of the Gounares-Horne agreement.

40. Llewellyn-Smith, *Ionian Vision*, 254–256.

41. Gedeon, Paschalidou, and Dima-Dimitrou, *A Concise History of the Campaign in Asia Minor*, 350–351.

42. Ibid., 328.

43. Ibid., 329.

44. Gedeon, Paschalidou, and Dima-Dimitrou, *A Concise History of the Campaign in Asia Minor*, 237–239, 334–335.

45. Ibid., 334–337.

46. Ibid., 337 and Erkal, *Büyük Taarruza Hazırlık ve Büyük Taarruz*, 171–174.

47. Gedeon, Paschalidou, and Dima-Dimitrou, *A Concise History of the Campaign in Asia Minor*, 337. The story of the succession of the command of the FAAM is worth detailing, as it is indicative of the deep problems for the Greeks at the strategic level. My colleague and friend Professor Konstantinos Travlos pieced it together, and I include his narrative herein. Papoulas initially suggested two officers as replacements—Viktor Dousmanes and Georgios Chatzanestes. They were the only remaining lieutenant generals in the army beyond Papoulas. Dousmanes had replaced Gouveles as chief of the Army Staff Service in 1921. While not willing to push for the supremacy of the staff service over field commands, as Gouveles had tried, he was still an active staff officer. He had considerable staff experience and, like Metaxas, was one of the few Greek officers to complete the German War Academy study program. But he lacked field command experience. Chatzanestes, on the other hand, was an eccentric character. He was known as a disciplinarian and had restored discipline of the 5th Division after its defeat at Sorovits during the First Balkan War. He had also caused a major mutiny during the 1914–1916 period with his harshness. In addition, he had left the army multiple times. From 1917 to 1920, he was one of the main propaganda agents of the exiled royal court. Both Dousmanes and Chatzanestes were committed to King Constantine. Initially, Theotokes asked Dousmanes for his suggestion for a replacement for Papoulas, and Dousmanes writes that he suggested one of the corps

commanders. Alas, he does not name him. Then the government asked Dousmanes to take command. He prepared for this, but was then told that he had been passed over for Chatzanestes. Dousmanes and Mihail Rodas both believe that he was not given command because of the machinations of Xenofon Strategos, now out of the army and a minister in the Protopapadakis government. Indeed, Georgios Merkoures told Dousmanes that Strategos threatened to resign, thus undermining the coalition government, if Dousmanes were made commander of FAAM. See Viktor Dousmanes (Βίκτωρ Δουσμάνης), *Η Εσωτερική όψη της μικρασιάτικης εμπλοκής (The Internal View of the Asia Minor Entanglement)* (Pyrsos, 1928), 158–161; and Mihail Rodas (Μιχαήλ Ρόδας), *Η Ελλάδα στην Μίκρα Ασία (Greece in Asia Minor)* (1950), 306. This might be the result of the fierce rivalry that developed between Dousmanes, Strategos, and Metaxas, all of whom had once worked together in the staff service of the Greek General Headquarters during the Balkan Wars (Metaxas had suggested Strategos as commander of the FAAM in 1920). It might also be because Dousmanes, unlike Chatzanestes, was not enamored of the idea of capturing Istanbul. Xenofon Strategos does not discuss these allegations in his own apologia, instead arguing that Chatzanestes was made commander of the Field Army of Thrace specifically for this project. See Xenofon Strategos (Ξενοφών Στρατηγός), *Η Ελλάδα στην Μικρά Ασία (Greece in Asia Minor)* (1925), 373. Having such a skeptical officer in command of the FAAM would have created a dangerous division of strategic vision. Finally, Chatzanestes was a loyal officer who would not push envelopes against the government. The Papoulas-*Amyna* affair might have soured the government against officers with their own ideas. It is thus that Chatzanestes, an extremely unpopular officer who had been out of the army for a long time and whose main merit was political loyalty, came to command both the FAAM and Field Army of Thrace.

48. Llewellyn-Smith, *Ionian Vision*, 264.
49. Mango, *Atatürk*, 337.
50. Timur, Atakan, Berktay, and Ertekin, *İdari Faaliyetler*, 383.
51. Mango, *Atatürk*, 332.
52. Shaw, *From Empire to Republic*, vol. 3, part 2, 1674.
53. Ibid.
54. Timur, Atakan, Berktay, and Ertekin, *İdari Faaliyetler*, 466.
55. Gedeon, Paschalidou, and Dima-Dimitrou, *A Concise History of the Campaign in Asia Minor*, 345.
56. Mango, *Atatürk*, 333.

57. Timur, Atakan, Berktay, and Ertekin, *İdari Faaliyetler*, 421–422.

58. Ibid., 384.

59. Erkal, *Büyük Taarruza Hazırlık ve Büyük Taarruz*, 114.

60. Ibid., 157–158, Kuruluş 7 (Organizational Chart 7 following page 160).

61. Görgülü, *On Yıllık Harbin Kadrosu*, 289.

62. Gedeon, Paschalidou, and Dima-Dimitrou, *A Concise History of the Campaign in Asia Minor*, 344.

63. Akyüz, "Legacy of the Stormtroop: The Influence of German Assault Troop Doctrines in the Great Offensive," 197–230.

64. Ökse, Baycan, and Sakaryalı, *Komutanların Biyografileri*, 124–126.

65. Erkal, *Büyük Taarruza Hazırlık ve Büyük Taarruz*, Kroki 26 (Sketch Map 26 following page 144); and Gedeon, Paschalidou, and Dima-Dimitrou, *A Concise History of the Campaign in Asia Minor*, 340.

66. Erkal, *Büyük Taarruza Hazırlık ve Büyük Taarruz*, 163.

67. Ökse, Baycan and Sakaryalı, *Komutanların Biyografileri*, 95–97.

68. Ibid., 130–132.

69. Mango, *Atatürk*, 334–335.

70. Erkal, *Büyük Taarruza Hazırlık ve Büyük Taarruz*, 169.

71. Ökse, Baycan, and Sakaryalı, *Komutanların Biyografileri*, 174–176.

72. Mango, *Atatürk*, 334–335.

73. Ökse, Baycan, and Sakaryalı, *Komutanların Biyografileri*, 29–31.

74. Erkal, *Büyük Taarruza Hazırlık ve Büyük Taarruz*, 175–178.

75. Ibid., Kroki 29 (Sketch Map 29 following page 178).

76. Ibid., 179–182.

77. Llewellyn-Smith, *Ionian Vision*, 273. With that assessment noted, the oft-repeated story that he thought he had "legs of glass," probably referred to his evaluation of the logistical situation of the FAAM, which he thought was conducting operations with inadequate support (the legs of glass).

78. Gedeon, Paschalidou, and Dima-Dimitrou, *A Concise History of the Campaign in Asia Minor*, 346–347, 529.

79. Ibid., 347.

80. Ibid., 348.

81. Llewellyn-Smith, *Ionian Vision*, 277; and Gedeon, Paschalidou, and Dima-Dimitrou, *A Concise History of the Campaign in Asia Minor*, 351–352.

82. Gedeon, Paschalidou, and Dima-Dimitrou, *A Concise History of the Campaign in Asia Minor*, 352.

83. Ibid., 352.

84. Llewellyn-Smith, *Ionian Vision*, 277–283.

85. Major General Sir Thomas Marden, "With the British Army in Constantinople, A Personal Narrative" (Part 2), *The Army Quarterly*, XXVII (October 1933 and January 1934): 43.

86. Erkal, *Büyük Taarruza Hazırlık ve Büyük Taarruz*, Kroki 33 (Sketch Map 33 following page 200) for map graphics of the Greek plan to occupy Istanbul.

87. Gedeon, Paschalidou, and Dima-Dimitrou, *A Concise History of the Campaign in Asia Minor*, 352.

88. Ibid., 369–371.

89. Ibid., 371.

90. "A Maze with no Exit" is Michael Llewellyn-Smith's title for chapter 12 of his book; see Llewellyn-Smith, *Ionian Vision*, 266–283.

TEN

The Great Offensive and the Pursuit to Izmir

The moment for which Mustapha Kemal has waited so stolidly had now arrived.[1]

Winston S. Churchill, March 1929

INTRODUCTION

Mustafa Kemal, Fevzi, and İsmet planned and executed a deliberate campaign of annihilation aimed at the encirclement and destruction of two army corps of the Greek FAAM. Their aim was to defeat the Greeks decisively to the point where they would have to evacuate their surviving forces from Asia Minor. What became the Great Offensive stands as one of the few examples of successfully completed operational-level encirclements conducted before World War II. It ranks with Tannenberg in 1914, Kut al Amara in 1915, and Megiddo in 1918 in scope but, in fact, exceeded these campaigns in terms of the decisive character of the defeat inflicted on the enemy.[2]

Every Nationalist commander at national, theater, army, and corps level, apart from First Army commander Nurettin, was a highly trained general staff officer educated at the Ottoman War Academy. It is also important to note that Ottoman Army doctrines mirrored those of the Germany Army, and the three-year curriculum of the Ottoman War Academy replicated that of the German War Academy.[3]

The term "decisive battle," which is generally ascribed to Henri Jomini, has come to be associated with the Prussian theorist Carl von Clausewitz and with German general and theorist Helmuth von Moltke (the Elder).[4] To summarize the concepts, these two theorists believed that decisive operations were necessary to render the enemy's forces incapable of further resistance. They theorized that the most effective way to accomplish this was through battles of annihilation, which meant the destruction of the enemy's main armies.[5] This led to a school of practice based on initiative and maneuver leading to battles of encirclement and annihilation.[6] These theories are often paraphrased as the German Way of War and became, by way of Prussian and German military assistance commissions, the intellectual foundation for thinking about war in both the Ottoman and the Greek armies. Ottoman commanders planned both tactical and operational-level encirclements in the Balkan Wars and in World War I[7] and Greek commanders planned operational-level encirclements in the war under study here.

NATIONALIST PREPARATIONS FOR THE GREAT OFFENSIVE

The Western Front Command continued planning for the Great Offensive throughout July 1922. On July 28, Kemal and Fevzi came from Ankara to İsmet's Western Front Command headquarters in Akşehir for a two-day conference finalizing the plans for the impending offensive. First and Second Army commanders Nurettin and Yakup Şevki attended, as did I, IV, and V Corps commanders İzzettin, Kemalettin Sami, and Fahrettin (who would all make the tactical main effort).[8] Accordingly, İsmet issued warning orders to the Western Front Command on August 6, outlining the concept and ordering preparations for the offensive.[9] During the preparation phase, the First Army would shift its I Corps to the army's left flank while İsmet would shift the V Cavalry Corps (under his direct command) to an assembly area in the I Corps rear area. The II Corps would remain in the Second Army area until ordered south while III and VI Corps and the Kocaeli Group conducted minor probing attacks to distract the Greek commanders. On the far southwestern flank (İsmet's extreme left flank), the independent 6th Division extended southwest of Uşak, and Kemal sent the 3rd Cavalry Division to operate in Menderes River Valley on the 6th Division's left flank. The 3rd Cavalry Division had been formed from the irregular bands of the Second Field Force and was poorly disciplined and not well trained.[10] Despite this, the 3rd Cavalry Division conducted harassing raids on the Izmir-Afyonkarahisar railway and blocked the trains on August 19 until driven off two days later.

On August 16, Fevzi arranged for a substantial loan from the Ottoman Bank, which Kemal provided to İsmet to pay soldiers' salaries and to hire additional transportation assets for the army. In his reply to Kemal, İsmet noted that, in addition to resolving the army's financial issues, the army's heavy artillery assets (105-mm, 120-mm, and 150-mm guns and howitzers) were arriving in their assault positions with 250 shells per howitzer on hand for the offensive.

İsmet had previously tasked the 25th Heavy Artillery Regiment (on July 31) to supervise artillery planning for the offensive. According to the campaign plan, the heavy artillery would be concentrated in the First Army sector and divided into four groups.[11] The 1st Group (22 howitzers) and the 2nd Group (42 howitzers) would support the IV Corps, while the 3rd Group (28 howitzers) and the 4th Group (19 howitzers) would support the I Corps. Over the next two weeks, intense planning began between the infantry commanders and the artillery commanders to develop the fire support plan, which was focused on the destruction of the enemy entrenchments. Special attention was given to ensure that observed fire procedures using field telephone communication between the observers and the artillery batteries were in place and ready. By the start of the offensive, the heavy artillery would have 300 shells per howitzer on hand, and, by August 25, the fire support plan integrated the regimental heavy machine guns in the indirect fire mode as well.

Between August 14 and 16, the Western Front Command issued its campaign plan for what the Turks would come call the Great Offensive (*Büyük Taarruz*). The mature plan reflected the classic hallmarks of Kemal and İsmet's German-style military education from their days as young officers in the Ottoman War Academy.[12] The plan employed economy of force (Second Army) while concentrating the bulk of the available combat strength in the main effort (First Army) (see Map 9.1). The highly mobile cavalry corps would be used to encircle the Greeks and finish them off in a Cannae-like battle of annihilation. The First Army would employ its I and IV Corps to break through the Greek lines, followed by the V Cavalry Corps exploiting to the north, with the II Corps in army reserve. The Second Army would conduct a supporting effort in the north employing the III and VI Corps, followed by cavalry exploiting to the west. However, lacking a cavalry division, the Second Army activated a Provisional

Cavalry Division on August 19 by consolidating the divisional cavalry detachments from the III and VI Corps infantry divisions. This gave Yakup Şevki's army a full cavalry division for his thrust east. On August 17, Kemal sent word that three squadrons of fighter aircraft would be ready for the operation and established August 24 as the date to be fully ready to attack, which was scheduled for August 26.[13]

Kemal left Ankara by automobile with Fevzi on the night of August 17/18, reaching İsmet's headquarters at Akşehir on August 20, where he established his own headquarters. To maintain secrecy, his staff maintained his social calendar in Ankara, including an August 21 tea party in Çankaya.[14] Mail was censored, and all subsequent army movements were conducted at night. The II Corps was detached from the Second Army on August 21 and began its march south to join the First Army. Its three divisions all arrived in their assembly areas by August 24 and became Nurettin's reserve. Also on that day, Nurettin moved his First Army headquarters to Şuhut (near the center of his army and close to the front). On August 25, Kemal joined the First Army's battle headquarters in Şuhut with İsmet and Fevzi, cutting off all communication with Ankara. At 12:30 a.m. that night, the Western Front Command issued its assault order to launch the Great Offensive on the morning of August 26.[15]

FIELD ARMY OF ASIA MINOR PREPARATIONS

Lieutenant General Chatzanestes dissolved the Northern and Southern groups on June 25 and subordinated all infantry divisions to his corps commanders.[16] Army Corps C, under Major General Soumilas (3rd, 10th, 11th, and Independent Divisions), guarded the northern Izmit-Eskişehir-Kütahya front. Army Corps B, under Major General Digenis (2nd, 9th, and 13th Divisions, with the 7th Division in reserve), was positioned north of Afyonkarahisar opposite Yakup Şevki's Second Army, and Army Corps A, under Major General Trikoupes (1st, 4th, 5th, and 12th Divisions), held the city of Afyonkarahisar and the southern front against Nurettin's First Army. Chatzanestes assigned Soumilas the mission to secure his sector while assigning Trikoupes and Digenis the mission of conducting an active defense in their sectors. In the event of a major enemy offensive in the southern sector, Chatzanestes specified that the senior commander, Major General Trikoupes, would take unified command of Army Corps A and B until Chatzanestes could arrive from the FAAM headquarters in Izmir to take command.[17]

The Greek intelligence services accurately plotted the changes in the reorganization and repositioning of İsmet's armies opposite the FAAM; however, good information could not compensate for the insufficient density of Greek forces along a very wide front. On August 14 (after the dispatch of the regiments to Army Corps D in Thrace), Army Corps C had 20 infantry battalions on the front line, with 18 in reserve covering a sector 245 kilometers in length; Army Corps B had 14 infantry battalions screening its front with 27 in reserve covering a sector 212 kilometers in length; and Army Corps A had 20 on the front line, with 22 in reserve, covering a sector 186 kilometers in length.[18] The Cavalry Division deployed as a screen south of Uşak coordinated with the Izmir command on a front of 140 kilometers. Altogether, the FAAM's front had a length of 783 kilometers, and General Chatzanestes retained no operational-level reserves whatsoever and would have to depend on laterally shifting divisions in the case of a major Nationalist offensive.

As finally matched, the Nationalists had an overall theater strength of 199,000 men, with 143,157 men, 15,687 cavalry, 748 machine guns, and 323 artillery pieces in the First and Second Army operational zones.[19] To oppose this force, the Greeks had overall theater strength of 218,000 men, with 123,864 men, 1,280 cavalry, 908 machine guns, and 262 artillery pieces in the 12 divisions of their three army corps and cavalry division.[20] More importantly than the raw numbers, the Western Front Command seized the initiative and could further concentrate its forces on narrow fronts, thus multiplying its superiority locally. For example, in the critical sector south of Afyonkarahisar, İsmet attacked the Greek 1st and 4th Divisions with seven infantry divisions and one cavalry division in his first-wave assault, as well as with the entire weight of the Nationalists' heavy artillery. It is also important to consider that the Turkmen mountain range, running northwest to southeast, separated the Eskişehir sector from the Afyonkarahisar-Kütahya axis, offering protection to the flanks of Nurettin's attacking forces for a counterattack by Army Corps C (see map 10.1).

THE GREAT OFFENSIVE

As rumors of the impending offensive spread, morale in the Nationalist regiments soared, and between midnight and dawn, İsmet's infantry quietly worked their way forward from assembly positions to assault positions. İsmet's artillery loaded their howitzers and guns at 4:30 a.m. and

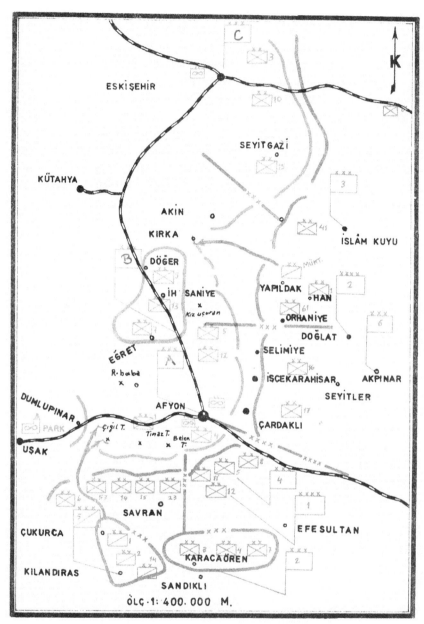

Map 10.1 Prebattle Prep (August 25, 1922)

On August 25, the First Army's V Cavalry Corps and the Second Army's Provisional Cavalry Division moved forward to their attack positions. Finding and exploiting a gap in the Greek lines, Fahrettin's V Cavalry Corps successfully occupied the Çigiltepe. This enabled the Nationalist cavalry to penetrate deep in the Greek rear areas at the very beginning of the offensive.

Courtesy of the Turkish General Staff Military History and Strategy Institute (ATASE).

trained them on their assigned targets.[21] The battle began at 5:00 a.m. on August 26, 1922, with an intense bombardment of artillery preparation fires on the Greek lines, after which the Nationalist infantry attacked at 6:00 a.m. Kemal, İsmet, Fevzi, and Nurettin gathered at dawn on the Koca Tepe, a hill in the IV Corps sector near its boundary with the I Corps, which dominated the front to observe the launching of the Great Offensive.[22] The Turkish artillery barrages were particularly devastating, which reflected the effectiveness of Kemal's emphasis on training and planning. In the First Army sector, Kemalettin Sami's IV Corps attacked the Greek 4th Division with the 11th, 5th Caucasian, and 8th Divisions (holding the 12th Division in corps reserve), and, to his west, İzzettin's I Corps attacked the Greek 1st Division with the 57th, 14th, 15th, and the 23rd Divisions.[23] On İzzettin's left flank, facing little initial opposition and with no heavy artillery support, Fahrettin's V Cavalry Corps began moving at 1:00 a.m. to positions on the Ahir Dağ heights. At dawn, the 14th Cavalry Division advanced into a 15-kilometer gap in the Greek 1st Division's sector and was followed by the 1st and 2nd Cavalry Divisions.[24] Colonel Ali Hikmet's (Ayerdem) II Corps, with the 3rd Caucasian, 4th, and 7th Divisions, remained in army reserve and immediately available.

Yakup Şevki established his Second Army headquarters in Doğlat in Kâzım's VI Corps sector, which attacked the Greek 5th Division with the 16th Division on August 26 (the 17th Division fixed but did not attack the Greek 12th Division).[25] The Second Army's main effort came from Şükrü Naili's III Corps attacking the seam between Greek 5th and 13th Divisions with the 61st Division, the Provisional Cavalry Division, and the 41st Division (with the 1st Division in corps reserve). On the army's far northern flank, the Kocaeli Group's 18th Division and cavalry maintained continuous pressure, as did the independent 6th Division and 3rd Cavalry Division on the army's far left (western flank).

According to the Concise Greek History, "The intensity and accuracy of the Turkish fires was such that the advanced Greek trenches were completely demolished and their defenders decimated . . . Never to that day had the Greek forces in Asia Minor experienced such sustained and accurate artillery fire."[26] Moreover, the Greek artillery was smothered by overwhelming Nationalist counterbattery artillery fires and could not react effectively. There were some exceptions; for example, in the Kalejik strongpoint, the six guns of the Ravtopoulos Battery were key in keeping the core of the position in Greek hands on the first day. On Afyonkarahisar's southern front, the Greek 1st and 4th Divisions put all three of their infantry regiments in the line, with only one battalion as a tactical reserve. By 7:00 a.m., Nationalist infantry seized most of the enemy forward trenches, and both Greek division commanders had committed most of their tactical reserves. To the city's north, Trikoupes's 5th Division had also lost its forward trenches and committed its own reserves. The three division commanders, who each faced an entire Nationalist army corps, requested reinforcements from Army Corps A.

In such an emergency, Lieutenant General Chatzanestes had designated Major General Trikoupes as the commander of both Army Corps A and B, and by 7:30 a.m., Trikoupes began to act. Trikoupes ordered the Plasteras Detachment from the 13th Division into the 4th Division's sector, and he ordered the 7th Division to send infantry battalions to the 1st Division.[27] At 8:30 a.m., Trikoupes subordinated his 5th Division to Army Corps B, giving Major General Digenis operational command of the battles to the north of Afyonkarahisar, as well as ordering counterattacks.[28] These were all tactically sound decisions. He also informed the FAAM at 8:15 a.m. that he intended to move part of the 9th Division to Afyonkarahisar. At 12:30 p.m., the FAAM directed Trikoupes not to move the 9th Division without army approval, but it was already too late. The order reached Digenis at 10:00 a.m., and he was already loading the 26th Infantry Regiment on trains for movement to Afyonkarahisar at 1:00 p.m.[29] Belatedly, Digenis halted the loading of the regiment, which, after many messages between the army and corps headquarters, resumed its movement at 3:00 a.m. on August 27, thus losing an entire day.

The relentless Nationalist attacks continued in the afternoon as Greek counterattacks recovered some of the lost ground. At 2:30 p.m., 7th Division commander Colonel Vasileois Kourousopoulos and one regiment arrived in the 1st Division sector and were met by division commander Major General Athanasios Frangou. Kourousopoulos and his regiment entered the fight while the rest of the 7th Division remained in reserve, distributed in battalions in the rear of the 1st Division. The group under Colonel Nikolaos Plasteras reached the 4th Division but did not fully enter the fight as Trikoupes had intended. As the day waned, General Trikoupes continued to order counterattacks and sent reports to the FAAM outlining the seriousness of his situation. However, these never reached Chatzanestes, who ordered Army Corps C and B to counterattack toward the east and then cabled Athens that "the combat is progressing smoothly."[30] Unaware of the true threat to Army Corps A, Chatzanestes believed that the Nationalist main effort was oriented toward Eskişehir.

At the end of the day of August 26, except for Yakup Şevki's 61st Division, none of İsmet's assaulting infantry had broken through the Greek lines.[31] The fight had been brutal, and casualties were severe. This did not sit well with Kemal who asked for situation reports directly from division commanders. In one tragic circumstance, Kemal called Colonel Reşat (Çiğiltepe), the commander of the 57th Division and an old comrade-in-arms from the Palestine and Syrian campaigns in World War I, asking why he had failed to capture the Çiğiltepe. In reply, Reşat promised to capture the hill within 30 minutes. Hearing nothing, Kemal later called the division headquarters and was read Reşat's suicide note, which explained, "I have decided to end my life because I have not kept my word."[32] However, on İsmet's left flank, the V Cavalry Corps was very successful, penetrating deep into the gap between the left flank regiments of the Greek 1st Division and reaching the Afyonkarahisar and Uşak rail line (see map 10.2). This disrupted not only rail traffic but cut telegraph communication between Chatzanestes and Trikoupes.[33] In response, Trikoupes ordered the 1st Cavalry Division to Dumlupınar to deal with the situation and to secure the army's rear. In the meantime, İsmet rested his assault troops and prepared to renew the offensive the following morning.

The Western Front Command resumed its offensive at dawn on August 27. The Greek 1st Division held its positions with difficulty, but the 4th Division lost its main defensive position on the high ground known as Küçük Kaleci at about 9:00 a.m. to assaults by Kemalettin Sami's 5th and 11th Divisions. Colonel Plasteras ordered counterattacks, but these failed, and, as the 4th Division's right flank collapsed, the division abandoned its artillery to the enemy. General Trikoupes scrambled unsuccessfully to reinforce the shattered 4th Division, sending the recently arrived 26th Infantry Regiment to its aid, as well as ordering the 12th Division to send the 46th Infantry Regiment. At approximately 10:00 a.m., Trikoupes, convinced that any resistance was impossible, ordered the withdrawal of the 1st, 4th, and 12th Divisions.[34] Due to the disruption of field telephone and wireless communication, Trikoupes's orders reached the 4th and 12th Divisions but not the 1st Division, causing that division to cling to its defensive positions. At 1:00 p.m., the 1st Division's main defenses were overrun by İzzettin's I Corps infantry, and the division commander ordered a withdrawal on his own authority. The Nationalists had broken the Greek front.

This was not the only disaster confronting Trikoupes on August 27. By the end of the day, Fahrettin's V Cavalry Corps had pushed its 14th and

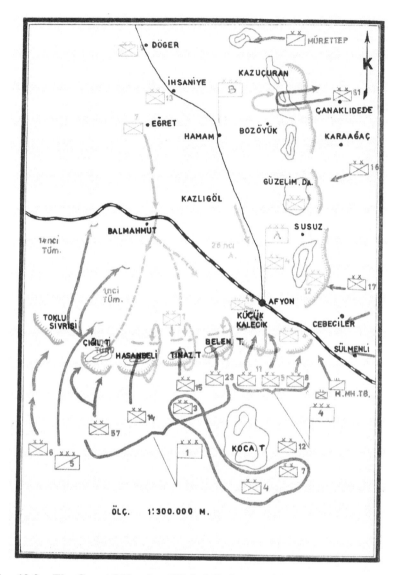

Map 10.2   The Great Offensive (Nightfall, August 26, 1922)

The Nationalist offensive began at 5:00 a.m., August 26 with intense artillery bombardments of the Greek trench lines, followed one hour later by Nationalist infantry assaults. While the Nationalists failed to gain their objectives that day, they held much of the Greek Army Corps A and B in place while the V Cavalry Corps advanced to hills overlooking the vital Afyonkarahisar-Uşak railroad, which supplied the Greeks. This destabilized the Greek position, leading to a disorganized retreat.

Courtesy of the Turkish General Staff Military History and Strategy Institute (ATASE).

2nd Cavalry Divisions north of the rail line and the 1st Cavalry Division east to block the retreating Greeks.[35] Fahrettin moved his own command post to the village of Yel Dâğ Ulucak (10 kilometers north of the rail line). In turn, Trikoupes ordered the 2nd Division to reinforce the Greek Cavalry Division at Dumlupınar to secure the rail line and restore communication. North of Afyonkarahisar, Army Corps B ordered the 5th and 13th Divisions, holding the line against Yakup Şevki's VI and III Corps, to withdraw as well. Turmoil erupted in Afyonkarahisar as more than 5,000 terrified Ottoman Armenians and Anatolian Greeks swarmed the army's trains or attempted to flee the city on foot.[36] Associated with this was "an event of great consequence," which occurred at about 12:30 p.m. when Army Corps A's wireless set was loaded on the wrong train.[37] The wireless was mounted on a motor vehicle, which was damaged, and the decision was made to move it by rail to Kazli Gol Hamam. However, due to a misunderstanding, the wireless was not unloaded there but was unloaded instead far to the north in Eskişehir. This left Trikoupes without communication with the FAAM or its divisions until the following afternoon when he was able to use the Army Corps B wireless.

The FAAM remained ignorant of the situation and sent a wireless message to Army Corps B at 5:30 p.m. ordering both army corps to counterattack and regain their positions.[38] As the day ended, Major General Frangou assumed control of both the 1st Division and part of the 7th Division and reported that he was withdrawing successfully but had lost about 2,000 men. Their retreat toward Dumlupınar continued, but, in the middle of the night, they were checked by Nationalist cavalry detachments at the Başkimse rail station. The Plasteras Detachment and the 4th Division had trouble breaking contact but, by midnight, had safely withdrawn to the heights west of Afyonkarahisar. At midnight, the Army Corps B chief of staff and operations officer reached Trikoupes's command post at Byram Gol. At the end of their meeting, Trikoupes gave them a situation report for wireless transmission to Izmir.

İsmet ordered the II Corps in army reserve into the gap created by the advances of the First and Second Armies.[39] The II Corps' 8th Division advanced into Afyonkarahisar itself on the evening of August 27, and Ali Hikmet moved his command post forward to Salar. At 3:00 a.m. on August 28, the Western Front Command ordered a pursuit with the objective of cutting off at least three Greek infantry divisions.[40] İsmet ordered the First Army to reorient Izzettin's I Corps from north to directly west and Kemalettin Sami's IV Corps from north to northwest. The Second Army was ordered to advance west as rapidly as possible with its Provisional Cavalry Division. On the morning of August 28, Kemal, Fevzi, and İsmet moved from the Koca Tepe into the city of Afyonkarahisar, observing large numbers of abandoned Greek vehicles, draft animals, and equipment. Cheered by the evident success of the operation, they sent messages to Ankara and ordered the heavy artillery battalions to pack up for movement in the wake of the advancing armies.

The Greeks were in a terrible position, and communication between the corps and their subordinate divisions had broken down to the point where messengers became the only possible means to convey orders and information. The Concise Greek History notes this phase as the "Break-up of the Greek forces" and Army Corps A and B's divisions and provisional groups were left on their own to withdraw to the east.[41] There were some localized successes—the Greek 4th Division launched an attack against Nurettin's 2nd Cavalry Division that inflicted many casualties and captured a battery of artillery. At 2:00 p.m., Lieutenant General Trikoupes met Major General Digenis at the Army Corps B command post in Olucak. Trikoupes had no information whatsoever regarding the position or the condition of the 1st and 7th Divisions, and he ordered the remnants of the 4th Division to remain in place. Digenis reported that his 9th and 13th Divisions were marching west toward his command post. In the meantime, the Plasteras Detachment reached the Frangou Group's position, and together they marched west toward the old Greek field fortifications at Dumlupınar.

In midafternoon, Frangou drove by automobile to Dumlupınar to find it had been guarded since morning by the Greek 1st Battalion, 38th Infantry Regiment. That evening, he brought his tired and hungry troops into the old defensive works. The night of August 28/29, 1922 "brought the complete and final break-up of the Greek forces into two groups: the Frangou group and the Trikoupes Group."[42] The Frangou Group at Dumlupınar was composed of the 1st and 2nd Divisions, five infantry battalions from the 4th Division, the 7th Division, two infantry battalions from the 12th Division, the Plasteras Detachment (three infantry battalions of the 5/42 Evzone Regiment), the Cavalry Division, and two artillery battalions. The Trikoupes Group at Olucak was composed of the 4th Division (four infantry battalions), the 5th and 9th Divisions, the 12th Division (minus two battalions), the 13th Division (minus the Plasteras detachment), and nine artillery battalions.[43]

The assembly of such a large force as the Trikoupes Group at Olucak brought some advantage to the Greeks by forcing Nurettin and the 2nd and

14th Cavalry Divisions north to Kurtköy and Osmaniye. This opened a path to the west for Trikoupes and his men, as well as split the V Cavalry Corps in half because the 1st Cavalry Division remained south of the railway.[44] However, by the end of the day on August 28, İzzettin's I Corps pushed its three infantry divisions directly west and made contact with Nurettin's 1st Cavalry Division while the IV Corps occupied the rail line and the Başkimse station. İsmet also ordered Ali Hikmet's II Corps (with three fresh infantry divisions) to march west through the night to a position south of the rail line. İsmet also ordered the Second Army to pivot Şükrü Naili's III Corps north to Döğer on the Afyonkarahisar-Eskişehir rail line for a pursuit north (rather than west). On İsmet's far left flank, the 3rd Cavalry Division and the 6th Infantry Division continued to raid and block the Uşak-Izmir rail line. In Yakup Şevki's Second Army sector, the Provisional Cavalry Division broke through and raced west past the Eskişehir-Afyonkarahisar rail line to Hacibeyli. As night fell on August 28/29, Kemal, Fevzi, and İsmet were convinced that the Western Front Command had defeated seven enemy divisions and was poised on the cusp of encircling them.[45] They ordered their tired infantry corps to continue marching west through the night while Lieutenant General Trikoupes gave orders for his group to continue retiring to the west at dawn, with the 9th Division as the advance guard and the 13th Division as the rear guard. It was all he could do, and it was better than staying in place while İsmet encircled him.

Unfortunately for Trikoupes not all his formations received their orders in the night, and the group was delayed in starting (except for the 9th Division, which marched at 4:30 a.m. on August 29, 30 minutes after dawn). The Greek advance guard encountered Nurettin's cavalry at Hamurköy several hours later, forcing the Greeks to bring up reserves. Trikoupes remained in Olucak until midmorning, vainly trying to communicate with the FAAM on the Army Corps B wireless as his divisions marched past in a long column.[46] Unfortunately for the Greeks, the IV Corps' the fast-marching 12th Division reached the Hamurköy battle in time to stop the Greek movement south, and, by 3:00 p.m., Ali Hikmet's fresh 7th Division reached Selkisaray Station on the rail line to block the westward path of the Trikoupes Group.[47] The IV Corps came on Ali Hikmet's right and Nurettin moved his First Army command post west to Akçaşehir. In the late afternoon, Kemalettin Sami's IV Corps and Ali Hikmet's II Corps attacked north to compress the Trikoupes Group, and Nurettin's 14th Cavalry Division did the same from the north. At the same time, Izzettin's I

Corps marched west to make contact with the Frangou Group while the 31st Cavalry Regiment blocked Trikoupes's road to the safety of Frangou's lines at Dumlupınar.[48]

At 6:00 p.m. on August 29, reports reached Trikoupes, who had moved the joint Army Corps A and B command post west to Hamurköy, indicating that his advance guard had been stopped and destroyed, and his group was now encircled in a pocket.[49] Moreover, the forces inside the shrinking pocket had lost their tactical integrity, and many of their leaders were in a state of disarray and confusion. Although his commanders pressed him to convene a council of war, Trikoupes believed that the road south through Salköy to Dumlupınar was not strongly held and could be forced open. He ordered the group to march through the night, but, due to the decreasing numbers of fit draft animals, Trikoupes ordered his heavy artillery abandoned and destroyed. His heavy engineering and transport equipment also became a liability and it too was abandoned and destroyed. The Trikoupes Group was now completely cut off from communication with the FAAM, as well as physically from the Frangou Group. Over the night of August 29/30, the Nationalists relentlessly compressed the Trikoupes Group into a shrinking perimeter around the village of Aliiören and a hill mass called Büyük and Küçük Ada Tepe (Big and Little Ada Hills).[50] Convinced that his infantry could contain Trikoupes, İsmet ordered Nurettin to disengage, move north, and capture the city of Kütahya with the III Corps.

THE COMMANDER IN CHIEF'S BATTLE

After discussions with İsmet and Fevzi on the evening of August 28, Mustafa Kemal decided to "go for a kill at Dumlupınar" and destroy Trikoupes's army.[51] Kemal sent Fevzi to join Kâzım's VI Corps in closing the northern pincer while he joined Nurettin in closing the southern pincer. On August 30, Kemal moved to a hill now called Zafer Tepe (Victory Hill), where he joined Nurettin and Kemalettin Sami to command the battle. Later Kemal would name this battle the Commander in Chief's Battle, while the Greeks know it as the Battle of Ali Veran (Aliiören).

Generals Trikoupes and Digenis arrived at Salköy (eight kilometers west of Hamurköy and at the western end of the pocket occupied by the Trikoupes Group) at 6:00 a.m. on August 30. There they came under heavy enemy artillery fire, forcing them back, where they conferred with the 4th, 9th, and 12th Division commanders. Trikoupes firmly intended to break through to join Frangou at Dumlupınar, and he issued orders to this effect at 7:30 a.m.[52] While Trikoupes was trying to decide what to do, Nurettin moved the First Army heavy artillery into position and opened fire. Shortly thereafter, Kemal ordered the assault. In the south, Kemalettin Sami's 11th, 5th Caucasian, and 23rd Divisions attacked with the support of the 25th Heavy Artillery Regiment.[53] Simultaneously Kâzım's 16th and 61st Divisions attacked the north perimeter of the Greek pocket. Nurettin's 14th Cavalry Division held the west side of the pocket but did not have the strength to completely seal the encirclement (see map 10.3). By the end of the day, the 23rd Division captured Büyük Ada Tepe while the 5th Caucasian and 11th Divisions captured Küçük Ada Tepe. The Greeks were pushed into the shelter of the numerous wooded ravines west of Salköy. Huddled there, the Trikoupes Group was out of food and fodder and almost out of ammunition.

By 4:00 p.m., the Greeks were so compressed that there was nowhere left to seek cover from the overwhelming enemy artillery bombardments. Shortly before 4:00 p.m., General Trikoupes realized that the Salköy-Dumlupınar road to the south was too strongly held and, with the recommendations of his division commanders, decided to break out directly west on the Banaz road. At 8:30 p.m. Trikoupes ordered the breakout that night, but he had lost the entire day trying to force the Salköy road open. His army, now reduced to about 20,000 men, began moving at around 11:00 p.m. on August 30, while İsmet ordered his infantry divisions to make their final assaults to crush the surviving Greeks the following day.

On the night of August 30/31, the Trikoupes Group survivors who were able to march were organized into three columns, marching separately and following separate routes. The wounded and those who were unable to march were left behind. Major General Demetrios Demaras and Colonel Perikles Kallidopoulas led 1,500 infantry and 600 cavalry survivors of the 4th and 12th Divisions.[54] The second column was composed of the 13th Division with Generals Trikoupes and Digenis in command, and the third column was comprised of Colonel Panagiotes Gardikas and the 9th Division. Demaras and Kallidopoulas kept going until 8:00 p.m. on September 1 before they were surrounded and forced to surrender some 1,700 officers and men. General Trikoupes led his group west toward Banaz but, discovering it had been captured by the enemy, turned south on the morning of September 2. Harried by the enemy and now surrounded, General Trikoupes decided to fight to the last man but then relented and was forced to surrender. At 5:00 p.m., Generals Trikoupes and Digenis, 13th Division commander Colonel Kaimpales, 190 officers, and 4,400 men (with six

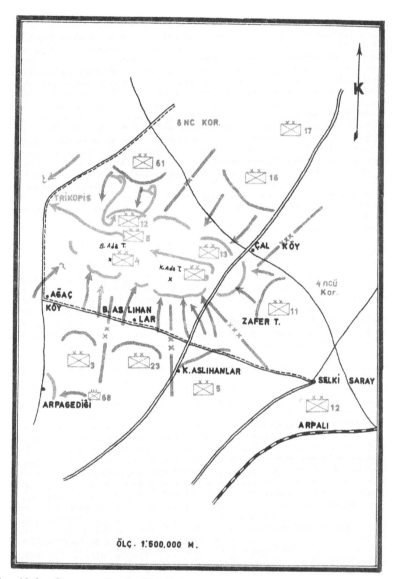

Map 10.3 Commander in Chief's Battle (August 28–29, 1922)

The sudden collapse of the Greek positional defense of the Afyonkarahisar salient led to disorganized groups of Greek soldiers retreating west in disarray. On August 28, Mustafa Kemal personally coordinated the encirclement of the remnants of five Greek divisions led by General Trikoupes. The assault the next day led to a partial surrender, but Trikoupes led the survivors out of the trap. Pursued by the Nationalists, Trikoupes surrendered on September 2—it was the end of Army Corps A and B.

Courtesy of the Turkish General Staff Military History and Strategy Institute (ATASE).

artillery pieces) went into captivity.[55] The Turkish official history reported that 391 officers, 4,385 enlisted men, and 700 draft animals surrendered and that on the following morning, the Nationalists recovered 5,000 rifles, 100 machine guns, 200 automatic rifles, 12 mountain howitzers, and thousands of rounds of ammunition.[56] The exhausted prisoners were collected by the 5th Caucasian Division and the sick and wounded given medical care. The Gardikas column, comprising the remnants of the 9th, 12th, and 4th Divisions, reached the bridge over the Gediz River, north of the town of Han, crossing into safe territory with some 5,000 officers and men.

THE FRANGOU GROUP

While Army Corps A and B endured their death throes in the mountains northwest of Dumlupınar, Major General Frangou occupied the old Greek defenses at Dumlupınar on August 29.[57] He ordered the Plasteras Detachment into the main northern positions on the high ground facing east, and, by noon, he had a solid defensive line. Altogether, the Frangou Group had 31 infantry battalions, 18 artillery batteries, and 1 heavy artillery battery in the line, with a reserve of 7 infantry battalions and two artillery batteries. It was a "dense and effective defense" of a front of only 25 kilometers.[58] However, the short length of the position was its undoing, as Kemalettin Sami's IV Corps swept around its right flank from the south.

On August 29, Kemalettin Sami's infantry divisions smashed the weak Greek defenses on Frangou's right flank, causing the Greeks to shift their reserves to a tall hill massive called the Kaplangı Dağı east of the Dumlupınar-Uşak railway. Realizing that he risked becoming encircled, Major General Frangou decided at 4:00 p.m. to withdraw to a line some 20 kilometers to the west during the night of August 29/30.[59] The next morning, the Nationalist 57th Division captured the Kaplangı Dağı peaks while the 14th Division to its north and the 5th Caucasian Division to its south pushed east, and the I Corps' 15th Division occupied the Greek defensive line.[60] General Frangou fell back to Banaz and İslamköy and reestablished his line, but it soon came under relentless attack by the I Corps. At 9:30 pm on August 30, the FAAM ordered Frangou to take command of the remnants of the 1st, 2nd, 4th, 7th, 12th, and 13th Divisions and to hold in place while the survivors from the east made their way to safety. However, this was impossible, and on August 31, the Frangou Group was withdrawing again to the town of Kapaklar (halfway between Dumlupınar and Uşak). Frangou continued to receive orders from Lieutenant General Chatzanestes in Izmir to defend his ground and tried to accomplish this by conducting local counterattacks, which briefly but unsuccessfully stopped the enemy. He decided to retreat once again and that evening Colonel Gardikas and the remnants of Army Corps B joined his force. According to the Concise Greek History, had Frangou remained in the Kapaklar position, there remained a chance that Trikoupes and Digenis could have escaped to safety.[61] However, there was too much pressure from the Western Front Command, and, on September 1, General Frangou abandoned the city of Uşak and began another withdrawal to the town of Takmak.

Far to the north Fahrettin's V Cavalry Corps was ordered to turn east while the III Corps continued north. On August 30, the Provisional Cavalry Division briefly occupied Kütahya while Şükrü Naili's III Corps infantry divisions marched on their left flank north along the rail line toward Eskişehir. To the south, the 3rd Cavalry Division captured Denizli and again interdicted the Greek lines of communication to Izmir. The next day, İsmet's aviation squadrons brought reports that the Greek formations near Uşak and Eskişehir were disorganized and were frantically withdrawing equipment and supplies by rail.[62] İsmet was promoted to lieutenant general on August 31, 1922 and ordered a pursuit to begin.

THE PURSUIT OPERATION

An actual doctrinal "pursuit" is a deliberate offensive operation undertaken after a decisive battle wherein the enemy army is badly defeated and retreating amid conditions of great disorganization. The pursuing army exploits its mobility by pressing the defeated army relentlessly. Often the pursued army is encircled and annihilated or simply disintegrates under pressure. An actual deliberate pursuit is rare in modern military history with the most well known being Napoleon's pursuit of the Prussians after Jena-Auerstedt in 1806, Grant's pursuit of Lee after Petersburg in 1865, Allenby's pursuit of the Ottomans after Megiddo in 1918, the German pursuit of the Soviets in Operation Barbarossa in 1941, and Eisenhower's pursuit of the Germans after the breakout from Normandy in August 1944. However, one of the most successful but little-known pursuits in the twentieth century was then-colonel Nurettin's brutally relentless pursuit of Major General Sir Charles Townshend's small Anglo-Indian army after the Battle of Ctesiphon in November 1915. Colonel Nurettin's continuous nine-day 170-kilometer pursuit of Townsend led to his encirclement in Kut al-Amara, where he remained surrounded until his surrender in April 1916.[63] That

Lieutenant General Nurettin (promoted from major general on August 31, 1922[64]) should command Kemal's First Army in a pursuit at this point in Ottoman-Turkish history is nothing short of remarkable.

On August 31, Fahrettin's V Cavalry Corps moved east to assembly areas a few kilometers east of Gediz while the victorious VI Corps moved behind it (see map 10.4). The victorious I Corps joined the II Corps and shared their headquarters at İslamköy. Kemal, İsmet, and Nurettin jointly moved their headquarters to the town of Dumlupınar with the IV Corps. They were cheered that day by the news that the Provisional Cavalry Division had captured the important city of Kütahya. Yakup Şevki moved forward as well and established his Second Army headquarters at Beşkarış.[65] Encouraged by resounding success, Kemal famously gave the command, "Armies, your first goal is the Mediterranean, Forward!"[66] The pursuit began in earnest on September 1 with the V Cavalry Corps crossing the Han River at Gediz and pushing the Greek 5th Division out of Hamidiye Hanı to the south. Nurettin's First Army advanced with the I Corps, capturing Uşak, and the II Corps moving west on his left flank. The next day, the V Cavalry Corps swept southwest to occupy Derbent and Keskin while the I and II Corps moved to confront Frangou's Takmak (Eşme) line.

On September 1/2, Lieutenant General Chatzanestes reorganized the front by activating the Southern Battle Group under the command of Major General Frangou while 2nd Division commander Colonel Stylianos Gonatas assumed command of a resurrected Army Corps A (composed of the remnants of 1st, 2nd, 4th, and 7th Divisions) and 5th Division commander Colonel Nikolaos Rokas assumed command of a resurrected Army Corps B (composed the remnants of the 5th, 9th, 12th, and 13th Divisions). They had not long to wait. Greek aerial reconnaissance on September 1 showed an alarming concentration of Nationalist cavalry assembled in the Han River Valley.[67] The FAAM became very concerned over the possibility of Frangou becoming outflanked and, on September 3, ordered 3,000 men with artillery under Colonel Charalampos Louphas to Kula to block the enemy cavalry. However, Frangou felt he could hold the Takmak line safely but ordered a 50-kilometer withdrawal to a new line on the Alaşehir River, 10 kilometers east of the city of Alaşehir (ancient Philadelphia) itself. The FAAM was determined to save as much of its transport and logistical elements as possible and ordered the service support elements to continue withdrawing to the city of Izmir.

By midday on September 4, the Southern Battle Group occupied its new defensive line after abandoning Kula and withdrawing the Louphas

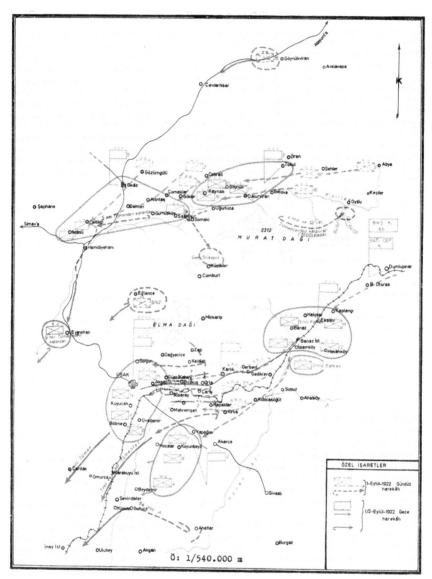

Map 10.4   Pursuit (September 2, 1922)

İsmet launched his pursuit operation on August 31, with the objective of capturing the city of Izmir and expelling the surviving Greeks from Anatolia. General Frangou led the remnants of the FAAM is a desperate, but successful, retreat to Izmir and to the safety of an evacuation by the Greek Navy. İsmet kept the V Cavalry Corps on his right flank in hopes of enveloping the retreating Greeks, but the long marches exhausted the horses, and this was never achieved.

Courtesy of the Turkish General Staff Military History and Strategy Institute (ATASE).

Detachment to cover the left flank.[68] Fahrettin's 14th Cavalry Division raced through Kula, bypassing the retreating Louphas Detachment to seize the high ground north of the rail line to the rear of Alaşehir while its sister cavalry divisions closely followed. Nurettin's fast-moving I and II Corps also marched hard and made contact with Frangou's front lines. Kemal, İsmet, and Nurettin rode west and established their joint command post in Takmak.[69] On September 5, Fahrettin sent his 3rd and 14th Cavalry Divisions on a wide envelopment around the Greek left flank to cut off the Greek retreat at the village of Salihli (on the rail line to Izmir) while his 2nd Cavalry Division attacked the rail line at Dereköy. However, Frangou had previously withdrawn the 8th Division to the village the night before and had ordered the Cavalry Division on September 4/5 there as well. In the early hours of September 5, a Greek telegraph section arrived at the Salihli train station to report it was largely undefended. This caused Colonel Plasteras to rush reinforcements there from the Cavalry Division, which arrived just in time to dismount and repel a dismounted assault at 8:30 a.m. by Fahrettin's 1st Cavalry Division.[70] Major General Frangou arrived at the Cavalry Division's command post at 1:00 p.m. in time to observe the 14th Cavalry Division launch another unsuccessful attack on the town. While these fights at Salihli raged, 10 kilometers to the east, the Greek 2nd Division repelled Fahrettin's 2nd Cavalry Division at Dereköy.[71] In truth, the V Cavalry Corps was not trained or equipped to assault enemy defensive positions, but these battles by determined Greek soldiers saved the Southern Battle Group from destruction.

Under such pressure, the FAAM decided to abandon the Alaşehir line, ordering the Southern Battle Group on September 5 to retreat the surviving units to Kasaba and Manisa (ancient Magnesia) respectively. Nurettin's I and II Corps crossed the river and occupied the city of Alaşehir on the night of September 5/6. During the next day, Frangou reestablished his defensive lines between Sart (Sardich, ancient Sardis) on the rail line and the Marmara Lake. Sart was the one of the last defensible positions protecting the city of Izmir, which was only 85 kilometers away. Nurettin drove his V Cavalry Corps, which was not in good condition by now and had been pushed to the limits of its endurance, west to make contact again with the Greek line.[72] By the end of the day, the I and II Corps arrived in support of the V Cavalry Corps, and Nurettin had established his First Army command post in Salihli. Overnight on September 6/7, the Southern Battle Group again retreated to a hasty line at Turgutlu, 50 kilometers east of Izmir. On September 7, Nurettin sent the V Cavalry Corps northwest toward Manisa while his I and II Corps occupied Ahmetli 10 kilometers east of the Greek line. Now in danger of being outflanked from the north, Frangou conducted another retreat, pulling his infantry back along the rail line to Kemalpaşa and his cavalry back through Manisa to Menemen. Kemalpaşa (then called Nif or by its ancient name, Nymphaion) lay in a gap between a range of hills 30 kilometers east of Izmir, and it was the last possible defensive position for the Greeks.

Throughout the agony of Army Corps A and B, the FAAM commander in chief Lieutenant General Georgios Chatzanestes refused to come forward to the front to command the battles. This caused a tremendous loss of confidence among his own staff and in the army's subordinate corps and divisions. On September 4, after the loss of the Dumlupınar line, the government in Athens decided to relieve him of command.[73] The government intended to replace him with Major General Trikoupes but, when notified the next day of Trikoupes's capture, assigned former Army Corps C commander Lieutenant General Georgios Polymenakos to command the FAAM. General Polymenakos and Minister of the Army Theotokes boarded a destroyer bound for Izmir that evening and arrived on the morning of September 6. They immediately convened a council of war, during which Chatzanestes was informed of his relief and during which he briefed them on the military situation. General Polymenakos immediately ordered Frangou to mount a determined defense and stop the Nationalists. Chatzanestes returned to Athens that night, followed on September 8 by Theotokes and Lieutenant General Dousmanes. The unfortunate Trikoupes, who had been treated well and enjoyed coffee and cigarettes with Kemal, "learnt in captivity that he had been appointed commander of the entire front. It was a joke in bad taste."[74]

On the morning of September 8, the V Cavalry Corps drove the Greek Cavalry Division out of Menemen to Mersinli (an eastern suburb of Izmir) while the II Corps drove Frangou's infantry out of the Kemalpaşa position. To Izmir's south, the Nationalist 3rd Cavalry Division advanced north to the town of Torbalı.[75] Standing with İsmet and Nurettin that evening in what would be renamed the Kemalpaşa gap, from where he could see the city of Izmir and the sea, Mustafa Kemal famously pointed to the Aegean Sea and ordered that as the army's objective for September 9, 1922.[76] In his comprehensive army orders issued at 10:00 p.m., İsmet ordered the V Cavalry Corps to attack the next morning at 10:30 a.m. to capture the city and stop the evacuation of as many Greek soldiers as possible.[77] These orders also contained instructions to Nurettin's First Army to occupy the city while the V Cavalry Corps pursued the enemy to Urla, and then to the small port of Çesme. Once this was accomplished, Fahrettin's cavalry would advance north to Edremit by July 15. İsmet also ordered Yakup Şevki's Second Army to concentrate at Akhisar and advance the III Corps toward Balıkesir and Bandırma.

THE PURSUIT TO ÇESME

The FAAM staff in Izmir began packing their headquarters records and equipment on September 1 and followed with explicit warnings to the garrison and to local Greeks to prepare for evacuation. This caused an immediate panic among the Greek and Armenian population of the city. Reinforcements in the way of the A Division from Edirne (Adrianople) in Thrace arrived on the evening of September 5; however, most of its agitated soldiers, upon learning of the army's disastrous retreat, refused to disembark.[78] These reinforcements were, in a phrase, too little too late, as the military situation had been irretrievably lost by that date. Panic followed as the Greek, Armenian, and international community of Izmir flocked to the quays and attempted to board any ship leaving the city.[79] By September 7, a "true exodus" was underway, with ships carrying three times their designed capacity departing the wharves.[80] On that day, the Greek Army hospitals were emptied of wounded men, who were put on ships bound for Piraeus, and General Polymenakos loaded the FAAM staff on two steamships in the harbor. The next morning, the Greek civil administration also loaded aboard Greek ships in the harbor, causing an outburst of anxiety among those Christians who had not left. Just before sundown on September 8, the transport ships carrying the military and civil administration, as well as the Greek gendarmerie, began to sail away. When they had cleared the harbor, the remaining Greek Navy ships also departed.

Previously, at 10:00 a.m. on September 8, General Polymenakos ordered the remaining FAAM to retreat west to the small port of Çesme for evacuation. General Frangou, with the remaining field forces, would retreat south of the city no later than noon on September 9, while the Cavalry Division would remain as a rear guard. Polymenakos's evacuation plan functionally divided responsibilities with Major General Andreas Plates, commander of the Izmir Higher Military Command, controlling the marshalling, embarkation, and evacuation of Greek forces and with General Frangou in command of his remaining combat-worthy forces holding the narrow isthmus of Lestren Dâğ (40 kilometers west of Izmir and 20 kilometers east of Çesme).[81]

Fahrettin's cavalry began moving earlier than ordered, at 6:30 a.m., and entered Izmir in the midmorning of September 9, 1922.[82] By midafternoon, the V Cavalry Corps occupied the city and had captured 35 Greek officers and 1,500 soldiers. First Army commander Nurettin entered the city in the late afternoon and was informed that over 4,000 enemy soldiers had been captured. There were still British, French, and Italian naval vessels in the harbor evacuating the international community of Izmir. On September 10, Kemal, İsmet, and Nurettin opened their headquarters in Izmir while Izzettin's I Corps took over the occupation, thus relieving Fahrettin's V Cavalry Corps to advance south and west. Fahrettin's cavalry pushed the Greek rear guards back and entered Urla (30 kilometers west of Izmir) at 7:30 a.m. on September 11. The next day, the 3rd and 14th Cavalry Divisions, accompanied by the 57th Infantry Division, pushed the Greek rear guards back again and advanced to the Lestren Dâğ defensive line.[83]

The Greeks reconfigured their defenses by assigning Major General Andreas Plates, the commander of the A Division, as the officer responsible for the defense of the entire Erythea Peninsula (the peninsula west of the Lestren Dâğ line).[84] Plates was directed to defend the first line and, as the force to be evacuated grew smaller, to defend a second line at the village of Alaçatı on the hills overlooking Çesme harbor itself. On the night of September 11/12, the remnants of Army Corps B encamped at Alaçatı Plates in preparation for evacuation. The Army Corps A survivors of the 1st, 2nd, and 7th Divisions and the fresh A Division took up defensive positions in the Lestren Dâğ line, with the 13th Division in reserve. On September 13, Army Corps B, with the noncombatant formations of Army Corps A, embarked from Çesme for the Greek island of Chios. The men and horses of the Cavalry Division were also embarked that day. This left only fighting men on the peninsula. Plates withdrew the 13th Division to the second defensive line at Alaçatı and placed it under a trusted officer, designating it the Plasteras Detachment.[85] Plates withdrew Army Corps A at 10:00 a.m. on September 14 and moved the 2nd and 7th Divisions into Alaçatı to join Colonel Plasteras. The final orders appointed Lieutenant Colonel Odysseas Maroulis with a detachment of 1,200 men and 2 artillery batteries to hold the port long enough to get the main body of surviving regiments safely away. On September 14 and 15, Plates withdrew his divisions and successfully embarked them under the cover of naval gunfire support from the Greek Navy's battleships and cruisers. The Maroulis Detachment withdrew into the port itself at 9:00 p.m. on September 15. In the early morning hours of September 16, Lieutenant Colonel Maroulis drew his men up on the quay at Çesme and departed for home.[86] Fahrettin's 3rd Cavalry Division occupied the port at 9:00 a.m. that morning.

According to the Concise Greek History, the 4th, 5th, 7th, and 12th Divisions evacuated 799 officers, 15,000 enlisted men, 5,562 animals, and 19 artillery pieces from Çesme.[87] It further stated that there are no reliable figures for the 1st, 2nd, 9th, and 13th Divisions and the Cavalry Division but "their strength was certainly very reduced in both personnel and equipment." The Turkish official history asserts that previously the Greeks evacuated about 20,000 men from Çesme and, moreover, had previously evacuated some 20–30,000 men from Izmir prior to September 9, while the Greek Independent Division evacuated 7,500 men from the port of Dikili. Later in the Bandırma battles the unevacuated Greek 3rd Division surrendered 3,500 men.[88]

While the last of the FAAM evacuated Çesme, one of the most controversial episodes during the Greek-Turkish War occurred in what is known today as the "Destruction of Smyrna" or the "Great Fire of Smyrna." There is a large extant literature about the events that occurred before, during, and after a disastrous fire started on the afternoon of September 13 in the Armenian quarter of Izmir.[89] How it started and who started it became a cause célèbre at the time, and these questions remain hotly contested by Turks, Greeks, and Armenians today. The fires raged uncontrollably for several days, forcing thousands of residents, Greeks, Armenians, and Turks alike, to flee to the waterfront or to one of the neutral steamships in the harbor in the hope of escaping the flames. The three communities all blame one another for the fire, and there are several conspiracy-like theories about whether it was started accidently or deliberately by malignant design. The actual number of dead is contested today, as is the actual amount of damage, with estimates of the deaths ranging from 10,000 to 100,000. After the evacuation of the Greek administration and gendarmerie, there was no civil authority, and the city was under martial law imposed by Nurettin's First Army. In the absence of trained and equipped firefighters, suppressing the fires before they became catastrophic and unstoppable was problematic at best. A case can certainly be made that Nurettin had no interest in fighting the fire and allowed the city to burn.[90] It has also been suggested that Nurettin, who had commanded the Central Army against the Pontic Greek uprisings, bore ill-will toward the Greek community, as evidenced by the lynching in Izmir on September 10 of the primate of the Greek Orthodox Church, Metropolitan Chrysostomos.

Similarly, as the Greeks retreated and the Nationalists advanced in summer and fall 1922, great devastation was inflicted on western Anatolia. The Turkish position is that the Greeks conducted scorch and burn tactics as they withdrew by deliberately destroying and burning villages, crops, orchards, and equipment. According to Andrew Mango, hundreds of villages and a whole string of market towns—from Uşak to Izmir—were burned down by the retreating Greeks.[91] Mango continued by stating that in Alaşehir, 4,300 out of 4,500 houses were destroyed, with the loss of 3,000 lives. In Manisa, only 1,400 out of 14,000 homes remained standing. Likewise, there is a Greek counternarrative that blames the Turks for the destruction and elaborates on the thousands of Anatolian-Greeks who were killed and robbed by the Nationalist armies as they recaptured western Anatolia.[92]

THE PURSUIT TO BANDIRMA

For all intents and purposes, Kemal and İsmet detached Şükrü Naili's III Corps from Yakup Şevki's Second Army on August 30 by ordering him north toward Eskişehir. On September 1, Şükrü Naili's Provisional Cavalry Division advanced from Kütahya toward the Bursa-Eskişehir rail line, while the 41st and 61st Divisions advanced toward the city of Eskişehir on the right flank.[93] Şükrü Naili located his corps command post in Sarıkaya, following his cavalry division's path of advance. Opposing him was Major General Soumilas's Army Corps C with its headquarters in Eskişehir and its subordinate Independent and 10th Divisions facing the III Corps and the 3rd and 11th Divisions facing the Kocaeli Group.[94] Soumilas had, over the course of the previous five days, received a series of orders from the FAAM to conduct counterattacks to relieve enemy pressure on Army Corps A and B, one of which, on August 27, ordered Colonel Demiterios Theotokes's Independent Division to Akin to counterattack south (the colonel was a cousin of the minister of war). This was exceptionally dangerous because in the interim, Şükrü Naili had moved north of Theotokes, isolating him from Army Corps C. The next day the FAAM ordered Soumilas to begin the evacuation of all unnecessary equipment and supplies by rail from Kütahya and Eskişehir and to withdraw to the old defensive lines just east of Bursa. At 10:00 a.m. on August 29, the FAAM ordered the Independent Division to march south to Dumlupınar to come under the command of Army Corps B.⁹⁵ However, recognizing the futility of that course of action, Soumilas pulled his remaining forces on August 30, along with thousands of panicked Christians, out of Kütahya, marching to the west toward Gediz and the Han River crossings.

Theotokes's Independent Division (composed of 244 officers, 7,400 enlisted men, 2,845 animals, 48 machine guns, and 14 artillery pieces) now began a 17-day odyssey that took it 600 kilometers by foot march to the small port of Dikili (100 kilometers north of Izmir on the Aegean coast) on September 12, where it loaded on steamers bound for the Greek island of Mytilene.⁹⁶ Theotokes fought a single battle at the Kütahya Pass on August 31, costing only about 150 casualties but otherwise remaining unengaged for the remainder of the campaign. However, while en route, he learned that İsmet's army had captured Dumlupınar, causing him to bolt west toward the sea. He did acquire some 2,500 Christian refugees from Kirkagaç and evacuated them and 6,000 Greek and Armenian refugees as well. Thus, Soumilas lost a quarter of his combat strength, and the FAAM lost the use of an entire infantry division.

Soumilas abandoned Eskişehir on September 1, and it fell to the Nationalists. Şükrü Naili's III Corps continued its rapid assault north, attacking with the 1st Division and the Provisional Cavalry Division to capture the now-famous village of İnönü from Soumilas's 10th Division on September 3. On the III Corps' right flank, the 61st Division advanced against the Greek 3rd Division. Şükrü Naili moved his corps' command post to İnönü the next day and continued to advance north while the Kocaeli Group advanced southeast of Lake Iznik.⁹⁷ Over the night of September 4/5, Soumilas withdrew his force pursued by Şükrü Naili. On September 6, Army Corps C occupied its old defensive lines east of Bursa, with the 11th Division holding the northern sector and the 3rd Division holding the south.⁹⁸ Soumilas kept the 10th Division in reserve, but he had already been ordered by the FAAM to evacuate Bursa with a view toward evacuation from the ports of Mudanya and Gemlik (Kios). Şükrü Naili now brought the formerly independent 18th Division under his command and attacked the Greek defensive position on September 7. Soumilas's infantry was able to hold the well-prepared line that day, and he was also informed that he was authorized to evacuate from the ports of Erdek (Artaki) or Bandırma (Panormos).

Logistics intervened when Soumilas learned that Gemlik had minimal port capacity and the changing weather made Mudanya problematic. Geography made the decision quite easy for Soumilas because Erdek was located on the Kapıdağ (Cyzicus) Peninsula in the Sea of Marmara, which was easily defensible at its narrow neck. Şükrü Naili continued to attack the fortified line from September 7 to 9, after which Soumilas decided to retreat. Screened by cavalry detachments, Army Corps C withdrew and abandoned Bursa on September 10.[99] Şükrü Naili's 1st Division occupied the city that same day while his Provisional Cavalry Division pursued the retreating Greeks west of Bursa. The Kocaeli Detachment also advanced southwest on September 10 and captured Gemlik. Army Corps C assigned the 11th Division the mission as rear guard while the remainder of the corps withdrew to Bandırma and Erdek.

On September 11, Şükrü Naili's 18th Division fixed the unlucky 11th Division in position while he sent the Provisional Cavalry Division to outflank it from the south. By the day's end, Nationalist cavalry reached the Mudanya rail line on the coast and the 1st Division's infantry closely followed.[100] The Greek 11th Division was now cut off and isolated in Mudanya. Oddly, there were French and British military representatives in the port, and the division commander, Major General Nikolaos Kladas, attempted to arrange a cease-fire and evacuation with the French. This failed, and Kladas held a council of war with his commanders to plan a breakout to the west. However, the morale and cohesion of the division had disintegrated, and at 1:30 pm on September 12, Kladas decided to surrender.[101] According to the Concise Greek History, the 11th Division surrendered about 4,500 men and 36 artillery pieces to Şükrü Naili; however, the Turkish official history asserts that 217 officers and 4,467 enlisted men from the 11th Division surrendered and an additional 1,500 men belonging to independent regiments also surrendered, bringing the total count of prisoners to over 6,000.[102]

Led by the Provisional Cavalry Division, Şükrü Naili's III Corps then advanced on September 13 and 14 west of Mudanya to the Greek defensive line 10 kilometers east of Bandırma. On September 15, the 18th Division made contact with the defensive perimeter Soumilas had built around Bandırma.[103] The next day, Şükrü Naili attacked Bandırma with his infantry regiments while he sent the Provisional Cavalry Division to the west in another attempt to outflank the retreating Greeks. From September 15 to 17, Army Corps C evacuated its noncombat personnel, its equipment, and its animals while the infantry and some artillery held the enemy at bay. Nevertheless, Bandırma fell on September 17 to the III Corps and Soumilas withdrew into the Kapıdağ Peninsula itself. Lieutenant General Polymenakos, the new commander of the FAAM, arrived in Erdek by steamship with his staff at about 2:00 p.m., September 17 to visit the front. After quickly visiting the 30th Infantry Regiment, Polymenakos became convinced that complete evacuation was the only remaining course of action, and he departed two hours later. Starting that night, Soumilas's remaining combat troops began to embark, and, by noon on September 18, the surviving 6,000 men of Army Corps C were evacuated to Tekirdağ (across the Sea of Marmara in Thrace). It was the end of the road for the Field Army of Asia Minor on the Anatolian mainland.

CONCLUSION

The voice of the Hellenic Army History Division is compelling: "The vision of Hellenism, the Great Idea (*Megala Idea*) of the Greek Nation to liberate the Greeks and unite them with the motherland was not fulfilled. It was extinguished with the passage of time and the evolution of events. It was buried in the battlefields of Asia Minor, together with those heroic dead of the Hellenic Field Army."[104] Michael Llewellyn-Smith titled his chapter about this period simply as "Catastrophe" and left it at that.[105] In a military sense, the Greek campaign after Sakarya was unwinnable under any circumstances, and the political indecision that left the Field Army of Asia Minor so exposed was criminal. Moreover, it is unlikely that Lieutenant General Georgios Chatzanestes, even had he come forward to command the battle after August 26, could have saved his army. The Nationalists were too well prepared, they enjoyed positional advantage, and they acquired all the military advantages accrued in seizing the initiative. Might the FAAM have engaged in some kind of fighting withdrawal to salvage more of their army than was evacuated? There is certainly room to argue that after late spring 1922, the Greek staffs should have focused on planning and developing several lines of linear defense in the rear areas. Overall, for the FAAM, the final campaign in Asia Minor was a disaster from which there was no possible recovery.

For the Nationalists (and the modern Turks), the Great Offensive was a triumph that restored much of their army's luster that had been lost over the preceding two centuries and enabled Mustafa Kemal to create the modern Republic of Turkey. Looking at the paper maps with large blue arrows drawn on them, it may seem fashionable to criticize İsmet's handling of the Western Front Command about the possibility of inflicting an even greater defeat of the Greeks. But one has only to travel to the operational area and battlefields to consider how geography limited options and controlled movement. When the difficult Anatolian geography is combined with the deficient road networks and primitive communications of the day—it is even more remarkable that Kemal, Fevzi, and İsmet emerged with the decisive victory that they achieved in such a short span of time.

NOTES

1. Churchill, *The Aftermath*, 418.

2. The Russian Army recovered after Tannenberg—as did the British and Indian armies after Kut al-Amara. Allenby's great victory destroyed the Ottoman Eighth Army but failed to destroy the Ottoman Seventh Army and, moreover, did not lead directly to the end of the war. The Nationalist Great Offensive inflicted a catastrophic defeat on the Greek Army from which it could not recover and led directly to the termination of the war, awarding the Nationalists almost every strategic aim they sought.

3. See Edward J. Erickson, *Defeat in Detail: The Ottoman Army in the Balkans, 1912–1913* (Westport, CT: Praeger Publishing, 2003), 55–60 for an explanation of Ottoman staffs and the Ottoman War Academy curriculum.

4. See, for example, Guenter E. Rothenberg, "Moltke, Schlieffen, and the Doctrine of Strategic Envelopment," in *Makers of Modern Strategy from Machiavelli to the Nuclear Age*, ed. Peter Paret (Princeton: Princeton University Press, 1986), 296–325; and Jehuda L. Wallach, *The Dogma of the Battle of Annihilation* (Westport, CT: Greenwood Press, 1986), 41–90.

5. Daniel J. Hughes and Richard L. DiNardo, *Imperial Germany and War, 1871–1918* (Lawrence: University of Kansas Press, 2018), 54–57. Hughes and DiNardo's magnificent work presents the finest explanation of the "German Way of Way" in the English language today (see chapter two, "The Prussian Theory of War from Clausewitz to Moltke").

6. Hughes and DiNardo, *Imperial Germany and War*, 67–73.

7. See Edward J. Erickson, "From Kirkilisse to The Great Offensive: Turkish Encirclement Operations 1912–1922," *Middle Eastern Studies* 40, no.1 (2004): 45–64 for a complete explanation of these operations. Apart from Kut al-Amara in 1915–1916, all these encirclement operations were unsuccessful.

8. Kemal Niş, *Türk İstiklâl Harbi IInci Cilt Batı Cephesi 6ncı Kısım IInci Kitap Büyük Taarruz (1–31 Ağustos 1922)* (Ankara: Genelkurmay Basımevi, 1968), 16–17.

9. Ibid., 21–23.

10. Ibid., 34–36.

11. Ibid., 30–32.

12. George W. Gawrych, "Kemal Atatürk's Politico-Military Strategy in the Turkish War of Independence, 1919–1922: From Guerrilla Warfare to the Decisive Battle," *Journal of Strategic Studies*, 11, no. 3 (1988): 318–341.

13. Niş, *Büyük Taarruz*, 29.

14. Mango, *Atatürk*, 339.

15. Western Front Command orders number 98, August 26, 1922, quoted in Niş, *Büyük Taarruz*, 53–54.

16. Gedeon, Paschalidou, and Dima-Dimitrou, *A Concise History of the Campaign in Asia Minor*, 350.

17. Ibid.

18. Ibid., 357–359.

19. Western Front Command General Strength, August 15, 1922. See Niş, *Büyük Taarruz*, Loj.Ek.2 (Logistics Table 2 following page 316).

20. Gedeon, Paschalidou, and Dima-Dimitrou, *A Concise History of the Campaign in Asia Minor*, 332–334, 359.

21. Niş, *Büyük Taarruz*, 54–57.

22. A fresh look, based on previously untapped Greek archival sources, at what exactly transpired on the tactical level in the key sector of what the Greeks called the Kalejik sector, and the Turks called the Erikman Hills, is being prepared by Vasileios Loumiotes. Excerpts are posted in Greek on the *Velisarios* blog, https://belisarius21.wordpress.com/. Once completed, it will provide one of the most complete tactical-level studies of one of the key sectors of the Great Offensive. Meanwhile, the amateur battlefield archeologist Serdar Aydin has been carefully visiting and cataloging the sites. I am grateful to Dr. Konstantinos Travlos for making me aware of both efforts.

23. Niş, *Büyük Taarruz*, 54–57, Kroki 10 and 11 (Sketch Maps 10 and 11 both following page 56).

24. The Concise Greek History notes the length and the existence of the "Karagozeli-Sinan Pasha" gap; however, it does not present the reason why the gap was undefended or was screened so lightly. See Gedeon, Paschalidou, and Dima-Dimitrou, *A Concise History of the Campaign in Asia Minor*, 358 and Sketch map 56 (following page 360); and Niş, *Büyük Taarruz*, Kroki 29 (Sketch Map 29 following page 120).

25. Niş, *Büyük Taarruz*, Kroki 17 (Sketch Map 17 following page 80).

26. Gedeon, Paschalidou, and Dima-Dimitrou, *A Concise History of the Campaign in Asia Minor*, 373.

27. Gedeon, Paschalidou, and Dima-Dimitrou, *A Concise History of the Campaign in Asia Minor*, 374.

28. As per the new research of Loumiotes (see note 22), there is over-whelming evidence that Plasteras did not execute his counterattack order.

29. Gedeon, Paschalidou, and Dima-Dimitrou, *A Concise History of the Campaign in Asia Minor*, 376.

30. Ibid., 381.

31. Niş, *Büyük Taarruz*, Kroki 29 (Sketch Map 29 following page 120).

32. Ökse, Baycan, and Sakaryalı, *Komutanların Biyografileri*, 63–65; and Mango, *Atatürk*, 340. Reşat's family later adopted the surname Çiğiltepe in honor of his last battle.

33. Llewellyn-Smith, *Ionian Vision*, 288–289; and Niş, *Büyük Taarruz*, Kroki 24 (Sketch Map 24 following page 104).

34. Gedeon, Paschalidou, and Dima-Dimitrou, *A Concise History of the Campaign in Asia Minor*, 384.

35. Niş, *Büyük Taarruz*, Kroki 32 (Sketch Map 32 following page 136).

36. Llewellyn-Smith, *Ionian Vision*, 289; and Gedeon, Paschalidou, and Dima-Dimitrou, *A Concise History of the Campaign in Asia Minor*, 388.

37. Gedeon, Paschalidou, and Dima-Dimitrou, *A Concise History of the Campaign in Asia Minor*, 388.

38. Ibid., 390–391.

39. Niş, *Büyük Taarruz*, 143–144, Kroki 36 (Sketch Map 36 following page 137).

40. Ibid., 145.

41. Gedeon, Paschalidou, and Dima-Dimitrou, *A Concise History of the Campaign in Asia Minor*, 394–395.

42. Ibid., 399.

43. Ibid. The term "division" is inclusive of divisional field artillery, engineers, cavalry, and supporting logistical formations.

44. Niş, *Büyük Taarruz*, 153–173, Kroki 39–42 (Sketch Maps 39–42 all following page 168).

45. Ibid., 181.

46. Gedeon, Paschalidou, and Dima-Dimitrou, *A Concise History of the Campaign in Asia Minor*, 404.

47. Niş, *Büyük Taarruz*, Kroki 44 (Sketch Map 44 following page 188).

48. Ibid., Kroki 45 (Sketch Map 45 following page 200).

49. Gedeon, Paschalidou, and Dima-Dimitrou, *A Concise History of the Campaign in Asia Minor*, 409.

50. Niş, *Büyük Taarruz*, Kroki 48 (Sketch Map 48 following page 216).

51. Mango, *Atatürk*, 341.

52. Gedeon, Paschalidou, and Dima-Dimitrou, *A Concise History of the Campaign in Asia Minor*, 416–417.

53. Niş, *Büyük Taarruz*, Kroki 51 (Sketch Map 51 following page 248).

54. Gedeon, Paschalidou, and Dima-Dimitrou, *A Concise History of the Campaign in Asia Minor*, 426–430.

55. Ibid., 429–430.

56. Kemal Niş and Reşat Söker, *Türk İstiklâl Harbi IInci Cilt Batı Cephesi 6ncı Kısım IIIncü Kitap, Büyük Taarruzda Takip Harekâtı (31 Ağustos–18 Eylül 1922)* (Ankara: Genelkurmay Basımevi, 1969), 53.

57. Ibid., 411–416.

58. Ibid., 412.

59. Ibid., 414–415.

60. Niş, *Büyük Taarruz*, Kroki 53 (Sketch Map 53 following page 264).

61. Gedeon, Paschalidou, and Dima-Dimitrou, *A Concise History of the Campaign in Asia Minor*, 435.

62. Niş and Söker, *Büyük Taarruzda Takip Harekâtı*, 3.

63. See Edward J. Erickson, *Ottoman Army Effectiveness in World War I* (Abingdon, OX: Routledge, 2007), 74–89 for a summary of Nurettin's pursuit of Townshend.

64. Ökse, Baycan, and Sakaryalı, *Komutanların Biyografileri*, 29–31.

65. Niş and Söker, *Büyük Taarruzda Takip Harekâtı*, Kroki 4 (Sketch Map 4 following page 24).

66. Şerif Güralp, *İstiklâl Savaşın'n İçyüzü* (Ankara: Polatlı Belediyesi Yayınları, 2007), 211.

67. Gedeon, Paschalidou, and Dima-Dimitrou, *A Concise History of the Campaign in Asia Minor*, 437.

68. Ibid., Sketch Map 65 (following page 424).

69. Niş and Söker, *Büyük Taarruzda Takip Harekâtı*, Kroki 12 (Sketch Map 12 following page 60).

70. Gedeon, Paschalidou, and Dima-Dimitrou, *A Concise History of the Campaign in Asia Minor*, 441–443; and Niş and Söker, *Büyük Taarruzda Takip Harekâtı*, Kroki 13 (Sketch Map 13 following page 88).

71. Gedeon, Paschalidou, and Dima-Dimitrou, *A Concise History of the Campaign in Asia Minor*, 444.

72. Niş and Söker, *Büyük Taarruzda Takip Harekâtı*, Kroki 17 (Sketch Map 17 following page 104); and Gedeon, Paschalidou, and Dima-Dimitrou, *A Concise History of the Campaign in Asia Minor*, 444.

73. Gedeon, Paschalidou, and Dima-Dimitrou, *A Concise History of the Campaign in Asia Minor*, 445.

74. Mango, *Atatürk*, 342–343.

75. Niş and Söker, *Büyük Taarruzda Takip Harekâtı*, Kroki 19 (Sketch Map 19 following page 112).

76. Ibid., 130.

77. Western Front Command orders number 104, 2200 hours, September 9, 1922, reprinted in Niş and Söker, *Büyük Taarruzda Takip Harekâtı*, 130–131.

78. Gedeon, Paschalidou, and Dima-Dimitrou, *A Concise History of the Campaign in Asia Minor*, 447; and Llewellyn-Smith, *Ionian Vision*, 301.

79. On July 22, 1922/August 4, 1922 the Greek government passed law 2870/1922, which made it illegal for Ottoman Greeks without Greek citizenship to cross over to Greece. The last government of Protopapadakis did order the implementation of the law, though it does not seem to have been obeyed.

80. Gedeon, Paschalidou, and Dima-Dimitrou, *A Concise History of the Campaign in Asia Minor*, 447.

81. Ibid., 448–449.

82. Niş and Söker, *Büyük Taarruzda Takip Harekâtı*, 125–128.

83. Ibid., Kroki 26 (Sketch Map 26 following page 152).

84. Gedeon, Paschalidou, and Dima-Dimitrou, *A Concise History of the Campaign in Asia Minor*, 450.

85. Ibid., 450–451.

86. Niş and Söker, *Büyük Taarruzda Takip Harekâtı*, Kroki 27 (Sketch Map 27 following page 152); and Llewellyn-Smith, *Ionian Vision*, 311.

87. Gedeon, Paschalidou, and Dima-Dimitrou, *A Concise History of the Campaign in Asia Minor*, 453.

88. Niş and Söker, *Büyük Taarruzda Takip Harekâtı*, 245.

89. While I recognize that Wikipedia is not a credible source, I would illustrate the contentious theories revolving around the Great Fire in Izmir by providing a link to the page "The Great Fire of Smyrna": https://en.wikipedia.org/wiki/Great_fire_of_Smyrna. Some of the more well-known published works are George Horton, *The Blight of Asia* (Indianapolis: The Bobbs-Merrill Company, 1926); Marjorie Housepian Dobkin, *Smyrna 1922: The Destruction of a City* (New York: Harcourt Brace Jovanovich, 1971); Milton Giles, *Paradise Lost—Smyrna 1922: The Destruction of a Christian City in the Islamic World* (New York: Basic Books, 2008); and Heinz A. Richter, *The Greek-Turkish War 1919–1922* (Ruhpolding, DE: Verlag Franz Philipp Rutzen, 2016). For short and balanced narratives, see also, Llewellyn-Smith, *Ionian Vision*, 307–313; Mango, *Atatürk*, 345–347;

and Fromkin, *A Peace to End All Peace*, 544–548. See also John C. Carr, R.H.N.S., *Averof: Thunder in the Aegean* (Barnsley, UK: Pen & Sword Maritime, 2014). Dr. Konstantinos Travlos argues that whatever the cause of the initial fire, the destruction of the Greek and Armenian quarters and the sparing of the Turkish one indicate at least a taking advantage of the situation by Nurettin Pasha to render it impossible for the Greek and Armenian communities to reconstitute themselves. The destruction assured that there would be no repetition of 1918, when Greek and Armenian expellees and refugees were able to return and reconstitute their communities, undoing the demographic gains that an element of the Committee of Union and Progress had sought to create during the war. The destruction would make it harder for demands for the return of refugees in the peace negotiations, forcing Greece to keep them. Nurettin Pasha had shown an enmity to the Ottoman Greek community, both during his service as *vali* of Izmir in 1919, by his actions against the Pontic Greek community, and finally by the arranged murder of Metropolitan Chrysostom. The actions also fit with patterns of intercommunal violence in the Balkans. Tasos Kostopoulos, in his book *War and Ethnic Cleansing* (see endnote 89), noted how during the 1890s Cretan conflict, both Turks and Greeks were willing to destroy the most prized possession on the island, the extremely difficult to re-create olive groves, in order to deny livelihood to their opponents and force them to move out of an area. Thus, destroying the Greek and Armenian quarters made strategic sense for those who saw the end of the political threat of minorities in the Ottoman Empire as a legitimate goal.

90. Mango, *Atatürk*, 344–345.

91. Mango, *Atatürk*, 343. Dr. Konstantinos Travlos notes how after 1920, the Greek campaign had elements of seventeenth-century European campaigns, as the cash-strapped army began to live off the land, with catastrophic results for the local population. For an understanding of the consequences of such a campaign, see Gregory Hanlon, *Italy 1636: Cemetery of Armies* (Oxford: Oxford University Press, 2016).

92. The most recent book in Greek to cover the atrocities committed by both sides is written by the left-wing journalist and author Tasos Kostopoulos. In his book *Πόλεμος και Εθνοκάθαρση 1912–1922* (*War and Ethnic Cleansing 1912–1922*) (Athens: Vivliorama, Vivliorama Ekdoseis: 2008), relying on firsthand accounts by soldiers, he tracks the destruction wrought by the Greek Army. He also covers Turkish atrocities. Kostopoulos holds some controversial positions in Greece, where the destruction of

the Ottoman Greek community is considered a genocide, but his primary account work on the activities of Greek soldiers is indispensable.

93. Niş and Söker, *Büyük Taarruzda Takip Harekâtı*, Kroki 29 (Sketch Map 29 following page 156).

94. Gedeon, Paschalidou, and Dima-Dimitrou, *A Concise History of the Campaign in Asia Minor*, 455–456.

95. Ibid., 459.

96. Ibid., 459, 462–466. See also Lewellyn-Smith, *Ionian Vision*, 298–299.

97. Niş and Söker, *Büyük Taarruzda Takip Harekâtı*, Kroki 30 and 31 (Sketch Maps 30 and 31 both following page 168).

98. Gedeon, Paschalidou, and Dima-Dimitrou, *A Concise History of the Campaign in Asia Minor*, 455–456.

99. Niş and Söker, *Büyük Taarruzda Takip Harekâtı*, 189–196.

100. Ibid., Kroki 38 (Sketch Map 38 following page 200).

101. Gedeon, Paschalidou, and Dima-Dimitrou, *A Concise History of the Campaign in Asia Minor*, 494–495.

102. Niş and Söker, *Büyük Taarruzda Takip Harekâtı*, 208.

103. Ibid., Kroki 42 (Sketch Map 42 following page 216).

104. Gedeon, Paschalidou, and Dima-Dimitrou, *A Concise History of the Campaign in Asia Minor*, 495.

105. Llewellyn-Smith, *Ionian Vision*, 284–311.

ELEVEN

The Advance to the Straits and the Armistice

Mustapha Kemal had paid no heed to the Paris Note or to the warnings of General Harrington, and continued to pour cavalry and perhaps artillery into the neutral zone.[1]

British Cabinet Conclusions, September 30, 1922

INTRODUCTION

The triumph of the Nationalists shocked the Great Powers in its speed and its completeness. The Nationalists' immediate advance to the straits (the Dardanelles and the Bosporus) compounded the sense of confusion among the Allies and created a diplomatic crisis of the first order. The town of Çanakkale on the Asian side of the Dardanelles, known to the Europeans as Chanak, gave the unexpected crisis a geographic focal point and a convenient name. Likewise, there were second-order effects when an unanticipated revolution in Greece overthrew the Gounares supported government of Protopapadakis. Thus, in a period of only one month, the status quo in Anatolia was turned upside down, and an entirely new dynamic unfolded to confront those who struggled to bring an end to the war. Kemal compounded the dilemma by advancing his armies to the straits (the term used by the Allies to identify the Dardanelles and the Bosporus) and the Neutral Zone (the area on both sides of the Dardanelles and

Bosporus occupied by the Allies).[2] A cease-fire conference was hastily arranged and convened at Mudanya, a port on the Sea of Marmara, which led to a localized armistice, ending the fighting.

DIPLOMACY AND POLICY

Greek hopes for ending the war on favorable terms hinged on intervention by the Great Powers, but, after the spring of 1922, their hopes rested exclusively on the actions of the British government. This was an outcome of increasingly anti-Greek positions taken by the French and the Italians. In turn, the pro-Greek elements in the British cabinet became increasingly marginalized, and British policy shifted to pro-Nationalist positions.

On July 26, 1922, Athens sent FAAM commander in chief Lieutenant General Georgios Chatzanestes a diplomatic note to be delivered to the Allied high commissioners in Istanbul, warning them of Greek intentions to occupy Istanbul (see chapter 9).[3] The note and the obvious Greek military preparations to occupy the city caused the British to react with alacrity by officially warning the Gounares government on July 29 that any violation of the Neutral Zone would be resisted by Allied forces. Now uncertain of how to proceed, the Greeks promised that they would not act without Allied approval, but they continued to mass the troops of Army Corps D in Thrace. As a result, the Allied high commissioners convened a council of war in Istanbul on July 30, 1922. The French position was profoundly anti-Greek, recommending that the Greek Army in Thrace and the military and naval mission in Istanbul withdraw entirely, as well as proposing a naval blockade of the principal Greek ports. The British position was simply to wait out the Greeks and, should they act, to join the French with severe sanctions. The high commissioners sent a strong warning to Chatzanestes at his headquarters in Tekirdağ. In the end, the Greek effort had been nothing more than a bluff, and it collapsed because of miscalculations regarding British policy.[4]

In 1922, Britain faced severe fiscal constraints, and its armed forces were stretched thin in global deployments. The competing human and monetary expenditures from World War I, the interventions in Russia and Poland, the Irish War of Independence, the perennial uprisings in Afghanistan, the imposition of the mandates in the Middle Fast, and Gandhi's noncooperation movement in British India had wearied the British public, its professional civil and military apparatus, and its elected politicians from undertaking new overseas obligations. Moreover, a new Soviet state had arisen from the ashes of Imperial Russia, and Britain retracted into a pre-twentieth century policy of blocking Soviet expansion in the same way it had done against the Russian Empire in the nineteenth century. Large among these concerns was keeping the Soviets out of the Mediterranean. Although Lloyd George was a friend of Greece, his cabinet was packed with men who backed a strong Turkish state, which had come to be seen as more realistic than supporting Greek expansion in Anatolia. These pro-Nationalist voices included Lord Curzon (foreign secretary), Austin Chamberlain (privy seal), Winston Churchill (secretary of state for the colonies), and the military and naval chiefs of staff—and they moved increasingly closer to an accommodation with the Ankara government.[5]

The commander in chief of the Allied Forces in Istanbul and the British Army of the Black Sea in 1922 was Major General Sir Charles Harrington, popularly known as "Tim" Harrington.[6] Because of Allied disagreements, the only force that Harrington actually had available was the British 28th Division (its sister 27th Division had been sent home earlier). Moreover, the division was much reduced in strength, having only two brigades (the 83rd and 84th Brigades) composed of six infantry battalions. Harrington also nominally commanded a large French contingent (seven infantry battalions, three artillery batteries, and a tank company) and a small Italian detachment (one infantry battalion) under generals Charles Charpy and Ernesto Mombelli, respectively.[7] Harrington planned to field a light covering force on the Kocaeli Peninsula (known to the British as the Ismid Peninsula) and defend Istanbul with his main force, but he had no real plan in place to hold the Dardanelles Neutral Zone (the Gallipoli Peninsula and Çanakkale). Despite this, on September 3, the British cabinet ordered Harrington to occupy the Gallipoli Peninsula.[8]

In early September, Harrington became increasingly anxious about a Nationalist seizure of the Dardanelles because he had only a single infantry battalion (the Loyals) in the Çanakkale garrison, under the command of 83rd Brigade commander Brigadier Digby I. Shuttleworth.[9] He ordered Shuttleworth to organize a defense and sent French and Italian detachments to Çanakkale, but these were soon withdrawn for political reasons. Harrington ordered Shuttleworth to maintain the integrity of the Neutral Zone along the Asian side of the Dardanelles, and he quickly sent Shuttleworth a second infantry battalion, an artillery battery, and a cavalry squadron. Harrington ordered Shuttleworth to prepare defensive positions suitable for a brigade-sized force, and then told him to prepare a plan to bring in an entire infantry division. However Shuttleworth grew anxious as the Nationalist forces drew nearer, and he recognized that his ad hoc brigade could do little to stop Kemal's army, even though the admiral commanding a Royal Navy battle squadron in the Dardanelles assured him of naval gunfire support.[10] Adding to Shuttleworth's dilemma, thousands of refugees poured into Çanakkale and had to be fed, watered, and medically cared for before he could evacuate them from the port.

The British cabinet determined on September 23 that it did not want to go to war with the Nationalists to save the Greeks. Although this conflicted with previous policy notes from Churchill, this news was relayed to Sir Horace Rumbold the British high commissioner in Istanbul. British policy officially now rested on four principles: (1) warning the Nationalists not to violate the armistice and the Neutral Zone, (2) British policy "was not in the smallest degree based on a desire to take up the cudgels on behalf of Greek interests in Thrace or elsewhere," (3) retain Çanakkale for the purpose of maintaining freedom of the straits, and (4) prevent the war from spreading into Europe.[11] While the cabinet debated, Shuttleworth dug entrenchments and laid barbed wire and, on September 23, sent his cavalry, the 3rd Squadron, King's Own Hussars under the command of Captain J. E. Petherick, forward some 60 kilometers down the Çanakkale-Izmir road to the town of Ezine as a show of force to deter the Nationalists. Nationalist cavalry crossed into the Neutral Zone, where they came in contact with Petherick's hussars. Shuttleworth motored out to see for himself what was going on and, after returning to his headquarters, sent a signal to Harrington asking permission to open fire if the Nationalists advanced on his men. He then went aboard the HMS *Benbow* (a modern battleship) and arranged for a naval gunnery officer to join Petherick to observe and direct naval gunfire. On the night of September 23/24, Harrington gave Shuttleworth permission to open fire if attacked.[12]

Finding Petherick's hussars difficult to resupply in Ezine, Shuttleworth brought them back inside his perimeter on the evening of September 24. Harrington deployed five more British infantry battalions with considerable artillery to Çanakkale, and, on September 26, Shuttleworth reported to Harrington that the "Turks were persistently aggressive but under strict orders to avoid conflict."[13] The next day, Harrington sent Major General T. O. Marsden to command the force, which had grown to nearly a full infantry division (Shuttleworth returned to command of his own brigade).[14] Reinforcements from Britain and Egypt poured into the straits region, and the Royal Navy deployed the Mediterranean Fleet and part of the Atlantic Fleet to the Aegean. The RAF sent aircraft and pilots. The War Office cabled Harrington on September 27 and assigned him four missions: (1) hold the Gallipoli Peninsula at all costs, (2) hold Çanakkale as long as possible without endangering the force, (3) evacuate the Kocaeli Peninsula when forced to by threat of serious attack, and (4) evacuate Constantinople when forced to.[15]

British policy coalesced on September 30 when the cabinet agreed on three "primary interests" that would guide British policy in what now being called the Chanak Crisis. These primary interests were: (1) achieving peace through mediation and a negotiated settlement, (2) securing freedom of navigation through the straits (the Dardanelles and the Bosporus), and (3) maintaining the alliance with France and Italy.[16] This cleared the way for an armistice, but, without British support, it also ended any notion of satisfying Greek interests or achieving Greek war aims.

THE ADVANCE TO THE STRAITS

The evacuation of Army Corps C from Erdek on September 18, 1922 set the stage for İsmet and his Western Front Command staff to examine the operational situation in conjunction with Kemal, who had remained in Izmir. That evening, the Western Front Command remained scattered in southwest Anatolia as a result of its pursuit of the Greek FAAM.[17] Nurettin's First Army headquarters in Izmir was composed of 10 infantry and 4 cavalry divisions, allocated to four army corps (I, II, IV, and V Corps). The I Corps (6th, 8th, and 15th Divisions) remained west of Izmir in Urla. The II Corps (4th, 14th, and 3rd Caucasian Divisions) had moved north to Ayvalık and Bergama, with the II Corps exercising tactical control of the 2nd Cavalry Division in Edremit. The IV Corps (11th, 12th, 23rd, and 5th Caucasian Divisions) lay near Akhisar and Soma. The V Cavalry Corps (1st, 3rd, and 14th Cavalry Divisions) was refitting south of Izmir. Yakup Şevki's Second Army headquarters, which lay to the north of Izmir in Balıkesir, was composed of six infantry divisions and one cavalry division allocated to two army corps and a tactical group (III and VI Corps and the Kocaeli Group). The III Corps (1st Division and the Provisional Cavalry Division) rested victoriously near Bandırma after its battles with Army Corps C. The VI Corps (16th and 17th Divisions) lay centered around Balıkesir near the army headquarters. The Kocaeli Group (18th Division and a Provisional Detachment) occupied the Kapıdağ Peninsula, collecting a few prisoners and abandoned Greek equipment. The Second Army headquarters retained direct command of the 41st and 61st Divisions at Balıkesir.

On September 19, İsmet issued a directive to the Western Front Command, which stated that "new operations would begin on 20 September."[18] Among the restaging of his armies, İsmet directed the following: the 2nd Cavalry Division will continue to operate toward Çanakkale, and the Kocaeli Group with the Provisional Cavalry Division will concentrate on the Kocaeli Peninsula and observe the area. On September 21, reports reached the Western Front Command headquarters that several hundred English cavalry had occupied Ezine. The V Cavalry Corps reached Manisa on September 22, while the 2nd Cavalry Division marched north to occupy Ayvalık. The next day, 2nd Cavalry Division's 20th Cavalry Regiment launched patrols toward Ezine and made contact with Petherick's hussars. At 6:00 a.m. on September 24, the patrols of the 20th Cavalry Regiment discovered that the English cavalry regiment had withdrawn to Erenköy.[19] Lieutenant Colonel Mehmet Zeki (Soydemir), commander of the 2nd Cavalry Division, then brought the 13th and 4th Cavalry Regiments north to establish a perimeter around Shuttleworth's garrison.

Farther north, on September 25, Colonel Halit's Kocaeli Group and Colonel Hacı Arif's (Örgüç) Provisional Cavalry Division moved from Bursa and Erdek toward the Kocaeli Peninsula.[20] The next day, Mehmet Zeki received a note from the British stating that they would observe a cease-fire if the Nationalists did not attempt to penetrate their lines. However, the noose was tightening around Çanakkale—on September 27, the VI Corps established its headquarters in Ezine, and its 16th Division reached Biga (northeast of Çanakkale), and the 17th Division occupied Bayramıç (east of Çanakkale and north of Ezine). The next day, the Western Front Command sent its evening report confirming that the perimeter around Çanakkale was firmly established and that the III Corps and II Corps occupied Bursa and Bergama respectively (see map 11.1). Moreover, the First Army headquarters moved north to Balıkesir. These deployments brought three Nationalist army corps within striking distance of Çanakkale. On September 29, the Provisional Cavalry Division moved into the Kocaeli Peninsula, and the 1st Division reached the city of Izmit. The next day, the Provisional Cavalry Division rode hard to occupy a line from the Black Sea port of Şile through Gebze to the town of Darica on the Sea of Marmara.[21] The rapidly marching infantry of the 1st and 61st Divisions followed behind. On October 2, the exhausted cavalry patrols of

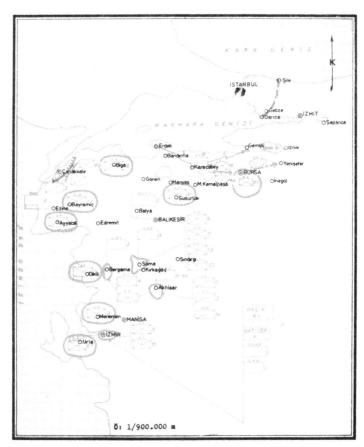

Map 11.1   Dardanelles (September 28, 1922)
By the end of September 1922, the victorious Nationalists had crushed the FAAM and expelled the survivors from Anatolia. İsmet pushed the V Cavalry Corps forward to make contact with the British force at Çanakkale and, shortly thereafter, moved infantry north to make contact with the Allied force on the Kocaeli Peninsula (Izmit Peninsula).
Courtesy of the Turkish General Staff Military History and Strategy Institute (ATASE).

Hacı Arif's Provisional Cavalry Division made contact with the Allied detachments manning the Neutral Zone on the Kocaeli Peninsula east of the Bosporus.[22] This brought Kemal's armies literally nose-to-nose with the French, Italians, and British on the Kocaeli Peninsula and with the British at Çanakkale.

NEGOTIATIONS FOR AN ARMISTICE

While İsmet focused on moving his armies to exploit the expulsion of the Greek Army from Anatolia, Mustafa Kemal focused on practicing coercive diplomacy as Bismarck had practiced the art. On the night of September 15, Colonial Secretary Winston Churchill sent telegrams to the prime ministers of Australia, New Zealand, South Africa, and Canada asking them to send military forces immediately to defend "freedom of the seas" and to stop "the Turk's threats to attempt aggression on Europe."[23] Only New Zealand responded positively, and a desperate Churchill publicly called for a conference between the Allies and the Ankara government. Churchill tried to reengage the dominions by reaffirming that the Neutral Zones protected the straits. Churchill reminded the dominions and the public to remember the sacrifices of the Gallipoli Campaign (1915–1916) and promised to resist any attack into the Neutral Zone. The British public was cool toward Churchill's appeal, and, making the situation more problematic for Britain, Kemal instructed his representative in Istanbul, Hamid Bey, on September 17 to inform the Allied high commissioners that the Nationalists had never agreed to and did not recognize "the so-called Neutral Zone."[24] Kemal further informed the Allies that his armies would take whatever action was necessary to fulfill the Turkish National Pact. In fact, Kemal was correct to point out that what the British called the Neutral Zone did not exist as an agreement or treaty but existed simply as a line drawn on the map by the Allied high commissioners themselves.

The British position greatly alarmed French prime minister Raymond Poincaré, who instructed General Maurice Pellé, the French high commissioner in Istanbul, to travel to Izmir to inform Kemal that France would not support British military action in the straits and ask for restraint until a peaceful solution could be found.[25] Kemal met with Pellé and restated his insistence on achieving the objectives of the Turkish National Pact, and Kemal also had Hamid Bey restate this to Harrington at the same time. On September 18, Poincaré ordered all French forces to withdraw from the Neutral Zone. Two days later, Poincaré informed Lord Curzon about Pellé's meeting with Kemal, noting that Kemal would attend a conference only if the Allies agreed in advance to turn over Istanbul and Thrace to the Nationalists. Curzon, of course, regarded this as blackmail and was furious at the French and Italians for their decisions to withdraw from the Anatolian side of the straits.

Kemal received Nationalist prime minister Rauf and General Ali Fuat, who led Kemal's party in the assembly, on September 21 in Izmir. He briefed Rauf and Ali Fuat on his strategy for the recovery of Istanbul and Thrace, which basically rested on separating the French from the British.[26] The visitors returned to Ankara and secured the approval of the assembly. Two days later, the Allies sent a joint note from Paris to Ankara (this is the basis for the epigraph at the beginning of this chapter) accepting the Meriç (Maritza) River as the western boundary of Turkey but asking that its occupation be delayed until after a peace had been concluded. Kemal deliberately delayed his reply and ordered Ismet to advance his armies to the Neutral Zone. On September 26, Kemal sent Harrington two telegrams expressing that he was doing his best to avoid bloodshed. Poincaré remained troubled by the crisis and sent the pro-Nationalist diplomat Henry Franklin-Bouillon to Izmir on September 28. Franklin-Bouillon assured Kemal that the Allies would force the Greeks to withdraw to the Meriç River before an actual peace treaty was signed and that Allied military forces would act as a buffer between the Greeks and the Nationalists. Unaware of Franklin-Bouillon's discussions with Kemal, the British government sent Harrington an ultimatum to be delivered to Kemal on September 29, demanding immediate evacuation of the Neutral Zone, or British troops would open fire. Much to the chagrin of Lloyd George, Curzon, and Churchill, Harrington wisely did not pass the note on to the Nationalists. On October 1, Kemal informed Poincaré that he had stopped the advance of his armies and proposed armistice negotiations, based on Franklin-Bouillon's assurances, begin promptly on October 3 at the Marmara port of Mudanya. Kemal left Izmir the next day and arrived in Ankara where he "was met as a conquering hero."[27]

The Greeks were doubly cursed by the Allied abandonment of their cause and by the festering discontent of military and naval officers who were enraged by the catastrophic defeat in Asia Minor. Among those unhappy officers, Colonel Nikolaos Plasteras, the "capable, courageous, and popular leader" of the detachment by the same name, led a conspiracy to overthrow the government.[28] General Polymenakos, having learned of the plot, unsuccessfully attempted to diffuse the situation by transferring Plasteras, but naval officers then carried the conspiracy forward. Undeterred, Plasteras, Colonel Panagiotes Gardikas, and Lieutenant Colonel Miltiades Koimeses formed a three-member revolutionary committee on September 22 on the island of Chios. They advanced the non-Venizelist Colonel Stylianos Gonatas as the head of the revolution, who accepted with the caveat that the king abdicate and a politically neutral government form. The revolution declared itself on September 24, and the plotters arrived in Piraeus on September 26. They announced their intentions, including putting political and military decision-makers on trial, by having an airplane drop leaflets over Athens while Colonel Gonatas delivered an ultimatum to the cabinet.[29] This triggered movements by the staunch anti-Constantinist ex-chief of staff of the FAAM major general Theodoros Pangalos in Athens. Besieged by multiple conspiracies, threatened by the landing of the revolutionary army, and facing an unwillingness of its partisans to fight, after some debate, the government resigned, and the king abdicated on September 27. The next day, despite the assurance of the revolutionaries to the contrary, prime ministers Gounares, Protopapadakis, Stratos (who had been prime minister only for a couple of days), Minister of Military Affairs Theotokes, Foreign Minister Baltatzes, ex–commander in chief General Chatzanestes, retired Admiral Goudas, and retired Major General Strategos were arrested and imprisoned. A new government, led by Prime Minister Sotirios Krokidas, was sworn on September 29. Thus, while Kemal maneuvered diplomatically and İsmet maneuvered militarily in search of an armistice, the Greek government collapsed.

This was not the end of the Greek tragedy. The revolutionaries, now divided into factions headed by the moderate Plasteras and hard-liner Pangalos and the parliament, enraged by the defeats and looking to blame someone so as to avert a social revolution headed by the refugees, undertook to press for a tribunal to punish the imprisoned leaders. Despite the protests of the Allied governments a military court-martial convened on November 13, with the accused being indicted for treason. The Krokidas government, predicting the conviction and punishment of the previous government, resigned on November 13. Colonel Gonatas formed a government, and the court-martial delivered its verdict at 7:30 a.m. that day. The unanimous sentences were carried out just five hours later, with Gounares, Protopapadakis, Stratos, Baltatzes, Theotokes, and Chatzanestes facing a firing squad, while Goudas and Strategos were sentenced to life imprisonment.[30]

THE MUDANYA ARMISTICE

The world owed much of the peaceful conclusion to what was called the Chanak Crisis to Tim Harrington, who had received a flurry of contradictory and confusing orders from London in the last few days of September 1922.[31] On October 1. Kemal notified Harrington that he would meet him in Mudanya two days hence. Harrington relayed this to London where, because he had already disobeyed direct orders, the cabinet quickly wrote instructions for the negotiations. These were sent from the War Office to Harrington and from the Foreign Office to Rumbold, who was ordered to instruct Harrington on what to do. London's principal outcome that Harrington was to deliver was an agreed-upon line for the Greek forces in Thrace to retreat behind, in return for which Ankara would agree not to attack the Neutral Zone or to cross into Europe. Harrington and a small entourage of officers left Istanbul on October 2 aboard the famed battleship HMS *Iron Duke* bound for Mudanya, while Rumbold stayed behind in the capital. General Charles Charpy and General Mombelli also departed on their own vessels to represent France and Italy, respectively. Kemal, as head of state, decided to send General İsmet rather than attend himself.[32]

The three Allied generals gathered in the town, which has been described as shabby and provincial, on October 3, and they met with İsmet the next day. Harrington initially underestimated the 39-year-old İsmet, who was a physically small man, but İsmet strictly adhered to Kemal's instructions and proved to be an able and tough negotiator.[33] The Greeks were invited but, because of a mechanical breakdown of their ship, had not arrived. Finally, the Royal Navy sent a destroyer to pick them up, and they arrived late on October 4/5.[34] The Greek delegation was led by Major General Alexandros Mazarakis-Ainian and included Sarrigiannis.[35] To their dismay, they learned that the Allies, led by Harrington, had taken decisions on their behalf in absentia. On the morning of October 5, the Greek delegation was invited to board HMS *Iron Duke* to be informed of the already agreed-upon decisions. Shocked by the decisions regarding a Greek withdrawal from Thrace and having been authorized only to negotiate a truce, the delegation refused to discuss the Allied-Turkish agreement. Faced with the Greek refusal, the three Allied generals returned to Istanbul that afternoon for discussions with the high commissioners. Major General Mazarakis sent the agreement to Athens, which contained the following: (1) hostilities would cease when the agreement went into effect, (2) the Greek Army would withdraw to the Line of the Hebrus (the Meriç/Maritsa River), (3) the Greek Army would complete its withdrawal within 13 days while the Allied secured order and allowed Nationalist gendarmes to maintain the rule of law.[36] Harrington and his colleagues returned to Mudanya on October 6 and that afternoon in Paris, Poincaré met with Lord Curzon and Italian diplomat and noted artist Carlo Galli to consider the way ahead. They agreed to support the proposed protocol, notifying both the high commissioners in Istanbul and former Prime Minister Venizelos, who led the Greek delegation in Paris, of their decision on October 7.

Over the following two days, Mazarakis received instructions from his government and from former prime minister Venizelos to accept the agreement with a two-kilometer adjustment to the proposed border and a request to extend the withdrawal period to 30 days (to allow for civilian evacuation). This was communicated to Harrington, who returned on October 10 with the same basic agreement as before. The Allies and the Nationalists then signed the protocol on October 11, 1922, but Mazarakis refused to sign and lodged a protest instead.[37] After a total of eight difficult meetings, negotiations ended with a partially signed agreement, which was formally called the Military Convention of Mudanya.[38] The unhappy Greek cabinet called Mazarakis to give an account of the facts when he returned to Athens but, in the end, decided to accept what had been unilaterally decided by the Allies. The cabinet ordered its high commissioner in Istanbul to sign the protocol on September 15.

One author described the terms as "simple" but, of course, in execution, these proved more difficult.[39] The Greeks would withdraw to the west side of the Meriç River, and the Allies would occupy the right bank. The Greek civil administration would hand over authority to the Allies, who would remain for 30 days, after which, the Nationalists were allowed to bring in 8,000 Jandarma (gendarmes) to establish civil authority. In return, the Nationalists would withdraw 15 kilometers from the Kocaeli Peninsula and Çanakkale Neutral Zones until a peace treaty was signed.

THE EVACUATION OF THRACE

In the wake of the evacuation of the Greek Army from Asia Minor, Army Corps C and 60,000 men disembarked in the Thracian port of Tekirdağ (Rodosto/Rhaedestus). After a short period of rest, its battered divisions moved inland, the 3rd Division to the Çatalca lines, the 12th Division to the Gallipoli Peninsula, and the Independent Division and the army corps headquarters to Lüleburgaz.[40] The Field Army of Asia Minor was officially dissolved on September 19 and the Field Army of Thrace resurrected, with Lieutenant General Polymenakos taking command. However, after the revolution, the new government removed him and returned Lieutenant General Konstantinos Nider to command on October 4.

Additionally, in the wake of the evacuation, the Greek war ministry decided to release the reservists from the classes of 1918 and earlier and to give the men of the classes of 1919–1922 10 days leave, after which they returned to their units. Sixty thousand reservists returned to their homes between September 14 and 21. Army Corps B on Chios collected and stored its surviving weapons and equipment in depots while the surviving units on Mytilene performed the same actions. Going into early October 1922, the Greek Army was composed of five infantry divisions, of which only two were at strength and ready to fight.

When the Greek high commissioner in Istanbul signed the Mudanya Armistice protocol on September 13, the ministry of war notified General Nider of its terms. The Greeks were certain that Kemal would violate the terms prohibiting the Nationalist Army from occupying Thrace, and Nider was ordered to maintain a posture, allowing him to attack while withdrawing his forces.[41] Working with the Allied generals, Nider negotiated an agreement that placed three British, three French, and one Italian battalion to secure the territory of the Field Army of Thrace as it withdrew, as well as establishing a bilateral Allied committee within his own headquarters to resolve any problems. The next day, Nider received instructions from Athens to begin withdrawal on October 16, with a completion date of October 28. The evacuation proceeded smoothly and under well-disciplined command; however, at the last moment, Nider had to ask for a three-day extension to allow the remaining civilian refugees time to evacuate. Except for the Gallipoli Peninsula, which was considered by the Allies as part of the Neutral Zone, the Greek evacuation of Thrace was completed on October 31. It took another three weeks for Greek residents of the Gallipoli peninsula to depart, but this was completed on November 24, 1922.[42]

After the Greek Army's evacuation from Thrace, the ministry of war undertook a major reorganization of forces by forming the Field Army of Hebrus under Lieutenant General Konstantinos Nider, with its headquarters in Alexandropoulis. The staff allocated two army corps headquarters to the field army, Army Corps D in Didymoteicho, composed of the 6th, 7th, and the 11th Divisions, and Army Corps C at Komotini, composed of the 3rd, 10th, and 12th Divisions.[43] Army Corps D held the frontier, while Army Corps C remained in reserve. Army Corps B reconstituted in Greek Macedonia, and Army Corps A was dissolved. Lieutenant General Nider fell ill in late December and was replaced by Major General Theodoros Pangalos, who had been the minister for the army after the revolution and was now one of the most powerful men in Greece. Pangalos continued the reorganization by imposing strict discipline and effective training but was hampered in his efforts by the massive losses of armaments, munitions, equipment, and draft animals during the evacuations from Asia Minor. In mid-January 1923, Pangalos moved his field army headquarters to Thessaloniki and began planning an invasion of eastern Thrace should peace negotiations break down. In his plan, Army Corps D would make the main effort, supported by Army Corps C while Army Corps B (the 4th and 14th Divisions) would land amphibiously south of Istanbul. Of course, it was predicated on the assumption that the Turks had not yet occupied the Thracian peninsula with İsmet's armies. On June 24, 1923, during the height of the peace negotiations, the Field Army of Hebrus was composed of 4,446 officers and 111,775 enlisted men completely equipped with armaments and equipment.[44]

On the Nationalist side, İsmet and Fevzi met on October 12 to plan how to reoccupy Thrace as the Greeks withdrew.[45] Over the course of the war, the existing Jandarma (gendarmerie) had been militarized and brought into the active army, and only one Jandarma regiment of 750 men was available immediately.[46] Fevzi and Ismet planned to transfer a total of 7,250 soldiers from the army to the resuscitated Jandarma to make up the shortfall. According to Fevzi, 400 newly conscripted men were available in six infantry battalions and 500 new conscripts in two cavalry regiments were available for training as Jandarma. Additionally, they determined that 16 infantry battalions (eight from First Army, four from Second Army, and four from the I Corps), two V Cavalry Corps cavalry regiments, and 15 machine gun detachments could be rerolled as Jandarma on a rapid basis. Men from the army's elite assault battalions (hücum taburları) were also to be selected on a case-by-case basis to complete the roster of 8,000 Jandarma allowed by the armistice protocols.[47] On October 25, the first six battalions from First Army arrived in Gemlik, and by October 30, the Second Army, I Corps, and V Cavalry Corps units arrived in Bandırma, where they were reorganized and reequipped as gendarmes.

Kemal had previously decided on October 9 to place Refet in command of establishing the Jandarma and civil authority in Thrace.[48] Refet rapidly took command and organized the Eastern Thrace Jandarma Command into four regimental areas: Edirne, Kırklareli, Tekirdağ, and Keşan.[49] He then organized 16 Jandarma battalions and 1 Jandarma cavalry regiment and placed them under the command of trusted army and ex-Jandarma officers. The Jandarma General Headquarters and the Edirne Jandarma Regiment arrived in Istanbul by ship on October 29, with two more regiments arriving by October 31. The remaining Jandarma forces were entirely deployed to Thrace by November 21. Refet arrived in Istanbul on October 19 to take personal command and coordinate the transfer of civilian authority to the Nationalists, as well as arrange a schedule for the arrival of civil officials in Thrace.[50] According to Refet's schedule and subject to the weather, civilian officials would arrive on October 30 in Silivri, Çorlu, and Saray; October 31 in Vize; November 1 in Demirköy; November 8 in Kırklareli, Lüleburgaz, Babaeski, and Pınarhısar; November 14 in Tekirdağ, Hayrabolu, and Malkara; and November 15 in the eastern Thracian border area.

While Refet organized the restoration of civil authority in Thrace, İsmet reorganized the field armies confronting the Allies. On October 12, İsmet ordered the First Army to take over the Kocaeli Peninsula facing the Neutral Zone (with the III and IV Corps, Kocaeli Group, and the Provisional Cavalry Division), with its headquarters in Izmit. The Second Army headquarters in Balıkesir faced the Çanakkale Neutral Zone (with the II and VI Corps). The III Corps and V Cavalry Corps remained in Western Front Command reserve and were ordered to prepare for movement by rail to either army should hostilities resume.[51] Colonel Halit's Kocaeli Groups was dissolved on October 19 and its units allocated to the First Army. At the same time, İsmet also established a Fortress Command in Izmir. Kemal returned to the Western Front Command headquarters in Izmir on October 25 to discuss further reorganization with İsmet. As finally configured on November 20, 1922, the First Army was composed of the III Corps (1st, 41st, and 61st Divisions) and the IV Corps (11th, 12th, and 5th Caucasian Divisions), while the Second Army was composed of the II Corps (3rd, 4th, and 7th Divisions) and the VI Corps (14th, 16th, and 17th Divisions). This balanced the field armies, with each having two army corps of three infantry divisions. The Western Front Command retained direct command of the I Corps (6th, 8th, and 15th Divisions) and the V Cavalry Corps (1st, 2nd, 3rd, and 14th Cavalry Divisions), the Izmir Fortress Command (57th Division), the 12th and 18th Independent Divisions, and the Provisional Cavalry Division.[52]

In the expectation of the reoccupation of the Gallipoli Peninsula and the Çanakkale fortifications, the Operations Division of the General Staff established a provisional Fortified Area Command headquarters.[53] The role of this command was to reoccupy and restore the former Ottoman fortifications at the Dardanelles, Edirne, and Çatalca.[54] It was composed of three heavy artillery regiments, an engineer battalion and a construction detachment, a naval mine detachment, communications and munitions detachments, and a naval air squadron.

There was one lingering active military front in October 1922 north of the disputed city of Mosul. The British organized an irregular force composed of 2,000 Nestorian Christians, 500 Armenian nationalists, 700 to 800 Indian Army soldiers, and 1,200 Arab gendarmes with two artillery batteries and 30 aircraft (altogether about 4,500 armed men).[55] They expanded their zone of control north to Zakho and Olmadiye and east to Kirkum. On October 19, Ankara ordered the Elcezire Front to push the irregulars back to the south, and the General Staff established two expeditionary forces, one from Cizre advancing southeast along the Euphrates River, and the second from Hakkârı advancing south along the Tigris River. These were not inconsequential forces. Ankara assembled troops from as far away as Kars and Sarıkamış and allocated each group three or four infantry regiments, an assault battalion, cavalry, and artillery detachments. Altogether, the Elcezire Front Command deployed 5,800 infantrymen, 1,350 cavalrymen, 86 heavy and light machine guns, and 16 artillery pieces, and the two groups marched south on November 22, 1922.[56] They advanced south to within 80 kilometers of Mosul when they were stopped by the government because of the impending Lausanne Conference.

CONCLUSION

In addition to the previously described revolution in Greece the Mudanya armistice affected British politics as well. On October 19, 1922, the Conservatives voted to leave Lloyd George's coalition government (partly because of Asia Minor but also because of the revolutionary situation in Ireland). He gave his resignation to the king that afternoon, and Andrew Bonar Law replaced him four days later. In the eloquent prose of Stanford Shaw, "So it was that the man who had done the most to stir a new war between Britain and Turkey and whose bigotry and blind passions had caused the deaths of thousands had passed into history. A new Conservative government led by Bonar Law was formed with Curzon remaining as Foreign Secretary with the task of picking up the pieces and attempting to bring the crisis to a final conclusion and to restore reasonably good relations between the two countries."[57]

NOTES

1. Conclusions of a Conference of Ministers held at 10, Downing Street, SW, on Saturday, September 30, 1922 at 5:00 p.m., 1, Cabinet 52/22, CAB/23/31, The National Archives, Kew, UK (TNA).

2. Edmonds, *The Occupation of Constantinople*, Map 2 on page 33.

3. Llewellyn-Smith, *Ionian Vision*, 277–283.

4. Ibid., 278.

5. Fromkin, *A Peace to End All Peace*, 543–544.

6. Charles Harrington, *Tim Harrington Looks Back* (London: John Murray, 1940), 108.

7. Conclusions of a Conference of Ministers held at 10, Downing Street, SW, on Friday, September 10, 1922 at 4:00 p.m., 3–6, Cabinet 49/22, CAB/23/31, TNA. See also Cecini, *Il Corpo di Spedizione Italiano*, 333–335 for the Italian contributions.

8. Conclusions of a Conference of Ministers held at 10, Downing Street, SW, on Thursday, September 7, 1922 at noon, 1, Cabinet 48/22, CAB/23/31, TNA.

9. Marden, "With the British Army in Constantinople," 43.

10. Harrington, *Tim Harrington Looks Back*, 112.

11. Conclusions of a Conference of Ministers held at 10, Downing Street, SW, on Saturday, September 23, 1922 at 11:00 a.m., 4–5, Cabinet 50/22, CAB/23/31, TNA.

12. Harrington, *Tim Harrington Looks Back*, 115.

13. Ibid., 116.

14. David Walder, *The Chanak Affair* (London: Hutchinson & Co Ltd., 1969), 204–210, 269–272; and Edmonds, *The Occupation of Constantinople*, 26–27.

15. WO to Harrington, 91247 cipher 28/9, 2200 hours, 28/9/1922, attached as Appendix , Draft Conclusions of a Conference of Ministers held at 10, Downing Street, SW, on Thursday, September 28, 1922 at 7:00 p.m., Cabinet 52/32, CAB/23/31.

16. Conclusions of a Conference of Ministers held at 10, Downing Street, SW, on Saturday, September 30, 1922 at 11:00 a.m., 4–5, Cabinet 50/22, CAB/23/31, TNA.

17. Abidin Tüzel, *Türk İstiklâl Harbi IInci Cilt Batı Cephesi 6nci Kısım IV Kitap, İstiklâl Harbinin Son Safhası (18 Eylül–1 Kasım 1923)* (Ankara: Genelkurmay Basımevi, 1969), 27–28.

18. Ibid., 28–29.

19. Ibid., 29 and Kroki 2 (Sketch Map 2 following page 28).

20. Ibid., 30; and Ökse, Baycan, and Sakaryalı, *Komutanların Biyografileri*, 190.

21. Tüzel, *Son Safhası*, Kroki 4 (Sketch Map 4 following page 36).

22. Ibid., 33–34.

23. Churchill Papers 17/28, quoted in Shaw, *From Republic to Empire*, vol. 4, 1754.

24. Shaw, *From Empire to Republic*, vol. 4, 1756–1757.

25. Ibid., 1759.

26. Mango, *Atatürk*, 325–323. See also Shaw, *From Empire to Republic*, vol. 4, 1760–1781 for a detailed narrative of the communication and correspondence between the British, French, and Nationalists.

27. Ibid., 353.

28. Gedeon, Paschalidou, and Dima-Dimitrou, *A Concise History of the Campaign in Asia Minor*, 499.

29. Ibid., 500. See also Llewellyn-Smith, *Ionian Vision*, 321–330 for a detailed narrative of British efforts to halt the courts-martial.

30. Ibid., 501–502. That the tribunal was political is indicated by the presence of retired Admiral Goudas, who had no role in the political and military affairs of the war but, together with Metaxas, had been the main political activist and propagandist for the Constantinists. It may be hypothesized that Chatzanestes also partly paid for his 1917–1920 political activity as much as his failure as commander in chief. Stratos, a once Venizelist politician, who had broken ranks during the National Schism, was also more of a political target than a military one. Further trials and inquiries on the Asia Minor debacle continued throughout the period 1923–1927.

31. Walder, *The Chanak Affair*, 298–299; and Edmonds, *The Occupation of Constantinople*, 27–28.

32. Tüzel, *Son Safhası*, 51–58.

33. Walder, *The Chanak Affair*, 314–317.

34. Shaw, *From Republic to Empire*, vol. 4, 1804.

35. Gedeon, Paschalidou, and Dima-Dimitrou, *A Concise History of the Campaign in Asia Minor*, 504–505.

36. Ibid., 505.

37. For an English language version of the complete agreement, see Shaw, *From Republic to Empire*, vol. 4, 1860–1862.

38. Shaw, *From Empire to Republic*, vol. 4, 1860.

39. Walder, *The Chanak Affair*, 317.

40. Ibid., 498–499.

41. Ibid., 506.

42. Ibid., 507. The Greek Concise History maintains that the withdrawal was particularly hard on the Thracian Greeks, who had inhabited the area since ancient times.

43. Gedeon, Paschalidou, and Dima-Dimitrou, *A Concise History of the Campaign in Asia Minor*, 507.

44. Ibid., 508.

45. Tüzel, *Son Safhası*, 90–91.

46. Ibid.

47. Ibid.

48. Ökse, Baycan, and Sakaryalı, *Komutanların Biyografileri*, 100.

49. Tüzel, *Son Safhası*, 92–93.

50. Shaw, *From Empire to Republic*, vol. 4, 1872–1876.

51. Western Front Command orders number 108, October 12, 1922, reproduced in Tüzel, *Son Safhası*, 94–95.

52. Tüzel, *Son Safhası*, 96–98.

53. Ibid., 96.

54. For information on the armaments and composition of these fortresses under the Ottoman Army, see Erickson, *Defeat in Detail*, 125–131, 154–155; and Erickson, *Gallipoli: The Ottoman Campaign*, 1–41

55. Tüzel, *Son Safhası*, 100.

56. Ibid., 101–102.

57. Shaw, *From Empire to Republic*, vol. 4, 1876.

TWELVE

The Treaty of Lausanne and the Establishment of the Turkish Republic

The Treaty of Lausanne followed in due course. It was a surprising contrast to the Treaty of Sèvres.[1]

Winston S. Churchill, 1929

INTRODUCTION

The terms of the Treaty of Lausanne delivered almost everything Kemal and the Nationalists had sought to secure from a durable and just peace. It upended the punitive Treaty of Sèvres by ending Greek aspirations to establish a Greater Greece that included eastern Thrace, Istanbul, western Asia Minor, and the Aegean littorals. The Treaty of Lausanne returned Greece to the position of a minor power while restoring the new Turkish Republic to a status previously enjoyed by the Ottoman Empire of being regarded as a significant regional power with an important geostrategic position. Moreover, the victory and its consequences gave Mustafa Kemal the power to impose his vision of a secular society on the emergent Republic of Turkey. Like a phoenix arisen from the ashes, the modern Turkish Republic emerged from the ruins of the Ottoman Empire. That this might happen, as most of the decision-makers of 1920 had not foreseen, was an astonishing outcome, which was itself a result of the Nationalist Army's campaigns of national liberation.

PLANNING THE PEACE CONFERENCE

On October 14, Lord Curzon proposed that a peace conference be convened to end the fighting with the people he called the Turks. Opinions differed as to where the conference ought to be held. Poincaré and Curzon advocated for Istanbul suburb, while Rumbold believed that such a venue was undesirable. In the end, the Allies invited the victorious Nationalists to a peace conference in Lausanne, Switzerland, on October 26, 1922. The "Sultan's phantom government in Istanbul" also received an invitation.[2] The invitations specified that the invited party provide a delegate, as did the Soviet and the Bulgarian invitations (rather than a fully participating representative), placing all four governments in the position of being nonvoting observers.[3] The British government suggested that the conference begin on November 13. The Grand National Assembly elected Lieutenant General İsmet (İnönü) as foreign minister on October 27, and the government reacted indeterminately to the invitation two days later.[4]

There were problems with the details, particularly with the issue of who spoke for Turkey. On October 29, Kemal's representative in Istanbul, Hamit Bey, protested the proposed verbiage, arguing that the Nationalists should attend as fully empowered representatives rather than as disempowered official delegates. Grand Vizier Tevfik Pasha cabled Kemal, proposing the Ottoman government and the Nationalist government for a joint delegation. In reply to this, Kemal sent Refet, who was already in Istanbul to reestablish civil authority, to the Sublime Porte for a meeting with the sultan that lasted four hours, during which Refet asked Tevfik Pasha to resign. Of course, Tevfik rejected this out of hand, and Refet informed him that the Grand National Assembly intended to abolish the sultanate and the caliphate to establish a republic. There were also problems within the Nationalist ranks because Kâzım Karabekir, the victorious commander of the eastern war against Armenia, had political aspirations and asked Kemal for the position of the Ankara government's official representative to the peace talks. Speaking to the Grand National Assembly on October 30, Kemal explained the exchange between Hamit Bey and Tevfik Pasha, which led to spirited debate in the chamber. A vote on November 1 reaffirmed as law the previous law of March 16, 1920 (when the Ottoman parliament dissolved), abolishing the sultanate, with all laws, treaties, and other acts signed by the sultanate as null and void.[5]

Tevfik Pasha asked Rumbold for advice on November 4 and was told that it was not within the purview of the Ankara government to abolish the sultanate. In any case, later that day, Tevfik and his quasi cabinet resigned, leaving civil administration in Istanbul entirely in Refet's hands. The next day, Refet notified the Allied high commissioners that he had assumed full control, and he asked them to withdraw their military forces from the city. On the same day (November 5), the respected but virulently anti-Nationalist author, newspaperman, and former foreign minister Ali Kemal was arrested in public by four plain clothes police from the Ankara government's secret service.[6] Ali Kemal was transported to Izmir where First Army commander and governor of Izmir, Nurettin, subjected him to a summary trial, followed by Ali Kemal's lynching by an angry mob. This sent shock waves through the Allied community, the pro-Ottoman constituency, and the Christian communities in Istanbul and Thrace. Moreover, now fearing for his safety, the 36th and last Ottoman sultan, Mehmet VI or Vahdettin, requested asylum from Tim Harrington on November 16. At dawn the next morning, Harrington smuggled Vahdettin, his son, a small entourage, and a fortune in gold and jewels out of the palace to safety on board the battleship HMS *Malaya*. Technically, Vahdettin was no longer the Ottoman sultan, but he remained caliph of the Islamic world. He sailed to Malta and eventually settled in San Remo. On learning of Vahdettin's flight, the Grand National Assembly declared the caliphate vacant and appointed his cousin, Abdülmecid the new caliph.[7]

Thus, by default, by the middle of November 1922, the Nationalist government in Ankara came to be the sole representative of the Turks in Lausanne. This was important for the future because Kemal and the Nationalists regarded themselves as the victors of a national war of liberation rather than as the representatives of the defeated Ottoman state of 1918 (hereafter the author will use the term "Turks" rather than "Nationalists"). The Grand National Assembly elected Foreign Minister İsmet, Dr. Rıza Nur, Hasan (Saka) Bey, and three additional counselors as the official party representing Ankara. Led by İsmet, the official party, accompanied by Hamit Bey, left Istanbul on the Orient Express on November 9, 1922 for the peace conference. They did not know that Curzon had delayed the conference by a week because of the pending election following the fall of the Lloyd George government. It was only after his arrival in Lausanne on November 12 that

İsmet learned of the delay. He protested unsuccessfully, and then went to Paris to speak with French officials while he waited.

THE TREATY OF LAUSANNE

İsmet and the official party came to the conference with the understanding that they would be treated as representatives of an established government and would be treated as full participants in all discussions and decisions. However, Curzon was not finished with his Machiavellian style of diplomacy and attempted to subvert this. On November 14, Curzon sent the French and Italian governments his proposal for a peace treaty, which, with minor modifications, restated many of the terms of the Treaty of Sèvres.[8] He threatened to withdraw from the conference if the Allies did not support his demands, which included demilitarizing the straits, the payment of indemnities and reparations, reinstating the Capitulations, and limiting Turkish sovereignty in Thrace and Istanbul. Although Poincaré had previously told İsmet that France would protect the Turks' interests, he backed off and acquiesced to Curzon's demands.[9] It was only on November 20, just before the conference opened, that Poincaré bothered to tell İsmet what the Allies intended the outcome of the conference to be. The president of the Swiss Confederation opened the conference on the afternoon of November 20, after which Curzon made a statement indicating that the three Allies were in agreement about the direction the conference would take. İsmet then approached the podium and gave a speech that contradicted Curzon by stating that Turkey was not a defeated nation that had to accept punishment. It was a shot across the bow that would frame the Turks' positions throughout the remainder of the conference and which meant trouble for Curzon.

The negotiations began on the morning of November 21, with Curzon chairing the conference. Curzon, supported by the French and the Italians, then established procedural rules that marginalized the Turks and to which İsmet lodged immediate objections. Pushing ahead without İsmet's blessings, Curzon then established specialized committees to examine the issues. There were three principal committees: territorial and military questions (chaired by Curzon himself); the regime of foreigners and minorities (chaired by Eugenio Garroni of Italy); and economic questions, ports, and railways (chaired by Camille Barrère of France).[10] İsmet protested again, insisting that a Turk ought to chair one of these committees.

Curzon then insisted that all discussions be held in secret, and, of course, İsmet again protested but to no avail. The territorial committee met the next day, while the capitulations and economics committees met in early December. Former Greek prime minister Venizelos, now consultant of foreign affairs for the new government in Greece, attended many committee meetings, consistently attempting to advance Greek interests, while İsmet protested every step along the way.[11]

The Turkish positions at Lausanne came directly from Mustafa Kemal in Ankara, and it is worth reviewing them here.[12] It is important to keep in mind that Kemal believed that he was negotiating on behalf of the Nationalists who had won the war of national liberation rather than on behalf of the Ottomans who had lost World War I. First and foremost on Kemal's agenda was foreign recognition of Turkey's full independence and sovereignty, which was nonnegotiable. Kemal regarded the eastern border as a settled issue, and Kemal's main priority in territorial issues was to establish the western border on the Meriç River with full Turkish sovereignty in Istanbul and eastern Thrace, including the Gallipoli Peninsula. Regarding western Thrace (today eastern Bulgaria and Greece from Thessaloniki [the Turkish view] or the Nestos River [the Greek view] to the Meriç River), Kemal supported a plebiscite, but he held that western Thrace was a strategic liability. He was also prepared to delay resolution of the status of Mosul, which was then occupied by the British, for the same reason (that it was valuable but that it was also a strategic liability). There were other territorial issues, such as the return of most of the Aegean islands and the demilitarization of the ones remaining in Greek hands. Kemal also opposed the revival of any legacy Greek, Armenian, or Kurdish territorial claims arising from the abandoned Treaty of Sèvres. Regarding economic issues, Kemal was determined to end the long-hated Capitulatory Regime, which granted unequal concessions and extraterritoriality to foreigners. Last, Kemal supported the exchange of ethnic populations between Greece and Turkey. Kemal explicitly instructed and trusted İsmet and his team to deliver these terms at Lausanne. With regard to a Turkish negotiation strategy, İsmet adopted a Fabian strategy of waiting until the enemy exhausted himself, and then striking the killing blow.

In early January 1923, as he had done previously at the Sèvres conference, Curzon presented a draft treaty, which ignored many of İsmet's conditions. Over the next few weeks, İsmet fought every day to revise Curzon's draft. On January 30, Curzon presented his final draft of a proposed treaty, the terms of which included many of İsmet's demands, including recognition and full sovereignty of Turkish authority in eastern Thrace; the denial of Greek, Armenian, and Kurdish claims based on Sèvres; and population exchanges. However, Curzon denied the Turks the Meriç River border; imposed a straits convention, including demilitarization of the Gallipoli Peninsula; abolished capitulations in name but left many legacy concessions; deferred the Mosul question to League of Nations arbitration; and imposed 12 million gold pounds in reparations.[13] İsmet refused to agree to the terms and asked for instructions from Ankara. Over the week that followed, the parties repeatedly met for discussions, during which İsmet asked for far more than the Allies were willing to accept. Some minor changes were made to appease the Turks, but Curzon was furious and unable to comprehend İsmet's intransigence. On February 7, Kemal instructed İsmet not to sign the treaty, mainly because Turkey had been treated like a defeated nation rather than as a victor. Curzon returned to London, and the British absolutely refused to make any further changes to Curzon's draft treaty.[14] The conference collapsed entirely when İsmet returned to Istanbul with his delegation on February 16.

While the main negotiations collapsed, there were bilateral issues between the Turks and the Greeks that were settled at Lausanne, one of the most contentious of which was the exchange of prisoners of war and the exchange of ethnic populations. On January 30, 1923, the Greek and Turkish delegates signed a treaty regarding the exchange of populations and prisoners of war.[15] Titled the Convention Concerning the Exchange of Greek and Turkish Populations (also known as Lausanne Peace Treaty VI), the agreement explicitly outlined a compulsory exchange of Orthodox Greeks from Turkey and Muslim Turks from Greece, excluding the Greeks of Istanbul and the Turks of western Thrace.[16] The exchanges were to be conducted in installments (as outlined in Article IV of the treaty) and would begin on May 1, 1923. Property was to be liquidated, sold, and its value adjudicated by a mixed commission. While this might have made sense to Venizelos and İsmet at the time and on paper, in execution it would prove arbitrary and brutal, with long-lasting consequences.[17]

The Greek and the diaspora Armenian delegations in Paris were "overjoyed at the breakdown of negotiations," while Kemal prepared to resume the war.[18] Not every politician in Ankara supported such a course of action, and, for the next two weeks, the Grand National Assembly met in secret to debate the future.[19] Once again, Prime Minister Rauf came to Kemal's aid by explaining and supporting his views. Kemal insisted that Ankara's negotiators needed the full support of the assembly if negotiations resumed. Consequently, on March 6, the Grand National Assembly gave the government an overwhelming vote of confidence to continue with negotiations in the direction articulated by Kemal. The next day, the Council of Ministers met in Ankara to write its own version of a draft treat. The result was a 100-page text that, first and foremost, demanded that future relations be based on the independence and sovereignty of the participating states. The proposed ministerial draft reaffirmed the Meriç River boundary; proposed a settlement for the Aegean islands disputes; reaffirmed the southern border in accordance with the previously signed Franco-Turkish treaty and placed Mosul into League of Nations arbitration; and contained draft agreements to end capitulations that included compensation for the Powers, repayment of the Ottoman debt, adjudicated reparations between Greece and Turkey directly without Allied interference, and amended other smaller clauses.[20] Ankara also invited the Powers to reconvene the peace conference anywhere at any time and sent the ministerial drafts to the Allied capitals.

While this was being settled, the Greeks and Turks again attempted to work bilaterally through the thorny issues of reparations, compensation, the Greco-Turkish border, and a more granular definition of the populations to be exchanged. At one such two-hour meeting between Venizelos and İsmet, they approached the issue of reparations as an equation of human lives lost being balanced by compensation for destroyed property but came to no agreement. For every demand Venizelos made, İsmet made a counterdemand. İsmet and the delegation returned to Lausanne on April 21, and the conference resumed two days later. Negotiations then continued, and many of the points of contention were handled through compromise.

In mid-May Greece demanded huge reparations and threatened to invade eastern Thrace. İsmet responded on May 18 by asserting that Turkey ought to receive compensation for the huge amount of damage Greece had inflicted in western Anatolia during its withdrawal from Afyonkarahisar. This led to a bilateral agreement directly between Venizelos and İsmet on May 26 regarding the adjudication of damages.[21] Despite these steps forward, the revolutionary government in Athens became increasingly frustrated and threatened to reinvade eastern Thrace if the Allies could not force the Turks to concede. Consequently, it ordered the Army of Hebrus to prepare for an offensive to seize Istanbul.[22] Moreover, some in the Greek government, including Pangalos, favored the public renunciation of the Mudanya agreement to help justify a new war. Trying to quell these tensions, the Allies sent Athens a strongly worded note on May 29, cautioning the government not to resume hostilities. However, the Greeks did not respond and, troubled by the absence of a reply, the British then demanded a meeting. In turn, a secret meeting between the Allies, the Greeks, and the Turks convened at 3:30 a.m. on June 8 in the offices of the British mission in Lausanne. Venizelos was persuaded to convince his government to return to negotiations rather than to restart the war. Two days later, Athens ordered its army and fleet to stand down.[23]

These kinds of tensions led the negotiating teams to meet continuously throughout June and early July, with the primary stumbling block being capitulations. The Turks succeeded in ending judicial and extraterritorial capitulations but could not budge the Allies on relinquishing economic concessions. Kemal instructed İsmet to return home. However, Curzon, at last reconciled to the idea that the Turks would not retreat from or concede their positions, agreed to Ankara's terms. The conference adjourned on July 17 with each delegate making a final statement. The Treaty of Lausanne, with 17 appendices (including separate peace treaties with Britain, Greece, Italy, France, Romania, and Japan), was signed by all the delegates on July 24, 1923.[24] The Grand National Assembly ratified the treaty a month later on August 24.

THE POSTWAR TURKISH ARMY

Throughout the period from the Mudanya Armistice and the signing of the Treaty of Lausanne, the Nationalist Army remained ready for the resumption of hostilities against both the Greeks and the Allies. However, on July 26, immediately after the signing of the peace treaty, the general headquarters of the Nationalist Army and the Western Front Command moved by rail to Ankara and immediately began to plan for a return to a peacetime posture.[25] Fevzi and the General Staff prepared a foundational reorganization plan (*Hazar Kuruluş ve Konuş Projesi*) on August 5, which transitioned the wartime army to a peacetime posture. On August 30, 1923, Fevzi published orders to take effect on September 1. The wartime front commands—the Western, Eastern, and Elcezire Front Commands—were inactivated, as were the two field armies, as the army transitioned to its traditional peacetime garrison configuration. Under the plan, the Turkish Army would again be composed of three army inspectorates that would have authority over the training and organization of the peacetime army, as well as the army's transition to wartime strength when activated by mobilization orders.[26] The army inspectorates would command nine army corps each of two infantry divisions. Additionally, three cavalry divisions would be assigned to army corps in frontier regions, and the famous V Cavalry Corps would transition to become a normal infantry corps (see table 12.1).

As planned, the Third Army Inspectorate on Turkey's eastern frontier was the largest in the army, with eight infantry and one cavalry division. This was in response to the creation of the Union of Soviet Socialist Republics in December 1922, which had absorbed the Transcaucasian and Transcaspian breakaway nations, and was again developing into a military threat. The First Army inspectorate followed with six infantry divisions

Table 12.1   The Turkish Republican Army in 1923

First Army Inspectorate (Ankara)		
II Corps	Balıkesir	4th Division—Edremit
		11th Division—Bursa
III Corps	Istanbul	1st Division—Üsküdar
		61st Division—Çorlu
		2nd Cavalry Division—Lüleburgaz
IV Corps	Eskişehir	8th Division—Ankara
		23rd Division—İzmit
Second Army inspectorate (Konya)		
I Corps	Afyonkarahisar	6th Division—Denizli
		57th Division—Izmir
V Corps	Konya	7th Division—Adana
		41st Division—Niğde
Third Army Inspectorate (Diyarbakır)		
VI Corps	Tokat	5th Division—Sivas
		15th Division—Samsun
VII Corps	Erzincan	2nd Division—Muş
		17th Division—Elazığ
		14th Cavalry Division—Urfa

Table 12.1   (continued)

VIII Corps	Erzincan	3rd Division—Trabzon
		16th Division—Erzincan
IX Corps	Erzurum	9th Division—Kars
		12th Division—Sarıkamış
		1st Cavalry Division—Karaköse
Fortress Commands*		Çatalca, Izmir, Kars, and Erzurum

*Because of the clauses in the Treaty of Lausanne regarding the demilitarization of the straits, the previous Ottoman Fortress Commands at the Dardanelles and the Bosporus were not reactivated as planned.

Source: Abidin Tüzel, *Türk İstiklâl Harbi Batı Cephesi: İstiklâl Harbinin Son Safhası (18 Eylül-1 Kasım 1923),* IInci cilt 6ncı kısım IV kitap (Ankara: Genelkurmay Basımevi, 1969), 268.

and one cavalry division. With tensions between Turkey, Greece, and Bulgaria settling down, only one infantry division and one cavalry division occupied garrisons in eastern Thrace. The Second Army Inspectorate did not maintain a presence on the land frontiers and acted as a central strategic reserve. The demobilization and movements back to the peacetime garrisons were completed by November 1. According to the last volume of the Turkish Army's official history, "For this reason it is appropriate to end the Turkish Independence War on July 24, 1923, and to end the Turkish Independence War Campaign on November 1, 1923."[27]

THE ESTABLISHMENT OF THE REPUBLIC OF TURKEY

The Treaty of Lausanne guaranteed full recognition of Turkey as the legal successor-state to the Ottoman Empire. In turn, the Grand National Assembly officially proclaimed the Republic of Turkey on October 29, 1923, with its capital in the remote Anatolian hill town of Ankara. Over the summer, Rauf and Kemal had a falling-out over the role that Kemal and İsmet would take in the new republic.[28] Both Rauf and Ali Fuat were concerned that when İsmet returned, Kemal would hand over the reins of power to him. This turned out to be true, and Rauf resigned as prime minister on August 4, ceding the position Fethi (Okyar). On August 13, İsmet returned in triumph from Lausanne, and, that day, the Grand National Assembly elected Kemal as its president.[29] He was unopposed. İsmet became the Republic of Turkey's first prime minister on October 30, 1923. The final legacy apparatus of the Ottoman state, the caliphate, was abolished on March 3, 1924, and Abdülmecid, the last caliph, left for exile in Switzerland.

There remained a number of lingering problems, such as the status of Mosul and Hatay Province, but the most compelling problem confronting the Turks after the war was the forced population exchange agreed upon by Venizelos and İsmet in January 1923.[30] There had already been a first wave of refugees in September and October 1922 from Izmir and the Aegean littoral, the total number of which remains contested today. However, the story of the mass evacuation of Anatolian Greeks and Armenians from Izmir is well known (and documented) today, and a total expulsion of a quarter million refugees is not an unreasonable estimate.[31] The Mudanya Armistice caused another smaller wave of mostly Christians to evacuate Istanbul and Thrace. Many of these refugees were children, women, and the elderly, and, according to one historian, one million refugees arrived in Greece prior to 1923.[32] Many of these were Ottoman Armenians and other minority groups who fled alongside Anatolian, Pontic, and Thracian Greeks.

The overall numbers of the exchanged populations are contested, but, according to the League of Nations administered Greek-Turkish Mixed Commission convened in 1934, one million people categorized as Orthodox Greeks had been uprooted from Anatolia and eastern Thrace immediately before and during the population exchange, which commenced in 1923, while 350,000 persons categorized as Muslim Turks had been removed from Greece and the Aegean islands.[33] These numbers have always looked lopsided, penalizing the Greeks, who appear to have lost far more in the way of valuable property and traditional land. However, it is important to consider that the Greek victory in the Balkan Wars of 1912–1913 resulted in the Greek acquisition of Epirus and some parts of southern Macedonia, within which lived a substantial Muslim population. After the Balkan Wars ended in summer 1913, a mass expulsion of Muslims forcibly removed perhaps as many as a quarter million persons to Ottoman territory from Greece.[34] According to the Turks, the expulsions and exchanges continued in 1914, which further forcibly removed and transferred another 100,000 Muslims from Greece to Anatolia and 45,000 ethnic Greeks from the Anatolian Aegean littorals to Greece.[35] Considering the entire span from 1912 through the mid-1920s, it is not unreasonable to think that the total numbers of expelled and exchanged populations were roughly equal.

The transfers were, in the words of American historian Sarah Shields, "internationally administered ethnic cleansing" in that an international treaty contained the operative mechanisms for forcible population transfers and the post-1923 exchanges were sanctioned and administered by the League of Nations.[36] The conditions for arriving refugees were abysmal on both sides of the Aegean, and, while the international community provided some help, it was not enough. Moreover, thousands of Pontic Greeks were transferred directly from the Nationalist Central Army's prison camps to marginally better camps in poverty-stricken Greece.

CONCLUSION

Time was on the Turk's side at Lausanne, and Kemal had everything to gain by holding out as long as possible. As at Mudanya, the physically diminutive İsmet proved a tough and relentless negotiator who wore his opponents down over a sustained period. Interestingly, after Mudanya, it became widely known that İsmet was mostly deaf, and he often ignored what was being said at Lausanne. It is unknown today whether this was a deliberate negotiating tactic or whether İsmet really could not hear. In any event, his disability seemed to help him in the long and drawn-out negotiations. The Turkish War of Independence, also called the Turkish National Struggle, ended, to the surprise of the world, with a resounding Nationalist victory. Looking into the future in early 1920, this was by no means a predictable outcome and can, in many ways, be attributed to the dynamic presence of Mustafa Kemal. It is hard to image the Nationalist victory without Kemal's inspiring, constant, and visionary leadership.

NOTES

1. Churchill, *The Aftermath*, 437.
2. Mango, *Atatürk*, 356.
3. Shaw, *From Empire to Republic*, vol. 4, 1882.

4. Ökse, Baycan, and Sakaryalı, *Komutanların Biyografileri*, 218.

5. Shaw, *From Empire to Republic*, vol. 4, 1883–1884.

6. Ibid., 1890; and Mango, *Atatürk*, 365. Ali Kemal (1867–1922) was the great-grandfather of British politician Boris Johnson.

7. Mango, *Atatürk*, 365–366.

8. Shaw, *From Empire to Republic*, vol. 4, 1904–1905.

9. Ibid., 1900–1913 for a comprehensive presentation of the Curzon-Poincaré discussions.

10. Shaw, *From Empire to Republic*, vol. 4, 1915–1916.

11. For the most comprehensive narrative of the Turkish positions during these discussions, see Shaw, *From Empire to Republic*, vol. 4, 1915–1940.

12. Mango, *Atatürk*, 366–367.

13. Shaw, *From Empire to Republic*, vol. 4, 1941–1943.

14. Eleftheria Daleziou, "Britain and the Greek-Turkish War and Settlement of 1919–1923: The Pursuit of Security by 'Proxy' in Western Asia Minor (inpublished PhD diss., University of Glasgow, 2002), 284–290. Daleziou makes the argument that Curzon's behavior was largely deliberate.

15. Gedeon, Paschalidou, and Dima-Dimitrou, *A Concise History of the Campaign in Asia Minor*, 509–510.

16. For the complete text of the Convention Concerning the Exchange of Greek and Turkish Populations, January 30, 1923 see the Republic of Turkey, Ministry of Foreign Affairs website at http://www.mfa.gov.tr/lausanne-peace-treaty-vi_-convention-concerning-the-exchange-of-greek-and-turkish-populations-signed-at-lausanne_.en.mfa.

17. See also Onur Yildirim, *Diplomacy and Displacement: Reconsidering the Turco-Greek Exchange of Populations, 1922–1934* (New York: Routledge, 2006).

18. Shaw, *From Empire to Republic*, vol. 4, 1950. The Republic of Armenia no longer existed, and the U.S.S.R. represented Soviet Armenia at the conference.

19. Shaw may have exaggerated the break. More specialist literature brings a more nuanced picture of controlled escalation by both sides. See John Darwin, "An Undeclared Empire: The British in the Middle East, 1918–39," *The Journal of Imperial and Commonwealth History* 27, no. 2 (1999): 159–176; and Michael M. Finefrock, "Ataturk, Lloyd George and the Megali Idea: Cause and Consequence of the Greek Plan to Seize Constantinople from the Allies, June–August 1922," *The Journal of Modern History* vol. 52, no. 1, On-Demand Supplement (March, 1980): D1047–D1066.

20. Shaw, *From Empire to Republic*, vol. 4, 1952–1953.

21. Ibid., 1956–1957.

22. Gedeon, Paschalidou, and Dima-Dimitrou, *A Concise History of the Campaign in Asia Minor*, 512.

23. Ibid., 513.

24. For the full text of the Treaty of Lausanne, July 24, 1923, see "Lausanne Treaty," Hellenic Resources Network, http://www.hri.org/docs/lausanne/.

25. Tüzel, *Son Safhası*, 267.

26. Ibid., 268–271.

27. Ibid., 272.

28. Mango, *Atatürk*, 385–389.

29. Shaw, *From Empire to Republic*, vol. 4, 1964–1965.

30. Clark, *Twice a Stranger*, 11–16.

31. Richter, *The Greek-Turkish War*, 169.

32. Ibid., 180; and Sean McMeekin, *The Ottoman Endgame: War, Revolution, and the Making of the Modern Middle East, 1908–1923* (New York: Penguin Press, 2015), 487–492.

33. Umit Özsu, "'A Thoroughly Bad and Vicious Solution': Humanitarianism, the World Court, and the Modern Origins of Population Transfer," *London Review of International Law* 1, no. 1 (2013): 99–110.

34. Igor Despot, "The Balkan Wars: An Expected Opportunity for Ethnic Cleansing," *Journal of Muslim Minority Affairs* 39, no. 3 (2019): 343–355; Justin McCarthy, *Death and Exile: The Ethnic Cleansing of Ottoman Muslims, 1821–1922* (Princeton: Darwin Press, 1995), 250–291.

35. Elçin Macar, "The Muslim Emigration in Western Anatolia," *Cahiers Balkaniques* (Online) 40 (2012), https://doi.org/10.4000/ceb.922; and Llewellyn-Smith, *Ionian Vision*, 30–32.

36. Sarah Shields, "The Greek-Turkish Population Exchange: Internationally Administered Ethnic Cleansing," *Middle East Report* no. 267 (2013): 2–6.

Conclusion

Over stony roads, through the defiles of thorny and rock-clad hills, across ochre deserts baking in the sun, the weary, sullen caravan of Facts kept pertinaciously jogging along.[1]

Winston S. Churchill, 1929

A WAR MADE OF WARS

To call these wars Total War may be somewhat misleading, but in all the important metrics it was a total war for the Armenians, the Greeks, and the Nationalists. It involved the nearly total mobilization of Armenia and Greece and the total mobilization of the remaining Ottoman citizens living in Anatolia under the Nationalists. Both sides fought to social, physical, and financial exhaustion, and it was a war that fought for an absolute—the right to claim lands in perpetuity. Defeat was ruinous to Armenia, Greece, and to the insurgent groups in Nationalist territory. As a precursor to the victimization of civilians in World War II, these wars proved deadly to civilians of all ethnicities when atrocities and criminality were perpetrated by rogue elements of every combatant state. Likewise, the massive population exchanges of 1923 presaged the expulsion of German and Eastern European populations in 1945–1946.

In the contemporary modern memory of Turkey, what is called the National Struggle has achieved a unitary narrative centering on the Ankara leadership's waging of the War of Independence. From the Turkish Nationalist perspective, the struggle might also be called a hybrid war because it contained elements of irregular war, counterinsurgency campaigning, multifront campaigning, secret diplomacy with the young Soviet Union, aligning domestic political activism, propaganda, and a revolt against the rump Ottoman government—all combined with conventional military operations against conventional armies. In truth, this was a "war made of wars," with a vast future hanging in the balance.[2]

GREAT MEN OR GREAT EVENTS?

There are schools of thought among historians regarding the question, Do great events create great men, or do great men create great events? Most of us believe that there is some truth in both ideas and that reality exists somewhere in the middle. But consider that throughout this book, the narrative hinges on the decisions of three men in particular, David Lloyd George, Eleutherios Venizelos, and Mustafa Kemal, all of whom emerge as powerful personalities driven by a complicated mix of patriotism, ability, vanity, and visionary ideas. As an outside force affecting these events, Lloyd George's shifting allegiances, first favoring a Greater Greece but later favoring a strong Turkey, certainly altered the outcome of the struggle. The principal players of the warring parties, Venizelos and Kemal shared the vision of creating modern nation-states in the Westphalian tradition, but these visions collided in western Anatolia, which, geographically, was vital to each man's dream. If you take these three leaders out of these events, it is hard to imagine the Greco-Turkish War lasting as long as it did. The other fronts certainly produced decisive and focused personalities and leaders—Karabekir, Nazarbekian, and Çerkez Ethem, for example—but their effect was always localized in time and space. We might also add that Gounares was also driven but consumed by his hate of Venizelos and, thus, focused too much on the war as a vehicle of domestic politics.

The Nationalist struggle was an inevitable outcome of the deliberate and self-serving political fragmentation of Anatolia written into the Treaty of Sèvres by the Allied powers. War became inevitable because of the meddling of the Allies, especially Great Britain and its championing of Greek interests under Lloyd George, as well as from Allied decisions to occupy significant parts of mainland Anatolia and America's refusal to participate in the League of Nations' mandates. Military intervention by Greece then followed, driven largely by the powerful personality of Eleutherios Venizelos and his obsessive vision of a trans-Aegean Greece. Unfortunately for Venizelos, who understood the risks but tried to leverage the imperialism of the Great Powers to achieve Greek goals, his country became a proxy for the ambitions of European powers seeking both advantage and territory among the ruins of the Ottoman Empire. Venizelos's personal calculations were upended by the loss of the 1920 election when he fell from power. In turn, Mustafa Kemal, whose appearance as a historical force could hardly have been predicted in 1919, led an unexpectedly successful Turkish Nationalist revival, which forced the Greeks into recapitalizing their strategic investment. Without Venizelos's strategic purpose and vision, what seemed to be straightforward decisions for Greece in 1919 turned into unsolvable dilemmas in 1922, from which there was no turning back.

STRATEGY AND OPERATIONS

Successful strategy always depends on a realistic balancing of ends, ways, and means (ends: what you want to accomplish; ways: how you intend to accomplish it; and means: the resources you will commit), as well as its corollary demands that decision-makers must continuously rebalance ends-ways-means, as the changing characteristics of the conflict evolve over time and in space. While understated in the Nationalist and Turkish narrative, the Nationalists pursued a Fabian strategy by the careful preservation of the army, weakening of the principal enemy (Greece), and then the turn to the strategic offensive. Such a strategy is essentially a point-to-point path that allows for rebalancing ends-ways-means in stride, and it is a strategy that favors the side unhindered by time constraints. Traditionally it has been a risk-averse strategy, which hinges on the enemy reaching an identifiable culmination point. In the Turkish War of Independence, the Nationalists gathered strength in the period 1918–1921 by avoiding defeat against the Greeks and eliminating the eastern and southern fronts with minimalist forces. After Sakarya, they spent almost a year preparing their army for decisive offensive operations against the Greeks, which successfully ended the war on Nationalist terms. The Nationalists had everything to gain by extending the war for several years and by trading space for force preservation.

Their enemies, on the other hand, clung to the idea of military victory, but they all grew weaker over time—the Armenians by the loss of external support, the French by the financial costs of the postwar occupation of the Middle East, and the Greeks by both internal financial and manpower constraints, as well as the loss of external support. Greek strategy used a conventional Jominian western approach to seek the decisive battle but, unfortunately for that country, came to a Clausewitzian culmination point beyond the Sakarya and Gök Rivers in the dangerous summer of 1921.

At the operational level, both the Greeks and the Nationalists calculated their objectives, and each sought to concentrate their armies at the decisive point in time and space. Ultimately, the Nationalists were more successful in this. Tactically, while there were trenches dug by the combatants, these wars were unlike World War I—this war was a war of maneuver. The conventional campaigns of these wars were characterized by large-scale forces maneuvering over large operational areas, and this created a tactical dynamic in which mobility and initiative multiplied combat effectiveness. In the end, the Nationalists were better at this as well. This was a result of the legacy of Ottoman Army command practices and its German-style professional military education system, as well as from the enormous reservoir of hard-won experiences accumulated by Ottoman officers on the fighting fronts from 1912 to 1918.

The importance of geography, as well as the positioning of the operational lines of communication of Asia Minor must be considered. In general, geography favored the Nationalists. There was ample space to trade for time as Kemal's armies retreated into Anatolia. Moreover, the Nationalists were not compelled tactically or emotionally to fight to the death for anything (as the French had fought for Verdun in 1916). The north-south orientation of many of the rivers created natural defensive lines for the Nationalist armies, as did the mountainous choke point at Dumlupınar. Moreover, the existence of such mountain chains served to compartmentalize enemy operations to the advantage of the Nationalists, particularly the Turkmen Mountains against the Greeks, the Amanus Mountains against the French, and the western Caucasus against the Armenians.

The critical importance of railroads in staging logistics and reinforcing armies in nineteenth- and twentieth-century military operations cannot be overstated. These served, especially in the Greco-Nationalist campaigns, to focus army operations along easily defined avenues of approach. Geography also penalized the Armenians, Greeks, and French by creating an unfavorable relationship of troops to task—there was simply too much space for their small and underequipped armies to control. The weather also became a factor, affecting operations at every level during the late fall-winter, early-spring seasons, which slowed down or halted military operations. This certainly favored the Nationalists in the winter of

1920–1921 by shielding the army from further Greek offensives and, then again, in 1921–1922 by providing an opportunity to refit and enlarge the army for offensive operations.

COMMANDERS AND ARMIES

The Nationalists were blessed to have a readily available pool of senior officers whose service and experiences in the Balkan Wars and in World War I ensured a first-rate command slate for the Nationalist armies. Those earlier wars had, to a certain extent, culled the herd, and the surviving senior officers were talented, aggressive, imperturbable in crisis, and experienced in modern war. The importance to the Nationalist cause of a cadre of trained and experienced senior Ottoman General Staff Officers (graduates of the elite Ottoman War Academy) cannot be overemphasized.

At the highest levels, İsmet proved himself to be a capable and active army group commander, especially when closely supported by Kemal and Fevzi. His performance as a field army commander was also characterized by focused and well-coordinated operations. Of note, İsmet was particularly effective in the operational-level counterattack, as shown at Eskişehir and Afyonkarahisar in 1921. It is certainly true that İsmet grew as a senior commander over time, and Kemal must receive credit for keeping him in command amid disaster, thus allowing him to grow in effectiveness.

Equally impressive was Kâzım Karabekir's handling of the independent operations of the XV Corps against Armenia, which amounted to a field army effort. Had Karabekir not demonstrated political aspirations, Kemal might have transferred him to army command against the Greeks in the west. In 1922, for much shorter periods under far more favorable circumstances. As a field army commander, Nurettin was a "closer" and known for getting the job done. Both he and Yakup Şevki also turned in admirable performances in the final campaigns of the war. At army corps level, the Nationalists also enjoyed an abundance of talented, aggressive, and capable commanders. These included Fahrettin, İzzettin, Kemalettin Sami, and Selahattin. These men were Ottoman General Staff officers and had enjoyed privileged assignments, which prepared them to exercise initiative on the battlefield. Also worthy of note was the Kocaeli Group commander, Colonel Halit, who did well in a corps-level equivalent command. At the divisional level, Şükrü Naili's 15th Division's magnificent stand on the Chal Dag during the hardest fighting of the Sakarya Campaign is worthy of note. It also must be said that rebel leaders Çerkez Ethem and

Demirci Mehmet Efe were charismatic and decisive commanders who understood their own strengths and weaknesses relative to the Nationalists, thus enabling and prolonging their rebellions.

At the highest levels, the Greeks were severely penalized by domestic politics, which disorganized national strategy and changed priorities. King Constantine was often at odds with the leaders of the army. According to Prince Andrew of Greece, Constantine's first choice was Stephanos Gennades, an able veteran with lots of command experience, but, in the end, Gennades took command of the police and interior security forces (an important position for the security of the new regime).[3]

In the Greek ranks, Anastasios Papoulas, the principal commander at field army level, was an ineffective commander. He was reluctant to make decisions, unable to plan operations, and most importantly, unable to impose his will on his own staff and his subordinates. He was fortunate to be backed up by deputy chief of staff Sarrigiannis, who was an able planner and had a good grasp of tactics and war. Moreover, Papoulas's unwillingness to make decisions led to the undercurrent of competition between Chief of Staff Pallis and his deputy Sarrigiannis to undermining Greek planning in 1921. However, his handling of the tactical retreat from the Sakarya was masterful, and we might characterize his strength as reactive under pressure. The team of Leonidas Paraskevopoulas and Theodoros Pangalos enjoyed a good working relationship and was very effective. The Greco-Turkish War might have achieved a better outcome had they been left in place to prosecute the campaign in the fall of 1920. The assignment of Georgios Chatzanestes led to strategic catastrophe. Of the army corps commanders, Konstantinos Nider and Georgios Polymenakos proved the most able. Alexandros Kontoulis failed to pursue Refet in March 1921, and Nikolaos Trikoupes failed to take active control before the Great Offensive and lost control quickly during the Nationalist attacks. At divisional level, Colonel Ioannes Trivilas (5th Division) and Colonel Athanasios Frangou (1st Division) stand out from the rest as courageous and resourceful commanders.

In Armenia, Tovmas Nazarbekian proved an able army commander. His reorganization of the republic's armed forces enabled them to stay in the field and operational longer than expected. But, at corps level, Harutium Hovsepian proved a failure while Grigorii Shelkovnikian (Sholkovnikov) was largely untested. Among the Allies, the French commander in Cilicia, Noël Marie Amédée Garnier-Duplessis proved able in very difficult circumstances. British commander in the Turkish Straits region, Tim Harrington's decisive analysis and diplomatic skills prudently diffused what could have erupted into a full-scale war.

In terms of understanding the capability of the various armies, the strength of the Nationalist Army was clearly its cadre of experienced senior commanders, while the strength of the Greek Army lay in its cadre of regimental commanders. Nothing would have saved the Armenians from Karabekir's offensive, and it is difficult to gauge their efforts. The French efforts in Cilicia reflected their vast global experiences in counter–irregular warfare, showcasing the initiative of their regimental officers. The British and Italians did not fight but proved able administrators of occupation forces.

CHIEFS OF STAFF AND LOGISTICIANS

The complementary relationship between the commander and his chief of staff is the subject of a wide and rich literature, with the German experience of 1870–1945 forming much of the core. The reason for this is that the General Staff system in use by all European armies in the early twentieth century was a Prussian and German military innovation and system. The most well-known such relationship today is that of Paul von Hindenburg (commander) and Erich von Ludendorff (chief of staff) in World War I. Hindenburg was steady and imperturbable and had commanding presence while Ludendorff was brilliant, volatile, and a good planner. In a short summary, their personalities and skills were complementary.

At the highest levels, the Nationalist pairing of Mustafa Kemal and Fevzi (chief of the Nationalist General Staff) proved to be a brilliant success in waging sustained total war. At the theater level, İsmet's chief of staff was the able and experienced Colonel Âsım (Gündüz). Colonel Âsım was a trained General Staff officer with service on the Ottoman General Staff who, during World War I, served as a division commander, a corps chief of staff, and a field army chief of staff. In İsmet's earlier battles, he was well served by Lieutenant Colonel Naci (Tınaz). On the Greek side, the most effective pairing of commander and chief of staff in the FAAM was that of Leonidas Paraskevopoulos and Theodoros Pangalos. They were followed by Anastasios Papoulas, an ineffective commander, who was fortunately backed up by the solid and able Colonel Ptolemaios Sarrigiannis, who was a very competent planner.

In the matter of logistics, the Nationalists empowered Minister of War Refet during the 1921–1922 strategic pause to coordinate the acquisition of munitions and supplies, as well as to consolidate and streamline the lines of communication. He did so with speed and efficiency. On the Greek side, Georgios Spyridonos, the logistics chief of the FAAM, did an excellent job overall, despite the operational overreach of the geographically overextended Greek Army.

MODERN MEMORY

The preponderance of western literature, factual and fictional, dealing with the events in Asia Minor/Anatolia during the period 1918–1923 highlights two themes: civilian victimization during the conflicts and the fatal outcomes of the massive forced population exchanges agreed to by the participants after the war. This literature is often characterized by the apportionment of blame and the assignment of responsibility. To say that it is polarized belies the fundamental disagreement in interpretation of the facts by the opposing narratives.

The problem of minority communities within the Ottoman Empire and within Greece began long before the 1920s. As parts of the Ottoman Empire, broken off in the nineteenth and early twentieth centuries, were absorbed by neighbors or became independent, Muslim communities were left behind. These communities numbered in the millions of inhabitants. Similarly, Christian and non-Turk communities had existed since ancient times in Anatolia—also numbering in the millions of inhabitants. The involuntary transfers and resettlements resulting from the Balkan Wars of 1912–1913 exaggerated this situation. Moreover, the ill-treatment of Ottoman Greeks, Ottoman Armenians, and other minorities at the hands of the Young Turks during the Great War further inflamed animosities and tensions. In the case of the Greek-Turkish War, the fundamental problem involved identifying and labeling constituent groups. There were subgroups of "others" who did not easily fit into one category or another—Ottoman Armenian refugees living in Greece, for example. Despite this, Greek and Nationalist decision-makers determined to homogenize ethnically their previously heterodox populations. Thus, because of this war, perhaps as many as 1.5 million "Greeks" were sent west, and .5 million "Turks" were sent east. The number of tragic stories and diaspora narratives produced as a result are staggering, as are the documented cases of crimes against these relocated peoples.

It is a sad but true statement that civilian victimization and a basic lack of humanitarian compassion for civilians often accompanied war in the twentieth century. As a military concern, civilian victimization and population exchanges did not figure into wartime strategic or operational decision-making in the struggle for Asia Minor/Anatolia. Neither did demographic engineering figure into political decisions to go to war or to continue the war. Arguably, at the time, the postwar population exchanges were thought to bring stability to the region by decreasing the problem of restive minorities in nation-states.

THE COST

Accurate statistics regarding military and civilian casualties, financial losses, and the cost of war damage to infrastructure and property are wildly disparate and heavily politicized. Many of the tabulations include statistics and data from the entire World War I period (1914–1923)—this is especially true of estimates regarding Turks and Armenians. Moreover, many of the numbers are suspiciously exact; for example, the Concise Greek History asserts that 9,362 Greek soldiers were killed in the campaigns in Asia Minor (from 1919–1923),[4] while Fahri Belen noted that 9,167 Nationalist soldiers were killed on the same front in the same time period.[5] It is difficult to reconcile these precise numbers with general numbers provided by other authors. For example, Heinz Richter asserted that 13,000 Greek soldiers were killed in the war, and 10,000 Greek soldiers were taken prisoner.[6] This is contradicted by Belen, who stated that 25–30,000 Greek officers and men were taken prisoner in the war.[7] Getting at actual and authentic hard data regarding casualties in the year 2021 is problematic at best.

Rather than inserting a recapitulation or summary into the text of the various estimates existing today, readers are referred to Appendix A: "Casualties," written by Professor Konstantinos Travlos and provided to the author. Professor Travlos's review and compilation of available data is, I believe, the most thorough in existence today, and I am proud to include it herein. It is also consequential to note that the financial cost to the participants was staggering. Britain, for example (which lost few soldiers), spent some £20,000,000 over the course of occupying the straits and in operations in Anatolia.[8]

FINIS

In a recently published book, Australian historian Jeremy Salt noted, "Precise detailed truth about the past is not attainable. The historian can only draw as close as possible to what he or she thinks is the truth. No wise historian would ever claim to *the* truth."[9] This book is not *the* truth—it is simply my interpretation of what happened in the struggles that occurred in Anatolia and Asia Minor after World War I, based on the sources that I am personally able to read. There is much research and work yet to be done by future historians and authors who will, no doubt, reinterpret and add further understanding to these great events.

In terms of agreed-upon historical interpretations, modern Turkey emerged from the crucible of war as a viable nation-state, while Greece found itself in reduced geopolitical circumstances. The Greek-Turkish War was as much a collision of obsessions and peoples as it was a collision of determined national leadership. For the Greeks, the war was a proactive militarized approach to an expansionist policy that could not be successfully negotiated. For the Nationalists, it was a reactive and instinctive military approach to the fragmentation of their Anatolian heartland by the Allies. The Eastern War extinguished the dream of a Greater Armenia, and the Republic of Armenia itself fell under the thrall of Soviet domination for the next 70 years. The British, French, and the Italians gave up their post–World War I claims to Ottoman territory but remained within the ranks of the Great Powers until World War II. That second war brought the Americans, who had wisely avoided entanglement in Anatolia in 1920–1921, back to the Middle East and set the stage for further American interventions. In the end, however, it is safe to say that the events in Asia Minor/Anatolia during 1919–1923 were truly a "war made of wars," which was conclusively won by the Turkish Nationalists.

NOTES

1. Churchill, *The Aftermath*, 375.

2. Applying the phrase "a war made of wars" to the Turkish War of Independence originates in the fertile mind of my friend and colleague, Professor Konstantinos Travlos. In my opinion, it is the perfect characterization for these events.

3. Professor Konstantinos Travlos, email correspondence, January 15, 2020.

4. Gedeon, Paschalidou, and Dima-Dimitrou, *A Concise History of the Campaign in Asia Minor*, 516.

5. Belen, *Türk Kurtuluş Savaşı*, 517.

6. Richter, *The Greek-Turkish War*, 152.

7. Belen, *Türk Kurtuluş Savaşı*, 517.

8. Busch, *Mudros to Lausanne*, 312.

9. Jeremy Salt, *The Last Ottoman Wars: The Human Cost, 1877–1923* (Salt Lake City: The University of Utah Press, 2020), 321.

APPENDIX A

Casualties

Konstantinos Travlos, Özyeğin University

INTRODUCTION

Before beginning this appendix, academic honesty demands that I state some things up front. The following appendix is not a full work of scholarship on the losses experienced by the militaries and civilian populations caught up in the wars of the War of Turkish Liberation. It is but a review of the minimum and maximum estimated casualties presented by various authors. I am not a demographer or a historian, instead being a political scientist, and I do not claim to be conducting a full review of the entire literature on these questions. I simply provide an estimate of estimates derived from the most prominent works and official histories. Furthermore, I am a believer in the Greek national idea and accept the Greek argument of a genocide committed against Ottoman Greeks in the period 1914–1922. With that said, I am also cognizant of the devastation and atrocities committed by either the Greek army or groups protected by the Greek army during the prosecution of the war against the Turkish Nationalist movement, a responsibility taken officially by Greece in the Treaty of Lausanne. I also recognize the right of the Muslim population of Anatolia to resist foreign rule and to a national state of their own, sovereign, and free of foreign domination. The Sèvres Ottoman Empire did not meet those requirements. It is up to the reader to decide if the above invalidate the following review of estimates or not. But my hope is that honesty will help bring a positive decision.

CIVILIAN LOSSES

Calculating the human loss of the various fronts of the Turkish War of Independence is extremely hard. When it comes to civilian losses, the usual process used by various scholars is to calculate population loss by comparing post-1923 censuses with the pre-1923 censuses. Since those censuses were done in 1914 or earlier, the population loss noted in comparison to post-1923 censuses contains the losses of World War I as well. Thus, disaggregating how much of that population loss was due to the events of 1919–1923 and how much due to the events of 1914–1918 is perhaps a hopeless task. Only estimates can be done, with few cases where loss of life can be unquestionably laid at the hands of specific actors. Moreover, the censuses themselves are not without their criticisms. Basically, they come down to either the Ottoman Census of 1914, with its various adjustments or the Patriarchal Census, though other even less honest population numbers are used.[1]

When it comes to Ottoman Greek civilian losses (including Pontic Greeks, who were known as *Karadeniz Rum* to the Ottomans), the most thorough comparison of existing figures is provided by left-wing journalist and scholar Tasos Kostopoulos as part of his polemics against the recognition of an Ottoman Greek Genocide (and Pontic Genocide) by the Greek State.[2] In his analysis, he noted a maximal Greek claim of 700,000 Ottoman Greeks lost in 1914–1923, with no distinction between the losses of World War I and the Turkish War of Independence. If we compare these numbers to Turkish academic Fuat Dündar's estimates of the Ottoman Greek population loss in 1914–1918 at 50,000 to 150,000, then the maximal Greek claim for 1919–1923 would be a population loss of about 550,000 to 650,000. These estimates include a maximum claim of 100,000–150,000 Ottoman Greek population loss in Izmir 1922.[3]

The official claim of the Greek state about the Pontic Greek population loss due to genocide in the entire 1914–1923 period is 353,000. There are two estimates noted by Kostopoulos given for 1919–1923, one by George Topalidis at 119,122, and one by Alexis Alexnadrakis at 116,000. Kostopoulos himself preferred a number between 100,000 and 150,000 Pontic Greek victims of what he called an ethnic cleansing campaign (but not genocide) for 1914–1923.

For the losses suffered at Izmir in 1922, Kostopoulos presented different numbers, which range from a minimum of 1,000–1,200 to a median of 12,000. Depending on which population estimate of Ottoman Greeks one starts with, and which estimate one accepts of Greek refugees and expellees arrived in Greece 1922–1923 (ranging from 1,335,121 to 1,500,000), one can estimate a minimal population loss of 138,889, a median of 269,670, and a maximum of 842,879. If we accept Dündar's estimate of population loss for 1914–1918, that translates into a population loss of as little as 88,000 and as large as 837,000 in the 1919–1923 time frame. A potential median estimate is between 119,000 and 219,000.

On the other hand, when it comes specifically to the Pontic Greeks/ *Karadeniz Rum*, Professor Justin McCarthy reported that 30,000 were deported into the interior of Asia Minor in 1920–1922, of which 8,000 died. He estimated a population loss of 65,000 between 1914–1922. McCarthy considered the actions of the Turkish Grand National Assembly to be inappropriate and out of proportion to the threat but did not call what happened ethnic cleansing or genocide.[4] That said, it should be noted that if his estimates are right, the population loss of Ottoman Greeks in the Pontus/Karadeniz region is at the level of 30–35 percent for the 1914–1922 period, based on the 1914 Ottoman Census population estimate, which is comparable to the Armenian one and much higher than the percentages for Ottoman Muslims.

When it comes to Muslims population loss, the best estimates are those of McCarthy, who argues for an estimated population loss of 1,246,068 Muslims between 1914 and 1922 in Anatolia, and arbitrarily ascribes 640,000 of those as occurring in the Greek and British zones of operation in 1919–1922.[5]

While it is hard to estimate numbers, the proportions seem to be similar across most estimations. It does seem possible that 10–15 percent of the Ottoman Greek population was lost specifically in 1919–1922. An 8–10 percent loss rate for the Muslim population of Asia Minor in 1919–1922 is also plausible. An important aspect to note is that of the estimated 100,000–160,000 Ottoman Greek males aged 15–45, who were deported into the interior of Asia Minor in 1922 by the victorious Nationalists, only a small number survived.[6]

Ultimately, the only observable result is that by 1922, the majority of Ottoman Greeks of Anatolia had either become refugees or had lost their lives. Only about 300,000 were actually exchanged in 1923–1924, the rest of those covered by the exchange having already arrived in Greece as refugees. Anatolia was emptied of Ottoman Greeks. As a counterpoint, while the Muslim population of the Balkans had also suffered acts of ethnic cleansing (reaching genocidal levels in certain localities), it has survived both in Greece and Bulgaria today.

Civilian losses in the Southern and Eastern Front theaters, as well as against the anti-Nationalist insurrections, are even harder to estimate. The Armenian population of Eastern Anatolia was largely decimated from the Committee of Union and Progress relocation policies of the 1914–1918 period, considered a genocide by many, including the author, while the Armeno-Turkish War (associated with atrocities to civilians from both sides) did not last long enough to cause massive civilian losses that can be differentiated from the awful heritage of 1914–1918 and the difficult post-war conditions faced by the Republic of Armenia. In the case of the Franco-Turkish war, there are some clear cases of massacres, but the numbers do not seem to climb above several thousand or tens of thousands.

In the end, civilians from all sides suffered, but only one national idea, the Turkish one, won the war of populations. In the vast struggle for Anatolia, the Armenian and Greek national ideas were extinguished and, with them, the populations they claimed to represent.

MILITARY CASUALTIES

One would think that estimating military losses would be a bit clearer. But, once more. there are differentiations in the numbers. When it comes to Greek military losses, the official Greek military tally is 24,250 dead and 48,880 wounded.[7] This equals a staggering loss rate of close to one-third of the Greek Army in Asia Minor in 1922. Celâl Erikan provided similar numbers of 23,287 dead and 38,477 wounded.[8] Where estimates differ is with the numbers of prisoners of war and missing in action. The official Greek military position claimed 18,095 missing in action, most of whom were prisoners of war (POWs) captured in 1922 and never repatriated. Greek sources argue that only 10,000 Greek military POWs were repatriated, the rest dying in captivity. Certain Greek sources claim a maximum of 55,000 Greek prisoners of war, while Erikan cites 49,853.[9] The official Turkish military history provided the number of Greek prisoners of war as 20,826. A moderate Greek estimate is that 25,000–27,000 Greek troops were captured in 1919–1922.[10] Cemalettin Taşkıran in his study (using only Turkish sources) of Greek and Turkish prisoners in the entire 1919–1922 period gave an estimate of 14,766 military prisoners and 10,527 civilian prisoners.[11]

The differences in numbers might be driven by the different treatment by the Turkish authorities of Greek soldiers who were Greek citizens and Greek soldiers who were Ottoman citizens (e.g., the bulk of the 10th and 11th Divisions and part of the 5th Division were composed of soldiers recruited from Ottoman territory). For the Greek side, all of these men were considered Greek prisoners of war, but, for the Turks, prisoners from the second category (those who were Ottoman citizens) were legally traitors and might have not been counted as prisoners of war. Whatever the estimates, between one-third and perhaps one-half of the Greek Army in Asia Minor became a casualty of the war.

When it comes to Turkish losses, the Turkish official tally is that the Army of the Turkish Grand National Assembly suffered 9,101 dead and 36,035 wounded in its war with the Greek Army.[12] Once more, estimates of prisoners of war vary. Erikan cited 7,084, while Greek sources claimed 18,000–20,000.[13] Taşkıran differentiated between 16,000 civil prisoners and 6,500–10,129 military prisoners. What we can safely say is that, like the Greek Army, the Army of the Turkish Grand National Assembly suffered about one-third losses, though only half the dead of the Greek Army.

The military losses for the Kuva-yi Milliye, which did the bulk of the fighting in 1919–1920, are also hard to estimate. The Greek official history claims to have inflicted about 3,000 casualties in the 1919–1920 time frame on enemy forces.[14] Equally, the military losses of the Armenian campaign are also hard to estimate, but seem to not have crossed the 1,000 threshold for either side, which explains the exclusion of the war from the data sets in the Correlates of War project.[15] When it comes to the conflict with France, the Correlates of War data set cited a number of 1,000 French military losses and 35,000 Turkish losses, which is surely an exaggeration of Turkish losses. What is clear is that the war on fronts other than the Greco-Turkish front was a sideshow when it came to the loss of human life. If we assume a number of 500,000 men to have passed through the colors for both the Greek and Turkish side between 1919 and 1922, then about 20 percent of the men who fought became casualties (see table A.1 for a summary of the different estimates).

CONCLUSION

The war over Anatolia followed a similar pattern of casualties with the other wars of succession fought over the legacy of the Ottoman Empire (with the noticeable exceptions of the Greek-Ottoman War of 1897 and the

Table A.1 Military Casualties

	Dead	Wounded	Prisoners	Sources
Greek Army	23,287	38,477	49,853	Celal Erikan 2018 (2008)
			Max. 55,000 (many Greek claims)	Papadimitriou 2002
			Realistic estimate 25–27,000 (Papadimitriou estimate)	
			Min. 20,826 (ATASE claim)	
			Only 10,000 repatriated (18,095 missing after 1923)	
			14,766 military prisoners	Taşkıran 2018
			10,527 civilian prisoners (perhaps Ottoman Greeks in service in the Greek Army?)	
	24,250	48,880	MIA 18,095	*Concise History*
Turkish Grand National Assembly Army–Western Front	9,101	36,035	7,084	Celal Erikan 2018 (2008)
			18-20,000	Papadimitriou 2002
			16,000 civil prisoners	Taşkıran 2018
			6,500–10,129 military prisoners	

Turkish Grand National Assembly Army-Armenian Front	Less than 1,000		Not listed in *Correlates of War* (=>1000 battle deaths); also see Hovannisian, *The Republic of Armenia*
Kuvay-i-Milliye-Western Front	2,248 (claimed)	500 (claimed)	*Concise History*
Turkish Forces Southern Front	35,000?		*Correlates of War*
Anti-TGNA forces			
Armenian Army	Less than 1,000		Not listed in *Correlates of War* (=>1000 battle deaths); also see Hovannisian
French Army	5,000		*Correlates of War*

Serbo-Bulgarian War of 1885–1886). The 1919–1923 war in Anatolia was deadly to the armies involved, and it was deadly for the civilians involved. Moreover, the result did not meet the expectations of the national ideas of the fighting sides. Even the victorious Turks had to give up territories considered central to their new national idea (Western Thrace, the Eastern Aegean Islands, Mosul, and Batum). It was even worse for the Bulgarians, Armenians, and Greeks, whose great expenditure in lives and treasure did not bring them their hoped-for territory. Nevertheless, compared to Greece, Armenia, and Bulgaria, the borders of modern Turkey are much closer to the ideas included in the National Pact of 1920. In the end, the final war of Ottoman succession was also the most successful war fought by the Turks since the seventeenth century.

NOTES

1. The war over numbers is ongoing in academic research and political activity. I will note here the literature on the issue of Greek and Turkish numbers, with which I am familiar, leaving out the issue of Armenians. For a general review, see Fuat Dündar, *Modern Türkiye'nin Şifresi: İttihat ve Terakki'nin Etnisite Mühendisliği (1913–1918)* (Istanbul: İletişim Yayınları, 2008). The discussion of the Greek translation I used, titled "Ο κώδικας της Σύγχρονης Τουρκίας," can be found on pages 38–40 and 85–115. The central line is drawn between those who accept as a basis the estimations of the Ottoman Census of 1914, which can be found in Kemal H. Karpat, *Ottoman Population, 1830–1914: Demographic and Social Characteristics* (Madison, WI: University of Wisconsin Press, 1985), or the Patriarchate estimation of 1910–1912 presented in Paschalis M. Kitromilides and Alexis Alexandris, "Ethnic Survival, Nationalism and Forced Migration," Δελτίο Κέντρου Μικρασιατικών Σπουδών, 6 (1986): 9–44. Examples of work supporting the use of the Ottoman Census as a realistic basis are Justin McCarthy, *Muslims and Minorities* (New York: New York University Press, 1983) and Servet Mutlu, "Late Ottoman Population and Its Ethnic Distribution," *Turkish Journal of Population Studies* 25, no. 1 (2003): 3–38. McCarthy is also the main critic of the Patriarchal Census. See Justin McCarthy, "Greek Statistics on the Ottoman Greek Population," *International Journal of Turkish Studies* 1, no. 2 (1980): 66–76. For the defence against this criticism, see Kitromilides and Alexandris, "Ethnic Survival," 23–34. Fuat Dündar, in considering all the parts of the

debate, believed that an estimate of about 2,000,000 Ottoman Greeks in the Ottoman Empire in 1914 is the most realistic number.

2. Tasos Kostopoulos, *War and Ethnic Cleansing 1912–1922* [Πόλεμος και Εθνοκάθαρση 1912–1922] (Athens: Vivliorama Ekdoseis, 2008). Despite the clear political bias of the author, his review of the population numbers debate in pages 252–265, is thorough and thus very useful.

3. See Stavros G. Karakaletsis, "Fall and Destruction of Smyrna (Η πτώση και καταστροφή της Σμύρνης)," in *Asia Minor Disaster* (Μικρασιατική Καταστροφή), eds. Nikos Giannopoulos and Vasilis Kambanis (Athens: Gnomon Ekdotiki, 2002), 50–58.

4. See Justin McCarthy, *Death and Exile: The Ethnic Cleansing of Ottoman Muslims, 1821–1922* (Princeton, NJ: Darwin Press, 1995). For his estimates on the Greek population, see footnote 138 (page 325) and footnote 195 (page 330). For his judgment of the Turkish state action, see pages 288–89. Essentially McCarthy, without being willing to do so in his own words, presents a basis for the Turkish authorities violating the legal principle of proportionality, which renders what happened technically a war crime.

5. See McCarthy, *Death and Exile*, 303.

6. McCarthy denies any significant population loss among the deportees of 1922. See McCarthy, *Death and Exile*, footnote 146, 326.

7. See Gedeon, Paschalidou, and Dima-Dimitrou, *A Concise History of the Campaign in Asia Minor* (Athens: Hellenic Army General Staff Army History Directorate, 2003), 517–18.

8. Celâl Erikan, *Kutrluş Savaşsı Tarihi (History of the War of Liberation)* (Istanbul: Türkiye İş Bankası, 2018).

9. See Erikan, *Kutrluş Savaşı Tarihi*; and Kostas Papadimitriou, "The Fate of Prisoners of War (Η τύχη των αιχμάλωτων στρατιωτικών)," in *Asia Minor Disaster* (Μικρασιατική Καταστροφή), Nikos Giannopoulos and Vasilis Kambanis (eds.) (Athens: Gnomon Ekdotiki, 2002).

10. Both numbers are from Papadimitriou, "The Fate of Prisoners of War," 61–65.

11. See Cemalettin Taşkıran, *Milli Mücadele'de Türk ve Yunan Esirler, 1919–1923* (Istanbul: Türkiye İş Bankası, 2018).

12. See Erikan, *Kuturluş Savaşı Tarihi*.

13. Papadimitriou, "The Fate of Prisoners of War."

14. See Gedeon, Paschalidou, and Dima-Dimitrou, *A Concise History of the Campaign in Asia Minor*.

15. See The Correlates of War Project website at https://correlatesof war.org/.

SOURCES

Dündar, Fuat. *Modern Türkiye'nin Şifresi: İttihat ve Terakki'nin Etnisite Mühendisliği (1913–1918)*. Istanbul: İletişim Yayınları, 2008.

Karakaletsis, Stavros G. "Fall and Destruction of Smyrna (Η πτώση και καταστροφή της Σμύρνης)." In *Asia Minor Disaster* (Μικρασιατική Καταστροφή), edited by Nikos Giannopoulos and Vasilis Kambanis. Athens: Gnomon Ekdotiki, 2002.

Karpat, Kemal H. *Ottoman Population, 1830–1914: Demographic and Social Characteristics*. Madison, WI: University of Wisconsin Press, 1985.

Kitromilides, Paschalis M., and Alexis Alexandris. "Ethnic Survival, Nationalism and Forced Migration." *Δελτίο Κέντρου Μικρασιατικών Σπουδών* 6 (1986): 9–44.

Kostopoulos, Tasos. *War and Ethnic Cleansing 1912–1922* (Πόλεμος και Εθνοκάθαρση 1912–1922). Athens: Vivliorama Ekdoseis, 2008.

McCarthy, Justin. *Death and Exile: The Ethnic Cleansing of Ottoman Muslims, 1821–1922*. Princeton, NJ: Darwin Press, 1995.

McCarthy, Justin. "Greek Statistics on the Ottoman Greek Population," *International Journal of Turkish Studies* 1, no. 2 (1980).

McCarthy, Justin. *Muslims and Minorities*. New York: New York University Press, 1983.

Mutlu, Servet. "Late Ottoman Population and Its Ethnic Distribution," *Turkish Journal of Population Studies* 25, no. 1 (2003): 3–38.

Papadimitriou, Kostas. "The Fate of Prisoners of War [Η τύχη των αιχμάλωτων στρατιωτικών]." In *Asia Minor Disaster* [Μικρασιατική Καταστροφή], edited by Nikos Giannopoulos and Vasilis Kambanis. Athens: Gnomon Ekdotiki, 2002.

Taşkıran, Cemalettin. *Greek and Turkish Prisoners during the National Renaissance 1919–1923 [Milli Mücadele'de Türk ve Yunan Esirler]*. Istanbul: Türkiye İş Bankası, 2018.

APPENDIX B

Campaigns of the Turkish War of Independence

INTRODUCTION

This appendix presents the author's appraisal of which major operations might be considered as the campaigns waged by the combatant armies during the Turkish War of Independence. In examining campaigns, it is necessary to recognize that there are three levels of war: the strategic, operational, and tactical. At the operational level of war, campaigns serve to connect tactical activities (usually battles and engagements) with the achievement of strategic goals. Commanders who plan and execute campaigns operate at the operational level of war are, for the most part, army group and field army commanders, although occasionally army corps fulfill this function when operating in an independent role.

It is also important to recognize that a battle is not a campaign, although in the Turkish War of Independence, some extended and large-scale battles took on campaign-like aspects. A campaign is a deliberately planned series of battles and engagements designed to achieve a strategic purpose. Campaigns are longer in time and space than battles and involve indirect command, which means that the commander does not personally conduct or supervise operations in the field. In such circumstances, command is conducted by assigning missions and objectives to subordinate commanders. Supervision (commonly called control) is exercised through staff procedures, although it was not uncommon for a high-level commander to intervene in emergency situations.

In the Turkish War of Independence, campaigns were generally planned and executed by field army or army group level headquarters. It is also important to consider that just because one side launches an offensive campaign, this does not automatically mean the reciprocal is true. For example, holding a defensive line against an enemy offensive campaign does not endow campaign status on the defender, because the battles and engagements cannot be planned in advance. The "bottom line" is that a campaign is planned in advance to achieve a strategic purpose.

While some may disagree, I have also listed a category called Major Operations, which have operational-level campaign-like aspects but are essentially opportunistic or reactive to the enemy situation and tactical conditions. In effect, these major offensive operations were hastily put together with minimal planning, and the major defensive operations were ad hoc reactions to enemy offensives.

Using these definitions, we may judge that the combatants planned and conducted 18 actual campaigns (14 offensive campaigns and 4 defensive campaigns) as well as conducted 11 major operations (9 offensive and 2 defensive) during the Turkish War of Independence (see table B.1). While there were some pitched battles using trenches, most of these campaigns and major operations were characterized by operational and tactical maneuver rather than by frontal attacks on heavily entrenched positions.

Table B.1   Campaigns of the Turkish War of Independence

Campaign/Inclusive Dates	Strategic Objective	Outcome
Armenian Army Major Offensive Operation		
Kars-Ardahan-Oltu 1919	Occupy territory	Successful
French Army Offensive Campaigns		
Cicilian Occupation 1919–1920	Occupy Cilicia	Successful
Gaziantepe Offensive 1920–1921	Recover and control territory	Successful*
Greek Army Offensive Campaigns		
Occupation of Izmir 1919	Occupy Izmir	Successful
First Greek Offensive 1920	Expand Izmir perimeter	Successful

Table B.1   (continued)

Campaign/Inclusive Dates	Strategic Objective	Outcome
Occupation of Thrace 1920	Occupy eastern Thrace	Successful
Uşak Offensive 1920	Political message	Unsuccessful
Reconnaissance in Force 1921	Confirm capabilities	Successful
Eskişehir Offensive 1921	Political message	Unsuccessful
Afyonkarahisar Offensive 1921	Political message	Unsuccessful
Kütahya-Eskişehir Offensive 1921	Destroy enemy army	Unsuccessful
Sakarya Offensive 1921	Destroy enemy army/capital	Unsuccessful
Greek Army Major Defensive Operations		
The Catastrophe 1922	Avoid destruction of army	Unsuccessful
Nationalist Army Offensive Campaigns		
Sarıkamış-Kars Offensive 1920	Recover territory	Successful
Nationalist Pursuit 1921	Destroy enemy army	Unsuccessful
Dumlupınar Campaign 1921	Destroy part of enemy army	Unsuccessful
The Great Offensive 1922	Annihilate enemy army	Successful
Advance to the Straits 1922	Occupy territory	Successful
Nationalist Army Major Offensive Operations		
Counterinsurgency Operations 1919–1922	Secure LOCs/area control	Successful
Uşak Counteroffensive 1920	Recover territory	Partial
First İnönü Counteroffensive 1921	Reestablish the front	Successful

(*continued*)

Table B.1   (continued)

Campaign/Inclusive Dates	Strategic Objective	Outcome
Kütahya Counteroffensive 1921	Recover territory	Unsuccessful
Sakarya Counteroffensive 1921	Recover territory	Successful
Pursuit to Izmir 1922	Expel enemy from Anatolia	Successful
Pursuit to Bandırma 1922	Expel enemy from Anatolia	Successful
Nationalist Army Defensive Campaigns		
Cicilia Defensive 1919–1921	Recover territory	Unsuccessful**
Second İnönü Campaign 1921	Defend territory	Successful
Nationalist Army Major Defensive Operations		
First İnönü 1921	Defend territory	Successful
Ottoman Army Major Offensive Operations		
Disciplinary Force Offensive 1920	Recovery territory	Unsuccessful

*The French campaigns were successful militarily in recovering Gaziantepe, Pozantı, and Urfa, but in the end, at the strategic level, the French could no longer afford the resources to maintain control of Cilicia and abandoned their effort.

**The Nationalist campaign in Cilicia was, in and of itself, unsuccessful in forcing the French to leave. My view is that external factors, such as postwar finances, disillusionment with the Greeks, and the lack of a strategic objective, were the primary reasons why the French abandoned Cilicia.

Source: Author's compilation

Bibliography

OFFICIAL DOCUMENTS

Harbord, James G. *Conditions in the Near East: Report of the American Military Mission to Armenia*. Washington, DC: Government Printing Office, 1920.

Intelligence Department, Naval Staff. *A Handbook of Asia Minor*, vol. 1 General. London: Royal Navy, July 1919.

Papian, Ara, and Davit O. Abrahamyan, eds. *Arbitral Award of the President of the United States of America Woodrow Wilson, Full Report of the Committee upon the Arbitration of the Boundary between Turkey and Armenia. Washington, November 22nd, 1920*. Armenia: Modus Vivendi, 2011.

OFFICIAL HISTORIES

Alpay, Hakkı, Şadi Sükan, and Kâmil Önalp. *Türk İstiklâl Harbi IInci Cilt Batı Cephesi 4ncü Kısım, Kütahya, Eskişehir Muharebeleri (15 Mayıs 1921–25 Temmuz 1921)*. Ankara: Genelkurmay Basımevi, 1974.

Apac'ca, Rahmi, Kâmil Önalp, and Selim Turhan. *Türk İstiklâl Hârbi IInci Cilt, Batı Cephesi, 3ncü Kısım (9 Kasım 1920–15 Nisan 1921)*. Ankara: Genelkurmay Basımevi, 1994.

Aykut, Fahri. *İstiklâl Savaşı'nda Kütahya ve Eskişehir Muharebeleri*. Ankara: Genelkurmay Basımevi, 2006.

Belen, Fahri. *Birinci Cihan Harbinde Türk Harbi 1914 Yılı Hareketleri, Vnci Cilt*. Ankara: Genelkurmay Basımevi, 1967.

Bell, Archibald C. *A History of the Blockade of Germany and of the Countries Associated with Her in the Great War: Austria-Hungary,*

Bulgaria, and Turkey 1914–1918, 5 vols. London: Her Majesty's Stationery Office, 1937.

Besbelli, Saim, and İhsan Göymen. *Türk İstiklâl Hârbi Vnci Cilt, Deniz Cephesi ve Hava Harekâtı.* Ankara: Genelkurmay Basımevi, 1964.

Bıyıklıoğlu, Tevfik. *Türk İstiklâl Harbi I, Mondros Mütarekesi ve Tatbikatı.* Ankara: Genelkurmay Basımevi, 1962.

Cecini, Giovanni. *Il Corpo di Spedizione Italiano in Anatolia (1919–1922).* Rome: Stato Maggiore Dell'Esercito, Ufficio Storico, 2010.

Edmonds, James E. *The Occupation of Constantinople 1918–1923 (Provisional).* (Draft manuscript written in 1944, transcribed by Neil J. Wells in 2009). Brambleside, East Sussex: The Naval and Military Press, 2010.

Ercan, Tefik. *Türk İstiklâl Hârbi IInci Cilt, Batı Cephesi, 2nci Kısım (4 Eylül 1919–9 Kasım 1920).* Ankara: Genelkurmay Basımevi, 1999.

Erkal, Şükrü. *Birinci Dünya Harbinde Türk Harbi VIncı, Hicaz, Asir, Yemen Cepheleri ve Libya Harekâtı 1914–1918.* Ankara: Genelkurmay Basımevi, 1978.

Erkal, Şükrü. *Türk İstiklâl Harbi IInci Cilt Batı Cephesi 6ncı Kısım Inci Kitap, Büyük Taarruza Hazırlık ve Büyük Taarruz (10 Ekim 1921–31 Temmuz 1922).* Ankara: Genelkurmay Basımevi, 1967.

Ertuna, Hamdi. *Türk İstiklâl Hârbi Vnci Cilt, İstiklâl Harbinde Ayaklanmalar (1919–1921).* Ankara: Genelkurmay Basımevi, 1974.

Falls, Cyril, and A. F. Becke. *Military Operations, Egypt & Palestine: From June 1917 to the End of the War.* London: Her Majesty's Stationery Office, 1930.

Falls, Cyril, and A. F. Becke. *Military Operations, Macedonia: From the Spring of 1917 to the End of the War.* London: Her Majesty's Stationery Office, 1935.

Gedeon, Demetrios, Eupraxia Paschalidou, and Angeliki Dima-Dimitrou. *A Concise History of the Campaign in Asia Minor 1919–1922* [English Edition]. Athens: Hellenic Army History Directorate, 2003.

Görgülü, Ismet. *Büyük Taarruz.* Ankara: Genelkurmay Basımevi, 1992.

Güvendik, Hakkı, Cihat Akçakayalıoğlu, and Selim Turhan. *Türk İstiklâl Hârbi IInci Cilt, Batı Cephesi, Inci Kısım (15 Mayıs–4 Eylül 1919).* Ankara: Genelkurmay Basımevi, 1999.

Koral, Necmi, Remzi Önal, Rauf Atakan, Nusret Baycan, and Selâttin Kızılırmak. *Birinci Dünya Harbı Idarı Faalıyetler ve Lojistik, Xncü Cilt.* Ankara: Genelkurmay Basımevi, 1962.

Le Ministère de la Guerre. *Les Armées Françaises dans la Grande Guerre: Tome IX-Ier Volume, Les Fronts Secondaires.* Paris: Imprimerie, 1936.

Niş, Kemal. *Türk İstiklâl Harbi IInci Cilt Batı Cephesi 6ncı Kısım IInci Kitap Büyük Taarruz (1–31 Ağustos 1922).* Ankara: Genelkurmay Basımevi, 1968.

Niş, Kemal, and Reşat Söker. *Türk İstiklâl Harbi IInci Cilt Batı Cephesi 6ncı Kısım IIIncü Kitap, Büyük Taarruzda Takip Harekâtı (31 Ağustos–18 Eylül 1922).* Ankara: Genelkurmay Basımevi, 1969.

Ökse, Necati, Nusret Baycan, and Salih Sakaryalı. *Türk İstiklâl Harbi'ne Katılan Tümen ve daha Üst Kademelerdeki Komutanların Biyografileri (İkinci Baskı).* Ankara: Genelkurmay Basımevi, 1989.

Önalp, Kâmil. *Türk İstiklâl Harbi IInci Cilt Batı Cephesi 5nci Kısım 1nci Kitap, Sakarya Meydan Muharebesinden Önceki Olaylar ve Mevzi İlerisindeki Harakât (25 Temmuz–22 Ağustos 1921).* Ankara: Genelkurmay Basımevi, 1972.

Saral, Ahmet Hulki, Atike Kaptan, and Alev Keskin. *Türk İstiklâl Harbi IV'üncü Cilt Güney Cephesi.* Ankara: Genelkurmay Basımevi, 2009.

Timur, Cevdet, Rauf Atakan, Alişan Berktay, and Veli Ertekin. *Türk İstiklâl Hârbi VIInci Cilt, İdari Faaliyetler (15 Mayıs 1919–2 Kasım 1923).* Ankara: Genelkurmay Basımevi, 1975.

Timural, Ahmet, Rauf Atakan, and Alişan Berktay. *Türk İstiklâl Harbi IInci Cilt Batı Cephesi 5nci Kısım 2nci Kitap, Sakarya Meydan Muharebesi (23 Ağustos–13 Eylül 1921) ve Sonraki Harekât (14 Eylül–10 Ekim 1921).* Ankara: Genelkurmay Basımevi, 1973.

Tugaç, Hüsamettin. *Türk İstiklâl Hârbi IIIncü Cilt, Doğu Cephesi (1919–1921).* Ankara: Genelkurmay Basımevi, 1965.

Tüzel, Abidin. *Türk İstiklâl Harbi IInci Cilt Batı Cephesi 6nci Kısım IV Kitap, İstiklâl Harbinin Son Safhası (18 Eylül–1 Kasım 1923).* Ankara: Genelkurmay Basımevi, 1969.

Ulusoy, Mümtaz. *İstiklâl Harbi'nde 2nci Kolordu (1918–1921).* Ankara: Genelkurmay Basımevi, 2006.

Vandemir, Baki. *Türk İstiklâl Savaşı'nda, Sakarya'dan Mudanya'ya.* Ankara: Genelkurmay Basımevi, 1972.

MEMOIRS

Baboian, Kevork. *The Heroic Battle of Aintab.* Translated by Ümit Kurt. London: Gomidas Institute, 2017.

Çalışlar, İzzetin. *İstiklâl Savaşı Hatıraları Sakarya Meydan Muharebesi'nde Inci Grup*. Ankara: Genelkurmay Basımevi, 2006.

Cebesoy, Ali Fuat. *Millı Mücadele Hatıraları*. Istanbul: Temel Yayınları, 2000.

Güralp, Şerif. *İstiklâl Savaşın'n İçyüzü*. Ankara: Polatlı Belediyesi Yayınları, 2007.

Harrington, Charles. *Tim Harrington Looks Back*. London: John Murray, 1940.

Karabekir, Kâzım. *İstiklâl Harbimiz 1. Cilt*. Istanbul: Yapı Kredi Yayınları, 2006.

Rawlinson, Anthony. *Adventures in the Near East, 1918–1922*. London: Andrew Melrose, 1924.

Vandemir, Baki. *Türk İstiklâl Savaşı'nda, Sakarya'dan Mudanya'ya*. Ankara: Genelkurmay Basımevi, 1972.

SECONDARY SOURCES

Akbıyık, Yaşar. *Milli Mücadelede Güney Cephesi (Maraş)*. Ankara: Kültür Bakanlığı Yayınları, 1990.

Allen, W. E. D., and Paul Muratoff. *Caucasian Battlefields: A History of the Wars on the Turco-Caucasian Border 1828–1921*. Cambridge: Cambridge University Press, 1953.

Anderson, Scott. *Lawrence in Arabia: War, Deceit, Imperial Folly and the Making of the Modern Middle East*. New York: Doubleday, 2013.

Ayışığı, Metin. *Mareşal Ahmet İzzet Paşa*. Ankara: Türk Tarih Kurumu Basımevi, 1997.

Belen, Fahri. *Türk Kurtuluş Savaşı*. Ankara: Başbakanlık Basımevi, 1971.

Bilgin, İsmail. *Medine Müdafaası: Çöl Kaplanı Fahrettin Paşa*. Istanbul: Timaş Yayınları, 2009.

Busch, Briton Cooper. *Mudros to Lausanne: Britain's Frontier in West Asia, 1918–1923*. Albany: State University of New York Press, 1976.

Carr, John C. *R.H.N.S. Averof: Thunder in the Aegean*. Barnsley, UK: Pen & Sword Maritime, 2014.

Churchill, Winston S. *The World Crisis: The Aftermath*, vol. 5. London: Thornton Butterworth Limited, 1929.

Çiloğlu, Fahrettin. *Kurtuluş Savaşı Sözlüğü*. Istanbul: Livane Yayınları, 2004.

Clark, Bruce. *Twice a Stranger: The Mass Expulsions that Forged Modern Greece and Turkey*. Cambridge: Harvard University Press, 2006.

Dobkin, Marjorie Housepian. *Smyrna 1922: The Destruction of a City.* New York: Harcourt Brace Jovanovich, 1971.

Dousmanes, Viktor (Βίκτωρ Δουσμάνης), *Η Εσωτερική όψη της μικρασιάτικης εμπλοκής (The Internal View of the Asia Minor Entanglement).* Pyrsos: 1928.

Dündar, Fuat. *Modern Türkiye'nin Şifresi: İttihat ve Terakki'nin Etnisite Mühendisliği (1913–1918).* Istanbul: İletişim Yayınları, 2008.

Erickson, Edward J. *Defeat in Detail: The Ottoman Army in the Balkans, 1912–1913.* Westport, CT: Praeger Publishing, 2003.

Erickson, Edward J. *Gallipoli: The Ottoman Campaign.* Barnsley, UK: Pen and Sword Military, 2010.

Erickson, Edward J. *Ordered to Die: A History of the Ottoman Army in the First World War.* Westport, CT: Greenwood Press, 2001.

Erickson, Edward J. *Ottoman Army Effectiveness in World War I.* Abingdon, UK: Routledge, 2007.

Erickson, Edward J. *Ottomans and Armenians: A Study in Counterinsurgency.* New York: Palgrave Macmillan, 2013.

Erickson, Edward J. *Palestine: The Ottoman Campaigns of 1914–1918.* Barnsley, UK: Pen and Sword Military, 2016.

Erikan, Celâl. *Kurtuluş Savaşı Tarihi (History of the War of Liberation).* Istanbul: Türkiye İş Bankası, 2018.

Erikan, Celâl. *100 Soruda Kurtuluş Savaşımızın Tarihi.* Istanbul: Gerçek Yayınevi, 1971.

Falls, Cyril. *The Great War.* New York: G.P. Putnam's Sons, 1959.

Fromkin, David. *A Peace to End All Peace: The Fall of the Ottoman Empire and the Creation of the Modern Middle East.* New York: Henry Holt & Company, 1989.

Gawrych, George W. *The Young Atatürk: From Ottoman Soldier to Statesman of Turkey.* London: I.B. Tauris, 2015.

Giannopoulos, Nikos, and Vasilis Kambanis. *Asia Minor Disaster (Μικρασιατική Καταστροφή).* Athens: Gnomon Ekdotiki, 2002.

Giles, Milton. *Paradise Lost—Smyrna 1922: The Destruction of a Christian City in the Islamic World.* New York: Basic Books, 2008.

Görgülü, Ismet. *On Yıllık Harbin Kadrosu 1912–1922.* Ankara: Türk Tarih Kurum Basımevi, 1993.

Güçlü, Yücel. *Armenians and the Allies in Cilicia, 1914–1923.* Salt Lake City: University of Utah Press, 2009.

Hanlon, Gregory. *Italy 1636: Cemetery of Armies.* Oxford University Press, 2016.

Hasanli, Jamil. *Foreign Policy of the Republic of Azerbaijan: The Difficult Road to Western Integration, 1919–1920*. London: Routledge, 2016.

Horton, George. *The Blight of Asia*. Indianapolis, IN: The Bobbs-Merrill Company, 1926.

Hovannisian, Richard G. *The Republic of Armenia: Between Crescent and Sickle: Partition and Sovietization*, vol. 4. Los Angeles: University of California Press, 1996.

Hovannisian, Richard G. *The Republic of Armenia: The First Year, 1918–1919*, vol. 1. Los Angeles: University of California Press, 1971.

Hovannisian, Richard G. *The Republic of Armenia: From London to Sèvres, February–August 1920*, vol. 3. Los Angeles: University of California Press, 1996.

Hovannisian, Richard G. *The Republic of Armenia: From Versailles to London, 1919–1920*, vol. 2. Los Angeles: University of California Press, 1982.

Hughes, Daniel J., and Richard L. DiNardo. *Imperial Germany and War, 1871–1918*. Lawrence: University of Kansas Press, 2018.

Jeffrey, Keith. *The Military Correspondence of Field Marshal Sir Henry Wilson*. Bodley Head: The Army Records Society, 1985.

Jowett, Phillip S. *Armies of the Greek-Turkish War 1919–1923*. Oxford: Osprey Publishing, 2015.

Karpat, Kemal H. *Ottoman Population, 1830–1914: Demographic and Social Characteristics*. Madison: University of Wisconsin Press, 1985.

Kostopoulos, Tasos. *Πόλεμος και Εθνοκάθαρση 1912–1922 (War and Ethnic Cleansing 1912–1922)*. Athens: Vivliorama Ekdoseis, 2008.

Llewellyn-Smith, Michael. *Ionian Vision: Greece in Asia Minor 1919–1922*. New York: St. Martin's Press, 1973.

Mango, Andrew. *Atatürk: The Biography of the Founder of Modern Turkey*. New York: The Overlook Press, 1999.

McCarthy, Justin. *Death and Exile: The Ethnic Cleansing of Ottoman Muslims, 1821–1922*. Princeton: Darwin Press, 1995.

McCarthy, Justin. *Muslims and Minorities*. New York: New York University Press, 1983.

McMeekin, Sean. *The Ottoman Endgame: War, Revolution, and the Making of the Modern Middle East 1908–1923*. New York: Penguin Press, 2015.

Özakman, Turgut. *Vahidettin, M. Kemal ve Milli Mücadele: Yalanlar, Yanlışlar, Yutturmacalar*. Istanbul: Bilgi Yayınevi, 1997.

Özçelik, İsmail. *Milli Mücadele'de Güney Cephesi: Urfa (30 Ekim 1918– 11 Temmuz 1920)*. Ankara: Kültür Bakanlığı, 1992.

Paret, Peter. *Makers of Modern Strategy from Machiavelli to the Nuclear Age*. Princeton: Princeton University Press, 1986.

Preston, R. M. P. *The Desert Mounted Corps*. New York: Houghton Mifflin Company, 1921.

Reynolds, Michael A. *Shattering Empires: The Clash and Collapse of the Ottoman and Russian Empires, 1908–1918*. Cambridge: Cambridge University Press, 2011.

Richter, Heinz A. *The Greek-Turkish War 1919–1922*. Ruhpolding, DE: Verlag Franz Philipp Rutzen, 2016.

Rodas, Mihail (Μιχαήλ Ρόδας). *Η Ελλαδα στην Μίκρα Ασία* (*Greece in Asia Minor*). 1950.

Salt, Jeremy. *The Last Ottoman Wars: The Human Cost, 1877–1923*. Salt Lake City: The University of Utah Press, 2020.

Savaş, Vural Fuat. *İstiklal Savaşının Finansmanı*. Ankara: Efil Yayınevi, 2017.

Shaw, Stanford J. *From Empire to Republic: The Turkish War of National Liberation. The Rise and Fall of the Ottoman Empire, 1918–1923*, 5 vols. Ankara: Türk Tarih Kurumu Basımevi, 2000.

Shaw, Stanford J., and Ezel Kural Shaw. *History of the Ottoman Empire and Modern Turkey: Reform, Revolution, and Republic: The Rise of Modern Turkey, 1808–1975*, vol. 2. Cambridge: Cambridge University Press, 1977.

Soysal, Ali. *On Binlerin Yürüyüşü Bir Yunan Tümeni'nin Kaçış Öyküsü*. Istanbul: Tarihçi Kitabevi, 2014.

Strategos, Xenofon (Ξενοφών Στρατηγός). *Η Ελλάδα στην Μικρά Ασία* (*Greece in Asia Minor*). Self-published in Greece, 1925.

Taşkıran, Cemalettin. *Milli Mücadele'de Türk ve Yunan Esirler, 1919–1923*. Istanbul: Türkiye İş Bankası, 2018.

Terraine, John. *Douglas Haig, The Educated Soldier*. London: Hutchinson, 1963.

Travlos, Konstantinos, ed. *Salvation and Catastrophe: The Greek-Turkish War, 1919–1922*. Lanham, Maryland: Lexington Books, 2020.

Trikoupis, Nikolaos (Τρικούπης, Νικόλαος). *Διοίκησης Μεγάλων Μονάδων εν Πολεμώ 1918–1922* (*Command of Major Units during War 1918–1922*), Athens: Eleftheris Skepsis, 2001[1935].

Türkmen, Zekeriya. *Mütareke Döneminde Ordunun Durumu ve Yeniden Yapılanması (1918–1920).* Ankara: Türk Tarih Kurumu Basımevi, 2001.

Uyar, Mesut. *The Ottoman Army and the First World War.* London: Routledge, 2021.

Walder, David. *The Chanak Affair.* London: Hutchinson & Co Ltd., 1969.

Wallach, Jehuda L. *The Dogma of the Battle of Annihilation.* Westport, CT: Greenwood Press, 1986.

Weisiger, Alex. *Logics of War: Explanations for Limited and Unlimited Conflicts,* Ithaca; London: Cornell University Press, 2013.

Yel, Selma. *Yakup Şevki Paşa ve Askerı Faaliyetleri.* Ankara: Atatürk Araştırma Merkezi, 2002.

Yildirim, Onur. *Diplomacy and Displacement: Reconsidering the Turco-Greek Exchange of Populations, 1922–1934.* New York: Routledge, 2006.

Yilmaz, Orhan. *Zile Insyanı.* Ankara: Veni, Vedi, Vici Yayınevi, 2014.

Zeidner, Robert F. *The Tricolor over the Taurus: The French in Cilicia and Vicinity, 1918–1922.* Ankara: Turkish Historical Society, 2005.

Zurcher, Erik-Jan. *The Young Turk Legacy and Nation Building.* New York: I.B. Tauris, 2010.

ARTICLES, CHAPTERS, AND MAPS

Akğun, Seçil Karal. "The General Harbord Commission and the American Mandate Question." In *Studies in Atatürk's Turkey, The American Dimension,* edited by George Harris and Nur Bilgi Criss, 83–96. Leiden: Brill Academic Publishers, 2009.

Akyüz, Doruk. "Legacy of the Stormtroop: The Influence of German Assault Troop Doctrines in the Great Offensive." In *Salvation and Catastrophe: The Greek-Turkish War, 1919–1922,* edited by Konstantinos Travlos, 197–230. Lanham: Maryland, Lexington Books, 2020.

Darwin, John. "An Undeclared Empire: The British in the Middle East, 1918–39." *The Journal of Imperial and Commonwealth History* 27, no. 2 (1999): 159–176.

Demirel, Demokaan. "Internal Rebellions during the National Struggle: The Case of Yozgat." *The Journal of International Social Research* 9, no. 45 (August 2016): 1–8.

Despot, Igor. "The Balkan Wars: An Expected Opportunity for Ethnic Cleansing." *Journal of Muslim Minority Affairs* 39, no. 3: 343–355.

Dyer, Gwynne. "The Origins of the 'Nationalist' Group of Officers in Turkey 1908–18." *Journal of Contemporary History* 8, no. 4 (1973): 121–164.

Erickson, Edward J. "Decisive Battles of the Asia Minor Campaign." In *Salvation and Catastrophe: The Greek-Turkish War, 1919–1922*, edited by Konstantinos Travlos, 173–196. Lanham: Maryland, Lexington Books, 2020.

Erickson, Edward J. "From Kirkilisse to The Great Offensive: Turkish Encirclement Operations 1912–1922." *Middle Eastern Studies* 40, no. 1 (January 2004): 45–64.

Finefrock, Michael M. "Ataturk, Lloyd George and the Megali Idea: Cause and Consequence of the Greek Plan to Seize Constantinople from the Allies, June–August 1922." *The Journal of Modern History* 52, no. 1, on-demand supplement (March 1980): D1047–D1066.

Gawrych, George W. "Kemal Atatürk's Politico-Military Strategy in the Turkish War of Independence, 1919–1922: From Guerrilla Warfare to the Decisive Battle." *Journal of Strategic Studies* 11, no. 3 (2008): 318–41, https://doi.org/10.1080/01402398808437345.

Gingeras, Ryan. "Notorious Subjects, Invisible Citizens: North Caucasian Resistance to the Turkish National Movement in Northwestern Anatolia, 1919–23." *International Journal of Middle East Studies* 40, no. 1 (2008): 89–108.

Gingeras, Ryan. "The Sons of Two Fatherlands: Turkey and the North Caucasian Diaspora, 1914–1923." *European Journal of Turkish Studies*, online edition (November 30, 2011). http://journals .openedition.org/ejts/4424.

Görgülü, İsmet. *Türk İstiklâl Harbi Haritası (15 Mayıs 1919–24 Temmuz 1923)*. Turkish War Academy Map created by Staff Major İsmet Görgülü, undated.

Güçlü, Yücel. "The Struggle for Mastery in Cilicia: Turkey, France and the Ankara Agreement of 1921." *The International History Review* 23, no. 3 (2010): 580–603.

Helmreich, Paul C. "Italy and the Anglo-French Repudiation of the 1917 St. Jean De Maurienne Agreement." *The Journal of Modern History* 48, no. 2 (1976): 99–139. Accessed November 11, 2020. http:// www.jstor.org/stable/1877819.

Jensen, Peter Kincaid. "The Greco-Turkish War, 1920–1922." *The International Journal of Middle East Studies* 10 (1979): 553–65.

Kitromilides, Paschalis M., and Alexis Alexandris. "Ethnic Survival, Nationalism and Forced Migration." *Δελτίο Κέντρου Μικρασιατικών Σπουδών* 6 (1986): 9–44.

Loumiotes, Vasileios (Λουμιώτης, Βασίλειος). "Η Ανώτατη Διεύθυνση των Επιχειρήσεων της Στρατιάς Μικράς Ασίας του Δεκέμβριου 1920 και του Μάρτιου 1921 (The Higher Direction of the Operations of the Field Army of Asia Minor in December 1920 and March 1921)." *Στρατηγειν* 1 (Summer 2019): 33–78.

Macar, Elçin. "The Muslim Emigration in Western Anatolia." Cahiers Balkaniques, online 40 (2012), http://journals.openedition.org/ceb /922, https://doi.org/10.4000/ceb.922.

Marden, Major General Sir Thomas. "With the British Army in Constantinople, A Personal Narrative" (Part 1). *The Army Quart*erly XXVI, no. 2 (July 1933): 263–74.

Marden, Major General Sir Thomas. "With the British Army in Constantinople, A Personal Narrative" (Part 2). *The Army Quarterly* XXVII (October 1933 and January 1934): 42–57.

McCarthy, Justin. "Greek Statistics on the Ottoman Greek Population." *International Journal of Turkish Studies* 1, no. 2 (1980): 66–76.

Mutlu, Servet. "Late Ottoman Population and Its Ethnic Distribution." *Turkish Journal of Population Studies* 25, no. 1 (2003): 3–38.

Niyazi, Taha. "The Bozkır Rebellions in the National Struggle." *Journal of the Institute of Social Sciences* 16, no. 1 (2004): 169–90.

Özsu, Umit. "'A Thoroughly Bad and Vicious Solution': Humanitarism, the World Court, and the Modern Origins of Population Transfer." *London Review of International Law* 1, no. 1 (2013): 99–127.

Salahaddin, Kaymakam. "Ikinci İnönü Meydan Muharebesi." *Askeri Mecmua* 31 (September 1, 1933): 5–160.

Shields, Sarah. "The Greek-Turkish Population Exchange: Internationally Administered Ethnic Cleansing." *Middle East Report* no. 267 (2013): 2–6, www.jstor.org/stable/24426444.

Siney, Marion C. "British Official Histories of the Blockade of the Central Powers during the First World War." *The American Historical Review* 68, no. 2 (1963): 392–401. https://doi.org/10.2307/1904539.

Tacar, Pulat, and Maxime Gauin. "State Identity, Continuity, and Responsibility: The Ottoman Empire, the Republic of Turkey and the Armenian Genocide: A Reply to Vahagn Avedian." *The European Journal of International Law* 23, no. 3 (2012): 821–835.

Travlos, Konstantinos. "The Correlates of Obsession: Selectorate Dynamics and the Decision of Venizelos for Military Intervention in Asia Minor." In *Salvation and Catastrophe: The Greek-Turkish War, 1919–1922*, edited by Konstantinos Travlos, 67–107. Lanham: Maryland, Lexington Books, 2020.

Tsirigotis, Dionysis. "The Impact of the Excess of the Culminating Point of Attack in the Greek Military Strategy on the Outcome of the Greek Campaign in Asia Minor (August 1921–August 1922)." *Defensor Pacis* 24 (June 2009): 143–175.

Tusan, Michelle. "'Crimes against Humanity': Human Rights, the British Empire, and the Origins of the Response to the Armenian Genocide." *The American Historical Review* 119, no. 1 (February 2014): 47–77.

Usta, Veysel. "A Criticism of the Memorandum Submitted to the Paris Conference by Trabzon Metropolitan Hrisantos." *International Periodical for the Languages, Literature and History of Turkish or Turkic* 6, no. 2 (Spring 2011): 973–84.

Zürcher, Erik-Jan. "The Ottoman Empire and the Armistice of Moudros." In *At the Eleventh Hour: Reflections, Hopes, and Anxieties at the Closing of the Great War, 1918*, edited by Hugh Cecil and Peter H. Liddle, 266–75. London: Leo Cooper, 1998.

UNPUBLISHED MATERIALS

Daleziou, Eleftheria. "Britain and the Greek-Turkish War and Settlement of 1919–1923: The Pursuit of Security by 'Proxy' in Western Asia Minor." Unpublished PhD diss. University of Glasgow, 2002.

Gauin, Maxime. "Imperialism, Revolution and Nationalism: The Relations between the French Republic and the Armenian Committees, from 1918 to 1923." Unpublished PhD diss. Middle Eastern Technical University, Ankara, Turkey, 2019.

Travlos, Konstantinos. "2nd Inonu and 1st Dulumpinar." Unpublished manuscript.

Travlos, Konstantinos, and Onur Buyuran. "Orders of Battle of the Turkish War of Independence." Unpublished manuscript.

Index

About the Author

Dr. Edward J. Erickson is a professor of international relations at Antalya Bilim University, a retired professor of military history from the Marine Corps University in Quantico, Virginia, and a retired U.S. Army lieutenant colonel who also qualified as a foreign area officer specializing in Turkey. During his career, he served in field artillery and general staff assignments in the United States, Europe, and the Middle East. Dr. Erickson has a doctorate in history from the University of Leeds, and he is widely recognized as one of the foremost specialists on World War I in the Middle East. He has published 16 books and numerous articles. The current book completes his well-regarded trilogy on the wars of the Ottoman and Turkish armies in the early twentieth century, the first two of which are *Defeat in Detail: The Ottoman Army in the Balkans, 1912–1913* (Praeger, 2003) and *Ordered to Die: A History of the Ottoman Army in the First World War* (Praeger, 2001).

Milton Keynes UK
Ingram Content Group UK Ltd.
UKHW020936090724
445317UK00007B/268